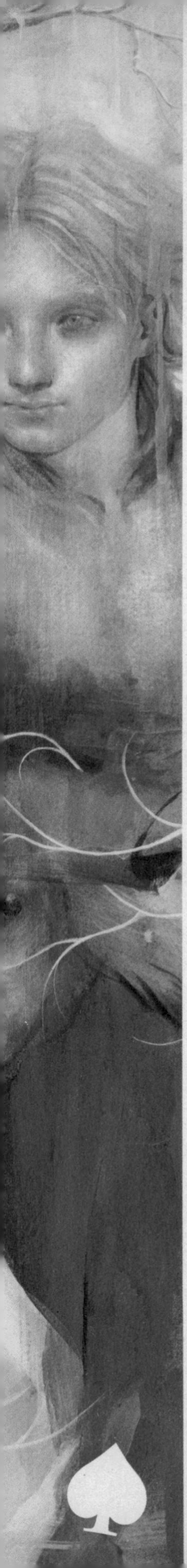

JACK
OF FABLES

JACK of HEARTS

BILL WILLINGHAM
MATTHEW STURGES
Writers

TONY AKINS
STEVE LEIALOHA
ANDREW PEPOY
Pencillers

ANDREW PEPOY
STEVE LEIALOHA
Inkers

LEE LOUGHRIDGE
DANIEL VOZZO
Colorists

TODD KLEIN
Letterer

JAMES JEAN
Original Series Covers

JACK OF FABLES
Created by Bill Willingham

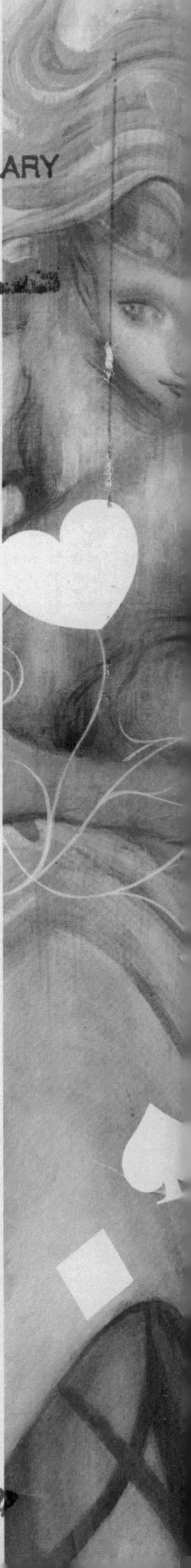

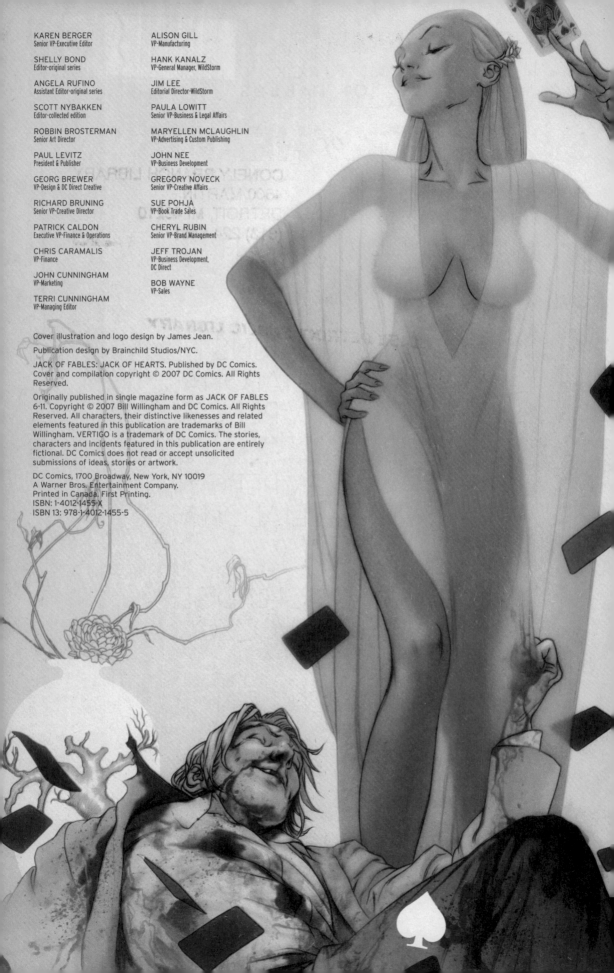

Cover illustration and logo design by James Jean.

Publication design by Brainchild Studios/NYC.

JACK OF FABLES: JACK OF HEARTS. Published by DC Comics.
Cover and compilation copyright © 2007 DC Comics. All Rights
Reserved.

Originally published in single magazine form as JACK OF FABLES
6-11. Copyright © 2007 Bill Willingham and DC Comics. All Rights
Reserved. All characters, their distinctive likenesses and related
elements featured in this publication are trademarks of Bill
Willingham. VERTIGO is a trademark of DC Comics. The stories,
characters and incidents featured in this publication are entirely
fictional. DC Comics does not read or accept unsolicited
submissions of ideas, stories or artwork.

DC Comics, 1700 Broadway, New York, NY 10019
A Warner Bros. Entertainment Company.
Printed in Canada. First Printing.
ISBN: 1-4012-1455-X
ISBN 13: 978-1-4012-1455-5

TABLE *of* CONTENTS

DRAMATIS PERSONAE

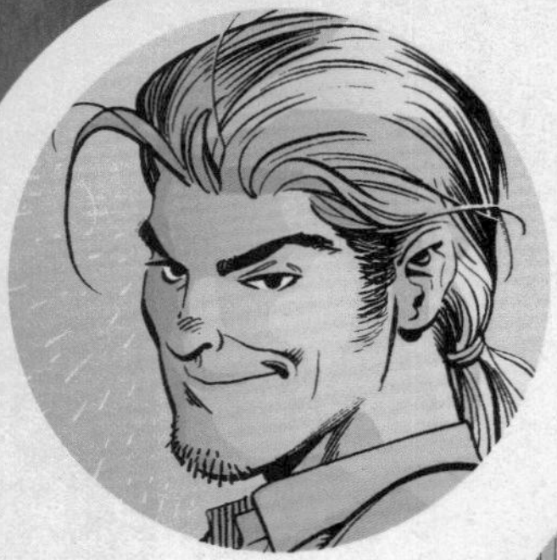

JACK

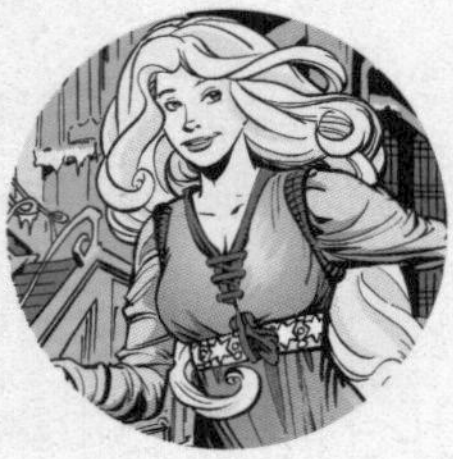

LUMI

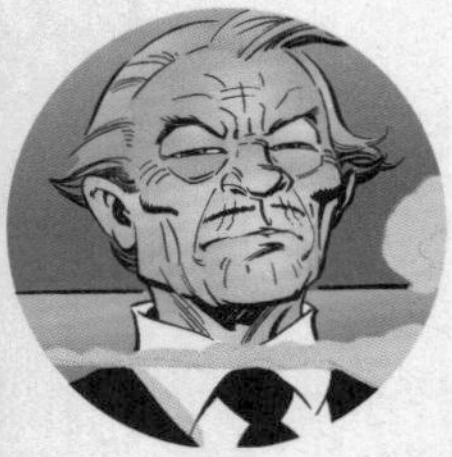

MR. REVISE

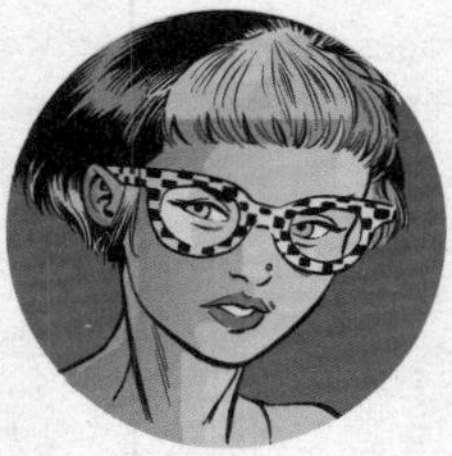

HILLARY PAGE

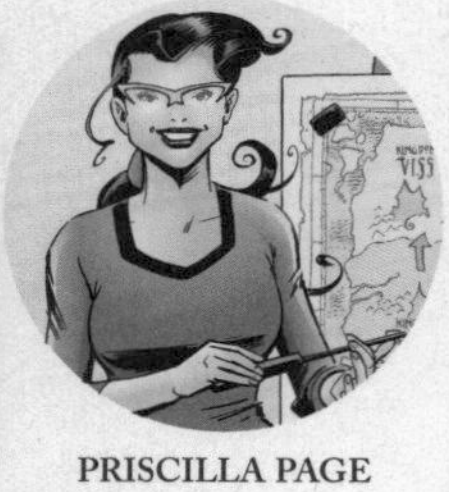

PRISCILLA PAGE

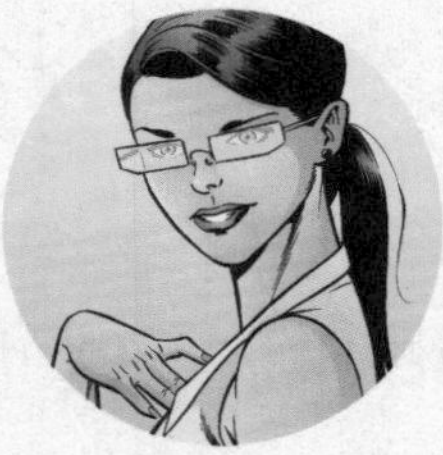

ROBIN PAGE

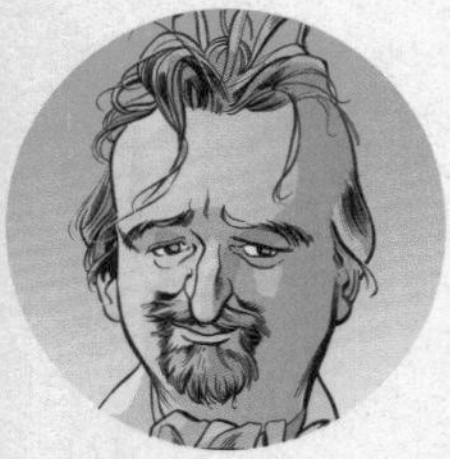

GARY

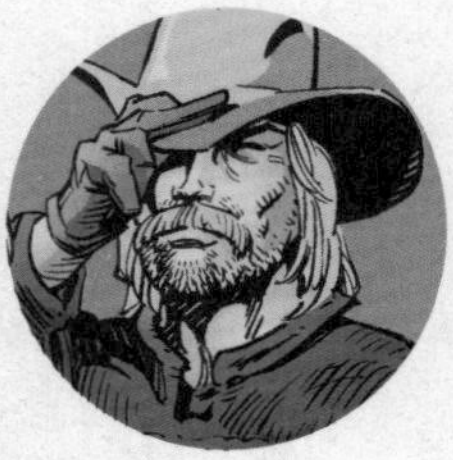

PECOS BILL

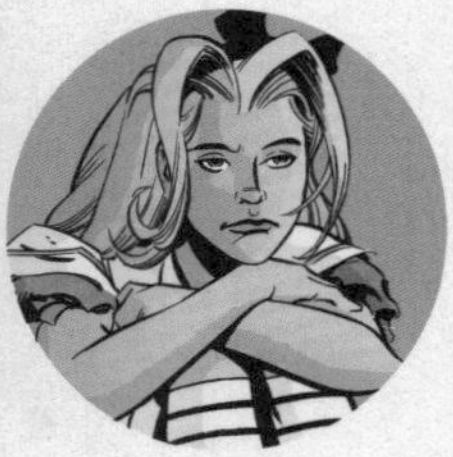

ALICE

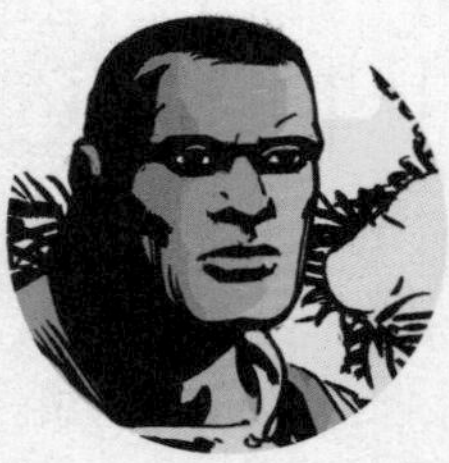

JOHN HENRY

JACK

Also known as Little Jack Horner, Jack B. Nimble, Jack the Giant Killer and countless other aliases, our hero Jack of Tales embodies the archetype of the lovable rogue (minus, according to many, the lovability).

LUMI, THE SNOW QUEEN

Now a key ally of the Adversary, this seasonal monarch was not always so cold-hearted.

MR. REVISE

Jack's current nemesis, dedicated to trapping Fables and draining their power in pursuit of a magic-free world.

THE PAGE SISTERS

Right-hand women to Mr. Revise and the chief librarians at his Fable prison, the Golden Boughs Retirement Village.

GARY, THE PATHETIC FALLACY

A timid, impressionable and warm-hearted fellow whose power over inanimate objects is matched only by his love of Sousa marches.

PECOS BILL

A cowboy who once rode a tornado and watered his ranch with the Rio Grande, now free after years of fenced-in life.

ALICE

A survivor of several adventures through a looking-glass, including a meal of questionable mushrooms.

JOHN HENRY

A steel-driving man, unemployed of late.

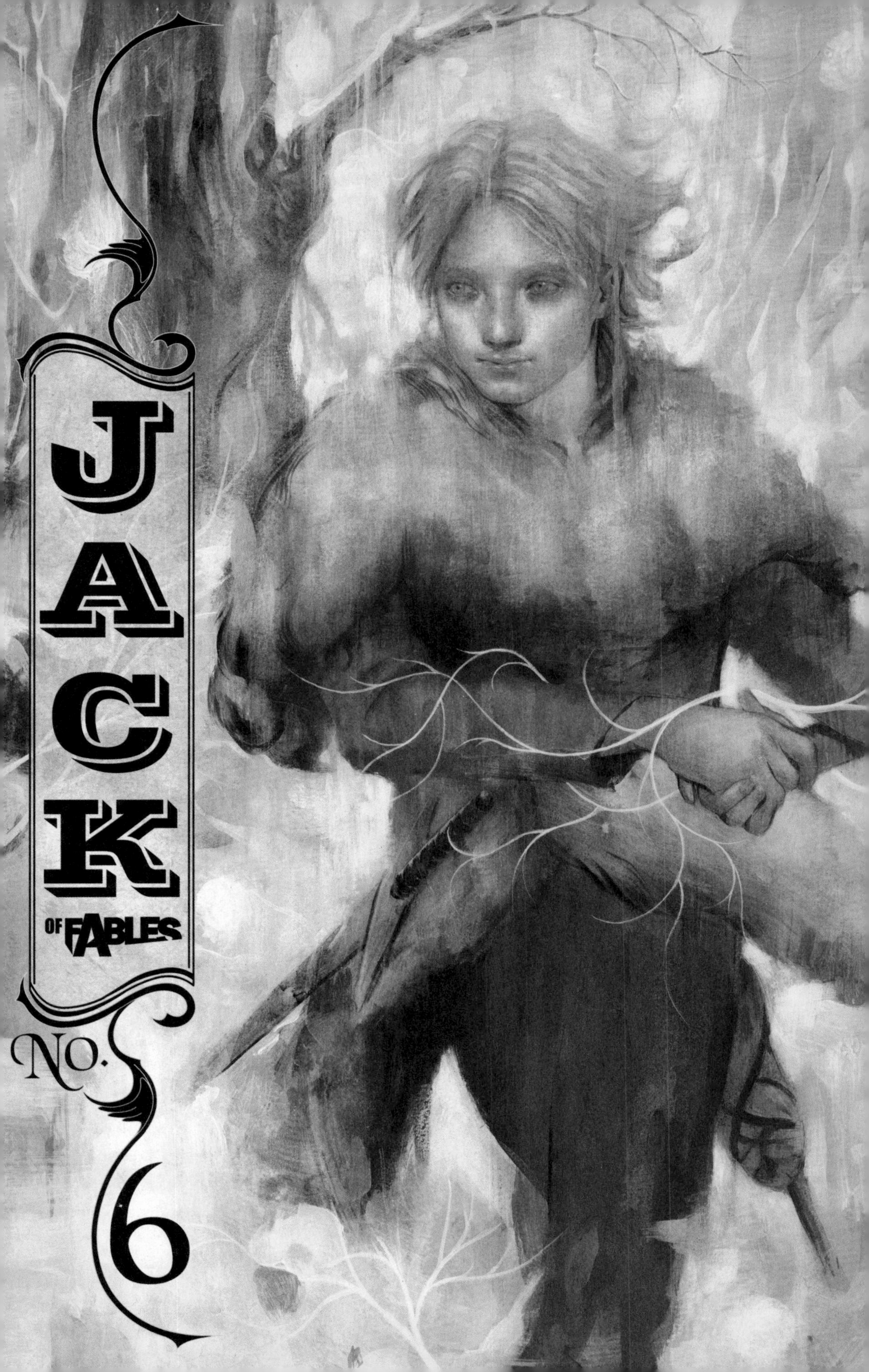
JACK
OF FABLES
NO.
6

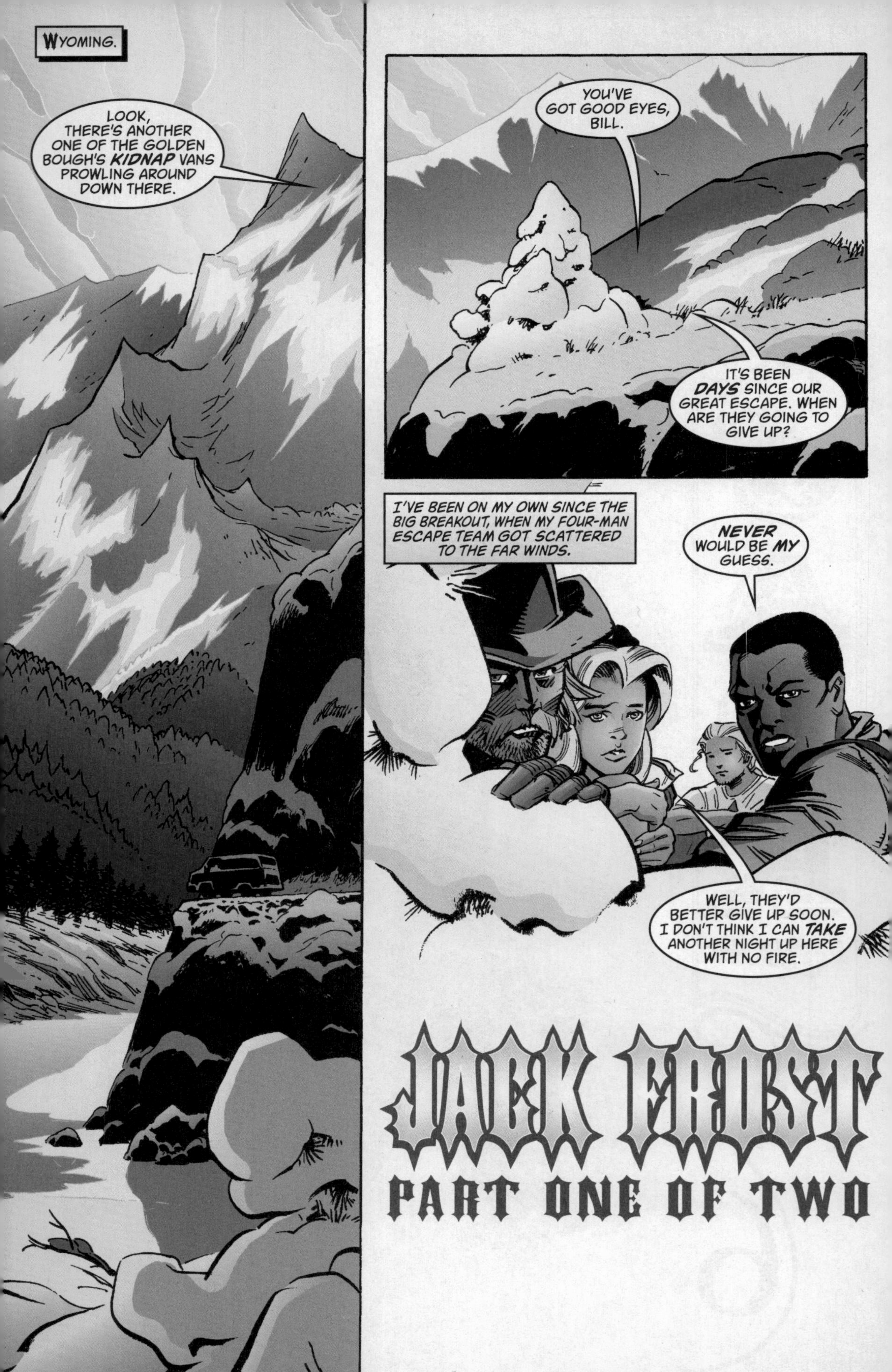
WYOMING.
LOOK, THERE'S ANOTHER ONE OF THE GOLDEN BOUGH'S KIDNAP VANS PROWLING AROUND DOWN THERE.
YOU'VE GOT GOOD EYES, BILL.
IT'S BEEN DAYS SINCE OUR GREAT ESCAPE. WHEN ARE THEY GOING TO GIVE UP?
I'VE BEEN ON MY OWN SINCE THE BIG BREAKOUT, WHEN MY FOUR-MAN ESCAPE TEAM GOT SCATTERED TO THE FAR WINDS.
NEVER WOULD BE MY GUESS.
WELL, THEY'D BETTER GIVE UP SOON. I DON'T THINK I CAN TAKE ANOTHER NIGHT UP HERE WITH NO FIRE.
JACK FROST
PART ONE OF TWO

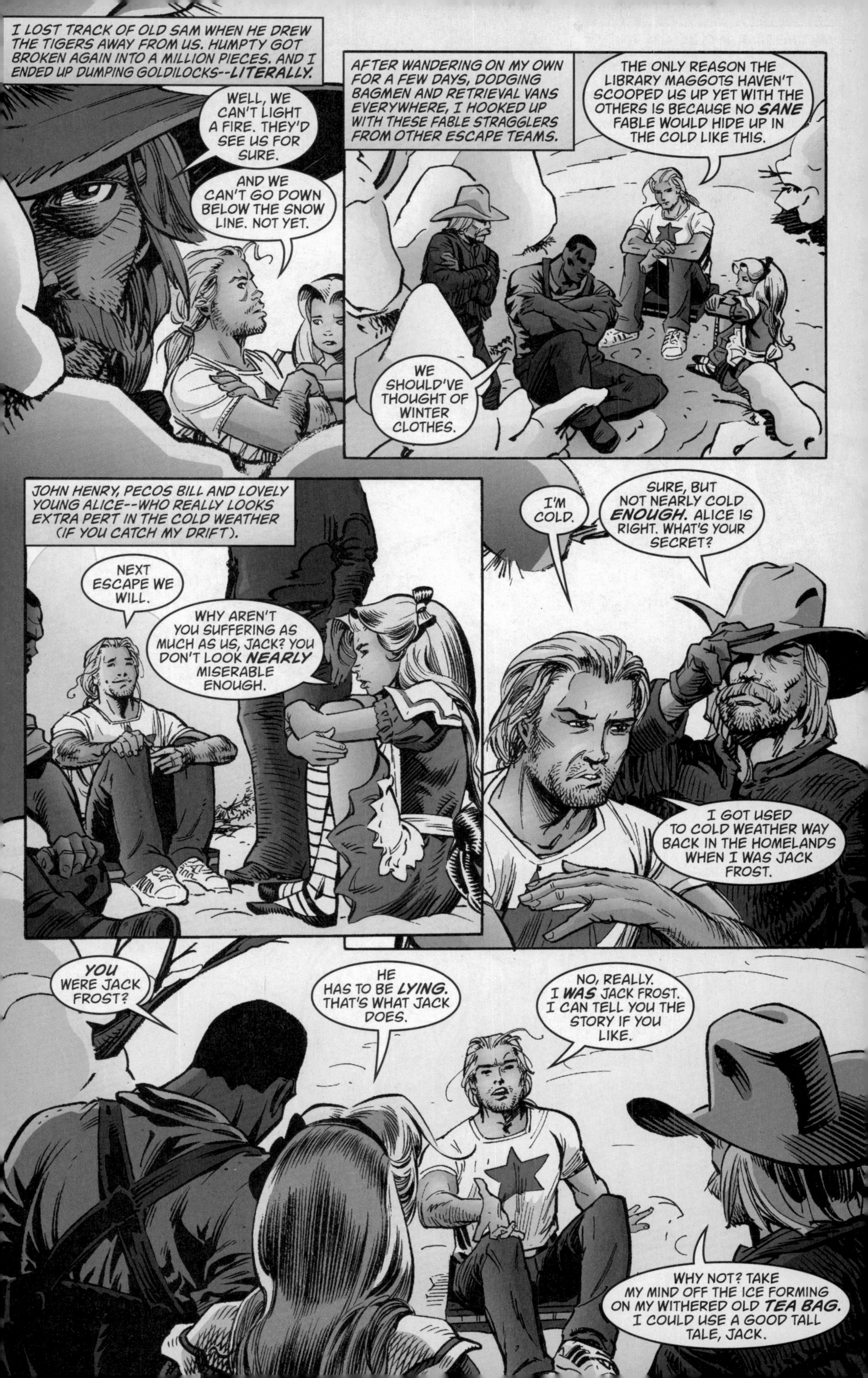

I LOST TRACK OF OLD SAM WHEN HE DREW THE TIGERS AWAY FROM US. HUMPTY GOT BROKEN AGAIN INTO A MILLION PIECES. AND I ENDED UP DUMPING GOLDILOCKS--LITERALLY.
WELL, WE CAN'T LIGHT A FIRE. THEY'D SEE US FOR SURE.
AND WE CAN'T GO DOWN BELOW THE SNOW LINE. NOT YET.
AFTER WANDERING ON MY OWN FOR A FEW DAYS, DODGING BAGMEN AND RETRIEVAL VANS EVERYWHERE, I HOOKED UP WITH THESE FABLE STRAGGLERS FROM OTHER ESCAPE TEAMS.
THE ONLY REASON THE LIBRARY MAGGOTS HAVEN'T SCOOPED US UP YET WITH THE OTHERS IS BECAUSE NO SANE FABLE WOULD HIDE UP IN THE COLD LIKE THIS.
WE SHOULD'VE THOUGHT OF WINTER CLOTHES.
JOHN HENRY, PECOS BILL AND LOVELY YOUNG ALICE--WHO REALLY LOOKS EXTRA PERT IN THE COLD WEATHER (IF YOU CATCH MY DRIFT).
NEXT ESCAPE WE WILL.
WHY AREN'T YOU SUFFERING AS MUCH AS US, JACK? YOU DON'T LOOK NEARLY MISERABLE ENOUGH.
I'M COLD.
SURE, BUT NOT NEARLY COLD ENOUGH. ALICE IS RIGHT. WHAT'S YOUR SECRET?
I GOT USED TO COLD WEATHER WAY BACK IN THE HOMELANDS WHEN I WAS JACK FROST.
YOU WERE JACK FROST?
HE HAS TO BE LYING. THAT'S WHAT JACK DOES.
NO, REALLY. I WAS JACK FROST. I CAN TELL YOU THE STORY IF YOU LIKE.
WHY NOT? TAKE MY MIND OFF THE ICE FORMING ON MY WITHERED OLD TEA BAG. I COULD USE A GOOD TALL TALE, JACK.

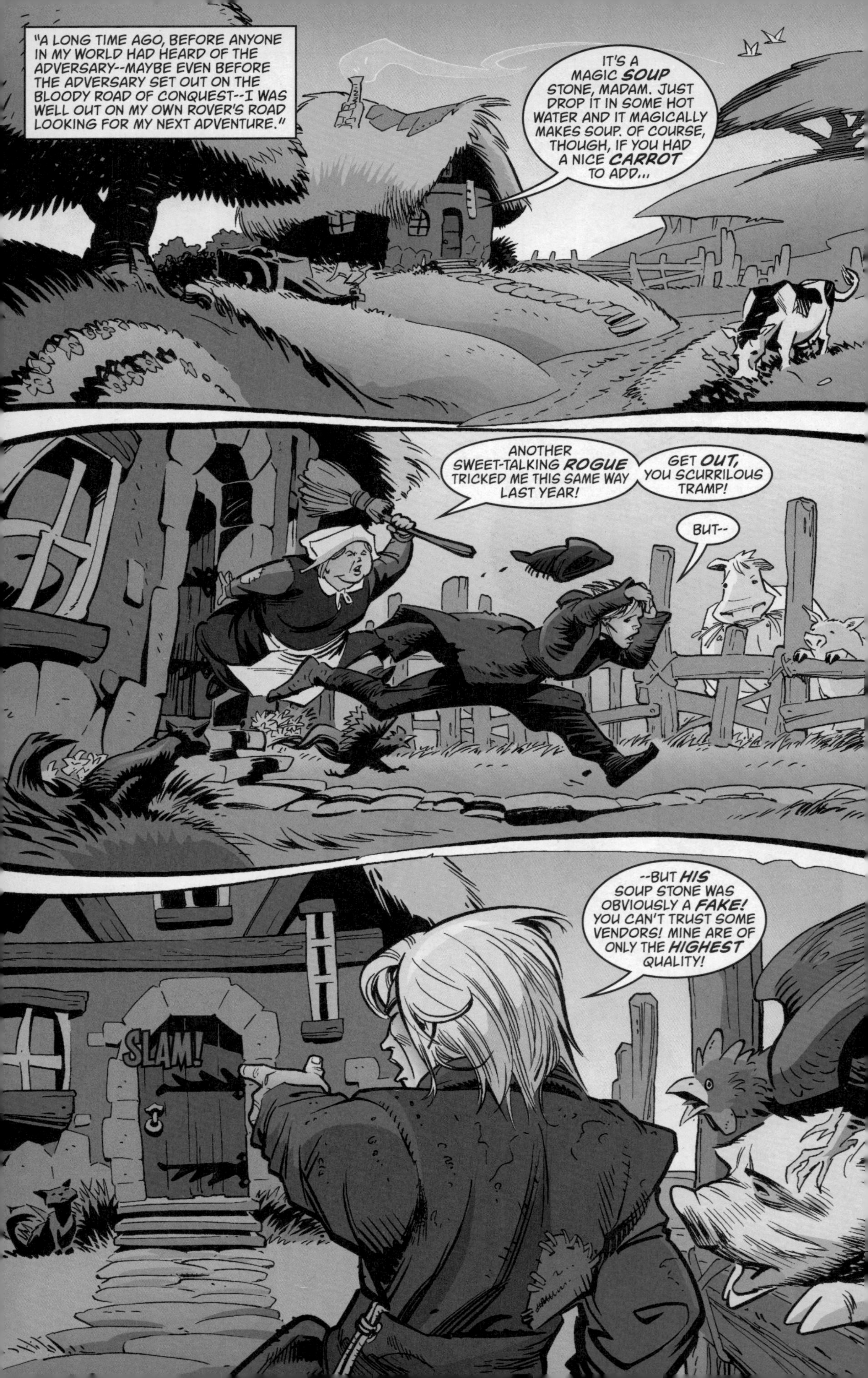
"A LONG TIME AGO, BEFORE ANYONE IN MY WORLD HAD HEARD OF THE ADVERSARY--MAYBE EVEN BEFORE THE ADVERSARY SET OUT ON THE BLOODY ROAD OF CONQUEST--I WAS WELL OUT ON MY OWN ROVER'S ROAD LOOKING FOR MY NEXT ADVENTURE."
IT'S A MAGIC SOUP STONE, MADAM. JUST DROP IT IN SOME HOT WATER AND IT MAGICALLY MAKES SOUP. OF COURSE, THOUGH, IF YOU HAD A NICE CARROT TO ADD...
ANOTHER SWEET-TALKING ROGUE TRICKED ME THIS SAME WAY LAST YEAR!
GET OUT, YOU SCURRILOUS TRAMP!
BUT--
--BUT HIS SOUP STONE WAS OBVIOUSLY A FAKE! YOU CAN'T TRUST SOME VENDORS! MINE ARE OF ONLY THE HIGHEST QUALITY!
SLAM!

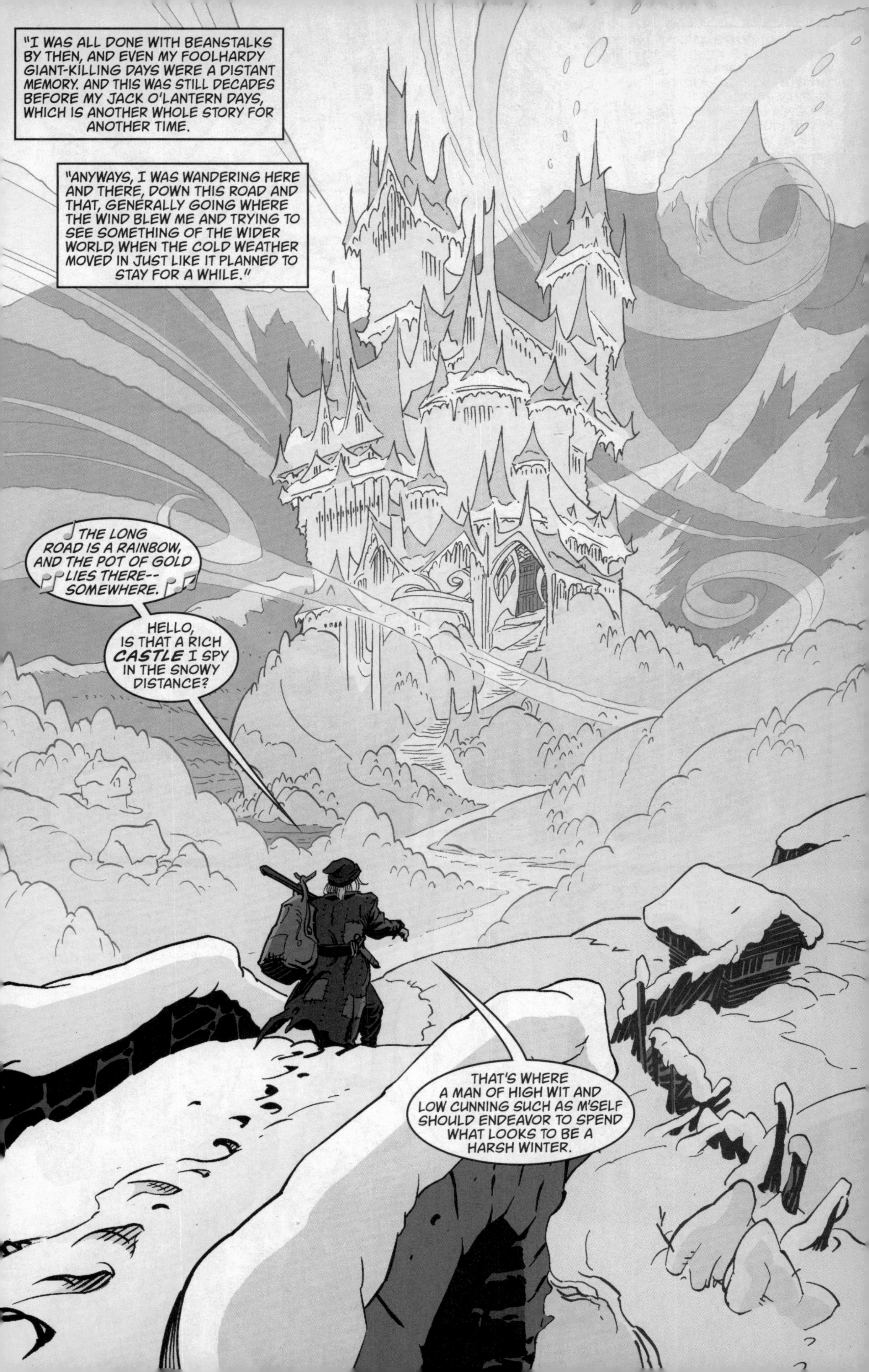
"I WAS ALL DONE WITH BEANSTALKS BY THEN, AND EVEN MY FOOLHARDY GIANT-KILLING DAYS WERE A DISTANT MEMORY. AND THIS WAS STILL DECADES BEFORE MY JACK O'LANTERN DAYS, WHICH IS ANOTHER WHOLE STORY FOR ANOTHER TIME.
"ANYWAYS, I WAS WANDERING HERE AND THERE, DOWN THIS ROAD AND THAT, GENERALLY GOING WHERE THE WIND BLEW ME AND TRYING TO SEE SOMETHING OF THE WIDER WORLD, WHEN THE COLD WEATHER MOVED IN JUST LIKE IT PLANNED TO STAY FOR A WHILE."
♩THE LONG ROAD IS A RAINBOW, AND THE POT OF GOLD LIES THERE-- SOMEWHERE.♫
HELLO, IS THAT A RICH *CASTLE* I SPY IN THE SNOWY DISTANCE?
THAT'S WHERE A MAN OF HIGH WIT AND LOW CUNNING SUCH AS M'SELF SHOULD ENDEAVOR TO SPEND WHAT LOOKS TO BE A HARSH WINTER.

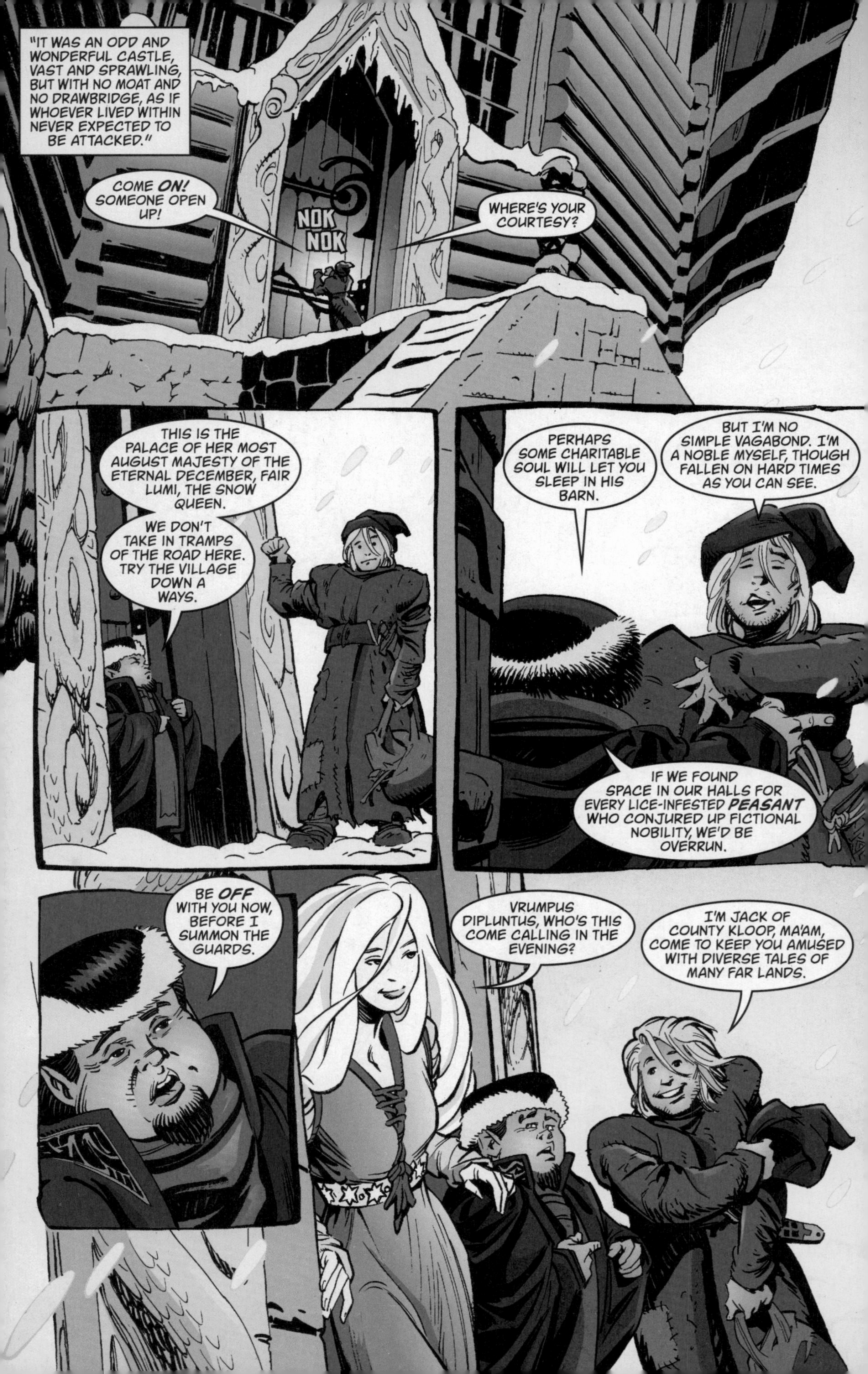

"IT WAS AN ODD AND WONDERFUL CASTLE, VAST AND SPRAWLING, BUT WITH NO MOAT AND NO DRAWBRIDGE, AS IF WHOEVER LIVED WITHIN NEVER EXPECTED TO BE ATTACKED."
COME ON! SOMEONE OPEN UP!
NOK NOK
WHERE'S YOUR COURTESY?
THIS IS THE PALACE OF HER MOST AUGUST MAJESTY OF THE ETERNAL DECEMBER, FAIR LUMI, THE SNOW QUEEN.
WE DON'T TAKE IN TRAMPS OF THE ROAD HERE. TRY THE VILLAGE DOWN A WAYS.
BUT I'M NO SIMPLE VAGABOND. I'M A NOBLE MYSELF, THOUGH FALLEN ON HARD TIMES AS YOU CAN SEE.
PERHAPS SOME CHARITABLE SOUL WILL LET YOU SLEEP IN HIS BARN.
IF WE FOUND SPACE IN OUR HALLS FOR EVERY LICE-INFESTED PEASANT WHO CONJURED UP FICTIONAL NOBILITY, WE'D BE OVERRUN.
BE OFF WITH YOU NOW, BEFORE I SUMMON THE GUARDS.
VRUMPUS DIPLUNTUS, WHO'S THIS COME CALLING IN THE EVENING?
I'M JACK OF COUNTY KLOOP, MA'AM, COME TO KEEP YOU AMUSED WITH DIVERSE TALES OF MANY FAR LANDS.

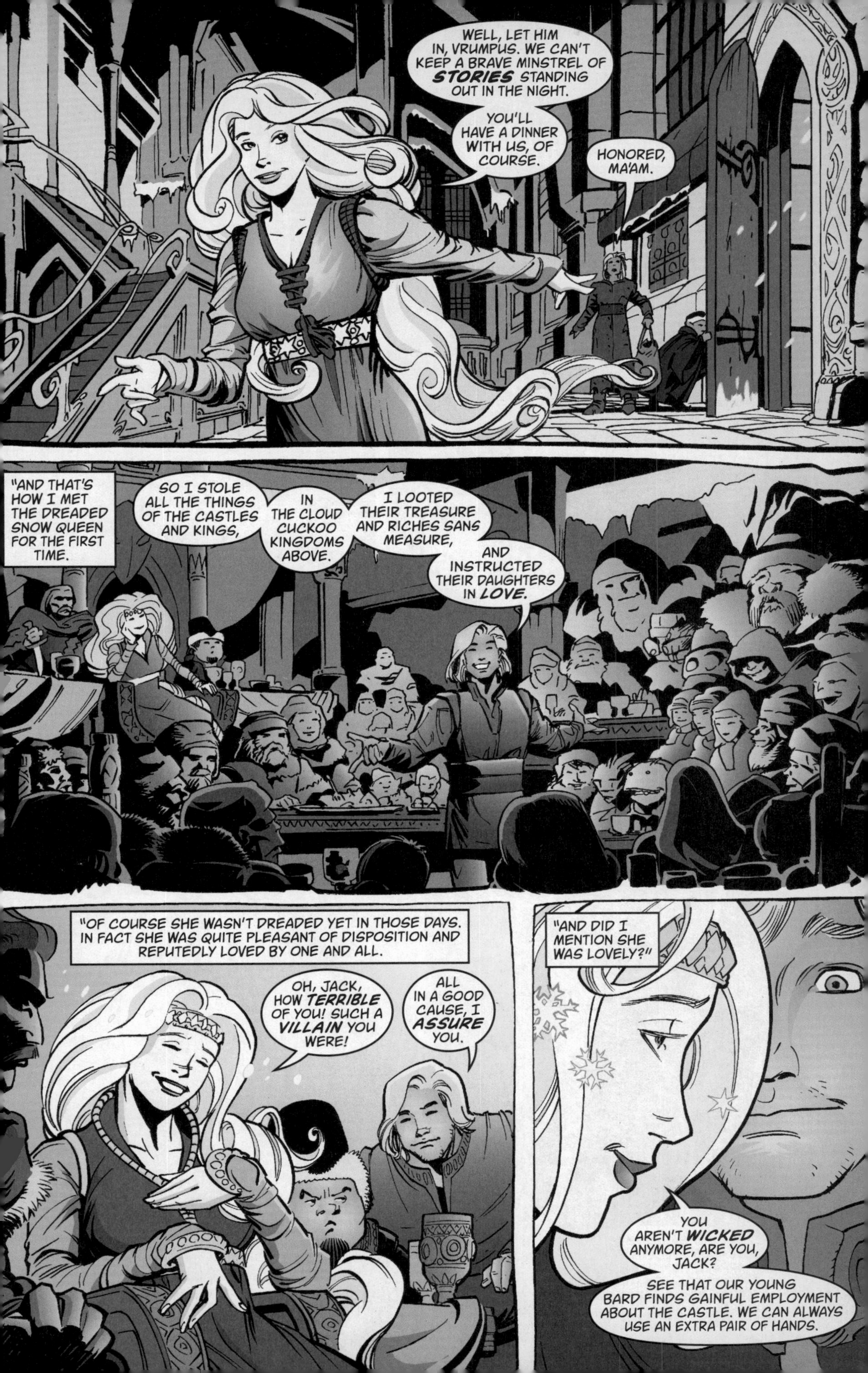
WELL, LET HIM IN, VRUMPUS. WE CAN'T KEEP A BRAVE MINSTREL OF STORIES STANDING OUT IN THE NIGHT.
YOU'LL HAVE A DINNER WITH US, OF COURSE.
HONORED, MA'AM.
"AND THAT'S HOW I MET THE DREADED SNOW QUEEN FOR THE FIRST TIME.
SO I STOLE ALL THE THINGS OF THE CASTLES AND KINGS,
IN THE CLOUD CUCKOO KINGDOMS ABOVE.
I LOOTED THEIR TREASURE AND RICHES SANS MEASURE,
AND INSTRUCTED THEIR DAUGHTERS IN LOVE.
"OF COURSE SHE WASN'T DREADED YET IN THOSE DAYS. IN FACT SHE WAS QUITE PLEASANT OF DISPOSITION AND REPUTEDLY LOVED BY ONE AND ALL.
OH, JACK, HOW TERRIBLE OF YOU! SUCH A VILLAIN YOU WERE!
ALL IN A GOOD CAUSE, I ASSURE YOU.
"AND DID I MENTION SHE WAS LOVELY?"
YOU AREN'T WICKED ANYMORE, ARE YOU, JACK?
SEE THAT OUR YOUNG BARD FINDS GAINFUL EMPLOYMENT ABOUT THE CASTLE. WE CAN ALWAYS USE AN EXTRA PAIR OF HANDS.

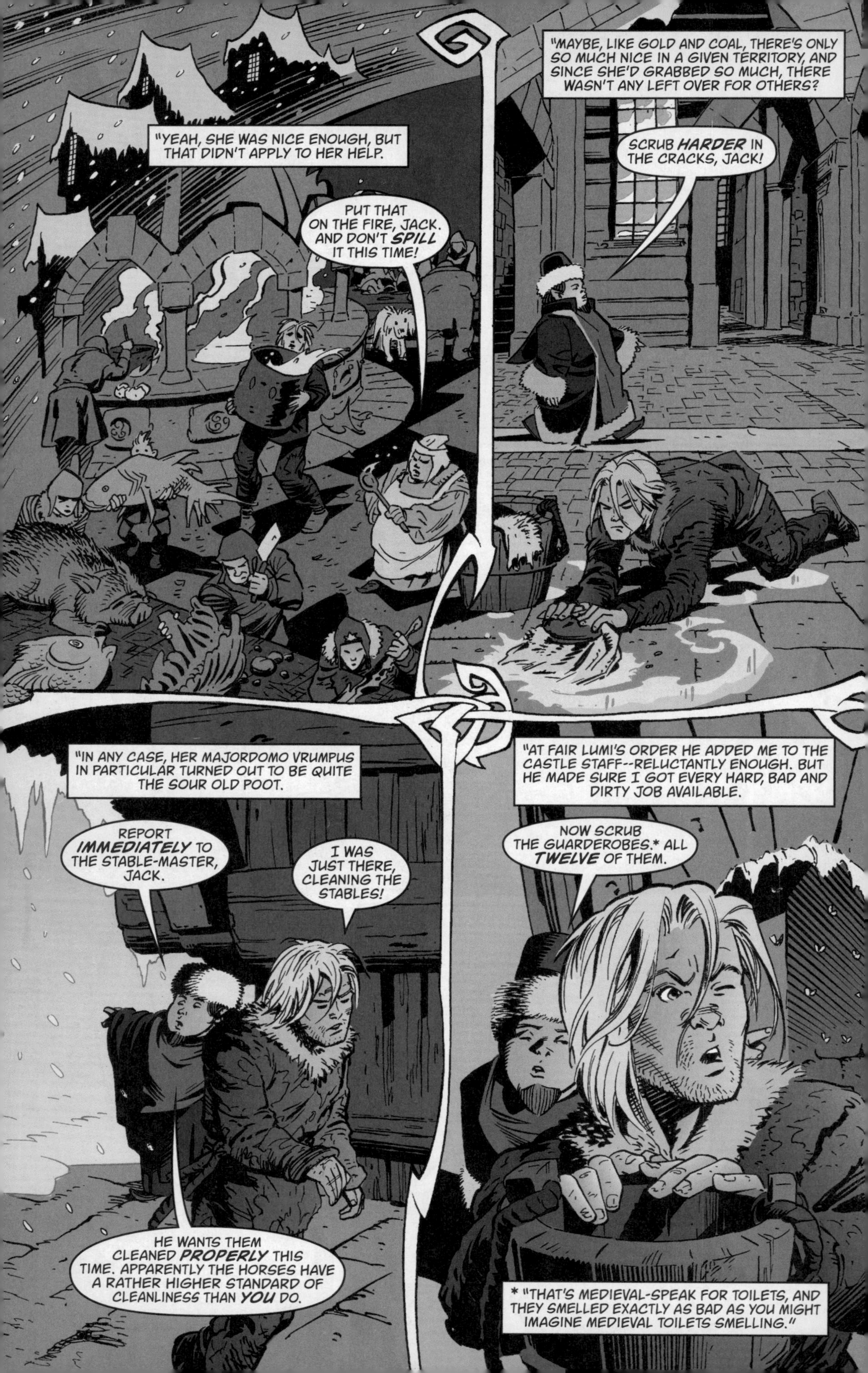
"YEAH, SHE WAS NICE ENOUGH, BUT THAT DIDN'T APPLY TO HER HELP.
PUT THAT ON THE FIRE, JACK. AND DON'T SPILL IT THIS TIME!
"MAYBE, LIKE GOLD AND COAL, THERE'S ONLY SO MUCH NICE IN A GIVEN TERRITORY, AND SINCE SHE'D GRABBED SO MUCH, THERE WASN'T ANY LEFT OVER FOR OTHERS?
SCRUB HARDER IN THE CRACKS, JACK!
"IN ANY CASE, HER MAJORDOMO VRUMPUS IN PARTICULAR TURNED OUT TO BE QUITE THE SOUR OLD POOT.
REPORT IMMEDIATELY TO THE STABLE-MASTER, JACK.
I WAS JUST THERE, CLEANING THE STABLES!
HE WANTS THEM CLEANED PROPERLY THIS TIME. APPARENTLY THE HORSES HAVE A RATHER HIGHER STANDARD OF CLEANLINESS THAN YOU DO.
"AT FAIR LUMI'S ORDER HE ADDED ME TO THE CASTLE STAFF--RELUCTANTLY ENOUGH. BUT HE MADE SURE I GOT EVERY HARD, BAD AND DIRTY JOB AVAILABLE.
NOW SCRUB THE GUARDEROBES.* ALL TWELVE OF THEM.
* "THAT'S MEDIEVAL-SPEAK FOR TOILETS, AND THEY SMELLED EXACTLY AS BAD AS YOU MIGHT IMAGINE MEDIEVAL TOILETS SMELLING."

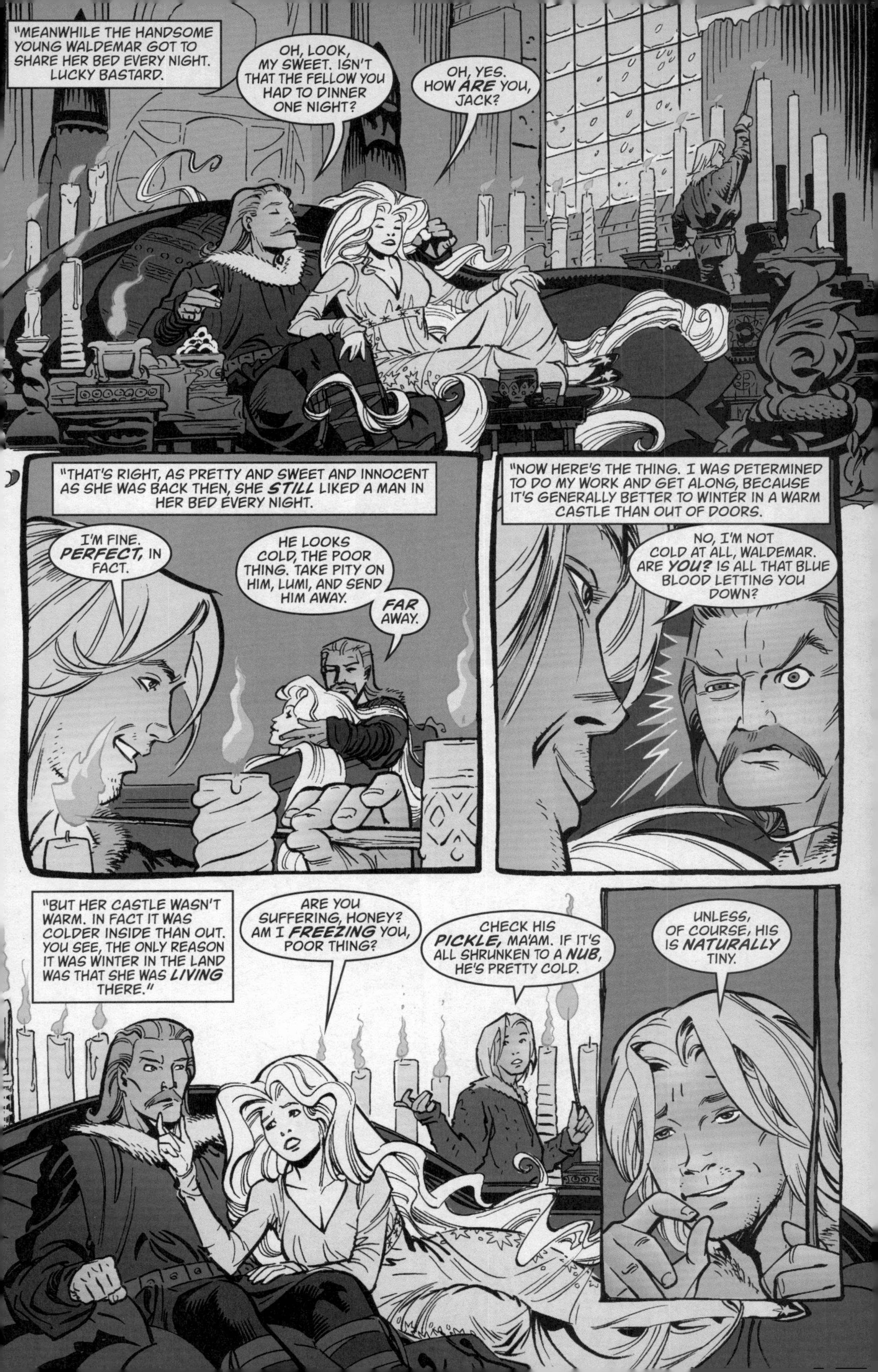
"MEANWHILE THE HANDSOME YOUNG WALDEMAR GOT TO SHARE HER BED EVERY NIGHT. LUCKY BASTARD.
OH, LOOK, MY SWEET. ISN'T THAT THE FELLOW YOU HAD TO DINNER ONE NIGHT?
OH, YES. HOW ARE YOU, JACK?
"THAT'S RIGHT, AS PRETTY AND SWEET AND INNOCENT AS SHE WAS BACK THEN, SHE STILL LIKED A MAN IN HER BED EVERY NIGHT.
I'M FINE. PERFECT, IN FACT.
HE LOOKS COLD, THE POOR THING. TAKE PITY ON HIM, LUMI, AND SEND HIM AWAY.
FAR AWAY.
"NOW HERE'S THE THING. I WAS DETERMINED TO DO MY WORK AND GET ALONG, BECAUSE IT'S GENERALLY BETTER TO WINTER IN A WARM CASTLE THAN OUT OF DOORS.
NO, I'M NOT COLD AT ALL, WALDEMAR. ARE YOU? IS ALL THAT BLUE BLOOD LETTING YOU DOWN?
"BUT HER CASTLE WASN'T WARM. IN FACT IT WAS COLDER INSIDE THAN OUT. YOU SEE, THE ONLY REASON IT WAS WINTER IN THE LAND WAS THAT SHE WAS LIVING THERE."
ARE YOU SUFFERING, HONEY? AM I FREEZING YOU, POOR THING?
CHECK HIS PICKLE, MA'AM. IF IT'S ALL SHRUNKEN TO A NUB, HE'S PRETTY COLD.
UNLESS, OF COURSE, HIS IS NATURALLY TINY.

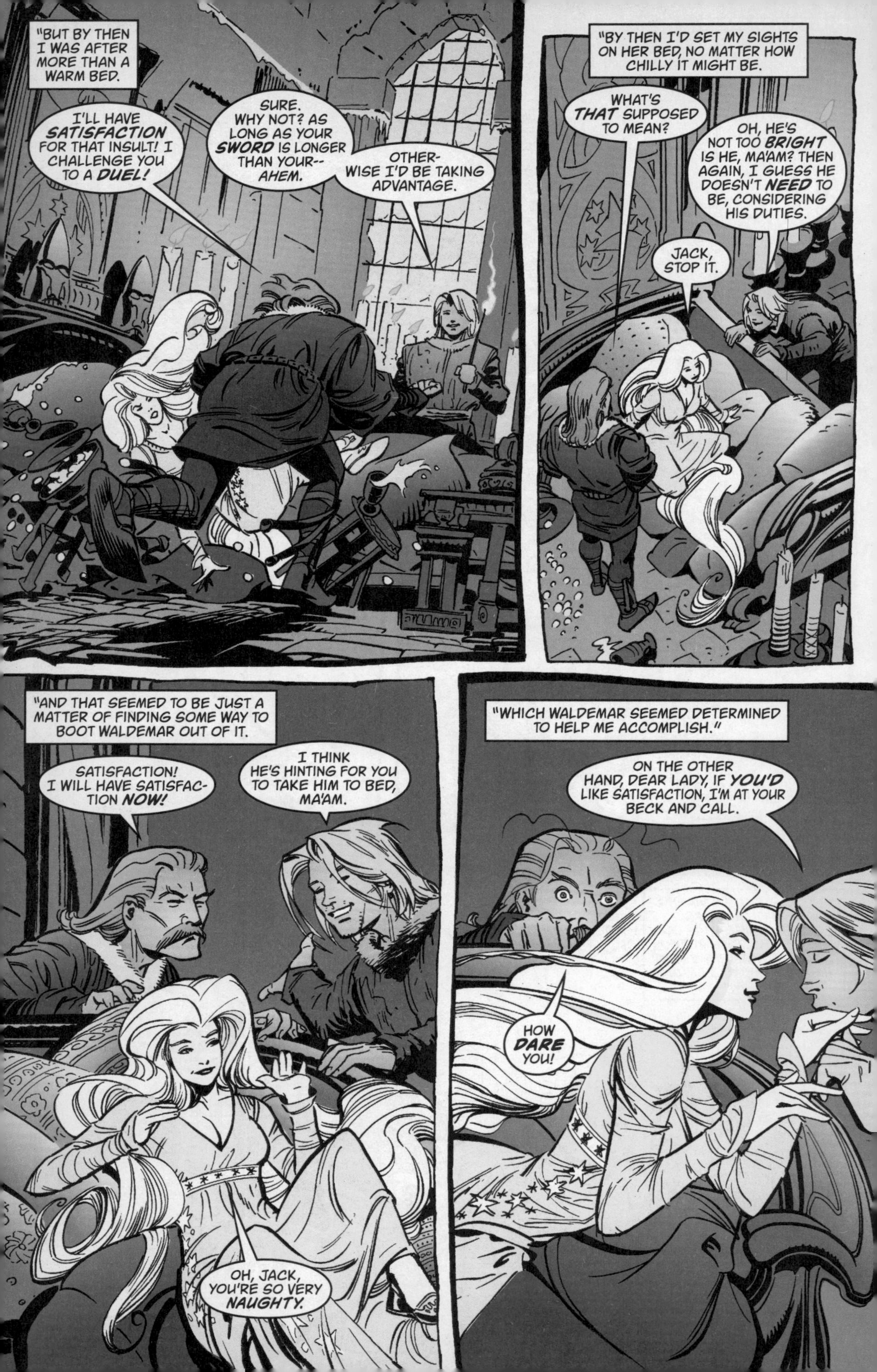
"BUT BY THEN I WAS AFTER MORE THAN A WARM BED.
I'LL HAVE SATISFACTION FOR THAT INSULT! I CHALLENGE YOU TO A DUEL!
SURE. WHY NOT? AS LONG AS YOUR SWORD IS LONGER THAN YOUR-- AHEM.
OTHER-WISE I'D BE TAKING ADVANTAGE.
"BY THEN I'D SET MY SIGHTS ON HER BED, NO MATTER HOW CHILLY IT MIGHT BE.
WHAT'S THAT SUPPOSED TO MEAN?
OH, HE'S NOT TOO BRIGHT IS HE, MA'AM? THEN AGAIN, I GUESS HE DOESN'T NEED TO BE, CONSIDERING HIS DUTIES.
JACK, STOP IT.
"AND THAT SEEMED TO BE JUST A MATTER OF FINDING SOME WAY TO BOOT WALDEMAR OUT OF IT.
SATISFACTION! I WILL HAVE SATISFACTION NOW!
I THINK HE'S HINTING FOR YOU TO TAKE HIM TO BED, MA'AM.
OH, JACK, YOU'RE SO VERY NAUGHTY.
"WHICH WALDEMAR SEEMED DETERMINED TO HELP ME ACCOMPLISH."
ON THE OTHER HAND, DEAR LADY, IF YOU'D LIKE SATISFACTION, I'M AT YOUR BECK AND CALL.
HOW DARE YOU!

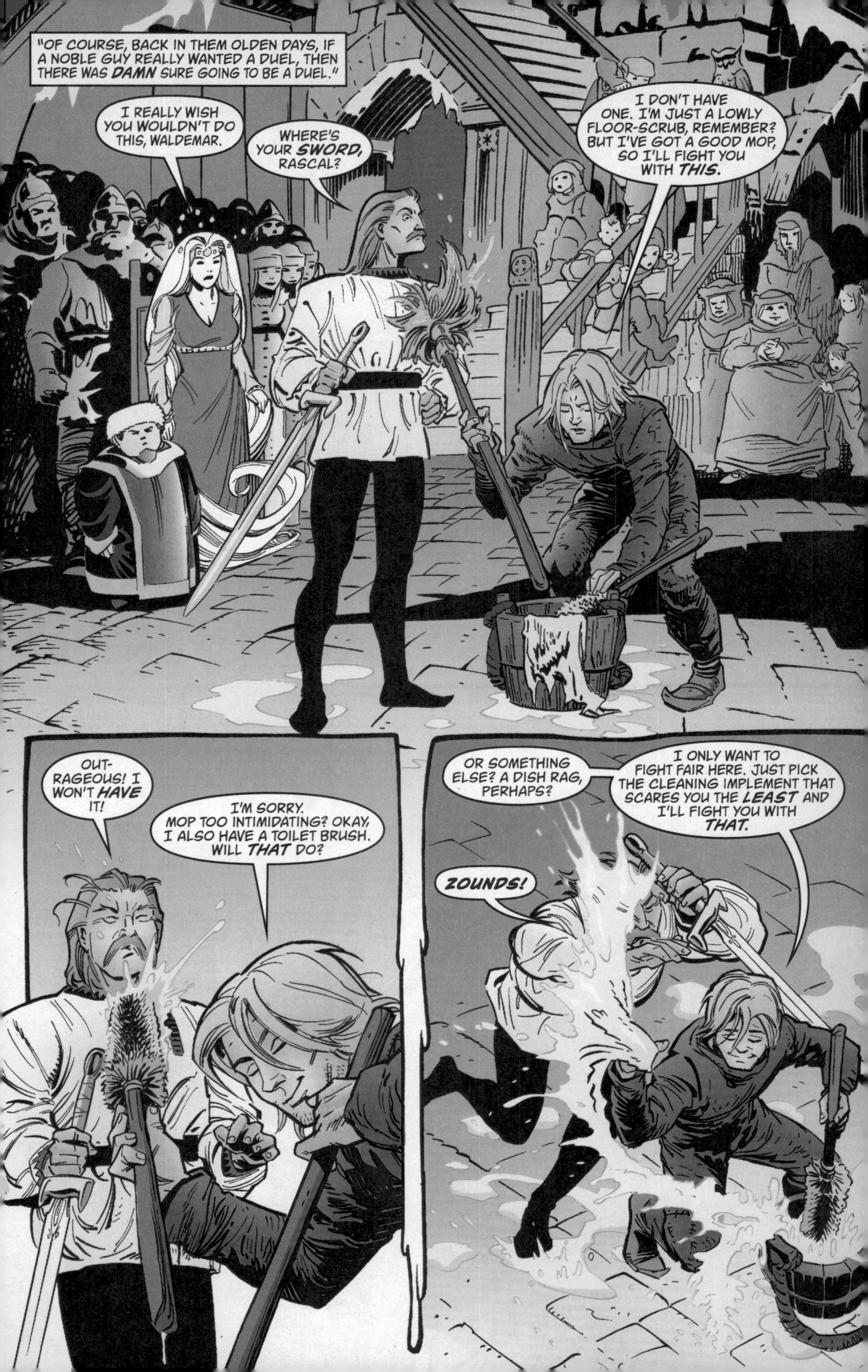
"OF COURSE, BACK IN THEM OLDEN DAYS, IF A NOBLE GUY REALLY WANTED A DUEL, THEN THERE WAS DAMN SURE GOING TO BE A DUEL."
I REALLY WISH YOU WOULDN'T DO THIS, WALDEMAR.
WHERE'S YOUR SWORD, RASCAL?
I DON'T HAVE ONE. I'M JUST A LOWLY FLOOR-SCRUB, REMEMBER? BUT I'VE GOT A GOOD MOP, SO I'LL FIGHT YOU WITH THIS.
OUT-RAGEOUS! I WON'T HAVE IT!
I'M SORRY. MOP TOO INTIMIDATING? OKAY, I ALSO HAVE A TOILET BRUSH. WILL THAT DO?
OR SOMETHING ELSE? A DISH RAG, PERHAPS?
I ONLY WANT TO FIGHT FAIR HERE. JUST PICK THE CLEANING IMPLEMENT THAT SCARES YOU THE LEAST AND I'LL FIGHT YOU WITH THAT.
ZOUNDS!

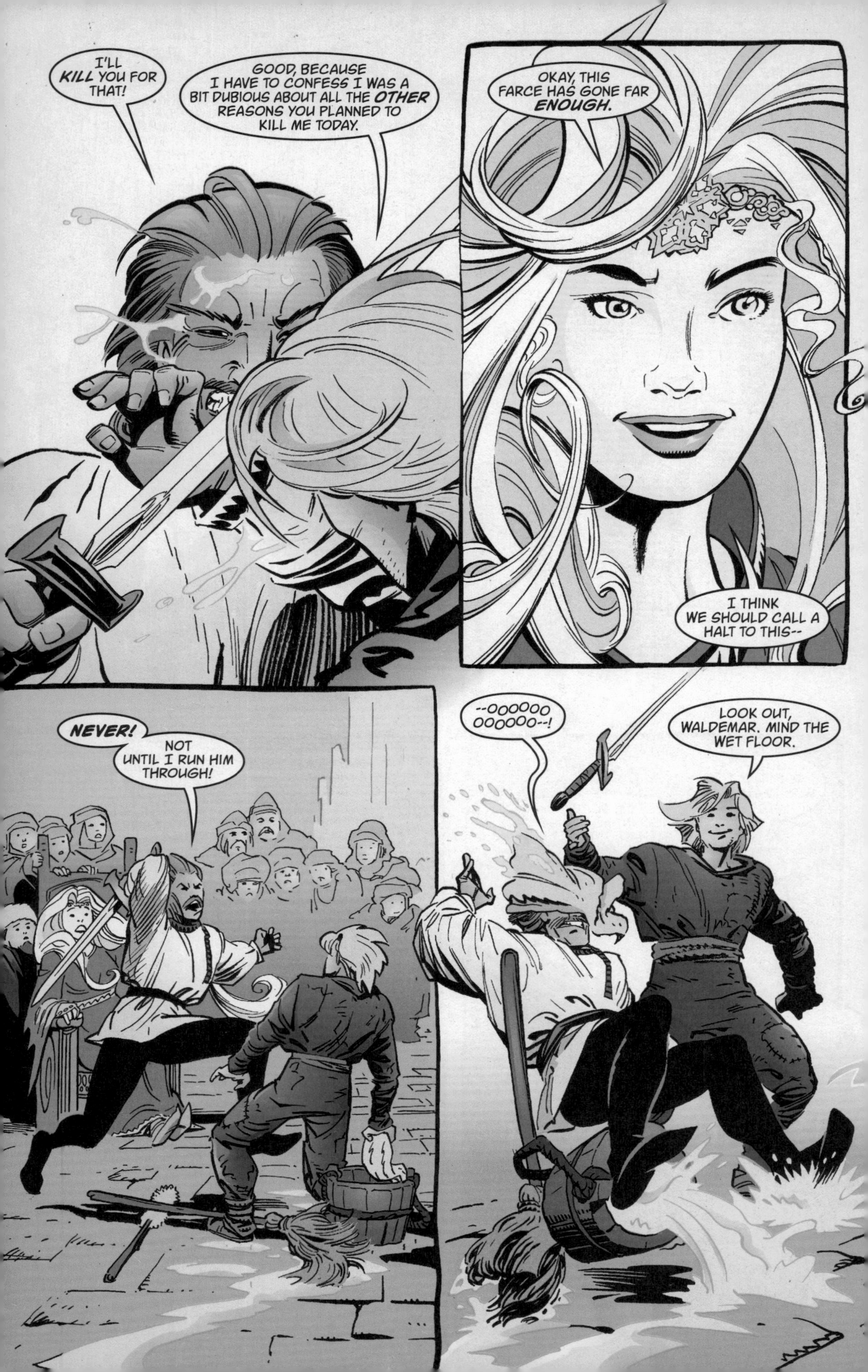
I'LL *KILL* YOU FOR THAT!
GOOD, BECAUSE I HAVE TO CONFESS I WAS A BIT DUBIOUS ABOUT ALL THE *OTHER* REASONS YOU PLANNED TO KILL ME TODAY.
OKAY, THIS FARCE HAS GONE FAR *ENOUGH.*
I THINK WE SHOULD CALL A HALT TO THIS--
NEVER!
NOT UNTIL I RUN HIM THROUGH!
--OOOOOO OOOOOO--!
LOOK OUT, WALDEMAR. MIND THE WET FLOOR.

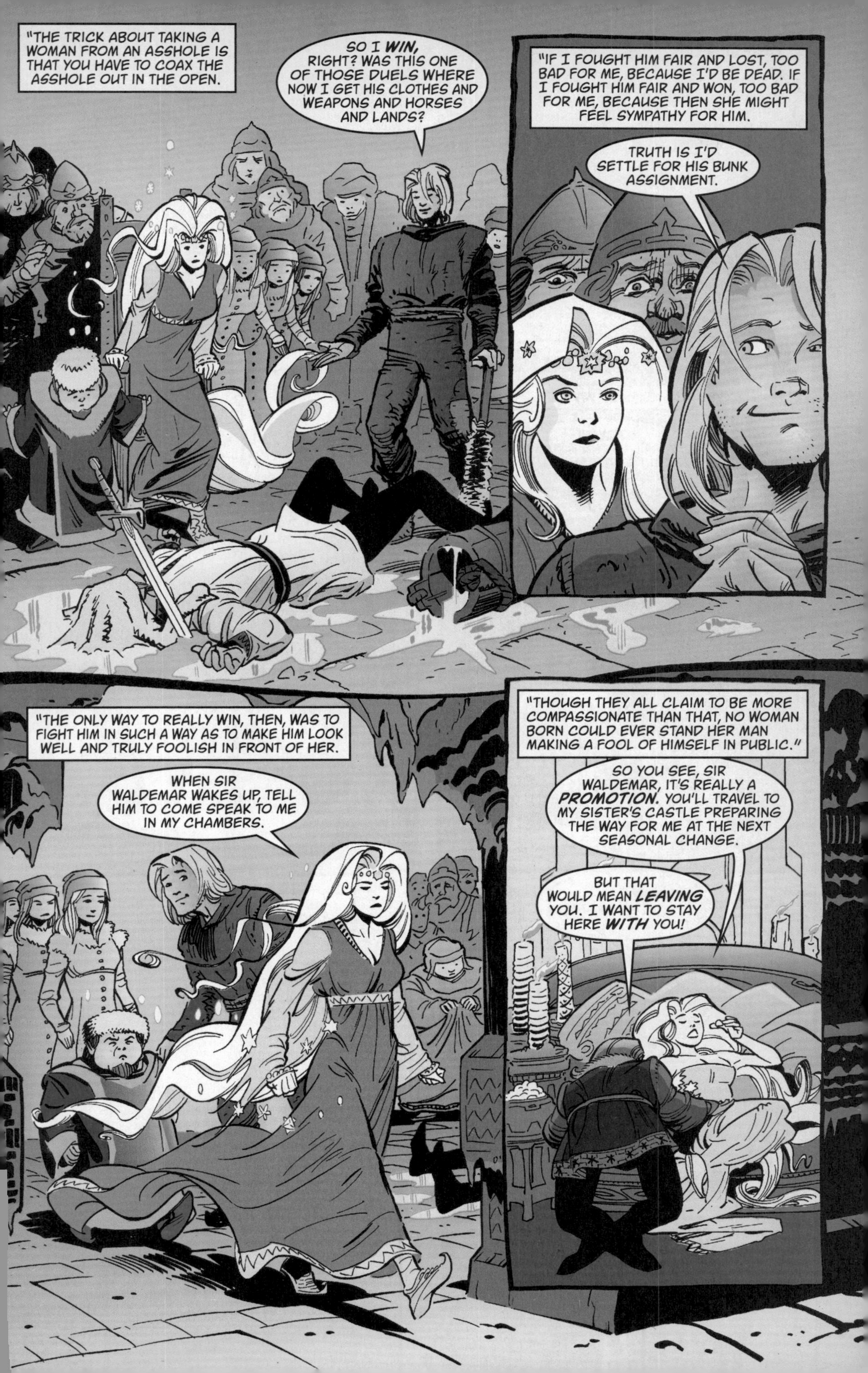
"THE TRICK ABOUT TAKING A WOMAN FROM AN ASSHOLE IS THAT YOU HAVE TO COAX THE ASSHOLE OUT IN THE OPEN.
SO I WIN, RIGHT? WAS THIS ONE OF THOSE DUELS WHERE NOW I GET HIS CLOTHES AND WEAPONS AND HORSES AND LANDS?
"IF I FOUGHT HIM FAIR AND LOST, TOO BAD FOR ME, BECAUSE I'D BE DEAD. IF I FOUGHT HIM FAIR AND WON, TOO BAD FOR ME, BECAUSE THEN SHE MIGHT FEEL SYMPATHY FOR HIM.
TRUTH IS I'D SETTLE FOR HIS BUNK ASSIGNMENT.
"THE ONLY WAY TO REALLY WIN, THEN, WAS TO FIGHT HIM IN SUCH A WAY AS TO MAKE HIM LOOK WELL AND TRULY FOOLISH IN FRONT OF HER.
WHEN SIR WALDEMAR WAKES UP, TELL HIM TO COME SPEAK TO ME IN MY CHAMBERS.
"THOUGH THEY ALL CLAIM TO BE MORE COMPASSIONATE THAN THAT, NO WOMAN BORN COULD EVER STAND HER MAN MAKING A FOOL OF HIMSELF IN PUBLIC."
SO YOU SEE, SIR WALDEMAR, IT'S REALLY A PROMOTION. YOU'LL TRAVEL TO MY SISTER'S CASTLE PREPARING THE WAY FOR ME AT THE NEXT SEASONAL CHANGE.
BUT THAT WOULD MEAN LEAVING YOU. I WANT TO STAY HERE WITH YOU!

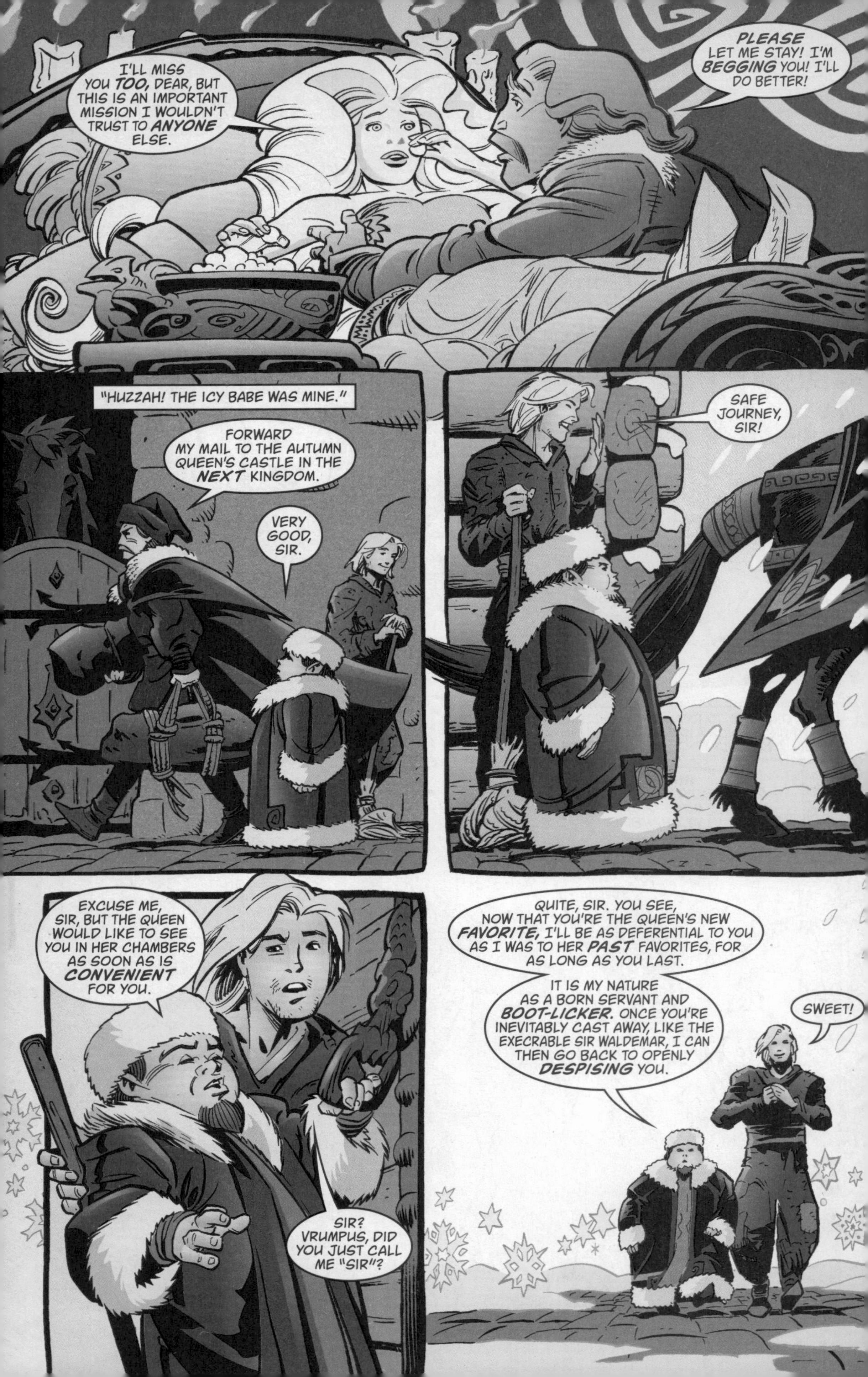
I'LL MISS YOU TOO, DEAR, BUT THIS IS AN IMPORTANT MISSION I WOULDN'T TRUST TO ANYONE ELSE.
PLEASE LET ME STAY! I'M BEGGING YOU! I'LL DO BETTER!
"HUZZAH! THE ICY BABE WAS MINE."
FORWARD MY MAIL TO THE AUTUMN QUEEN'S CASTLE IN THE NEXT KINGDOM.
VERY GOOD, SIR.
SAFE JOURNEY, SIR!
EXCUSE ME, SIR, BUT THE QUEEN WOULD LIKE TO SEE YOU IN HER CHAMBERS AS SOON AS IS CONVENIENT FOR YOU.
SIR? VRUMPUS, DID YOU JUST CALL ME "SIR"?
QUITE, SIR. YOU SEE, NOW THAT YOU'RE THE QUEEN'S NEW FAVORITE, I'LL BE AS DEFERENTIAL TO YOU AS I WAS TO HER PAST FAVORITES, FOR AS LONG AS YOU LAST.
IT IS MY NATURE AS A BORN SERVANT AND BOOT-LICKER. ONCE YOU'RE INEVITABLY CAST AWAY, LIKE THE EXECRABLE SIR WALDEMAR, I CAN THEN GO BACK TO OPENLY DESPISING YOU.
SWEET!

We briefly interrupt this funnybook for a few important words of explanation.

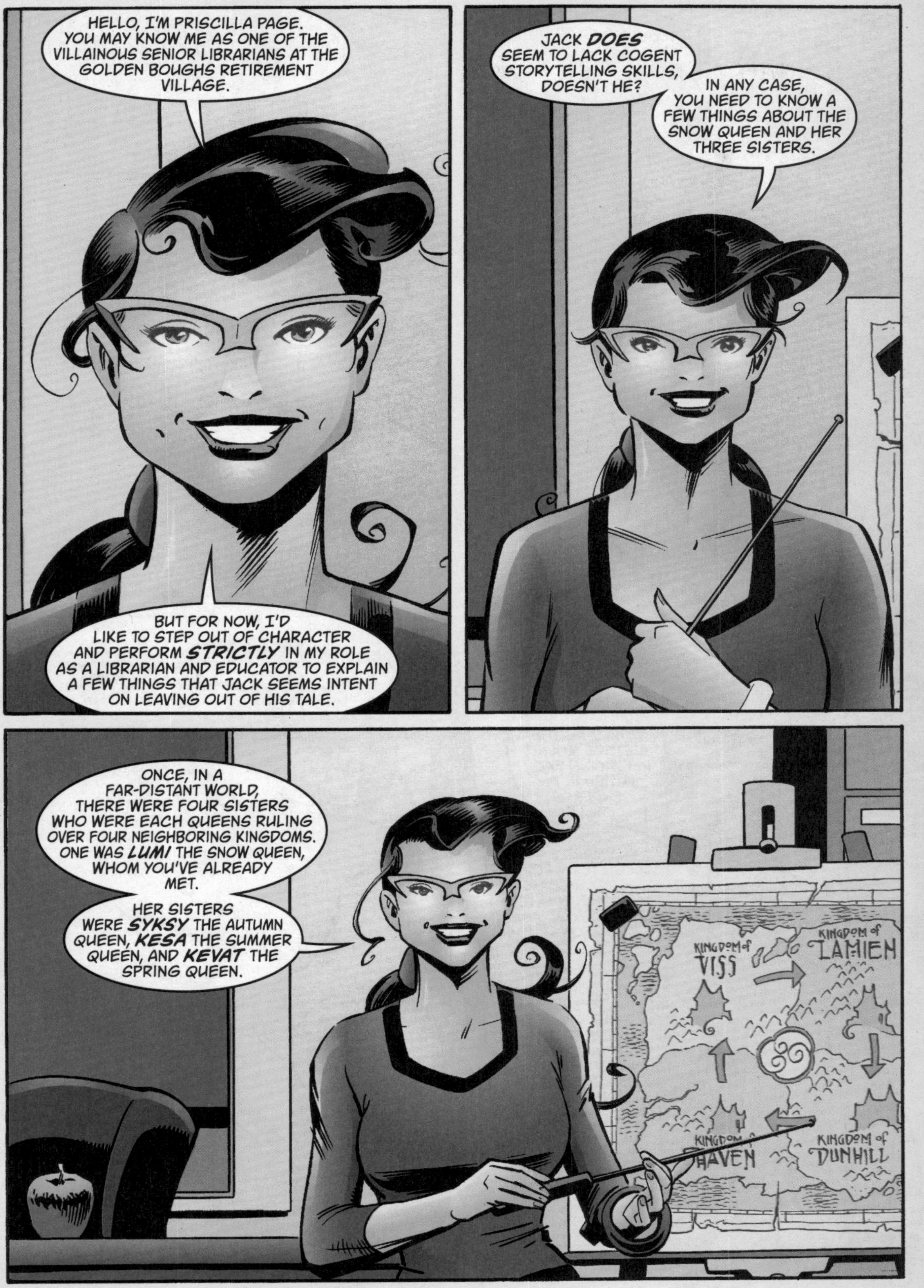
HELLO, I'M PRISCILLA PAGE. YOU MAY KNOW ME AS ONE OF THE VILLAINOUS SENIOR LIBRARIANS AT THE GOLDEN BOUGHS RETIREMENT VILLAGE.
BUT FOR NOW, I'D LIKE TO STEP OUT OF CHARACTER AND PERFORM *STRICTLY* IN MY ROLE AS A LIBRARIAN AND EDUCATOR TO EXPLAIN A FEW THINGS THAT JACK SEEMS INTENT ON LEAVING OUT OF HIS TALE.
JACK *DOES* SEEM TO LACK COGENT STORYTELLING SKILLS, DOESN'T HE?
IN ANY CASE, YOU NEED TO KNOW A FEW THINGS ABOUT THE SNOW QUEEN AND HER THREE SISTERS.
ONCE, IN A FAR-DISTANT WORLD, THERE WERE FOUR SISTERS WHO WERE EACH QUEENS RULING OVER FOUR NEIGHBORING KINGDOMS. ONE WAS *LUMI* THE SNOW QUEEN, WHOM YOU'VE ALREADY MET.
HER SISTERS WERE *SYKSY* THE AUTUMN QUEEN, *KESA* THE SUMMER QUEEN, AND *KEVAT* THE SPRING QUEEN.
KINGDOM of VISS
KINGDOM of LAMIEN
KINGDOM HAVEN
KINGDOM of DUNHILL

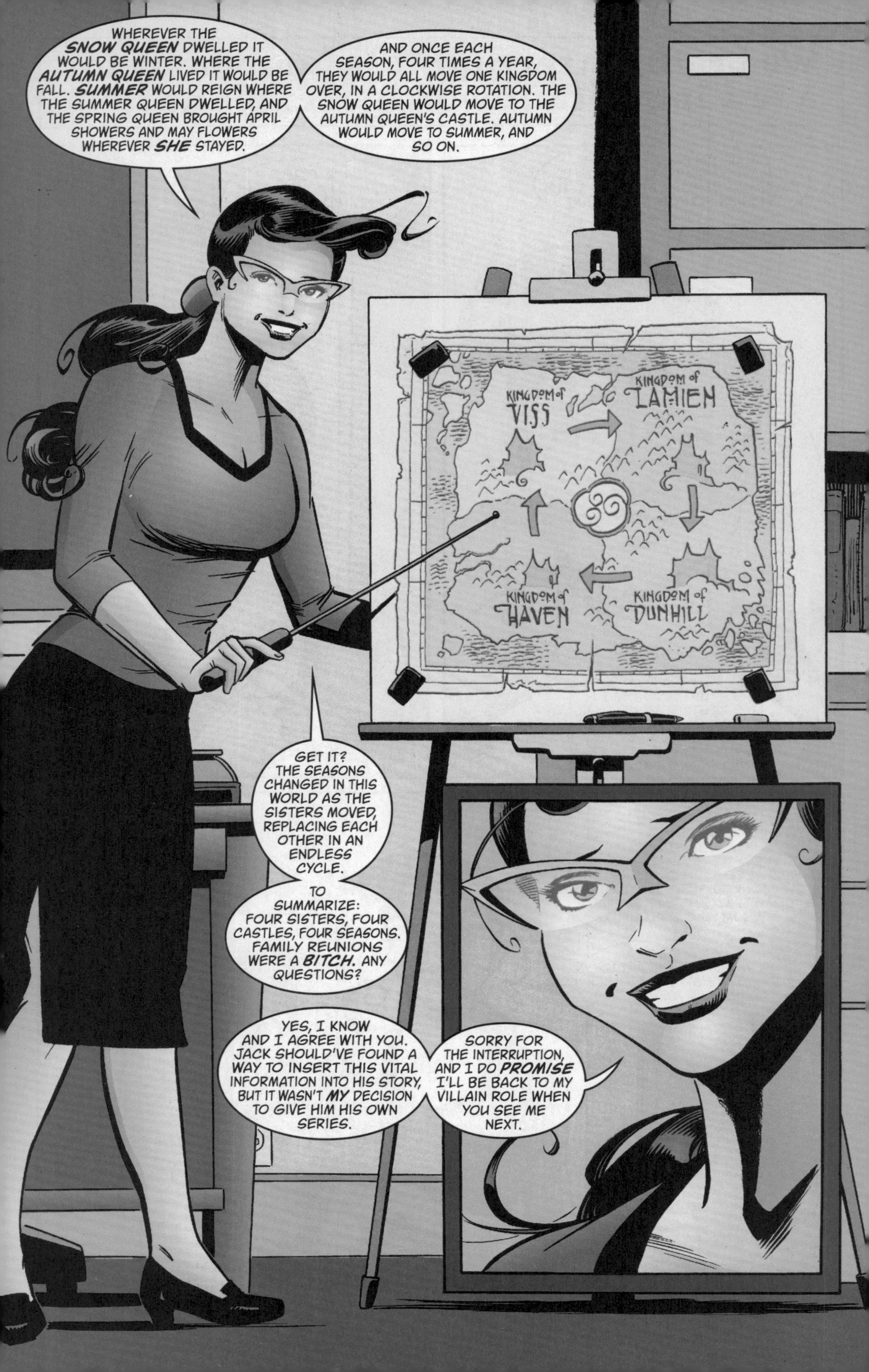
WHEREVER THE SNOW QUEEN DWELLED IT WOULD BE WINTER. WHERE THE AUTUMN QUEEN LIVED IT WOULD BE FALL. SUMMER WOULD REIGN WHERE THE SUMMER QUEEN DWELLED, AND THE SPRING QUEEN BROUGHT APRIL SHOWERS AND MAY FLOWERS WHEREVER SHE STAYED.
AND ONCE EACH SEASON, FOUR TIMES A YEAR, THEY WOULD ALL MOVE ONE KINGDOM OVER, IN A CLOCKWISE ROTATION. THE SNOW QUEEN WOULD MOVE TO THE AUTUMN QUEEN'S CASTLE. AUTUMN WOULD MOVE TO SUMMER, AND SO ON.
KINGDOM of VISS
KINGDOM of LAMIEN
KINGDOM of HAVEN
KINGDOM of DUNHILL
GET IT? THE SEASONS CHANGED IN THIS WORLD AS THE SISTERS MOVED, REPLACING EACH OTHER IN AN ENDLESS CYCLE.
TO SUMMARIZE: FOUR SISTERS, FOUR CASTLES, FOUR SEASONS. FAMILY REUNIONS WERE A BITCH. ANY QUESTIONS?
YES, I KNOW AND I AGREE WITH YOU. JACK SHOULD'VE FOUND A WAY TO INSERT THIS VITAL INFORMATION INTO HIS STORY, BUT IT WASN'T MY DECISION TO GIVE HIM HIS OWN SERIES.
SORRY FOR THE INTERRUPTION, AND I DO PROMISE I'LL BE BACK TO MY VILLAIN ROLE WHEN YOU SEE ME NEXT.

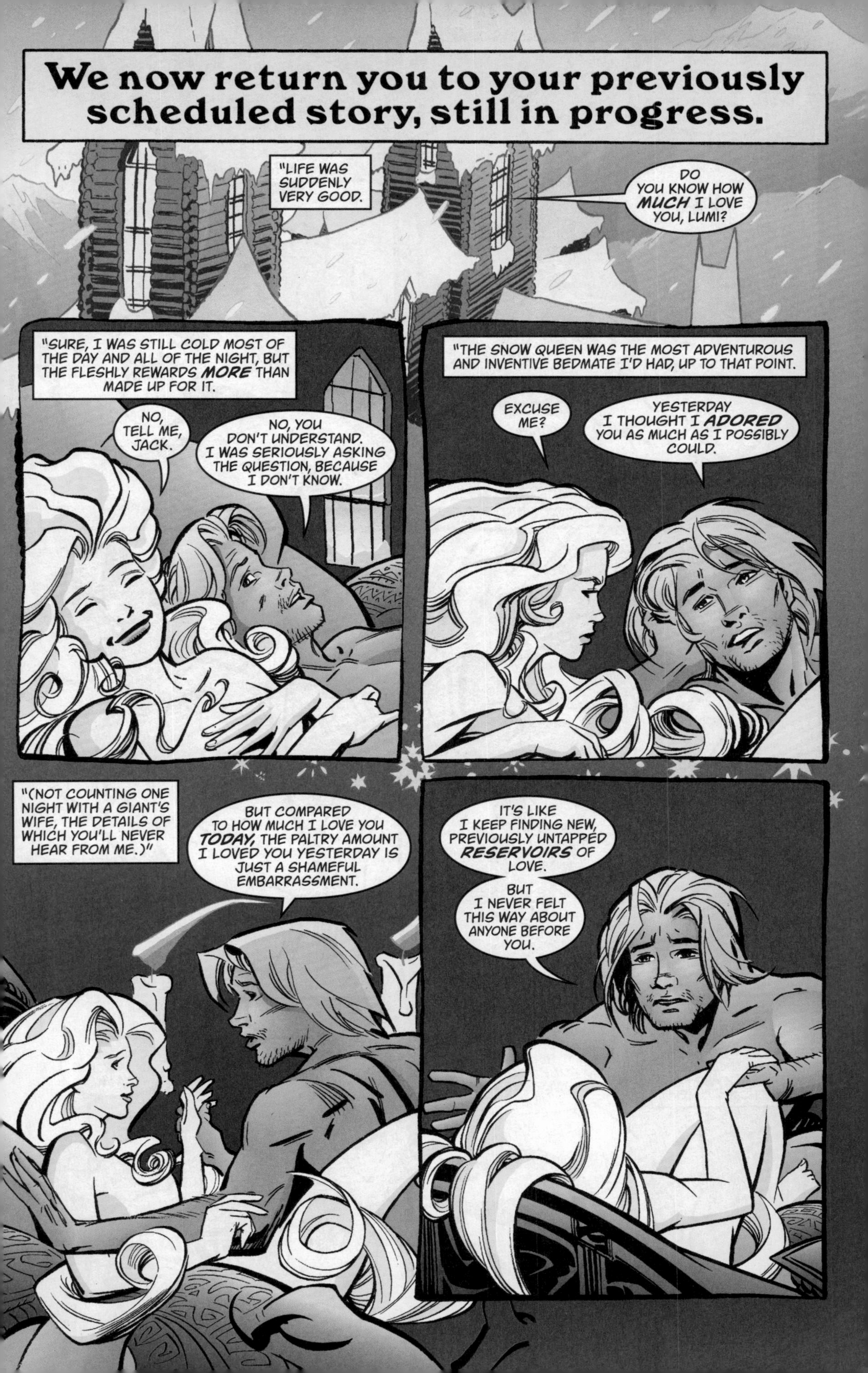
We now return you to your previously scheduled story, still in progress.
"LIFE WAS SUDDENLY VERY GOOD.
DO YOU KNOW HOW MUCH I LOVE YOU, LUMI?
"SURE, I WAS STILL COLD MOST OF THE DAY AND ALL OF THE NIGHT, BUT THE FLESHLY REWARDS MORE THAN MADE UP FOR IT.
NO, TELL ME, JACK.
NO, YOU DON'T UNDERSTAND. I WAS SERIOUSLY ASKING THE QUESTION, BECAUSE I DON'T KNOW.
"THE SNOW QUEEN WAS THE MOST ADVENTUROUS AND INVENTIVE BEDMATE I'D HAD, UP TO THAT POINT.
EXCUSE ME?
YESTERDAY I THOUGHT I ADORED YOU AS MUCH AS I POSSIBLY COULD.
"(NOT COUNTING ONE NIGHT WITH A GIANT'S WIFE, THE DETAILS OF WHICH YOU'LL NEVER HEAR FROM ME.)"
BUT COMPARED TO HOW MUCH I LOVE YOU TODAY, THE PALTRY AMOUNT I LOVED YOU YESTERDAY IS JUST A SHAMEFUL EMBARRASSMENT.
IT'S LIKE I KEEP FINDING NEW, PREVIOUSLY UNTAPPED RESERVOIRS OF LOVE.
BUT I NEVER FELT THIS WAY ABOUT ANYONE BEFORE YOU.

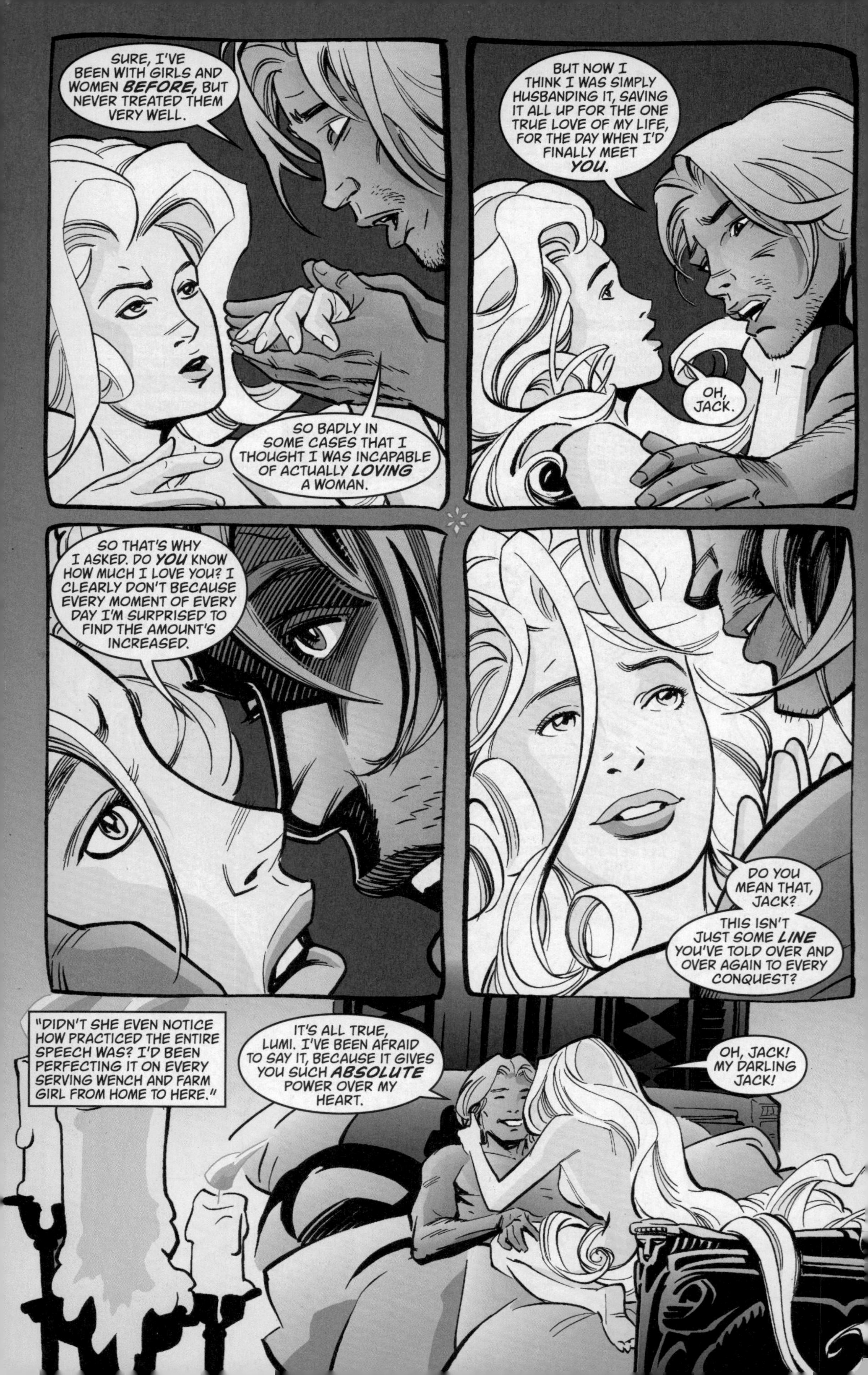
SURE, I'VE BEEN WITH GIRLS AND WOMEN BEFORE, BUT NEVER TREATED THEM VERY WELL.
SO BADLY IN SOME CASES THAT I THOUGHT I WAS INCAPABLE OF ACTUALLY LOVING A WOMAN.
BUT NOW I THINK I WAS SIMPLY HUSBANDING IT, SAVING IT ALL UP FOR THE ONE TRUE LOVE OF MY LIFE, FOR THE DAY WHEN I'D FINALLY MEET YOU.
OH, JACK.
SO THAT'S WHY I ASKED. DO YOU KNOW HOW MUCH I LOVE YOU? I CLEARLY DON'T BECAUSE EVERY MOMENT OF EVERY DAY I'M SURPRISED TO FIND THE AMOUNT'S INCREASED.
DO YOU MEAN THAT, JACK?
THIS ISN'T JUST SOME LINE YOU'VE TOLD OVER AND OVER AGAIN TO EVERY CONQUEST?
"DIDN'T SHE EVEN NOTICE HOW PRACTICED THE ENTIRE SPEECH WAS? I'D BEEN PERFECTING IT ON EVERY SERVING WENCH AND FARM GIRL FROM HOME TO HERE."
IT'S ALL TRUE, LUMI. I'VE BEEN AFRAID TO SAY IT, BECAUSE IT GIVES YOU SUCH ABSOLUTE POWER OVER MY HEART.
OH, JACK! MY DARLING JACK!

Once again we're forced to interrupt this story for an important announcement.

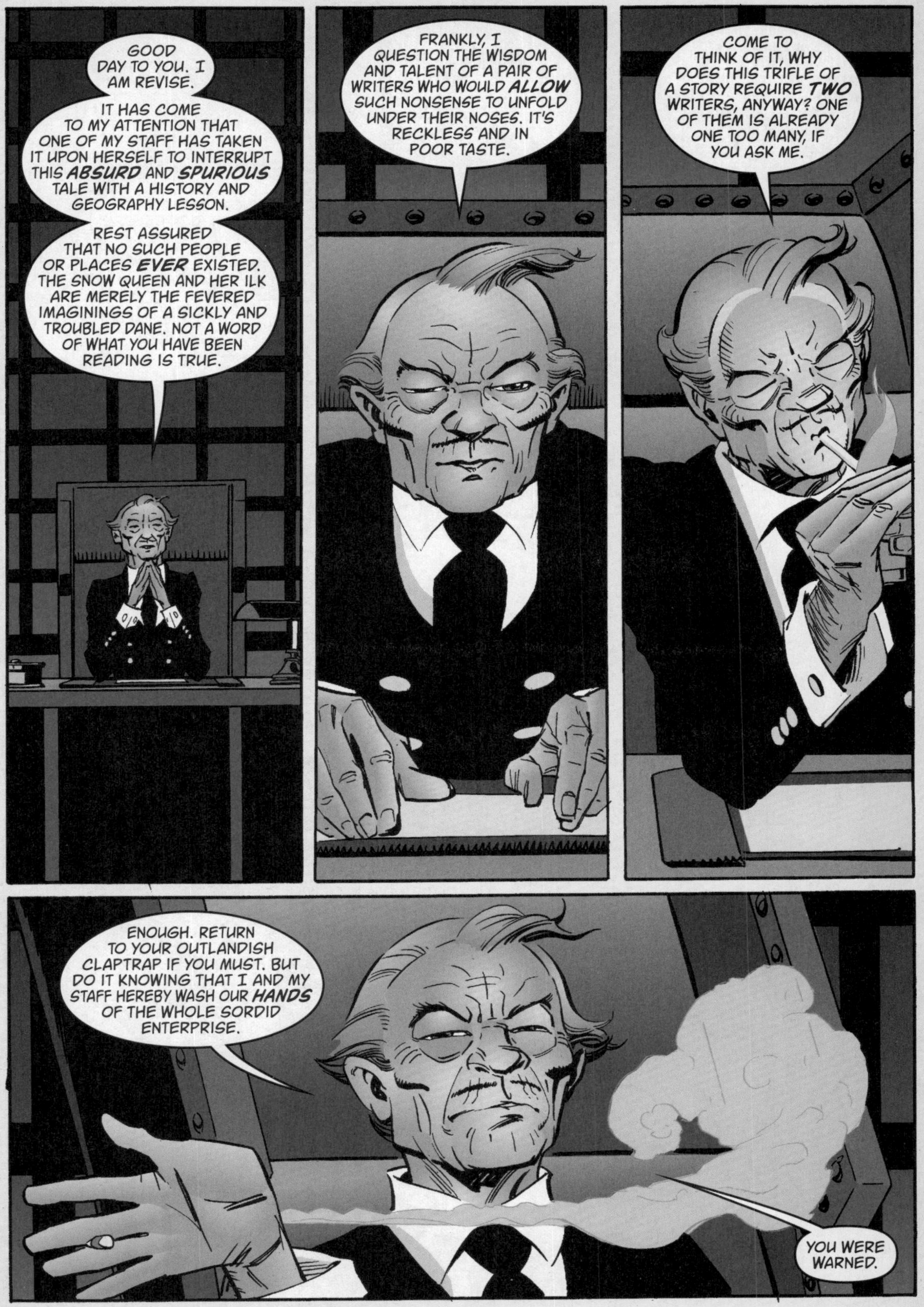
GOOD DAY TO YOU. I AM REVISE.
IT HAS COME TO MY ATTENTION THAT ONE OF MY STAFF HAS TAKEN IT UPON HERSELF TO INTERRUPT THIS ABSURD AND SPURIOUS TALE WITH A HISTORY AND GEOGRAPHY LESSON.
REST ASSURED THAT NO SUCH PEOPLE OR PLACES EVER EXISTED. THE SNOW QUEEN AND HER ILK ARE MERELY THE FEVERED IMAGININGS OF A SICKLY AND TROUBLED DANE. NOT A WORD OF WHAT YOU HAVE BEEN READING IS TRUE.
FRANKLY, I QUESTION THE WISDOM AND TALENT OF A PAIR OF WRITERS WHO WOULD ALLOW SUCH NONSENSE TO UNFOLD UNDER THEIR NOSES. IT'S RECKLESS AND IN POOR TASTE.
COME TO THINK OF IT, WHY DOES THIS TRIFLE OF A STORY REQUIRE TWO WRITERS, ANYWAY? ONE OF THEM IS ALREADY ONE TOO MANY, IF YOU ASK ME.
ENOUGH. RETURN TO YOUR OUTLANDISH CLAPTRAP IF YOU MUST. BUT DO IT KNOWING THAT I AND MY STAFF HEREBY WASH OUR HANDS OF THE WHOLE SORDID ENTERPRISE.
YOU WERE WARNED.

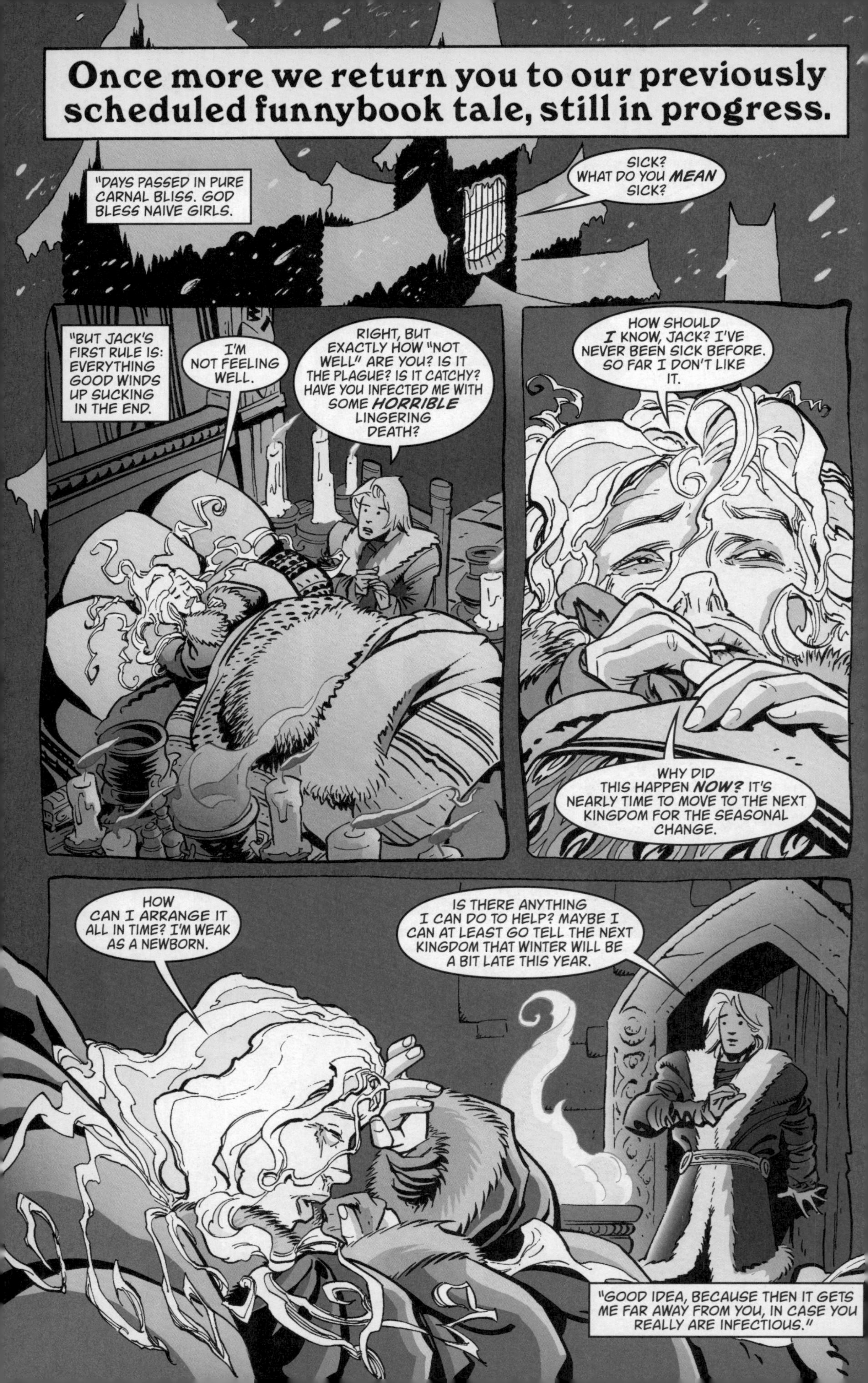

Once more we return you to our previously scheduled funnybook tale, still in progress.
"DAYS PASSED IN PURE CARNAL BLISS. GOD BLESS NAIVE GIRLS.
SICK? WHAT DO YOU MEAN SICK?
"BUT JACK'S FIRST RULE IS: EVERYTHING GOOD WINDS UP SUCKING IN THE END.
I'M NOT FEELING WELL.
RIGHT, BUT EXACTLY HOW "NOT WELL" ARE YOU? IS IT THE PLAGUE? IS IT CATCHY? HAVE YOU INFECTED ME WITH SOME HORRIBLE LINGERING DEATH?
HOW SHOULD I KNOW, JACK? I'VE NEVER BEEN SICK BEFORE. SO FAR I DON'T LIKE IT.
WHY DID THIS HAPPEN NOW? IT'S NEARLY TIME TO MOVE TO THE NEXT KINGDOM FOR THE SEASONAL CHANGE.
HOW CAN I ARRANGE IT ALL IN TIME? I'M WEAK AS A NEWBORN.
IS THERE ANYTHING I CAN DO TO HELP? MAYBE I CAN AT LEAST GO TELL THE NEXT KINGDOM THAT WINTER WILL BE A BIT LATE THIS YEAR.
"GOOD IDEA, BECAUSE THEN IT GETS ME FAR AWAY FROM YOU, IN CASE YOU REALLY ARE INFECTIOUS."

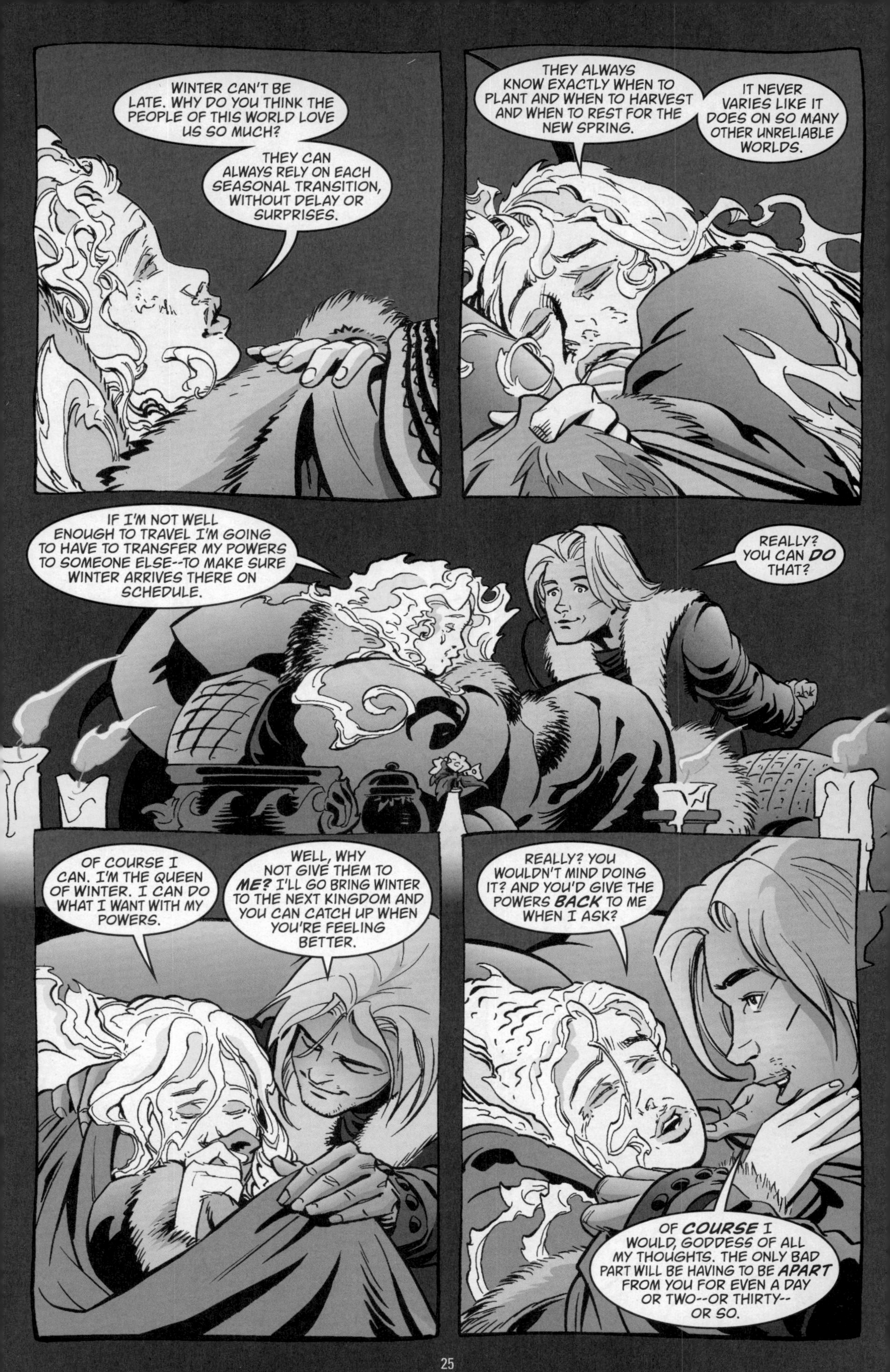
WINTER CAN'T BE LATE. WHY DO YOU THINK THE PEOPLE OF THIS WORLD LOVE US SO MUCH?
THEY CAN ALWAYS RELY ON EACH SEASONAL TRANSITION, WITHOUT DELAY OR SURPRISES.
THEY ALWAYS KNOW EXACTLY WHEN TO PLANT AND WHEN TO HARVEST AND WHEN TO REST FOR THE NEW SPRING.
IT NEVER VARIES LIKE IT DOES ON SO MANY OTHER UNRELIABLE WORLDS.
IF I'M NOT WELL ENOUGH TO TRAVEL I'M GOING TO HAVE TO TRANSFER MY POWERS TO SOMEONE ELSE--TO MAKE SURE WINTER ARRIVES THERE ON SCHEDULE.
REALLY? YOU CAN DO THAT?
OF COURSE I CAN. I'M THE QUEEN OF WINTER. I CAN DO WHAT I WANT WITH MY POWERS.
WELL, WHY NOT GIVE THEM TO ME? I'LL GO BRING WINTER TO THE NEXT KINGDOM AND YOU CAN CATCH UP WHEN YOU'RE FEELING BETTER.
REALLY? YOU WOULDN'T MIND DOING IT? AND YOU'D GIVE THE POWERS BACK TO ME WHEN I ASK?
OF COURSE I WOULD, GODDESS OF ALL MY THOUGHTS. THE ONLY BAD PART WILL BE HAVING TO BE APART FROM YOU FOR EVEN A DAY OR TWO--OR THIRTY--OR SO.

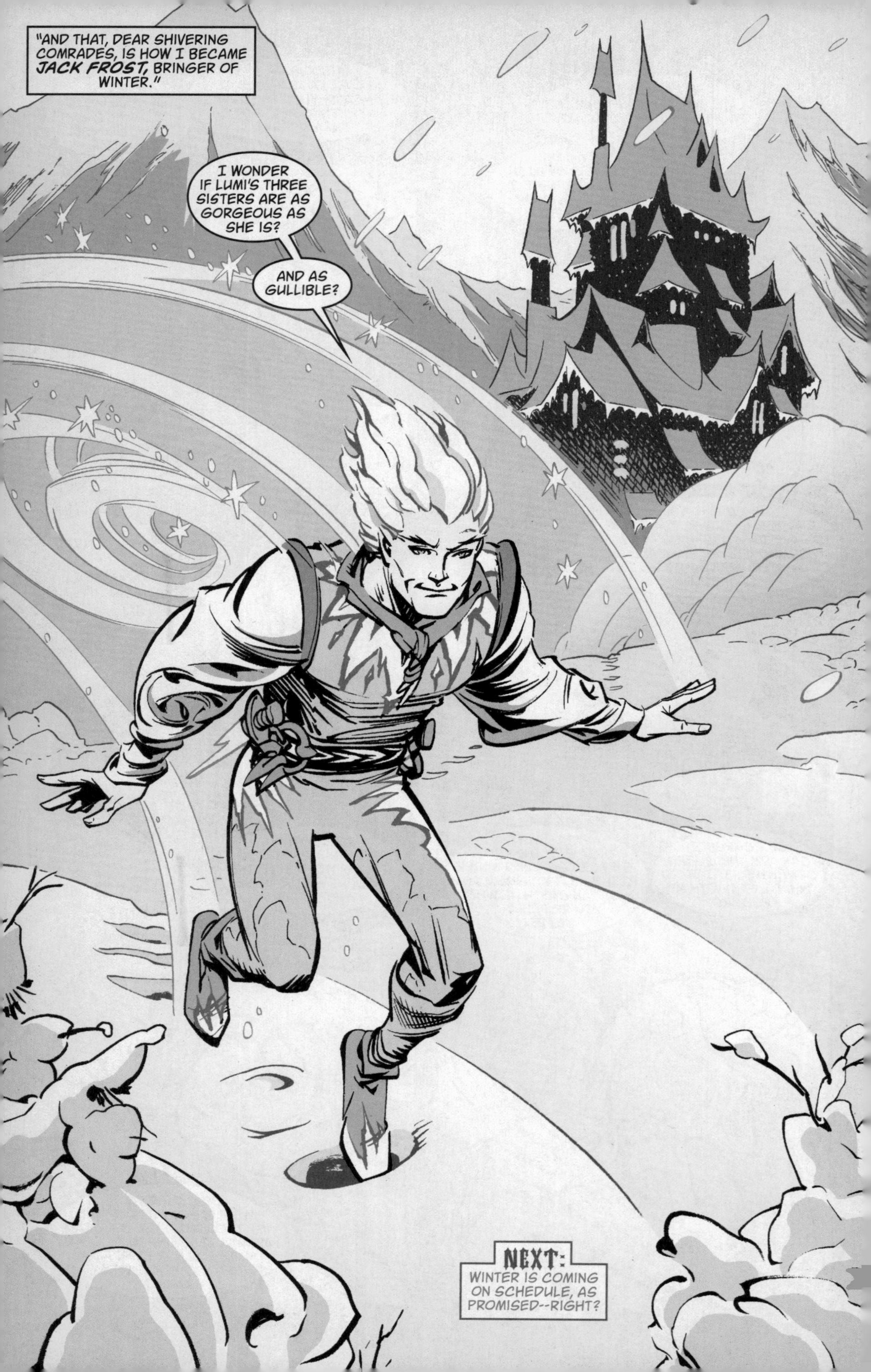
"AND THAT, DEAR SHIVERING COMRADES, IS HOW I BECAME JACK FROST, BRINGER OF WINTER."
I WONDER IF LUMI'S THREE SISTERS ARE AS GORGEOUS AS SHE IS?
AND AS GULLIBLE?
NEXT:
WINTER IS COMING ON SCHEDULE, AS PROMISED--RIGHT?

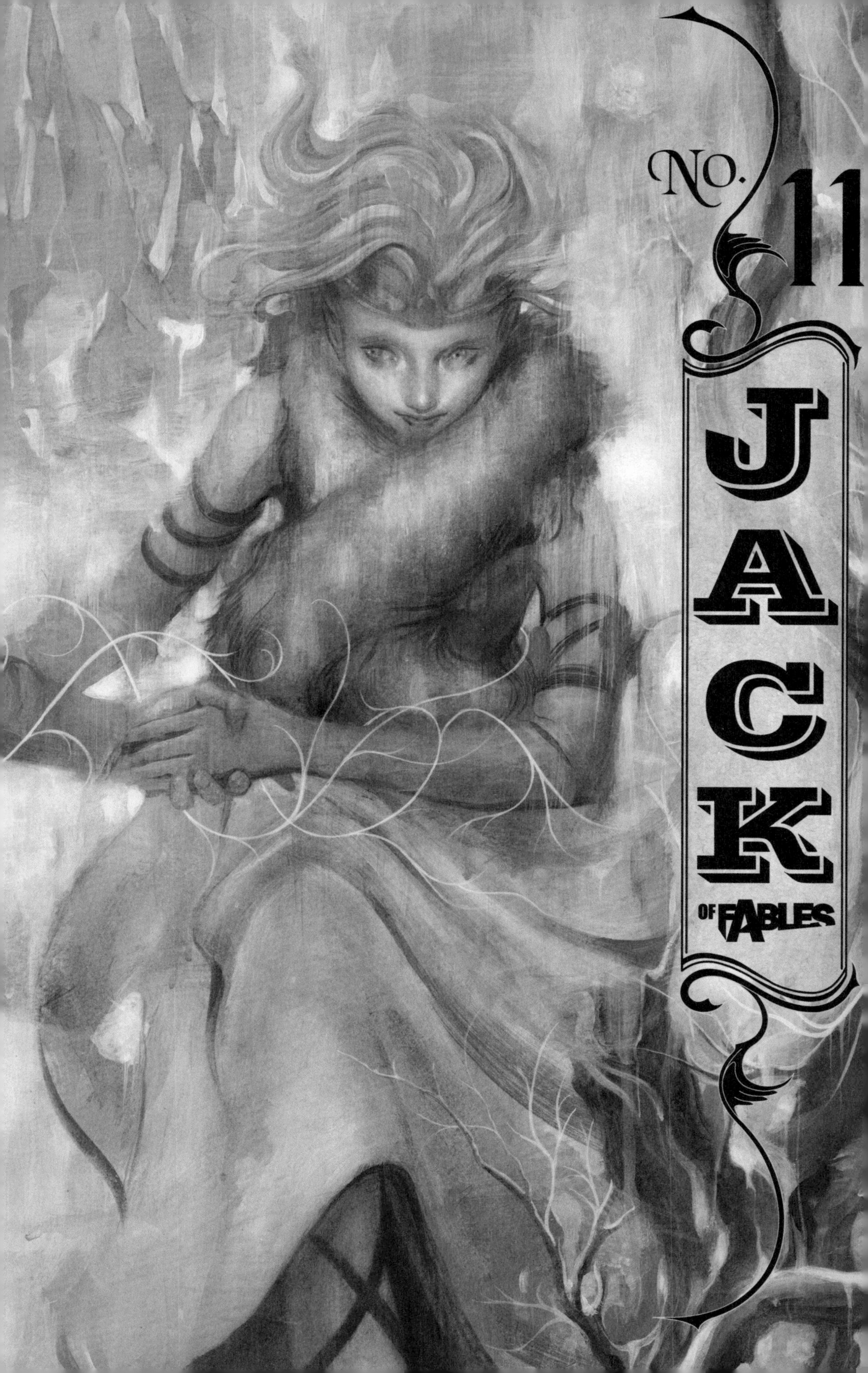

NO. 11
JACK
OF FABLES

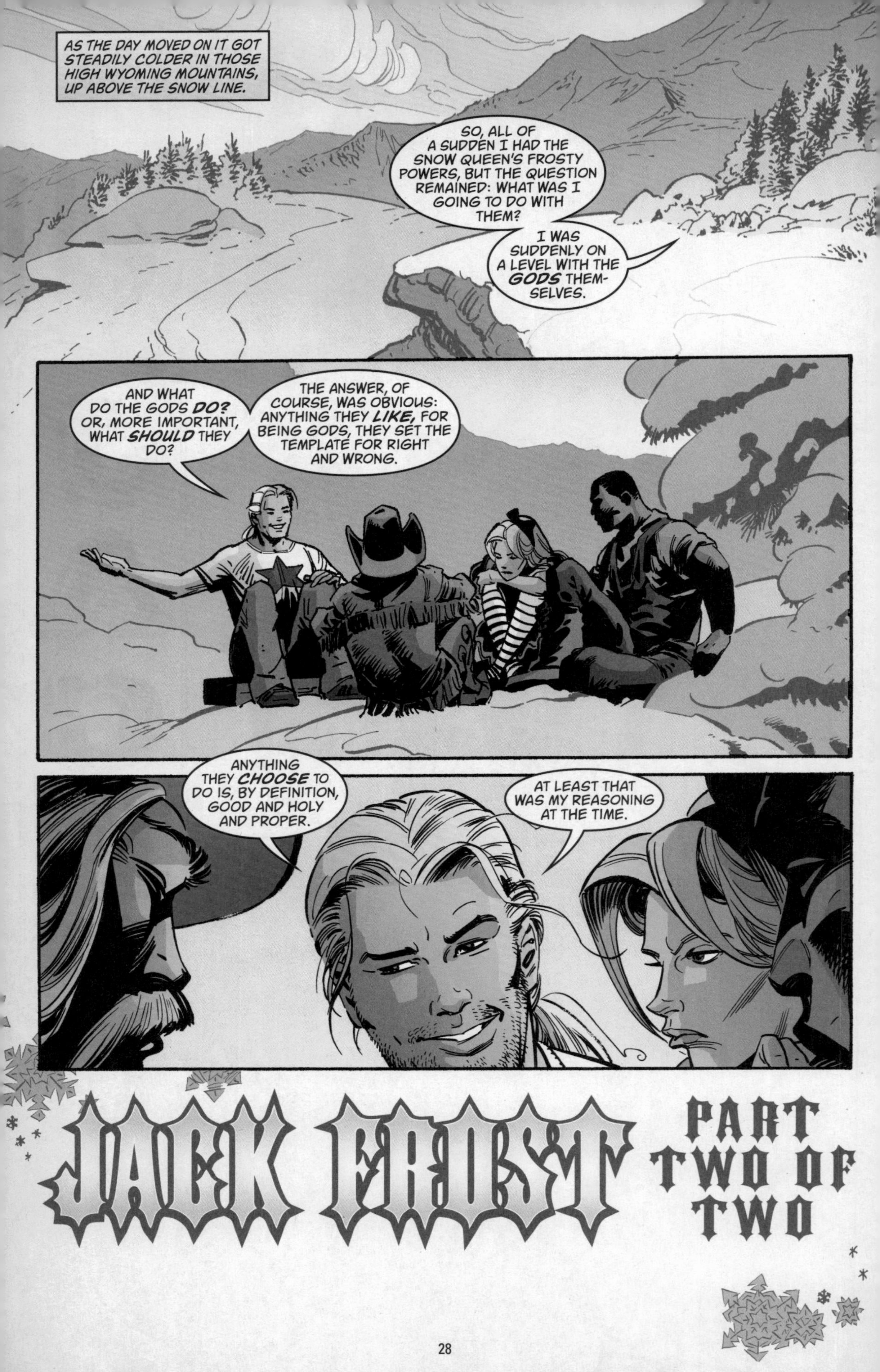
AS THE DAY MOVED ON IT GOT STEADILY COLDER IN THOSE HIGH WYOMING MOUNTAINS, UP ABOVE THE SNOW LINE.
SO, ALL OF A SUDDEN I HAD THE SNOW QUEEN'S FROSTY POWERS, BUT THE QUESTION REMAINED: WHAT WAS I GOING TO DO WITH THEM?
I WAS SUDDENLY ON A LEVEL WITH THE GODS THEM-SELVES.
AND WHAT DO THE GODS DO? OR, MORE IMPORTANT, WHAT SHOULD THEY DO?
THE ANSWER, OF COURSE, WAS OBVIOUS: ANYTHING THEY LIKE, FOR BEING GODS, THEY SET THE TEMPLATE FOR RIGHT AND WRONG.
ANYTHING THEY CHOOSE TO DO IS, BY DEFINITION, GOOD AND HOLY AND PROPER.
AT LEAST THAT WAS MY REASONING AT THE TIME.
JACK FROST
PART TWO OF TWO

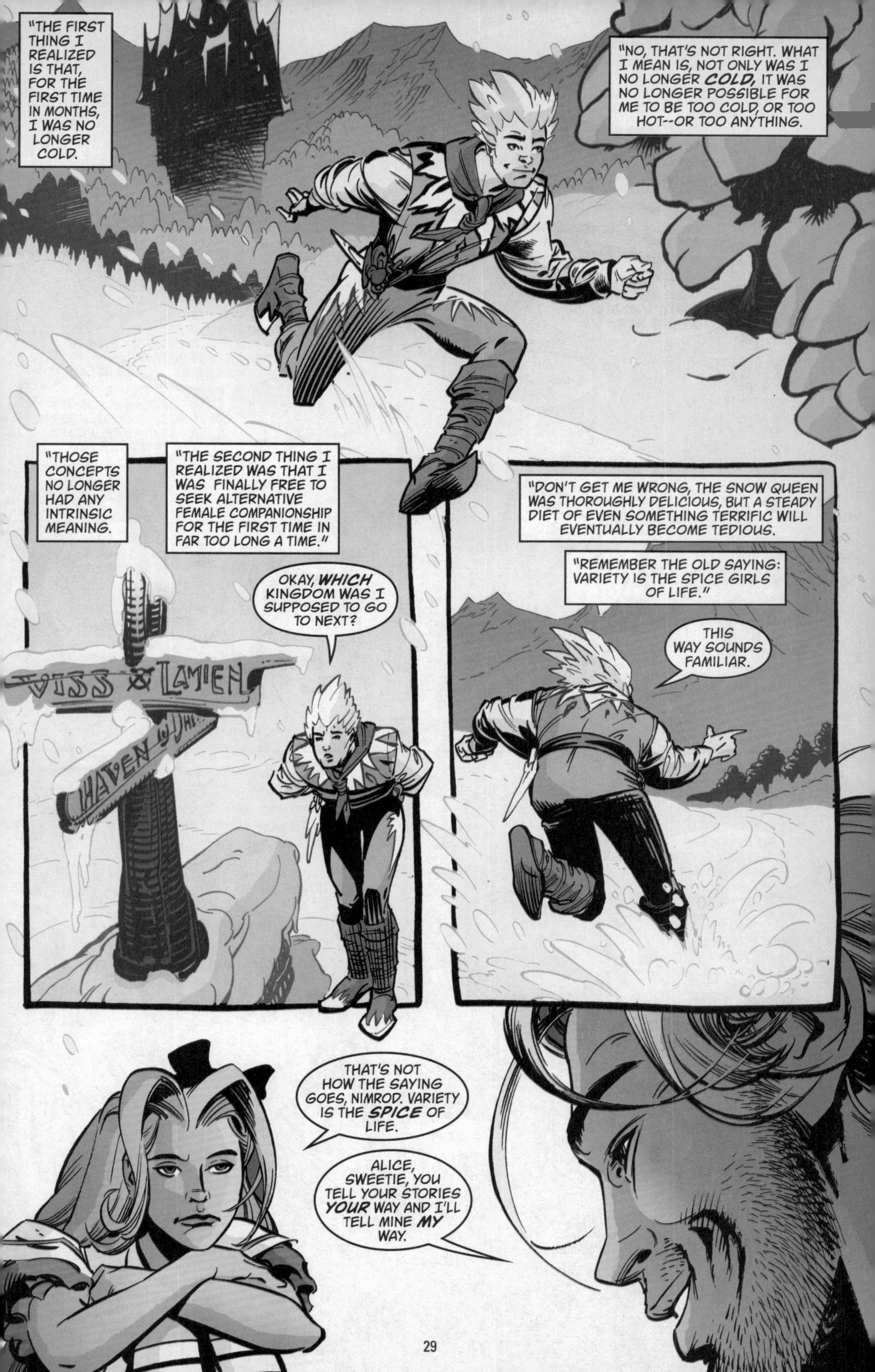
"THE FIRST THING I REALIZED IS THAT, FOR THE FIRST TIME IN MONTHS, I WAS NO LONGER COLD.
"NO, THAT'S NOT RIGHT. WHAT I MEAN IS, NOT ONLY WAS I NO LONGER COLD, IT WAS NO LONGER POSSIBLE FOR ME TO BE TOO COLD, OR TOO HOT--OR TOO ANYTHING.
"THOSE CONCEPTS NO LONGER HAD ANY INTRINSIC MEANING.
"THE SECOND THING I REALIZED WAS THAT I WAS FINALLY FREE TO SEEK ALTERNATIVE FEMALE COMPANIONSHIP FOR THE FIRST TIME IN FAR TOO LONG A TIME."
VISS
LAMIEN
HAVEN
OKAY, WHICH KINGDOM WAS I SUPPOSED TO GO TO NEXT?
"DON'T GET ME WRONG, THE SNOW QUEEN WAS THOROUGHLY DELICIOUS, BUT A STEADY DIET OF EVEN SOMETHING TERRIFIC WILL EVENTUALLY BECOME TEDIOUS.
"REMEMBER THE OLD SAYING: VARIETY IS THE SPICE GIRLS OF LIFE."
THIS WAY SOUNDS FAMILIAR.
THAT'S NOT HOW THE SAYING GOES, NIMROD. VARIETY IS THE SPICE OF LIFE.
ALICE, SWEETIE, YOU TELL YOUR STORIES YOUR WAY AND I'LL TELL MINE MY WAY.

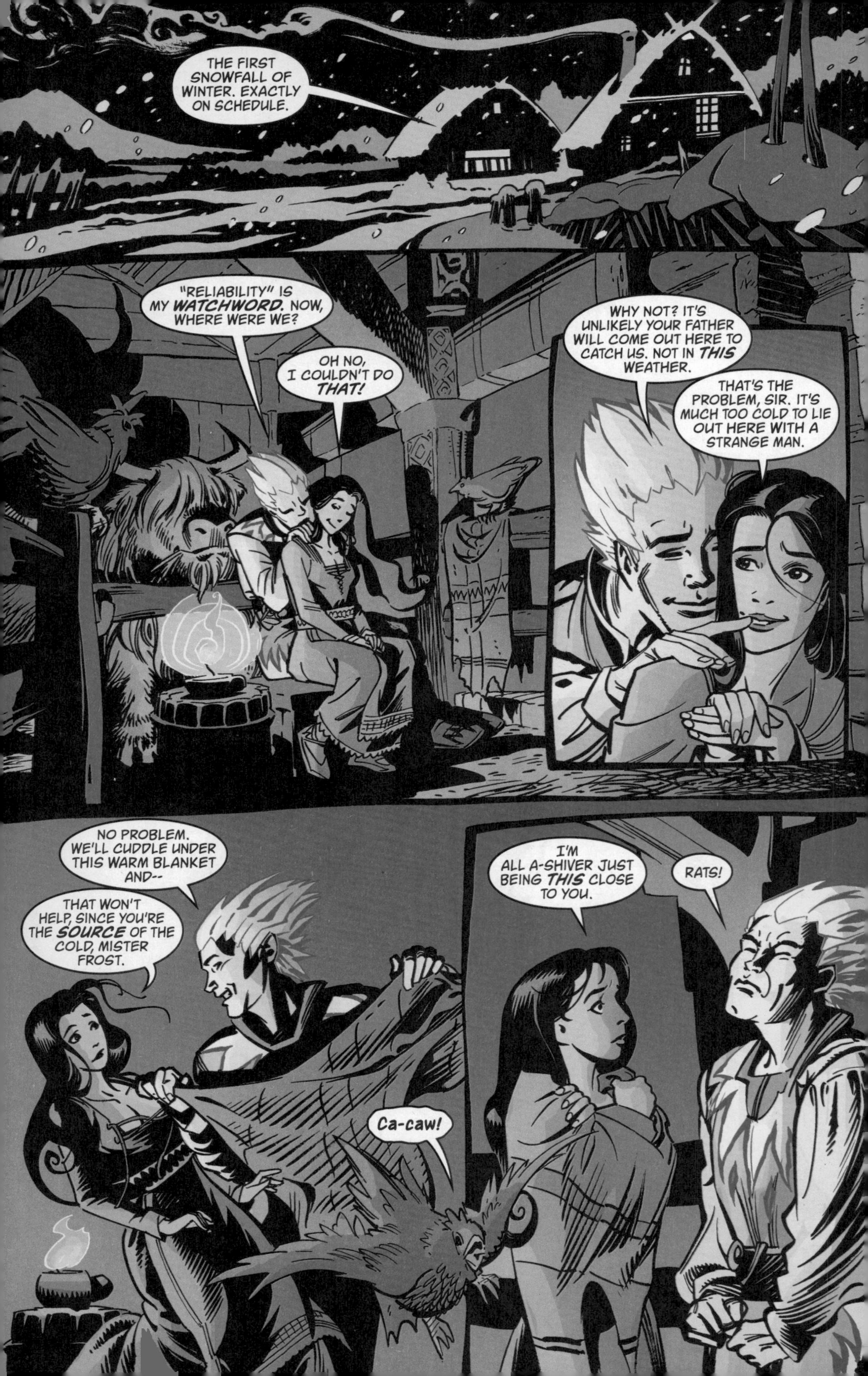
THE FIRST SNOWFALL OF WINTER. EXACTLY ON SCHEDULE.
"RELIABILITY" IS MY WATCHWORD. NOW, WHERE WERE WE?
OH NO, I COULDN'T DO THAT!
WHY NOT? IT'S UNLIKELY YOUR FATHER WILL COME OUT HERE TO CATCH US. NOT IN THIS WEATHER.
THAT'S THE PROBLEM, SIR. IT'S MUCH TOO COLD TO LIE OUT HERE WITH A STRANGE MAN.
NO PROBLEM. WE'LL CUDDLE UNDER THIS WARM BLANKET AND--
THAT WON'T HELP, SINCE YOU'RE THE SOURCE OF THE COLD, MISTER FROST.
Ca-caw!
I'M ALL A-SHIVER JUST BEING THIS CLOSE TO YOU.
RATS!

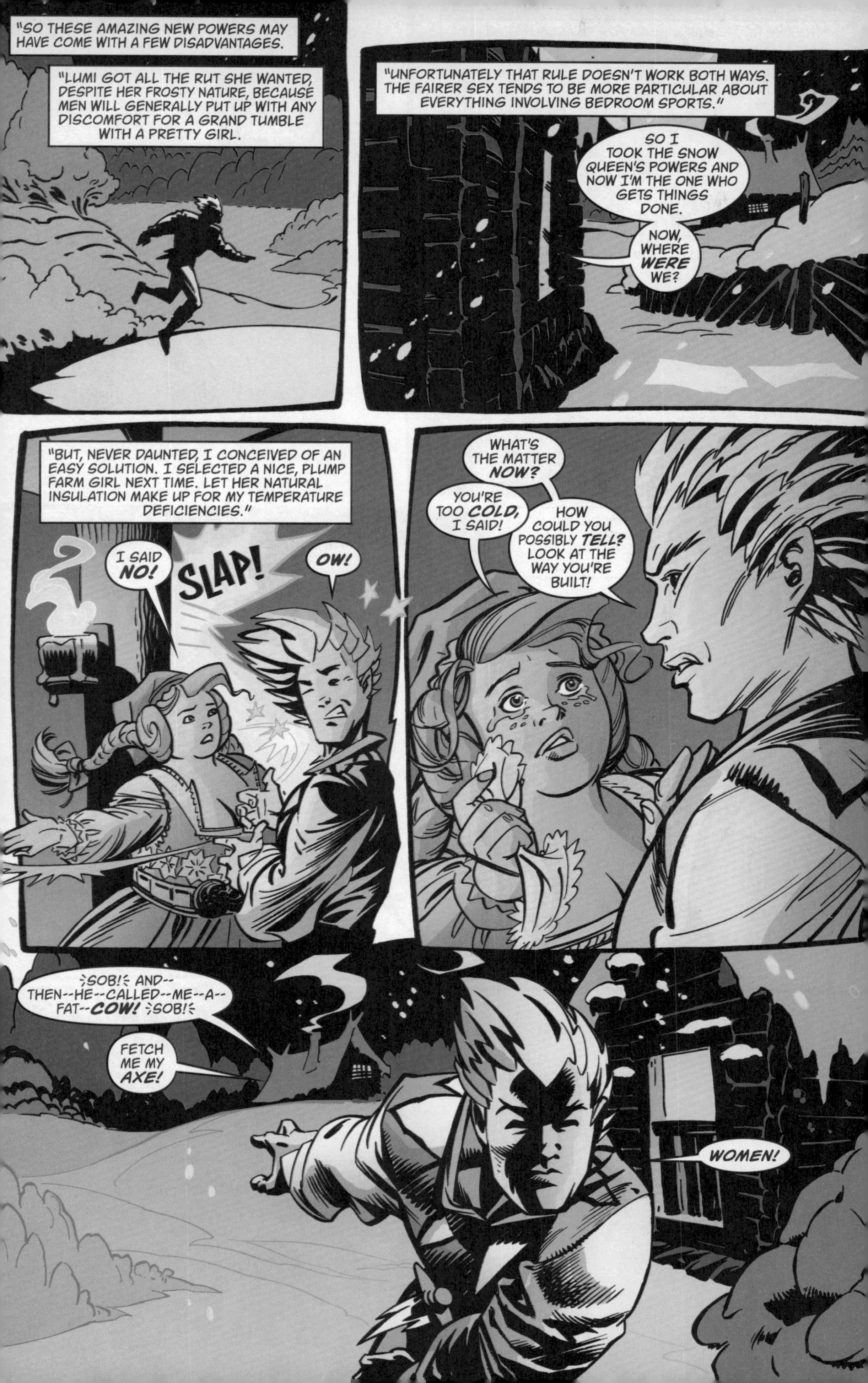
"SO THESE AMAZING NEW POWERS MAY HAVE COME WITH A FEW DISADVANTAGES.
"LUMI GOT ALL THE RUT SHE WANTED, DESPITE HER FROSTY NATURE, BECAUSE MEN WILL GENERALLY PUT UP WITH ANY DISCOMFORT FOR A GRAND TUMBLE WITH A PRETTY GIRL.
"UNFORTUNATELY THAT RULE DOESN'T WORK BOTH WAYS. THE FAIRER SEX TENDS TO BE MORE PARTICULAR ABOUT EVERYTHING INVOLVING BEDROOM SPORTS."
SO I TOOK THE SNOW QUEEN'S POWERS AND NOW I'M THE ONE WHO GETS THINGS DONE.
NOW, WHERE *WERE* WE?
"BUT, NEVER DAUNTED, I CONCEIVED OF AN EASY SOLUTION. I SELECTED A NICE, PLUMP FARM GIRL NEXT TIME. LET HER NATURAL INSULATION MAKE UP FOR MY TEMPERATURE DEFICIENCIES."
I SAID *NO!*
SLAP!
OW!
WHAT'S THE MATTER *NOW?*
YOU'RE TOO *COLD,* I SAID!
HOW COULD YOU POSSIBLY *TELL?* LOOK AT THE WAY YOU'RE BUILT!
SOB! AND--THEN--HE--CALLED--ME--A--FAT--*COW!* SOB!
FETCH ME MY *AXE!*
WOMEN!

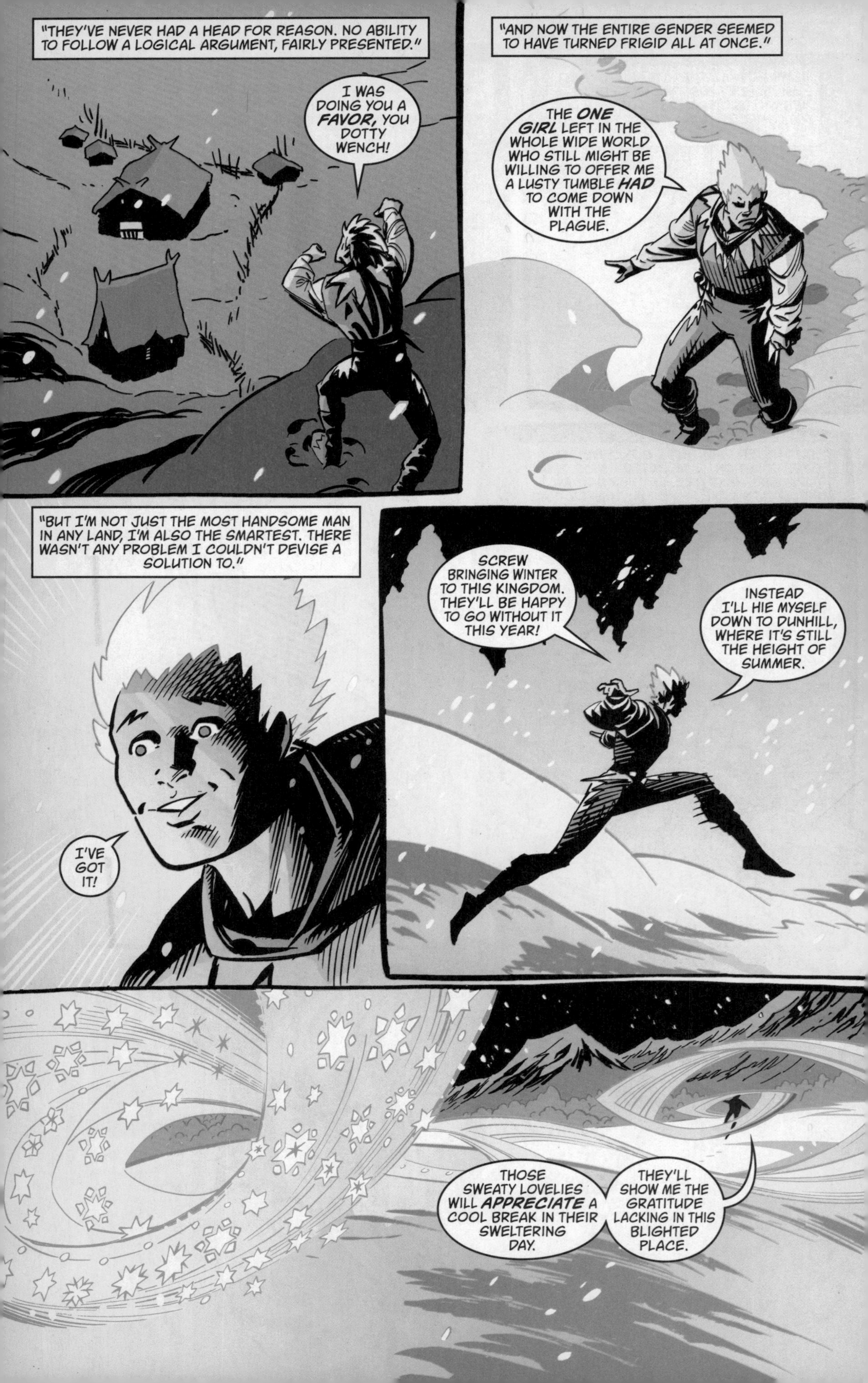
"THEY'VE NEVER HAD A HEAD FOR REASON. NO ABILITY TO FOLLOW A LOGICAL ARGUMENT, FAIRLY PRESENTED."
I WAS DOING YOU A FAVOR, YOU DOTTY WENCH!
"AND NOW THE ENTIRE GENDER SEEMED TO HAVE TURNED FRIGID ALL AT ONCE."
THE ONE GIRL LEFT IN THE WHOLE WIDE WORLD WHO STILL MIGHT BE WILLING TO OFFER ME A LUSTY TUMBLE HAD TO COME DOWN WITH THE PLAGUE.
"BUT I'M NOT JUST THE MOST HANDSOME MAN IN ANY LAND, I'M ALSO THE SMARTEST. THERE WASN'T ANY PROBLEM I COULDN'T DEVISE A SOLUTION TO."
I'VE GOT IT!
SCREW BRINGING WINTER TO THIS KINGDOM. THEY'LL BE HAPPY TO GO WITHOUT IT THIS YEAR!
INSTEAD I'LL HIE MYSELF DOWN TO DUNHILL, WHERE IT'S STILL THE HEIGHT OF SUMMER.
THOSE SWEATY LOVELIES WILL APPRECIATE A COOL BREAK IN THEIR SWELTERING DAY.
THEY'LL SHOW ME THE GRATITUDE LACKING IN THIS BLIGHTED PLACE.

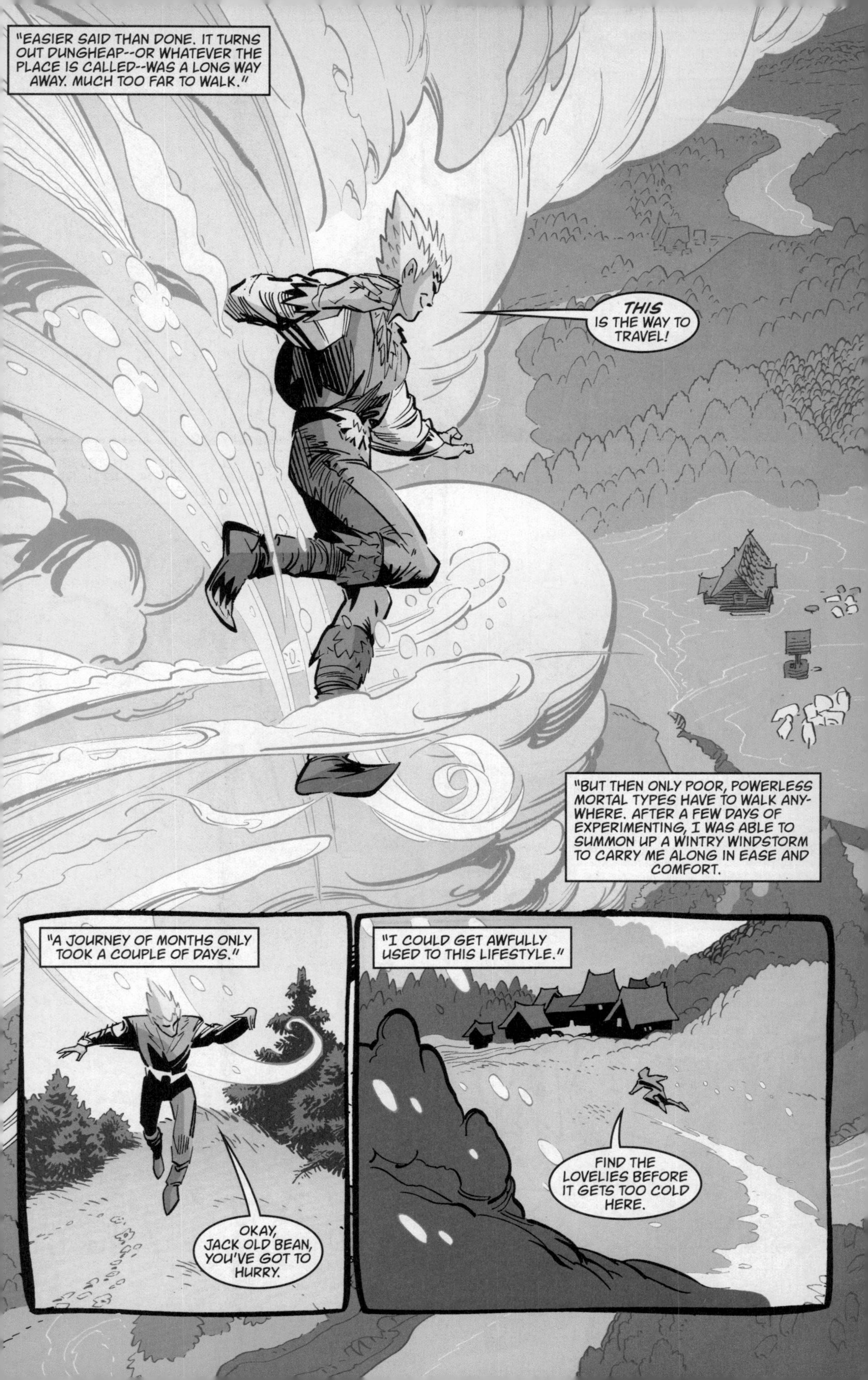
"EASIER SAID THAN DONE. IT TURNS OUT DUNGHEAP--OR WHATEVER THE PLACE IS CALLED--WAS A LONG WAY AWAY. MUCH TOO FAR TO WALK."
THIS IS THE WAY TO TRAVEL!
"BUT THEN ONLY POOR, POWERLESS MORTAL TYPES HAVE TO WALK ANYWHERE. AFTER A FEW DAYS OF EXPERIMENTING, I WAS ABLE TO SUMMON UP A WINTRY WINDSTORM TO CARRY ME ALONG IN EASE AND COMFORT.
"A JOURNEY OF MONTHS ONLY TOOK A COUPLE OF DAYS."
OKAY, JACK OLD BEAN, YOU'VE GOT TO HURRY.
"I COULD GET AWFULLY USED TO THIS LIFESTYLE."
FIND THE LOVELIES BEFORE IT GETS TOO COLD HERE.

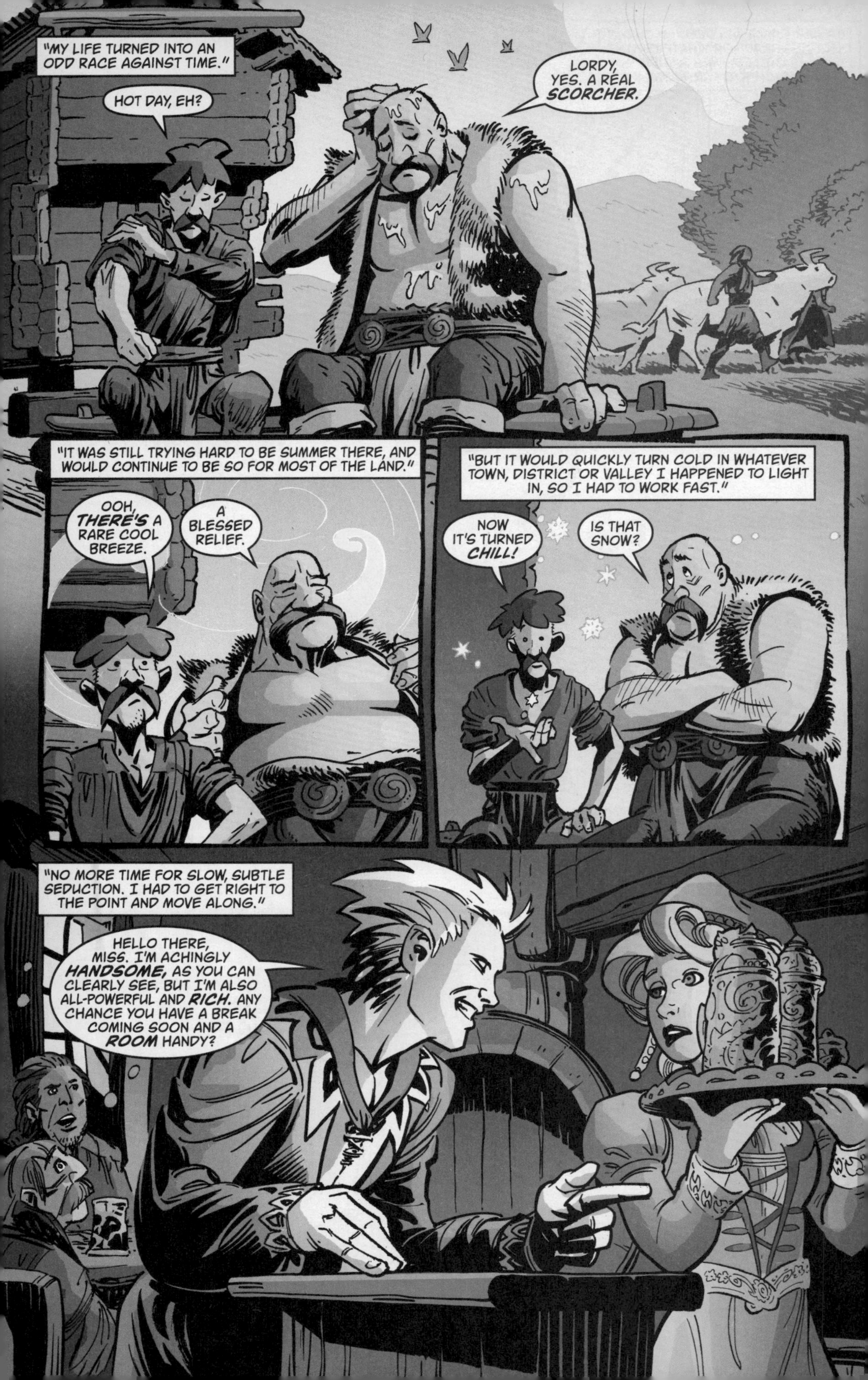
"MY LIFE TURNED INTO AN ODD RACE AGAINST TIME."
HOT DAY, EH?
LORDY, YES. A REAL SCORCHER.
"IT WAS STILL TRYING HARD TO BE SUMMER THERE, AND WOULD CONTINUE TO BE SO FOR MOST OF THE LAND."
OOH, THERE'S A RARE COOL BREEZE.
A BLESSED RELIEF.
"BUT IT WOULD QUICKLY TURN COLD IN WHATEVER TOWN, DISTRICT OR VALLEY I HAPPENED TO LIGHT IN, SO I HAD TO WORK FAST."
NOW IT'S TURNED CHILL!
IS THAT SNOW?
"NO MORE TIME FOR SLOW, SUBTLE SEDUCTION. I HAD TO GET RIGHT TO THE POINT AND MOVE ALONG."
HELLO THERE, MISS. I'M ACHINGLY HANDSOME, AS YOU CAN CLEARLY SEE, BUT I'M ALSO ALL-POWERFUL AND RICH. ANY CHANCE YOU HAVE A BREAK COMING SOON AND A ROOM HANDY?

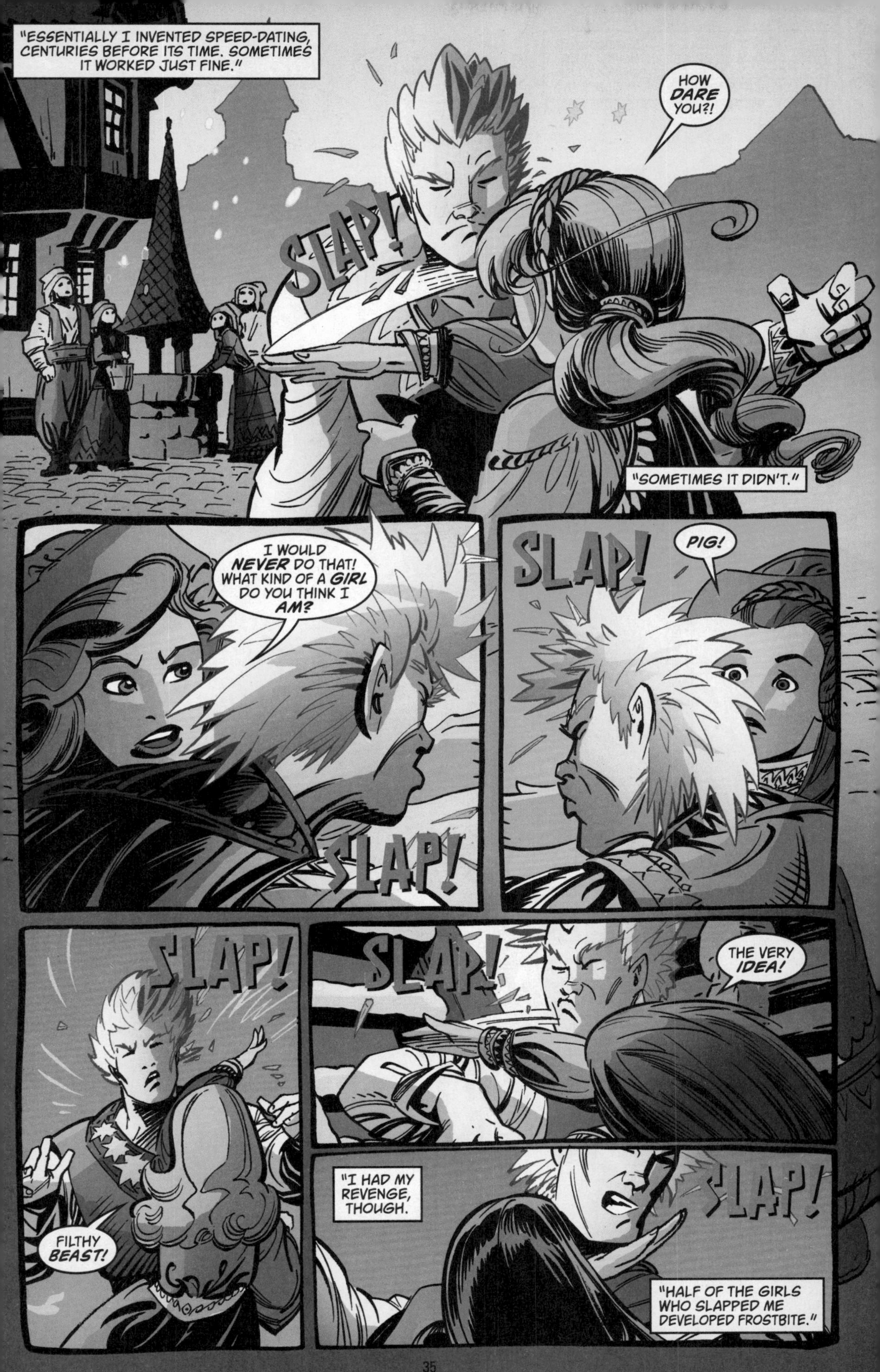
"ESSENTIALLY I INVENTED SPEED-DATING, CENTURIES BEFORE ITS TIME. SOMETIMES IT WORKED JUST FINE."
HOW DARE YOU?!
SLAP!
"SOMETIMES IT DIDN'T."
I WOULD NEVER DO THAT! WHAT KIND OF A GIRL DO YOU THINK I AM?
SLAP!
SLAP!
PIG!
SLAP!
FILTHY BEAST!
SLAP!
THE VERY IDEA!
"I HAD MY REVENGE, THOUGH.
SLAP!
"HALF OF THE GIRLS WHO SLAPPED ME DEVELOPED FROSTBITE."

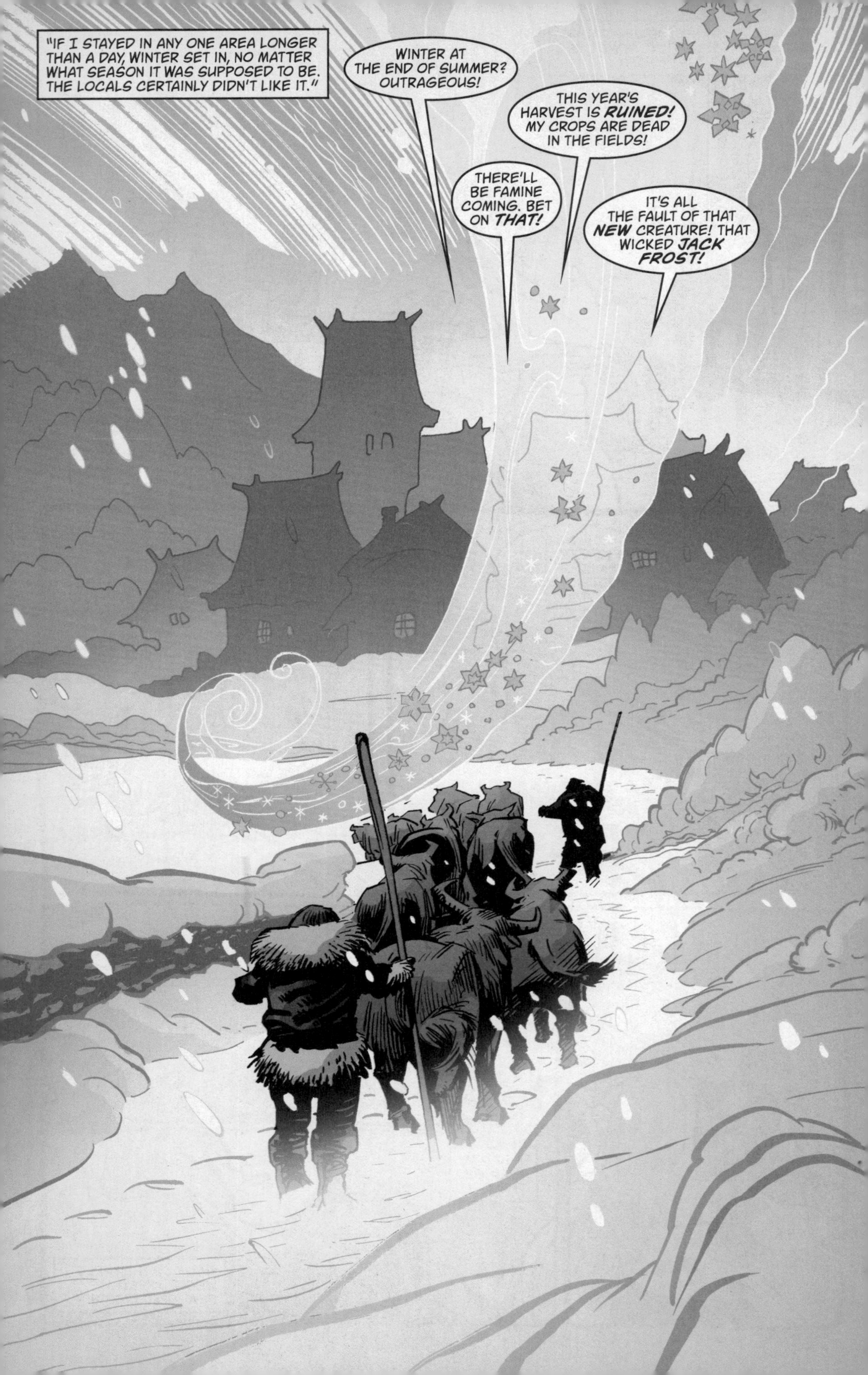
"IF I STAYED IN ANY ONE AREA LONGER THAN A DAY, WINTER SET IN, NO MATTER WHAT SEASON IT WAS SUPPOSED TO BE. THE LOCALS CERTAINLY DIDN'T LIKE IT."
WINTER AT THE END OF SUMMER? OUTRAGEOUS!
THIS YEAR'S HARVEST IS RUINED! MY CROPS ARE DEAD IN THE FIELDS!
THERE'LL BE FAMINE COMING. BET ON THAT!
IT'S ALL THE FAULT OF THAT NEW CREATURE! THAT WICKED JACK FROST!

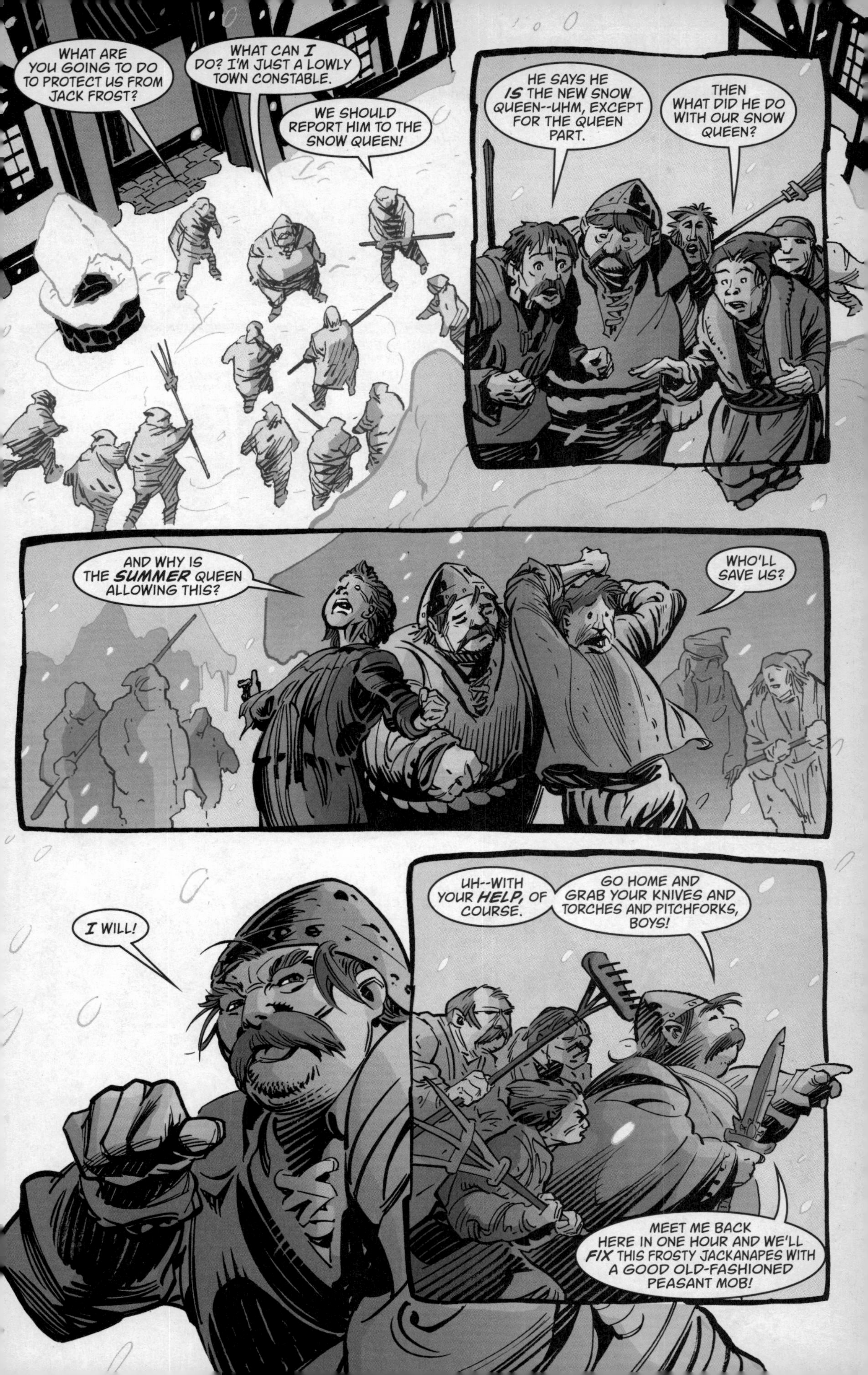
WHAT ARE YOU GOING TO DO TO PROTECT US FROM JACK FROST?
WHAT CAN I DO? I'M JUST A LOWLY TOWN CONSTABLE.
WE SHOULD REPORT HIM TO THE SNOW QUEEN!
HE SAYS HE IS THE NEW SNOW QUEEN--UHM, EXCEPT FOR THE QUEEN PART.
THEN WHAT DID HE DO WITH OUR SNOW QUEEN?
AND WHY IS THE SUMMER QUEEN ALLOWING THIS?
WHO'LL SAVE US?
I WILL!
UH--WITH YOUR HELP, OF COURSE.
GO HOME AND GRAB YOUR KNIVES AND TORCHES AND PITCHFORKS, BOYS!
MEET ME BACK HERE IN ONE HOUR AND WE'LL FIX THIS FROSTY JACKANAPES WITH A GOOD OLD-FASHIONED PEASANT MOB!

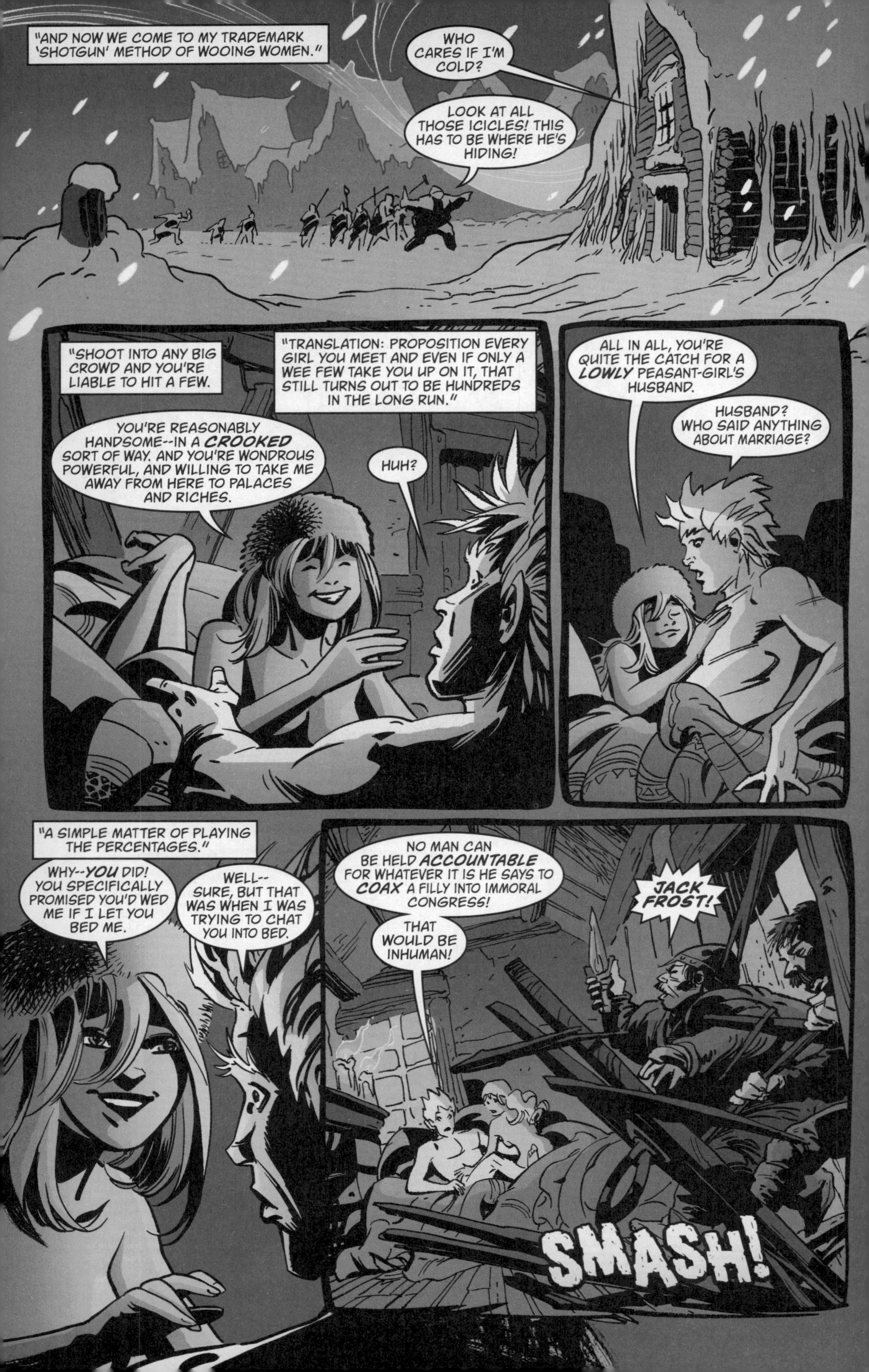
"AND NOW WE COME TO MY TRADEMARK 'SHOTGUN' METHOD OF WOOING WOMEN."
WHO CARES IF I'M COLD?
LOOK AT ALL THOSE ICICLES! THIS HAS TO BE WHERE HE'S HIDING!
"SHOOT INTO ANY BIG CROWD AND YOU'RE LIABLE TO HIT A FEW.
"TRANSLATION: PROPOSITION EVERY GIRL YOU MEET AND EVEN IF ONLY A WEE FEW TAKE YOU UP ON IT, THAT STILL TURNS OUT TO BE HUNDREDS IN THE LONG RUN."
YOU'RE REASONABLY HANDSOME--IN A *CROOKED* SORT OF WAY. AND YOU'RE WONDROUS POWERFUL, AND WILLING TO TAKE ME AWAY FROM HERE TO PALACES AND RICHES.
HUH?
ALL IN ALL, YOU'RE QUITE THE CATCH FOR A *LOWLY* PEASANT-GIRL'S HUSBAND.
HUSBAND? WHO SAID ANYTHING ABOUT MARRIAGE?
"A SIMPLE MATTER OF PLAYING THE PERCENTAGES."
WHY--*YOU* DID! YOU SPECIFICALLY PROMISED YOU'D WED ME IF I LET YOU BED ME.
WELL-- SURE, BUT THAT WAS WHEN I WAS TRYING TO CHAT YOU INTO BED.
NO MAN CAN BE HELD *ACCOUNTABLE* FOR WHATEVER IT IS HE SAYS TO *COAX* A FILLY INTO IMMORAL CONGRESS!
THAT WOULD BE INHUMAN!
JACK FROST!
SMASH!

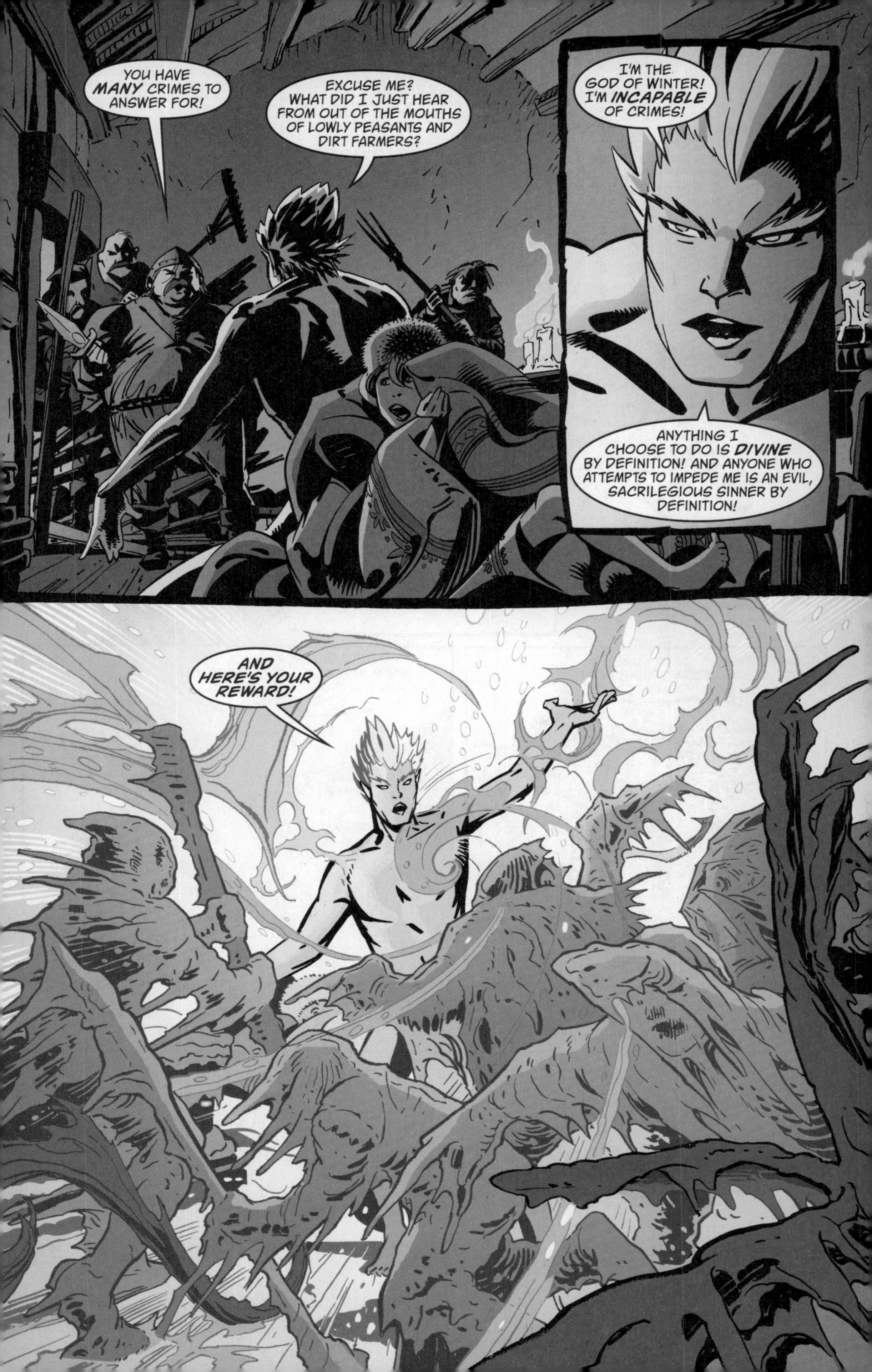
YOU HAVE MANY CRIMES TO ANSWER FOR!
EXCUSE ME? WHAT DID I JUST HEAR FROM OUT OF THE MOUTHS OF LOWLY PEASANTS AND DIRT FARMERS?
I'M THE GOD OF WINTER! I'M INCAPABLE OF CRIMES!
ANYTHING I CHOOSE TO DO IS DIVINE BY DEFINITION! AND ANYONE WHO ATTEMPTS TO IMPEDE ME IS AN EVIL, SACRILEGIOUS SINNER BY DEFINITION!
AND HERE'S YOUR REWARD!

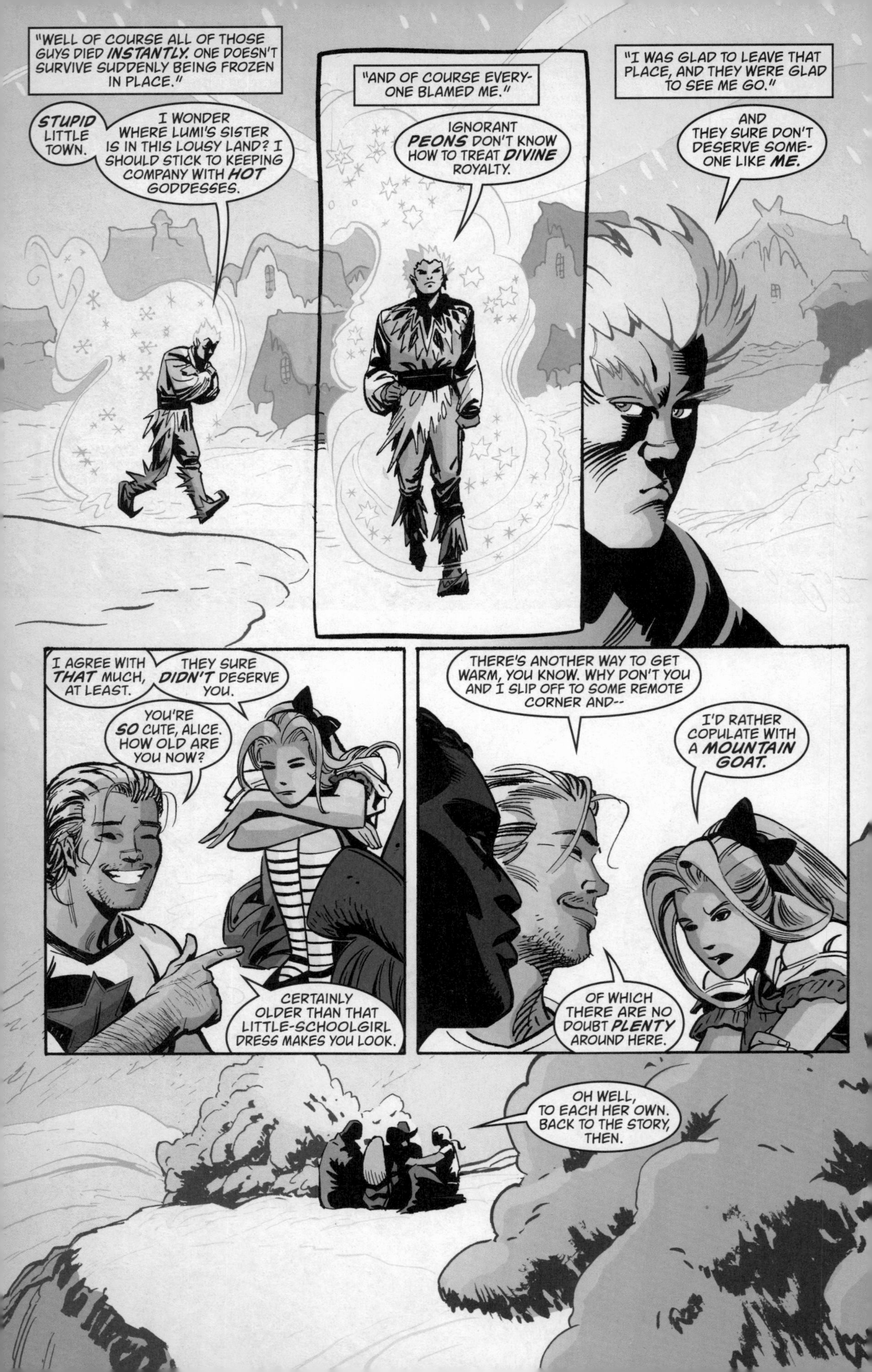
"WELL OF COURSE ALL OF THOSE GUYS DIED INSTANTLY. ONE DOESN'T SURVIVE SUDDENLY BEING FROZEN IN PLACE."
STUPID LITTLE TOWN.
I WONDER WHERE LUMI'S SISTER IS IN THIS LOUSY LAND? I SHOULD STICK TO KEEPING COMPANY WITH HOT GODDESSES.
"AND OF COURSE EVERY-ONE BLAMED ME."
IGNORANT PEONS DON'T KNOW HOW TO TREAT DIVINE ROYALTY.
"I WAS GLAD TO LEAVE THAT PLACE, AND THEY WERE GLAD TO SEE ME GO."
AND THEY SURE DON'T DESERVE SOME-ONE LIKE ME.
I AGREE WITH THAT MUCH, AT LEAST.
THEY SURE DIDN'T DESERVE YOU.
YOU'RE SO CUTE, ALICE. HOW OLD ARE YOU NOW?
CERTAINLY OLDER THAN THAT LITTLE-SCHOOLGIRL DRESS MAKES YOU LOOK.
THERE'S ANOTHER WAY TO GET WARM, YOU KNOW. WHY DON'T YOU AND I SLIP OFF TO SOME REMOTE CORNER AND--
I'D RATHER COPULATE WITH A MOUNTAIN GOAT.
OF WHICH THERE ARE NO DOUBT PLENTY AROUND HERE.
OH WELL, TO EACH HER OWN. BACK TO THE STORY, THEN.

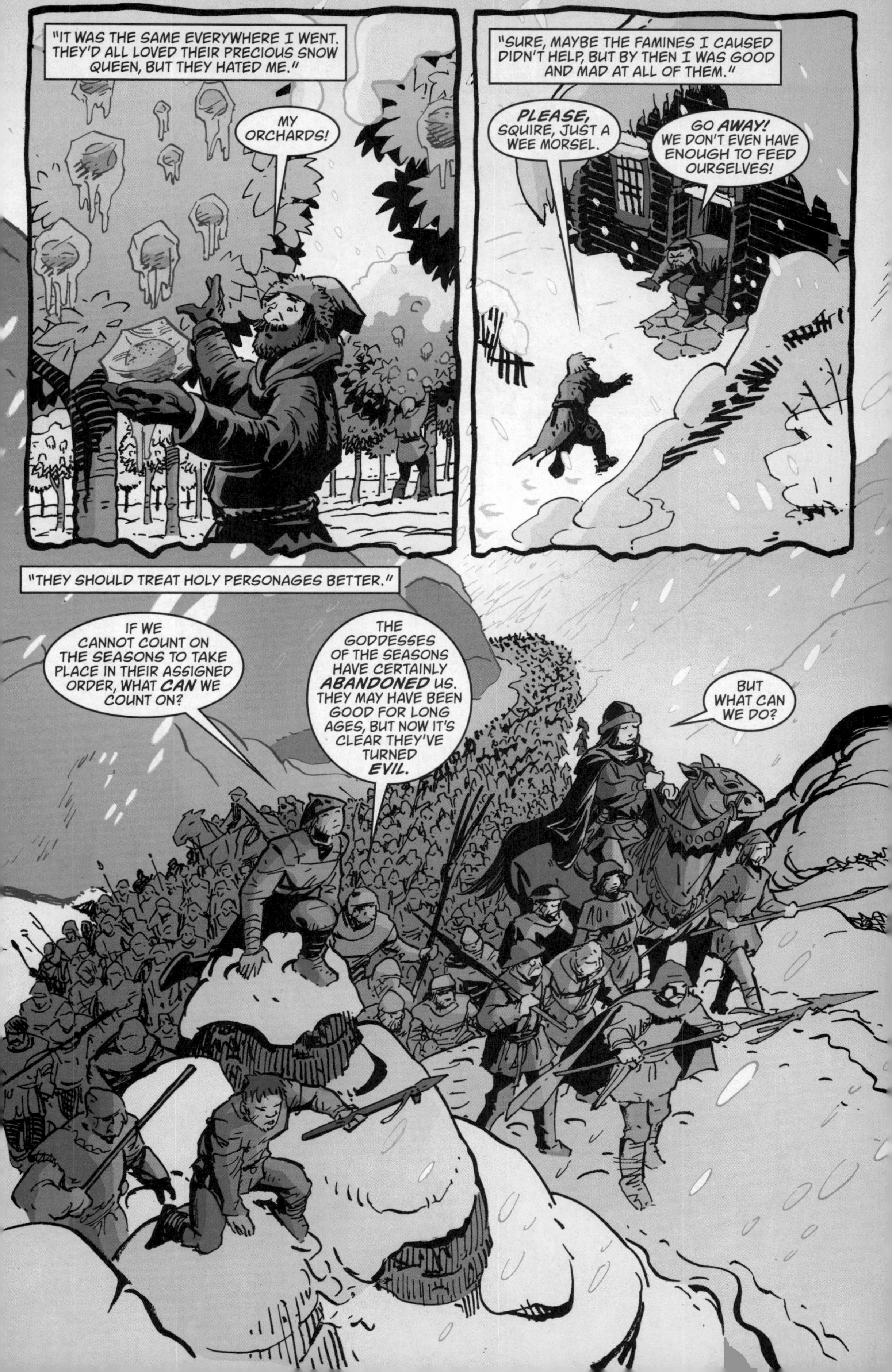
"IT WAS THE SAME EVERYWHERE I WENT. THEY'D ALL LOVED THEIR PRECIOUS SNOW QUEEN, BUT THEY HATED ME."
MY ORCHARDS!
"SURE, MAYBE THE FAMINES I CAUSED DIDN'T HELP, BUT BY THEN I WAS GOOD AND MAD AT ALL OF THEM."
PLEASE, SQUIRE, JUST A WEE MORSEL.
GO AWAY! WE DON'T EVEN HAVE ENOUGH TO FEED OURSELVES!
"THEY SHOULD TREAT HOLY PERSONAGES BETTER."
IF WE CANNOT COUNT ON THE SEASONS TO TAKE PLACE IN THEIR ASSIGNED ORDER, WHAT CAN WE COUNT ON?
THE GODDESSES OF THE SEASONS HAVE CERTAINLY ABANDONED US. THEY MAY HAVE BEEN GOOD FOR LONG AGES, BUT NOW IT'S CLEAR THEY'VE TURNED EVIL.
BUT WHAT CAN WE DO?

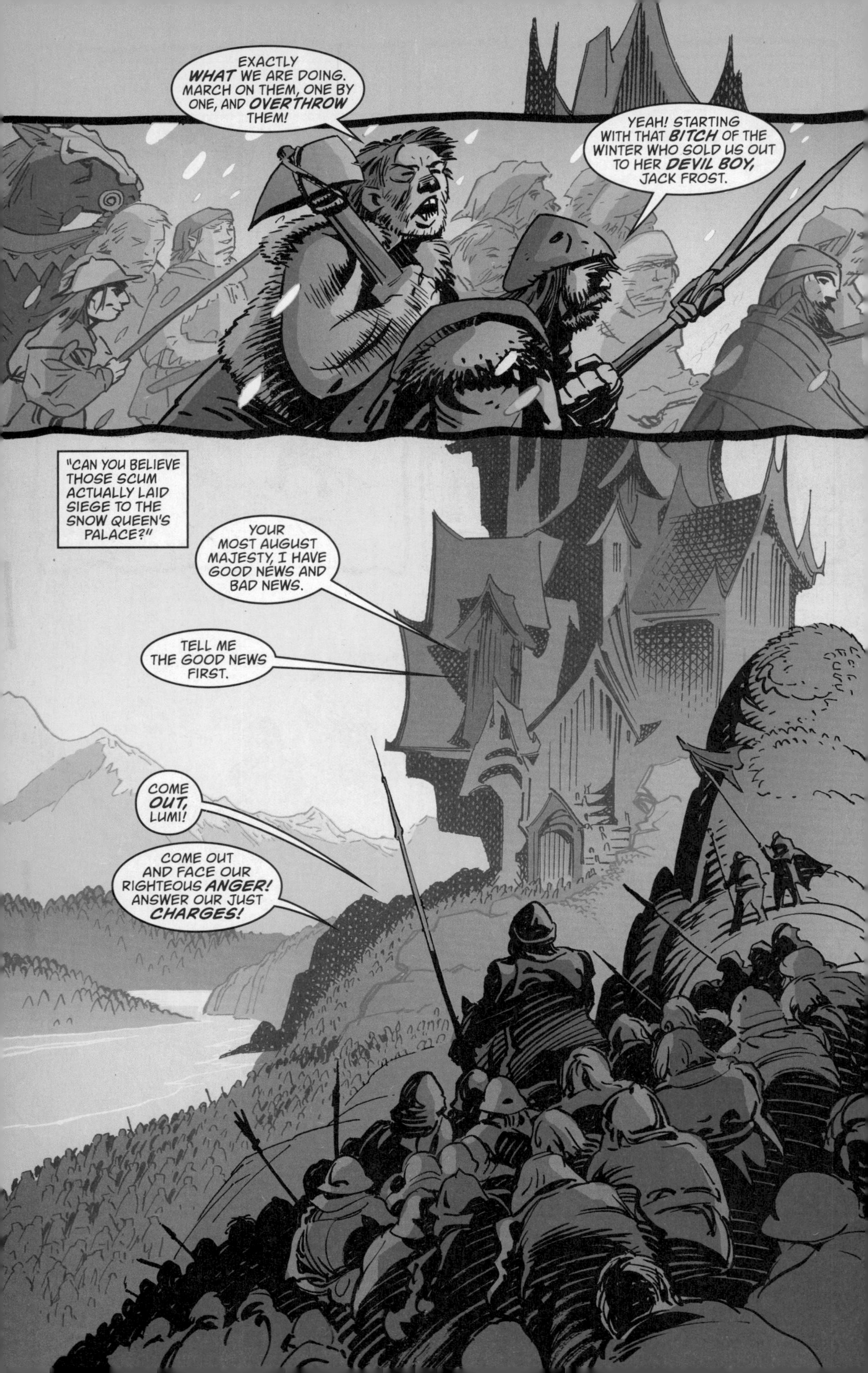
EXACTLY WHAT WE ARE DOING. MARCH ON THEM, ONE BY ONE, AND OVERTHROW THEM!
YEAH! STARTING WITH THAT BITCH OF THE WINTER WHO SOLD US OUT TO HER DEVIL BOY, JACK FROST.
"CAN YOU BELIEVE THOSE SCUM ACTUALLY LAID SIEGE TO THE SNOW QUEEN'S PALACE?"
YOUR MOST AUGUST MAJESTY, I HAVE GOOD NEWS AND BAD NEWS.
TELL ME THE GOOD NEWS FIRST.
COME OUT, LUMI!
COME OUT AND FACE OUR RIGHTEOUS ANGER! ANSWER OUR JUST CHARGES!

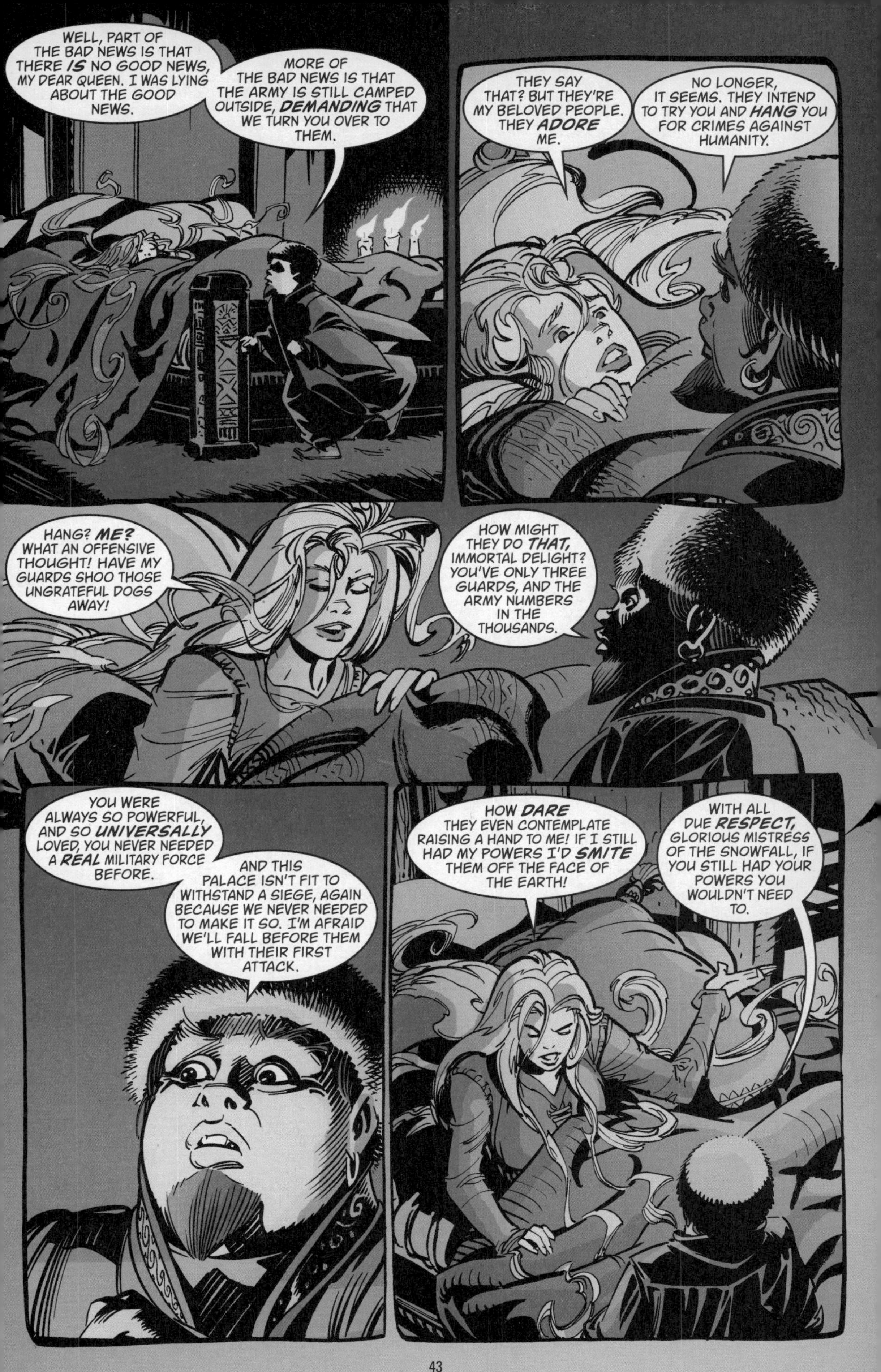
WELL, PART OF THE BAD NEWS IS THAT THERE *IS* NO GOOD NEWS, MY DEAR QUEEN. I WAS LYING ABOUT THE GOOD NEWS.
MORE OF THE BAD NEWS IS THAT THE ARMY IS STILL CAMPED OUTSIDE, *DEMANDING* THAT WE TURN YOU OVER TO THEM.
THEY SAY THAT? BUT THEY'RE MY BELOVED PEOPLE. THEY *ADORE* ME.
NO LONGER, IT SEEMS. THEY INTEND TO TRY YOU AND *HANG* YOU FOR CRIMES AGAINST HUMANITY.
HANG? *ME?* WHAT AN OFFENSIVE THOUGHT! HAVE MY GUARDS SHOO THOSE UNGRATEFUL DOGS AWAY!
HOW MIGHT THEY DO *THAT,* IMMORTAL DELIGHT? YOU'VE ONLY THREE GUARDS, AND THE ARMY NUMBERS IN THE THOUSANDS.
YOU WERE ALWAYS SO POWERFUL, AND SO *UNIVERSALLY* LOVED, YOU NEVER NEEDED A *REAL* MILITARY FORCE BEFORE.
AND THIS PALACE ISN'T FIT TO WITHSTAND A SIEGE, AGAIN BECAUSE WE NEVER NEEDED TO MAKE IT SO. I'M AFRAID WE'LL FALL BEFORE THEM WITH THEIR FIRST ATTACK.
HOW *DARE* THEY EVEN CONTEMPLATE RAISING A HAND TO ME! IF I STILL HAD MY POWERS I'D *SMITE* THEM OFF THE FACE OF THE EARTH!
WITH ALL DUE *RESPECT,* GLORIOUS MISTRESS OF THE SNOWFALL, IF YOU STILL HAD YOUR POWERS YOU WOULDN'T NEED TO.

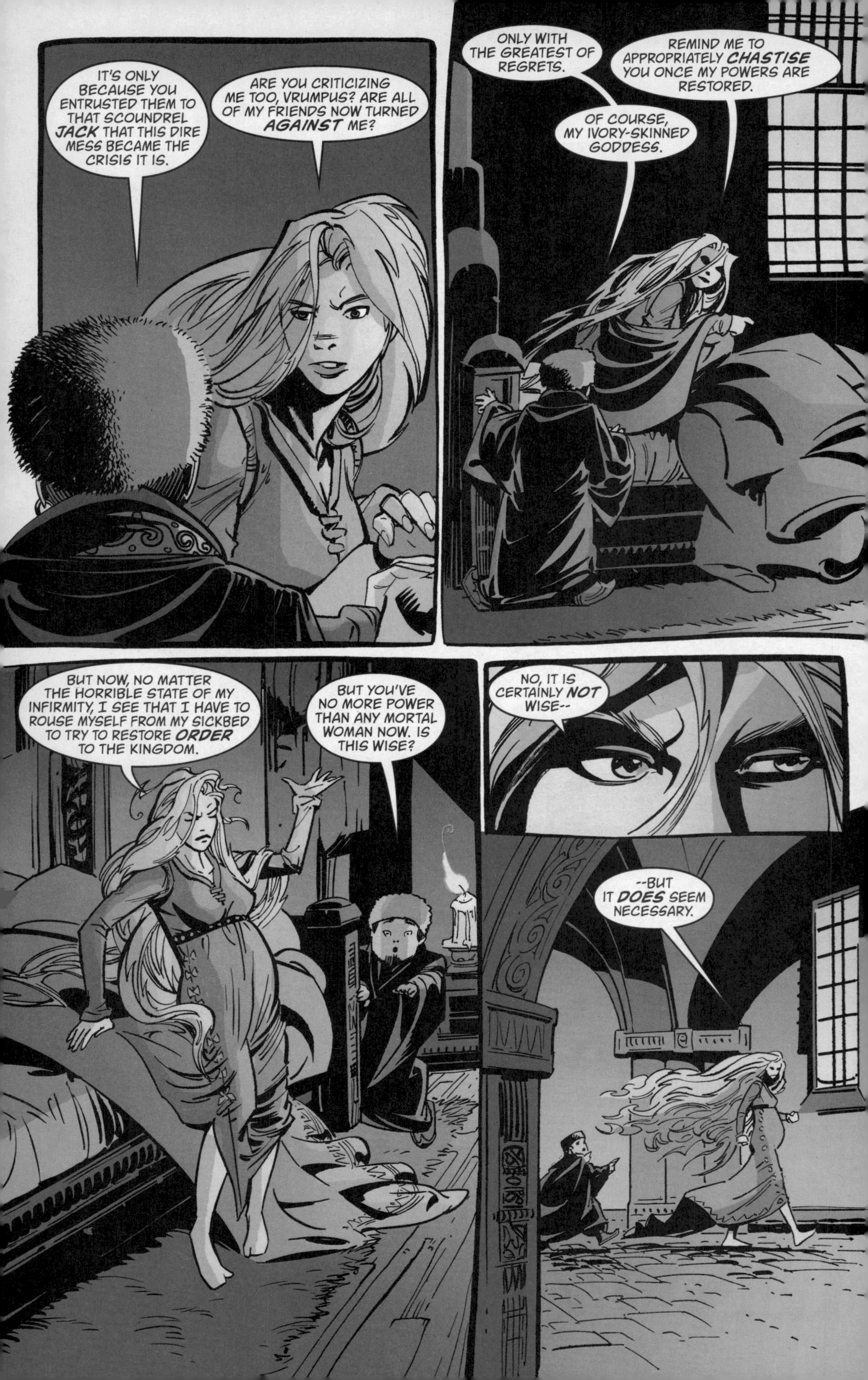
IT'S ONLY BECAUSE YOU ENTRUSTED THEM TO THAT SCOUNDREL JACK THAT THIS DIRE MESS BECAME THE CRISIS IT IS.
ARE YOU CRITICIZING ME TOO, VRUMPUS? ARE ALL OF MY FRIENDS NOW TURNED AGAINST ME?
ONLY WITH THE GREATEST OF REGRETS.
REMIND ME TO APPROPRIATELY CHASTISE YOU ONCE MY POWERS ARE RESTORED.
OF COURSE, MY IVORY-SKINNED GODDESS.
BUT NOW, NO MATTER THE HORRIBLE STATE OF MY INFIRMITY, I SEE THAT I HAVE TO ROUSE MYSELF FROM MY SICKBED TO TRY TO RESTORE ORDER TO THE KINGDOM.
BUT YOU'VE NO MORE POWER THAN ANY MORTAL WOMAN NOW. IS THIS WISE?
NO, IT IS CERTAINLY NOT WISE--
--BUT IT DOES SEEM NECESSARY.

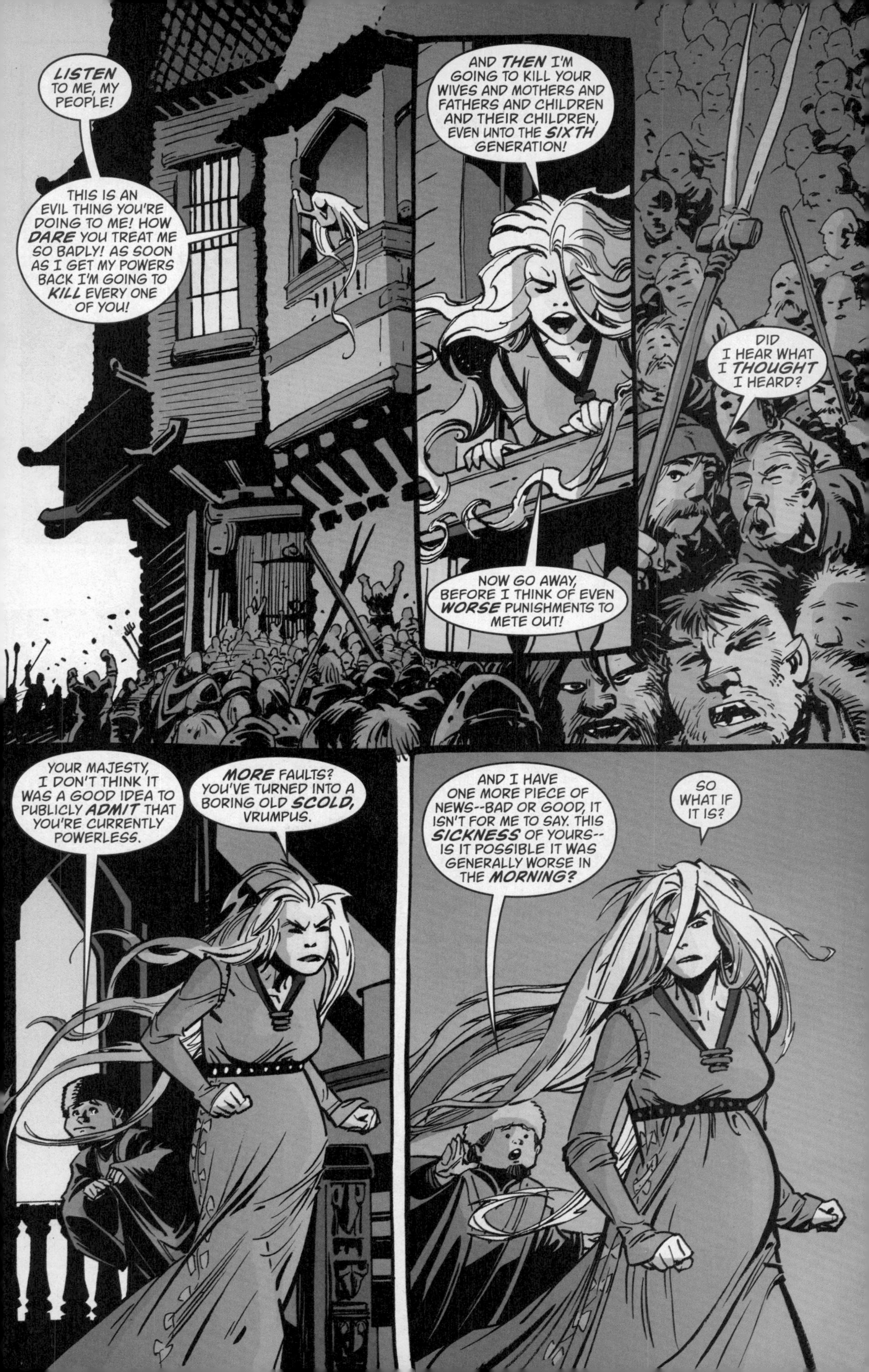
LISTEN TO ME, MY PEOPLE!
THIS IS AN EVIL THING YOU'RE DOING TO ME! HOW DARE YOU TREAT ME SO BADLY! AS SOON AS I GET MY POWERS BACK I'M GOING TO KILL EVERY ONE OF YOU!
AND THEN I'M GOING TO KILL YOUR WIVES AND MOTHERS AND FATHERS AND CHILDREN AND THEIR CHILDREN, EVEN UNTO THE SIXTH GENERATION!
NOW GO AWAY, BEFORE I THINK OF EVEN WORSE PUNISHMENTS TO METE OUT!
DID I HEAR WHAT I THOUGHT I HEARD?
YOUR MAJESTY, I DON'T THINK IT WAS A GOOD IDEA TO PUBLICLY ADMIT THAT YOU'RE CURRENTLY POWERLESS.
MORE FAULTS? YOU'VE TURNED INTO A BORING OLD SCOLD, VRUMPUS.
AND I HAVE ONE MORE PIECE OF NEWS--BAD OR GOOD, IT ISN'T FOR ME TO SAY. THIS SICKNESS OF YOURS--IS IT POSSIBLE IT WAS GENERALLY WORSE IN THE MORNING?
SO WHAT IF IT IS?

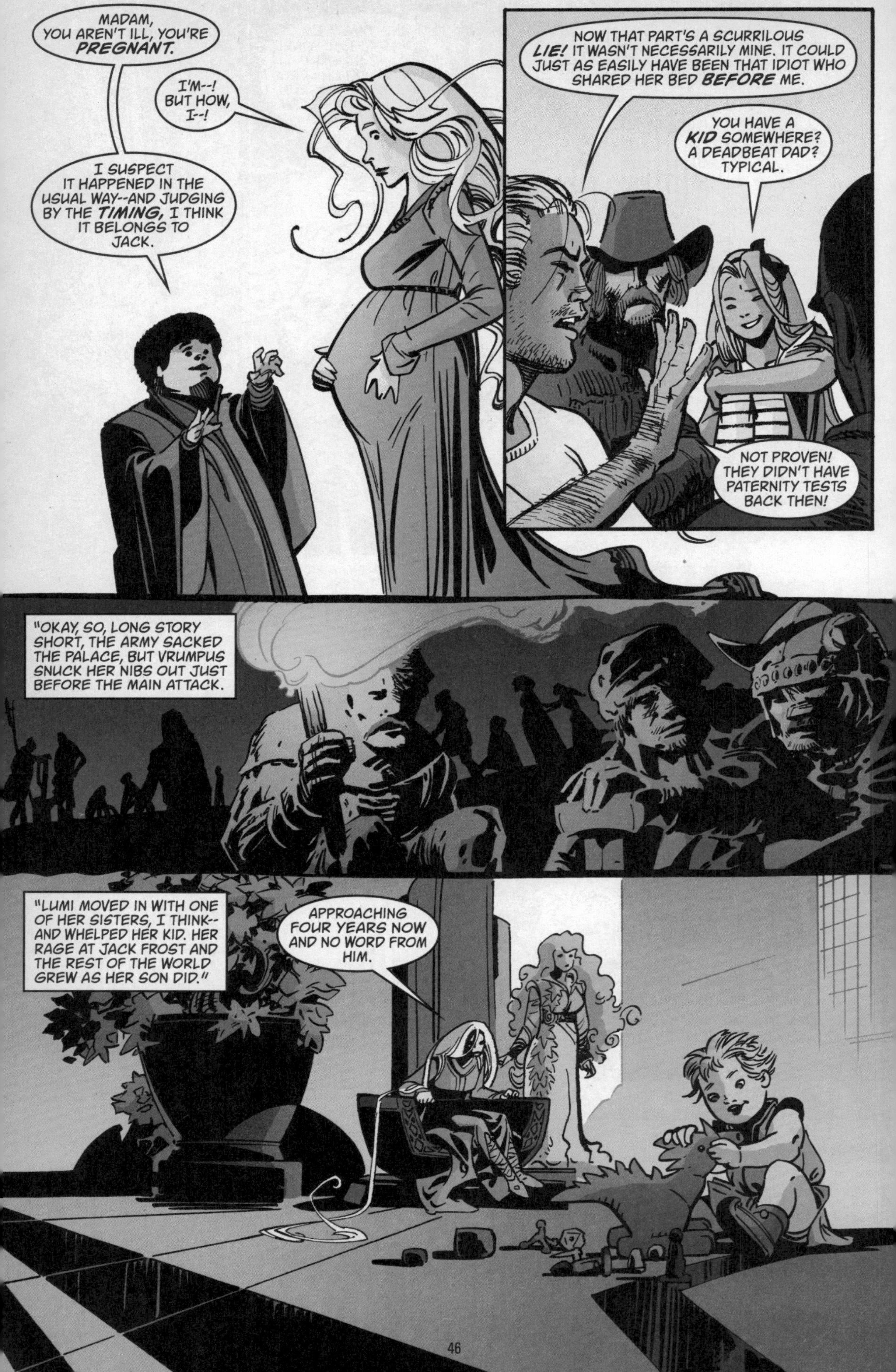
MADAM, YOU AREN'T ILL, YOU'RE PREGNANT.
I'M--! BUT HOW, I--!
I SUSPECT IT HAPPENED IN THE USUAL WAY--AND JUDGING BY THE TIMING, I THINK IT BELONGS TO JACK.
NOW THAT PART'S A SCURRILOUS LIE! IT WASN'T NECESSARILY MINE. IT COULD JUST AS EASILY HAVE BEEN THAT IDIOT WHO SHARED HER BED BEFORE ME.
YOU HAVE A KID SOMEWHERE? A DEADBEAT DAD? TYPICAL.
NOT PROVEN! THEY DIDN'T HAVE PATERNITY TESTS BACK THEN!
"OKAY, SO, LONG STORY SHORT, THE ARMY SACKED THE PALACE, BUT VRUMPUS SNUCK HER NIBS OUT JUST BEFORE THE MAIN ATTACK.
"LUMI MOVED IN WITH ONE OF HER SISTERS, I THINK--AND WHELPED HER KID. HER RAGE AT JACK FROST AND THE REST OF THE WORLD GREW AS HER SON DID."
APPROACHING FOUR YEARS NOW AND NO WORD FROM HIM.

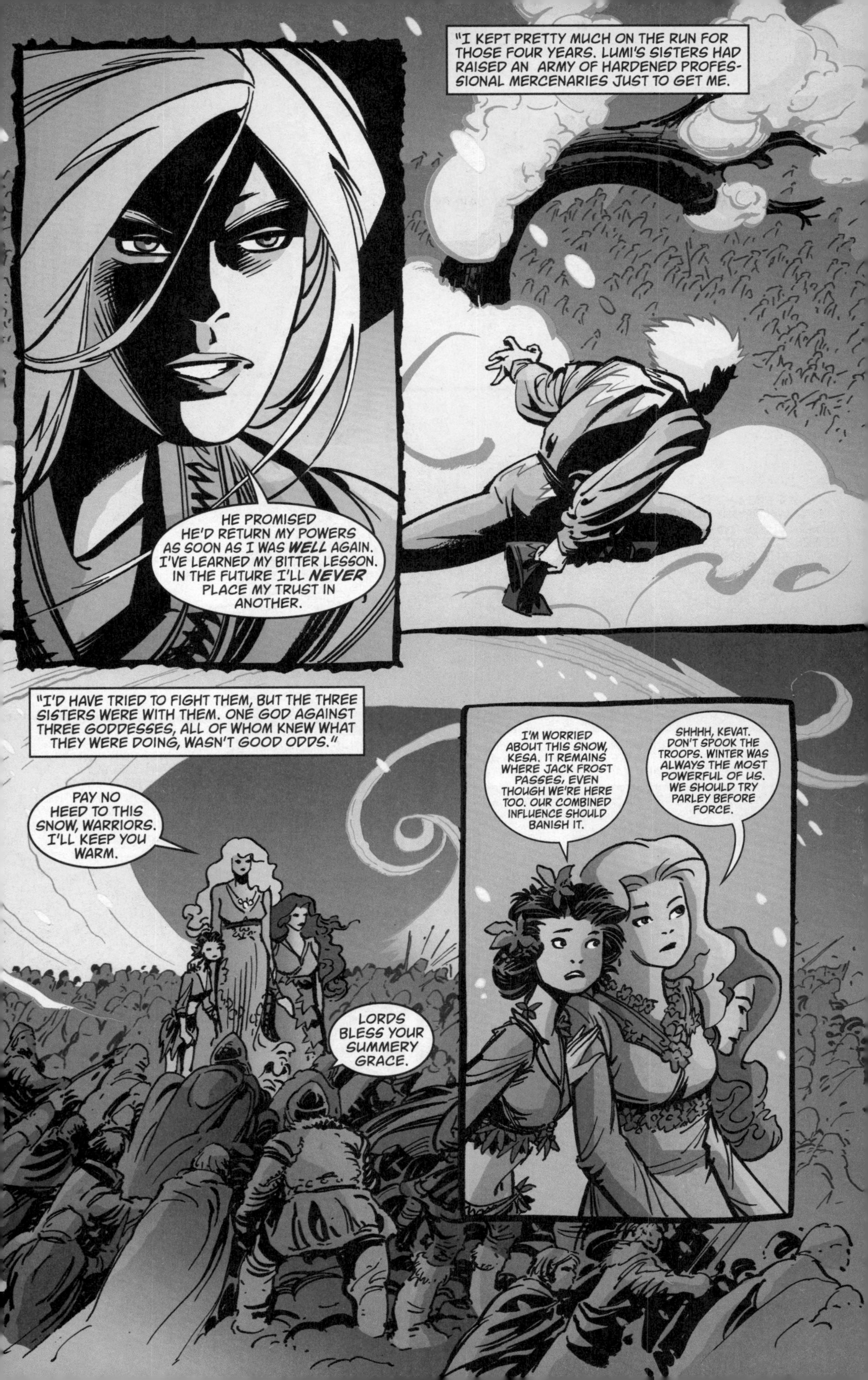
"I KEPT PRETTY MUCH ON THE RUN FOR THOSE FOUR YEARS. LUMI'S SISTERS HAD RAISED AN ARMY OF HARDENED PROFESSIONAL MERCENARIES JUST TO GET ME.
HE PROMISED HE'D RETURN MY POWERS AS SOON AS I WAS WELL AGAIN. I'VE LEARNED MY BITTER LESSON. IN THE FUTURE I'LL NEVER PLACE MY TRUST IN ANOTHER.
"I'D HAVE TRIED TO FIGHT THEM, BUT THE THREE SISTERS WERE WITH THEM. ONE GOD AGAINST THREE GODDESSES, ALL OF WHOM KNEW WHAT THEY WERE DOING, WASN'T GOOD ODDS."
PAY NO HEED TO THIS SNOW, WARRIORS. I'LL KEEP YOU WARM.
LORDS BLESS YOUR SUMMERY GRACE.
I'M WORRIED ABOUT THIS SNOW, KESA. IT REMAINS WHERE JACK FROST PASSES, EVEN THOUGH WE'RE HERE TOO. OUR COMBINED INFLUENCE SHOULD BANISH IT.
SHHHH, KEVAT. DON'T SPOOK THE TROOPS. WINTER WAS ALWAYS THE MOST POWERFUL OF US. WE SHOULD TRY PARLEY BEFORE FORCE.

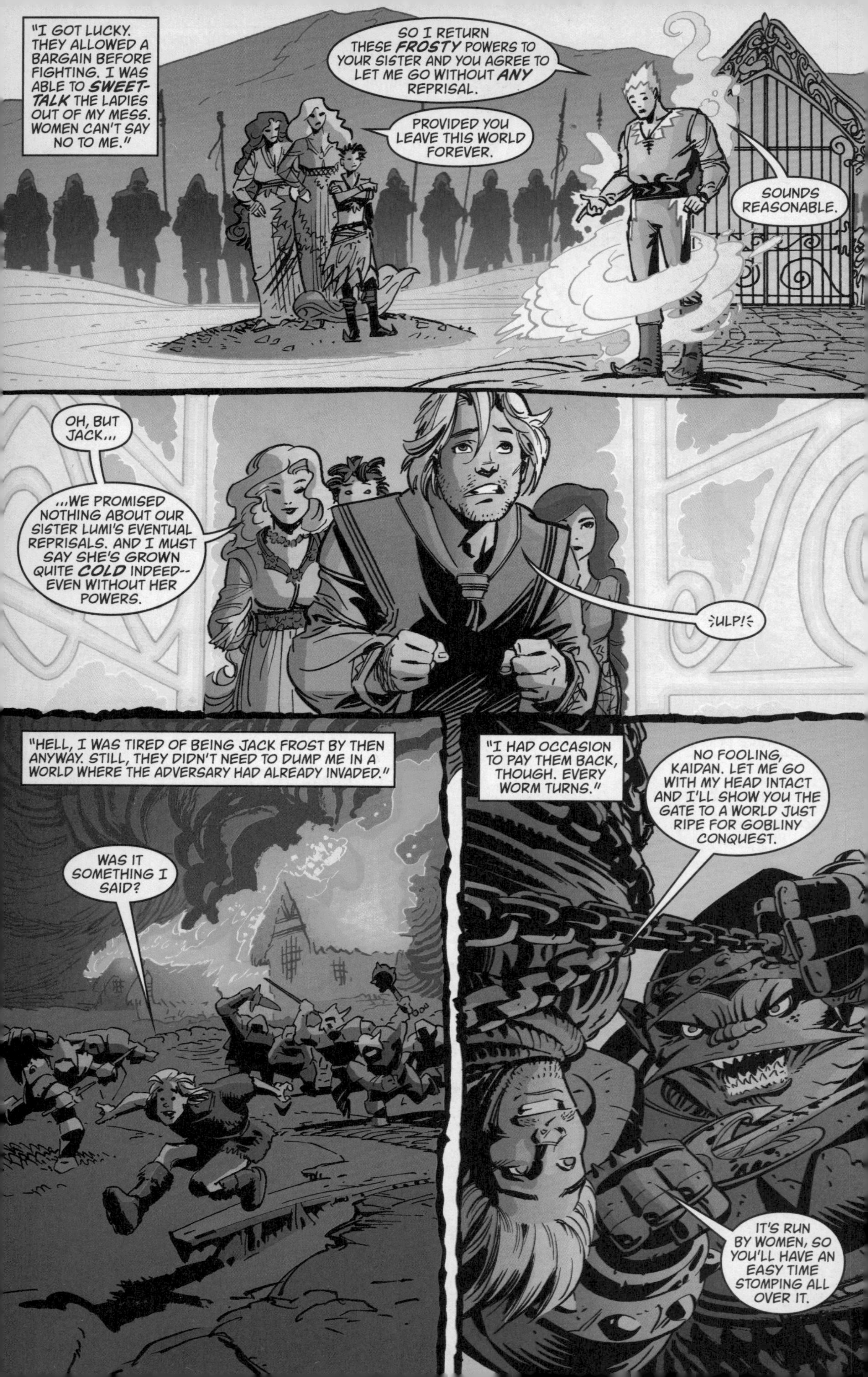
"I GOT LUCKY. THEY ALLOWED A BARGAIN BEFORE FIGHTING. I WAS ABLE TO SWEET-TALK THE LADIES OUT OF MY MESS. WOMEN CAN'T SAY NO TO ME."
SO I RETURN THESE FROSTY POWERS TO YOUR SISTER AND YOU AGREE TO LET ME GO WITHOUT ANY REPRISAL.
PROVIDED YOU LEAVE THIS WORLD FOREVER.
SOUNDS REASONABLE.
OH, BUT JACK...
...WE PROMISED NOTHING ABOUT OUR SISTER LUMI'S EVENTUAL REPRISALS. AND I MUST SAY SHE'S GROWN QUITE COLD INDEED-- EVEN WITHOUT HER POWERS.
ULP!
"HELL, I WAS TIRED OF BEING JACK FROST BY THEN ANYWAY. STILL, THEY DIDN'T NEED TO DUMP ME IN A WORLD WHERE THE ADVERSARY HAD ALREADY INVADED."
WAS IT SOMETHING I SAID?
"I HAD OCCASION TO PAY THEM BACK, THOUGH. EVERY WORM TURNS."
NO FOOLING, KAIDAN. LET ME GO WITH MY HEAD INTACT AND I'LL SHOW YOU THE GATE TO A WORLD JUST RIPE FOR GOBLINY CONQUEST.
IT'S RUN BY WOMEN, SO YOU'LL HAVE AN EASY TIME STOMPING ALL OVER IT.

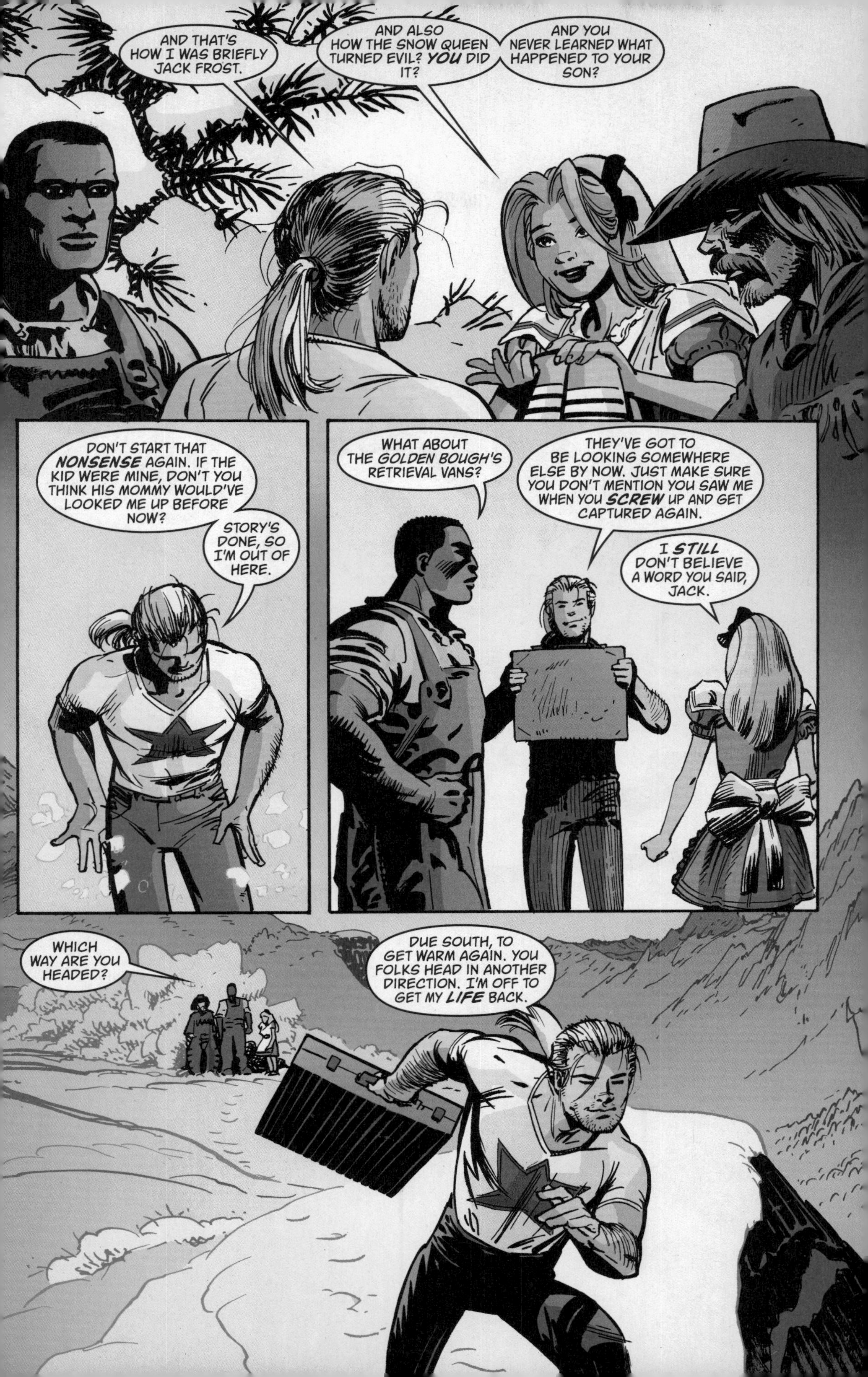
AND THAT'S HOW I WAS BRIEFLY JACK FROST.
AND ALSO HOW THE SNOW QUEEN TURNED EVIL? YOU DID IT?
AND YOU NEVER LEARNED WHAT HAPPENED TO YOUR SON?
DON'T START THAT NONSENSE AGAIN. IF THE KID WERE MINE, DON'T YOU THINK HIS MOMMY WOULD'VE LOOKED ME UP BEFORE NOW?
STORY'S DONE, SO I'M OUT OF HERE.
WHAT ABOUT THE GOLDEN BOUGH'S RETRIEVAL VANS?
THEY'VE GOT TO BE LOOKING SOMEWHERE ELSE BY NOW. JUST MAKE SURE YOU DON'T MENTION YOU SAW ME WHEN YOU SCREW UP AND GET CAPTURED AGAIN.
I STILL DON'T BELIEVE A WORD YOU SAID, JACK.
WHICH WAY ARE YOU HEADED?
DUE SOUTH, TO GET WARM AGAIN. YOU FOLKS HEAD IN ANOTHER DIRECTION. I'M OFF TO GET MY LIFE BACK.

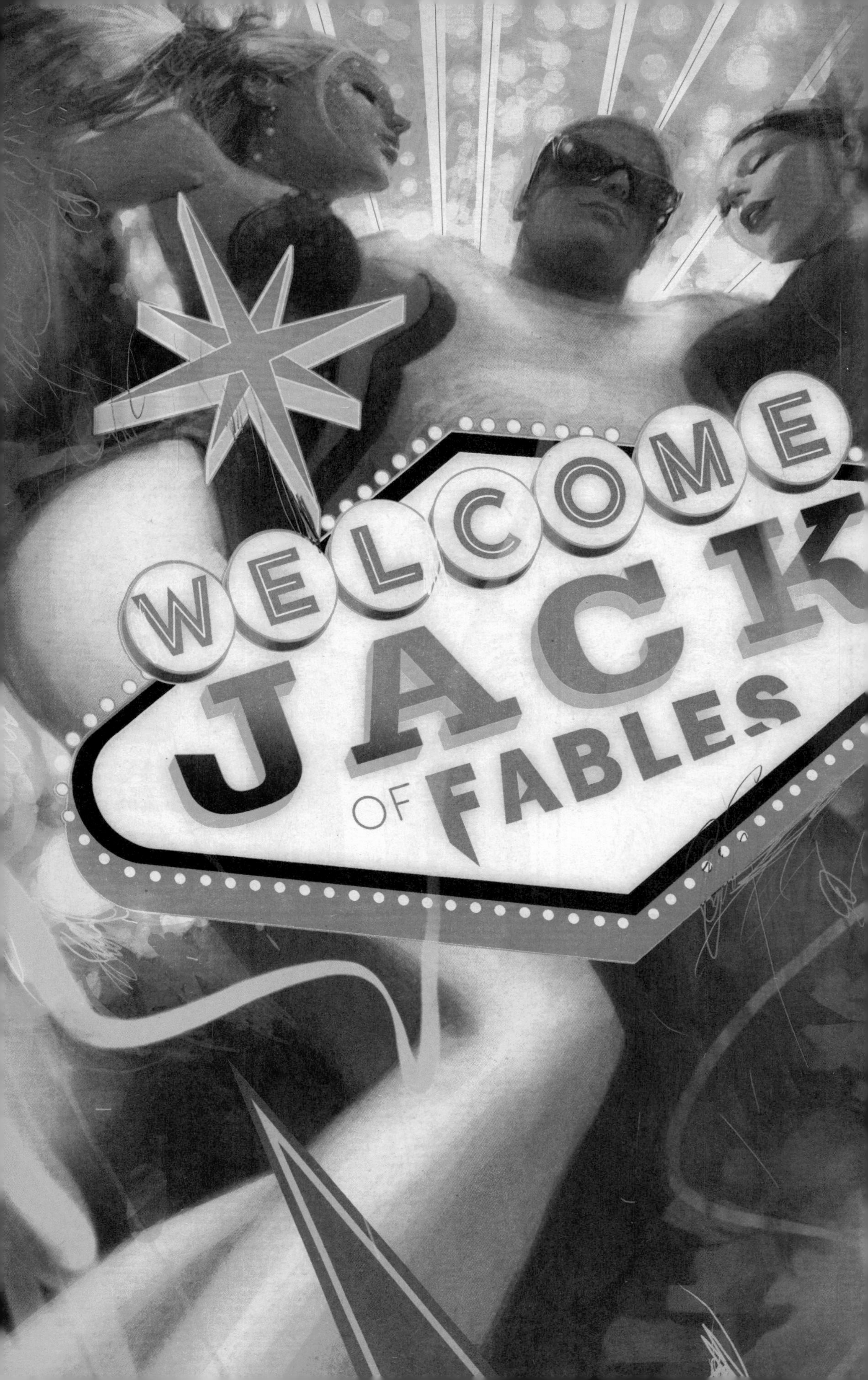
WELCOME
JACK
OF FABLES

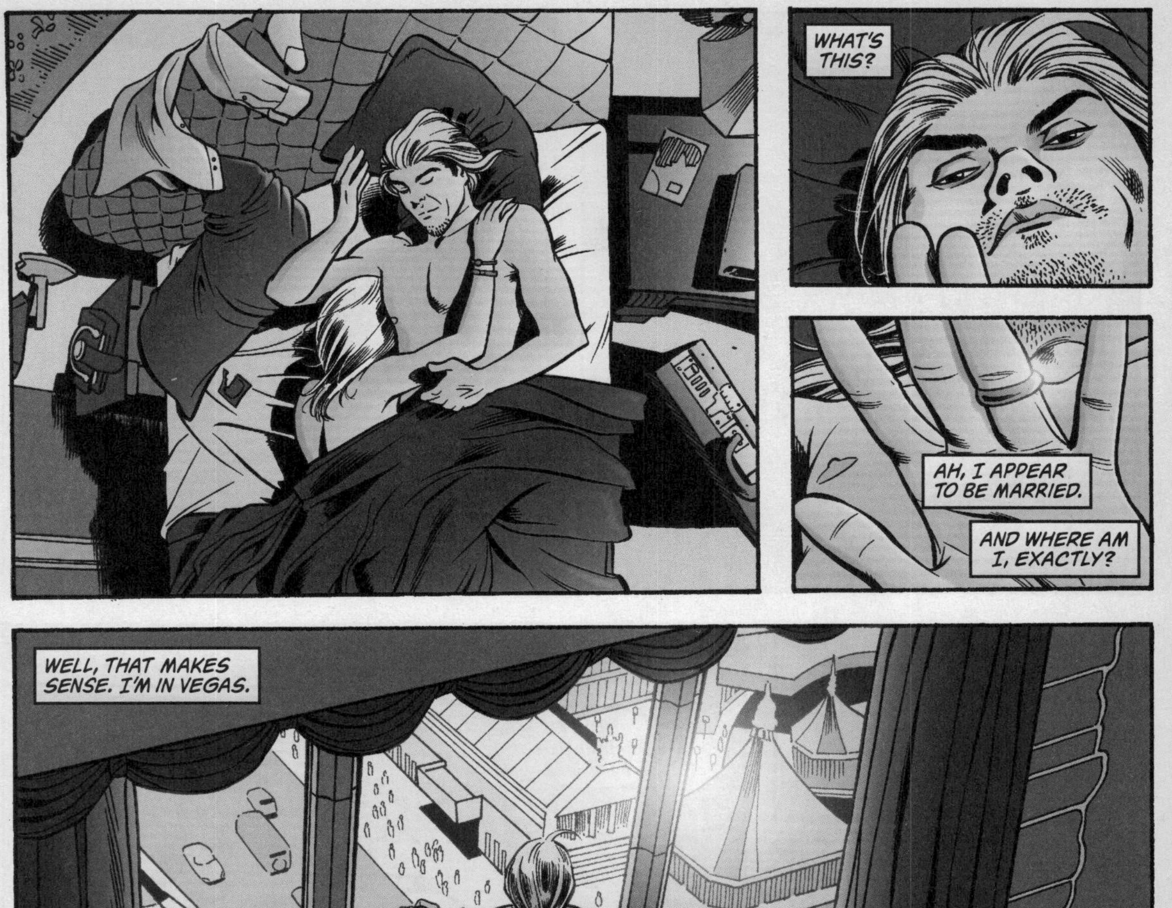
WHAT'S THIS?
AH, I APPEAR TO BE MARRIED.
AND WHERE AM I, EXACTLY?
WELL, THAT MAKES SENSE. I'M IN VEGAS.
MORNING, BABY.
WHY DON'TCHA COME BACK TO BED AND DO SOME MORE CONSUMMATING?

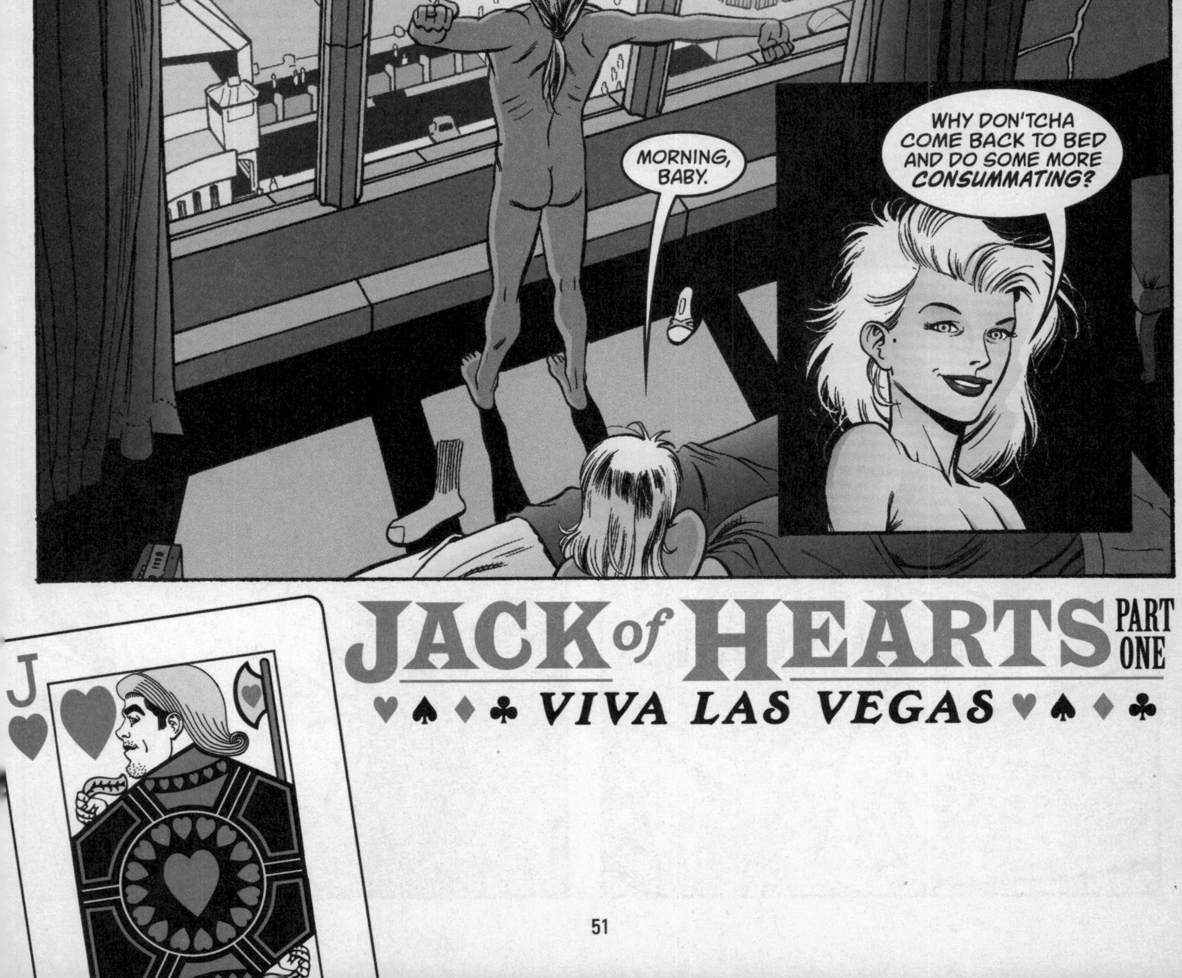

JACK of HEARTS PART ONE
♥ ♠ ♦ ♣ VIVA LAS VEGAS ♥ ♠ ♦ ♣

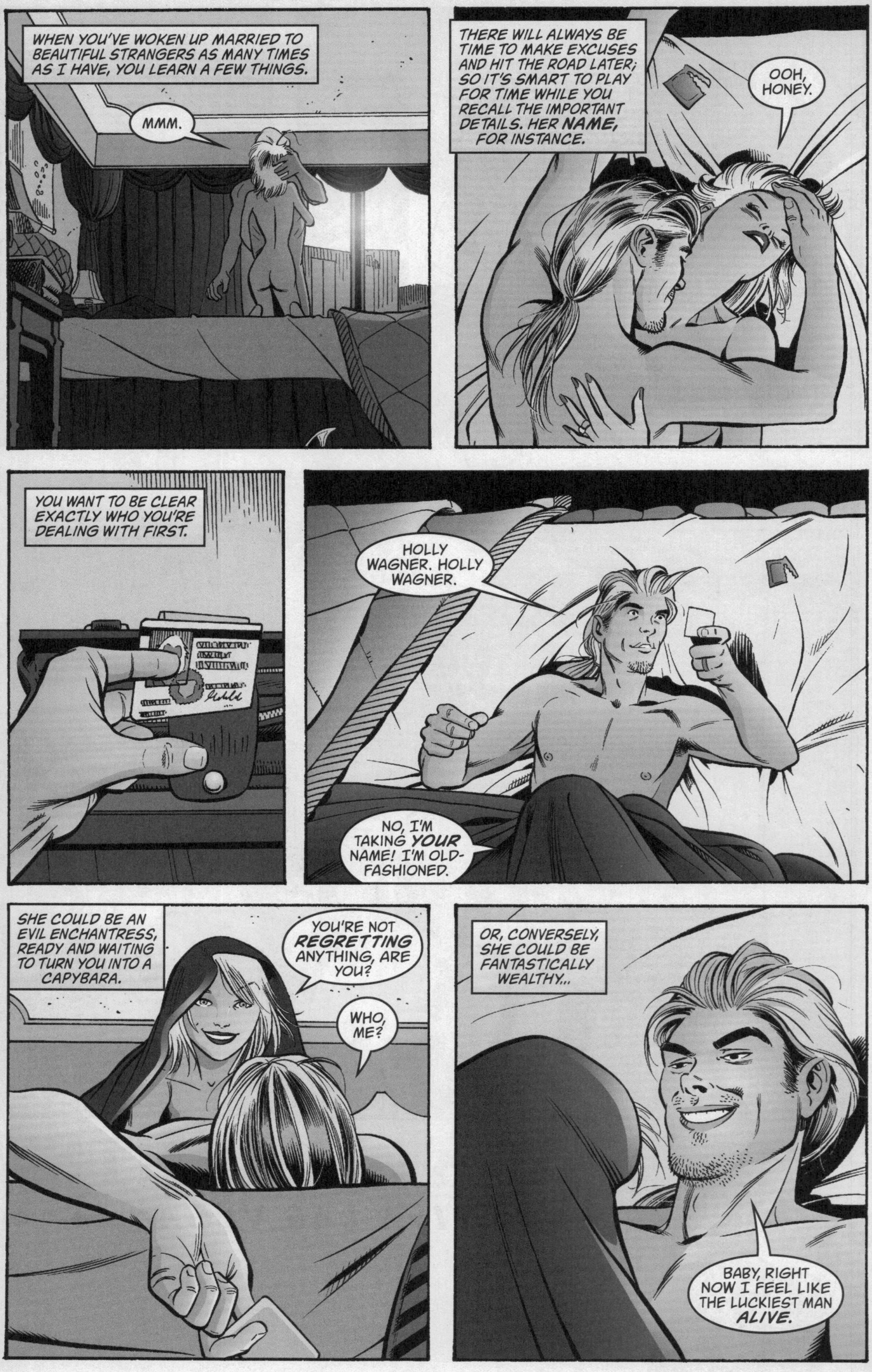
WHEN YOU'VE WOKEN UP MARRIED TO BEAUTIFUL STRANGERS AS MANY TIMES AS I HAVE, YOU LEARN A FEW THINGS.
MMM.
THERE WILL ALWAYS BE TIME TO MAKE EXCUSES AND HIT THE ROAD LATER; SO IT'S SMART TO PLAY FOR TIME WHILE YOU RECALL THE IMPORTANT DETAILS. HER NAME, FOR INSTANCE.
OOH, HONEY.
YOU WANT TO BE CLEAR EXACTLY WHO YOU'RE DEALING WITH FIRST.
HOLLY WAGNER. HOLLY WAGNER.
NO, I'M TAKING YOUR NAME! I'M OLD-FASHIONED.
SHE COULD BE AN EVIL ENCHANTRESS, READY AND WAITING TO TURN YOU INTO A CAPYBARA.
YOU'RE NOT REGRETTING ANYTHING, ARE YOU?
WHO, ME?
OR, CONVERSELY, SHE COULD BE FANTASTICALLY WEALTHY...
BABY, RIGHT NOW I FEEL LIKE THE LUCKIEST MAN ALIVE.

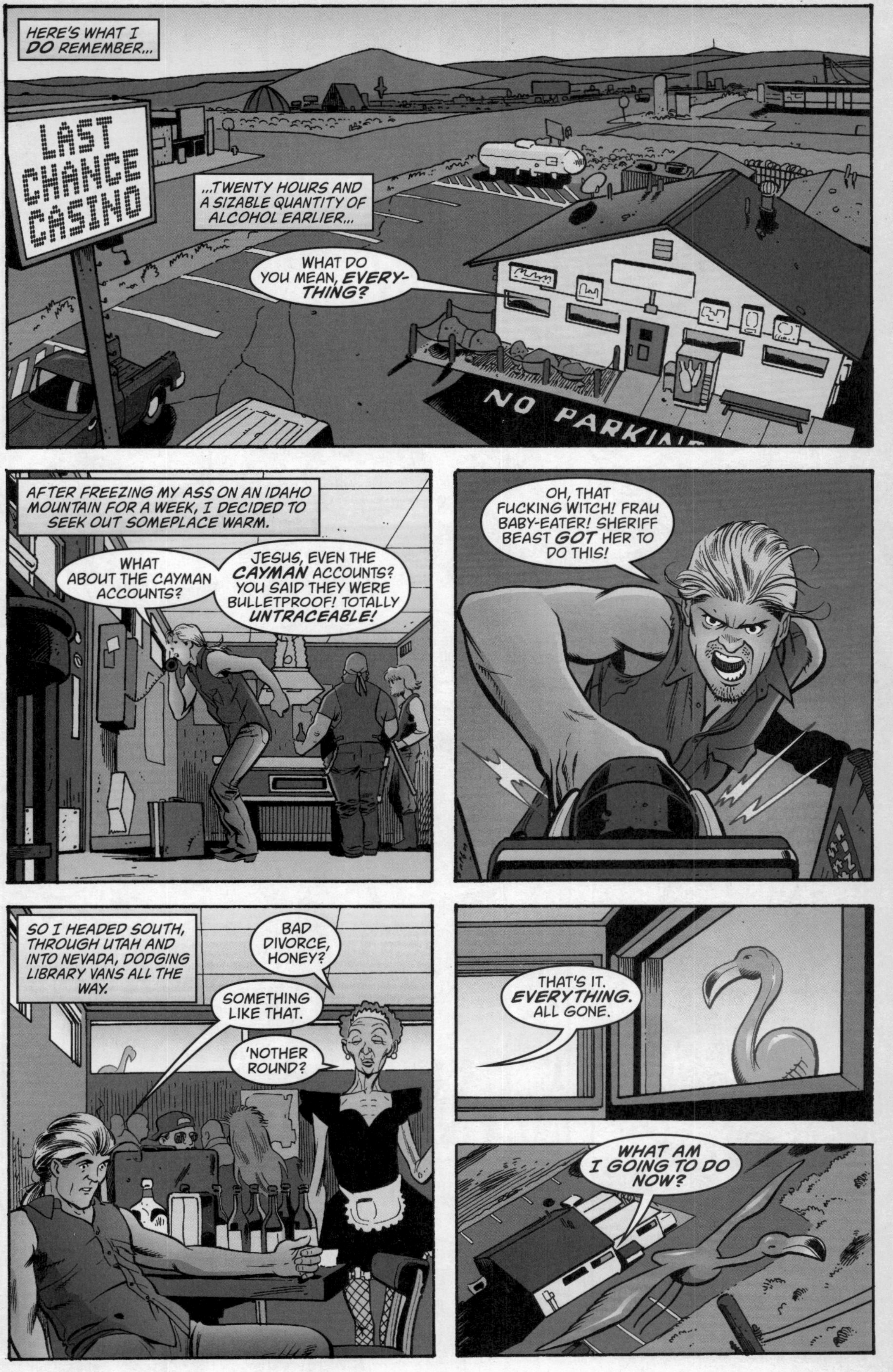
HERE'S WHAT I DO REMEMBER...
LAST CHANCE CASINO
...TWENTY HOURS AND A SIZABLE QUANTITY OF ALCOHOL EARLIER...
WHAT DO YOU MEAN, EVERY-THING?
NO PARKIN
AFTER FREEZING MY ASS ON AN IDAHO MOUNTAIN FOR A WEEK, I DECIDED TO SEEK OUT SOMEPLACE WARM.
WHAT ABOUT THE CAYMAN ACCOUNTS?
JESUS, EVEN THE CAYMAN ACCOUNTS? YOU SAID THEY WERE BULLETPROOF! TOTALLY UNTRACEABLE!
OH, THAT FUCKING WITCH! FRAU BABY-EATER! SHERIFF BEAST GOT HER TO DO THIS!
SO I HEADED SOUTH, THROUGH UTAH AND INTO NEVADA, DODGING LIBRARY VANS ALL THE WAY.
BAD DIVORCE, HONEY?
SOMETHING LIKE THAT.
'NOTHER ROUND?
THAT'S IT. EVERYTHING. ALL GONE.
WHAT AM I GOING TO DO NOW?

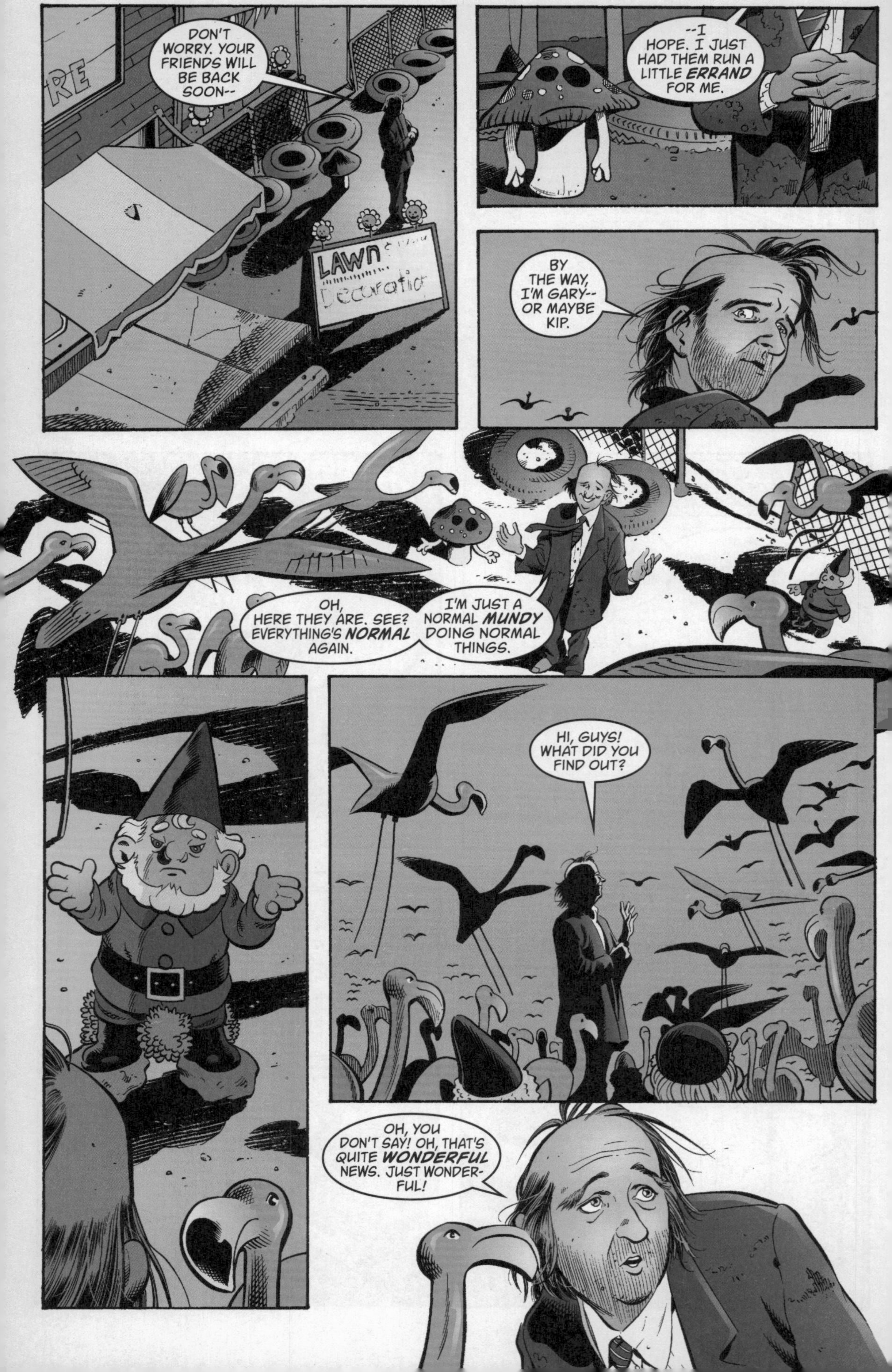
DON'T WORRY. YOUR FRIENDS WILL BE BACK SOON--
LAWN
Decoratio
--I HOPE. I JUST HAD THEM RUN A LITTLE ERRAND FOR ME.
BY THE WAY, I'M GARY--OR MAYBE KIP.
OH, HERE THEY ARE. SEE? EVERYTHING'S NORMAL AGAIN.
I'M JUST A NORMAL MUNDY DOING NORMAL THINGS.
HI, GUYS! WHAT DID YOU FIND OUT?
OH, YOU DON'T SAY! OH, THAT'S QUITE WONDERFUL NEWS. JUST WONDERFUL!

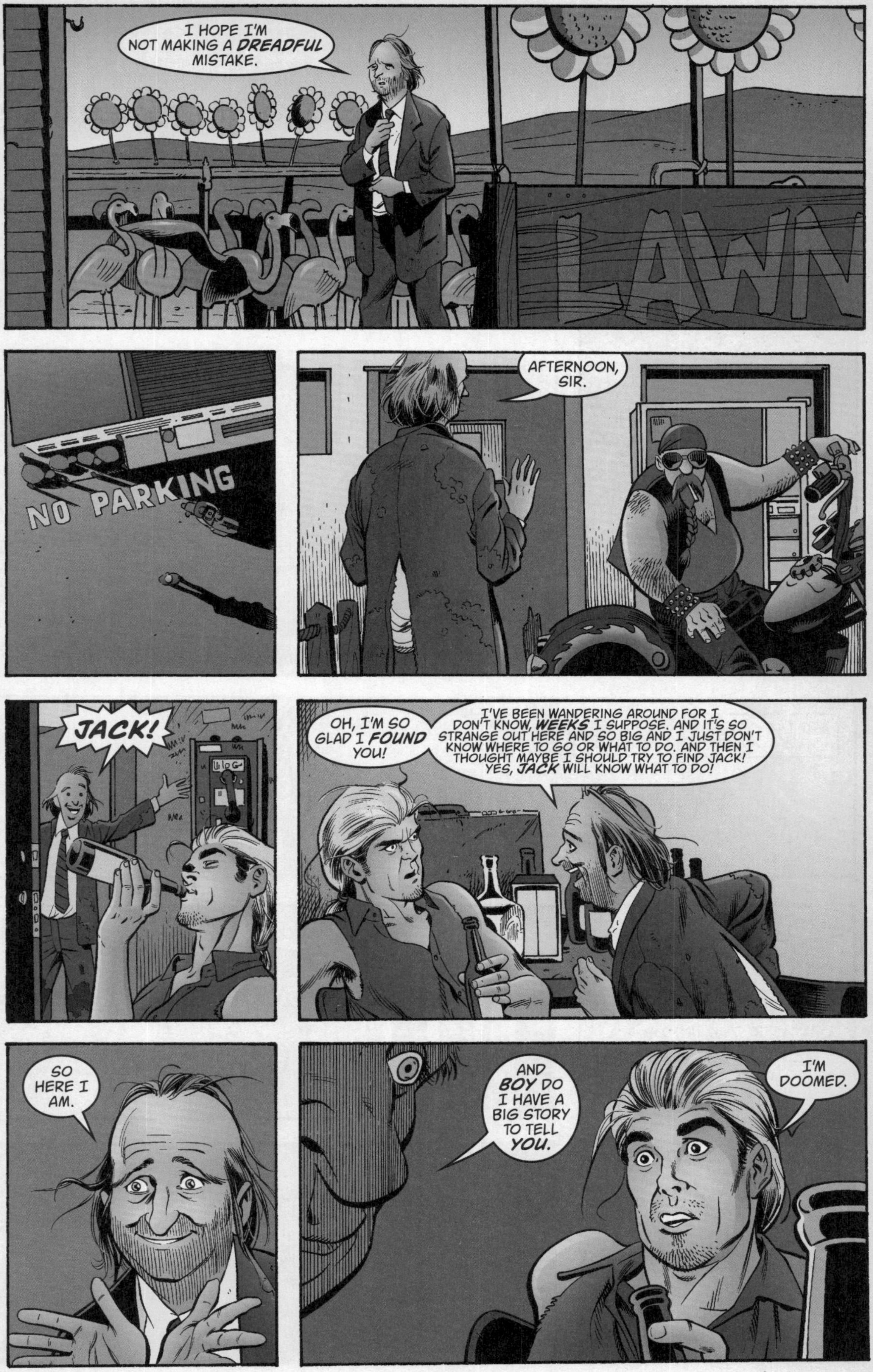
I HOPE I'M NOT MAKING A DREADFUL MISTAKE.
LAWN
NO PARKING
AFTERNOON, SIR.
JACK!
OH, I'M SO GLAD I FOUND YOU!
I'VE BEEN WANDERING AROUND FOR I DON'T KNOW, WEEKS I SUPPOSE. AND IT'S SO STRANGE OUT HERE AND SO BIG AND I JUST DON'T KNOW WHERE TO GO OR WHAT TO DO. AND THEN I THOUGHT MAYBE I SHOULD TRY TO FIND JACK! YES, JACK WILL KNOW WHAT TO DO!
SO HERE I AM.
AND BOY DO I HAVE A BIG STORY TO TELL YOU.
I'M DOOMED.

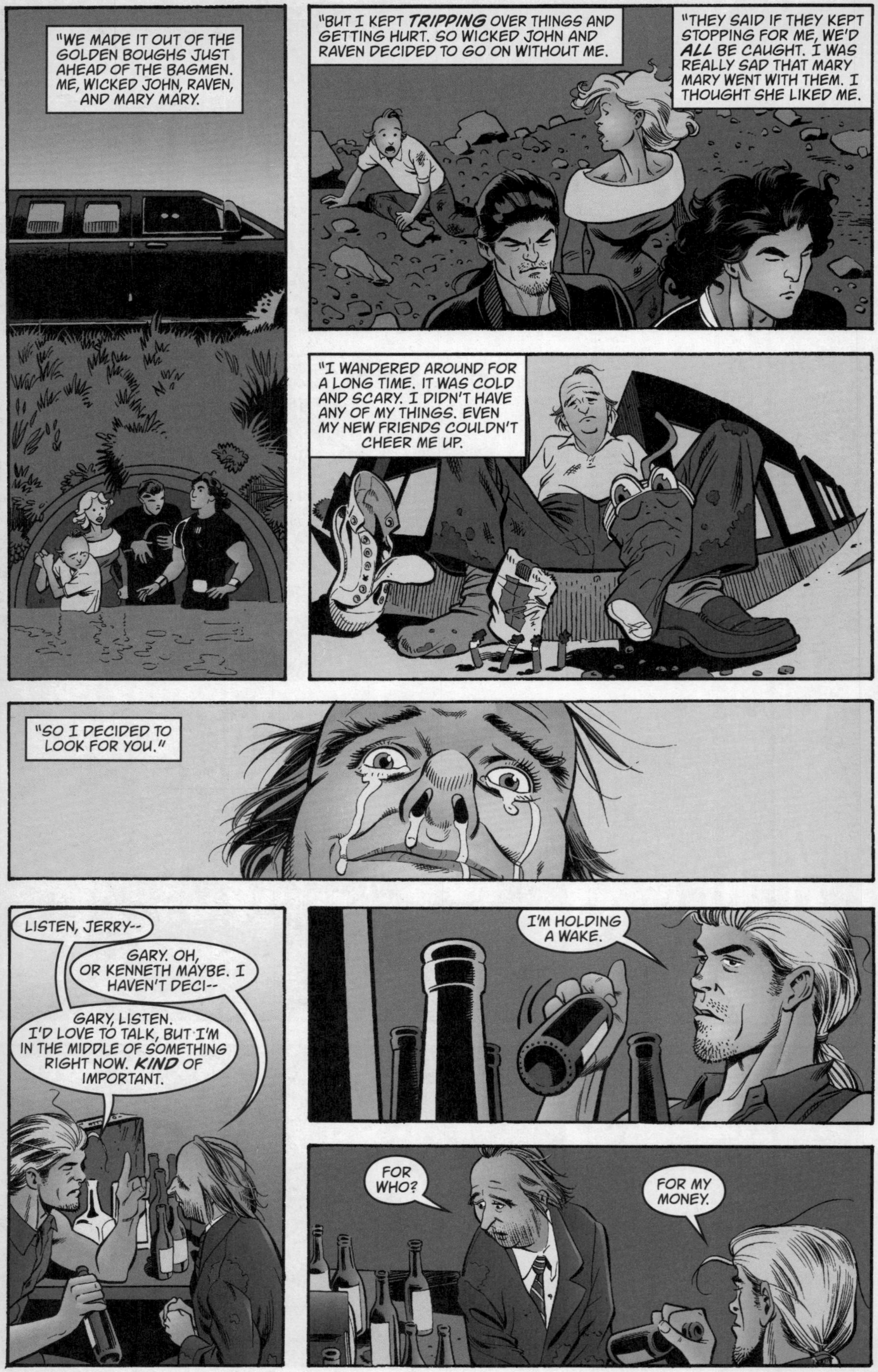
"WE MADE IT OUT OF THE GOLDEN BOUGHS JUST AHEAD OF THE BAGMEN. ME, WICKED JOHN, RAVEN, AND MARY MARY.
"BUT I KEPT TRIPPING OVER THINGS AND GETTING HURT. SO WICKED JOHN AND RAVEN DECIDED TO GO ON WITHOUT ME.
"THEY SAID IF THEY KEPT STOPPING FOR ME, WE'D ALL BE CAUGHT. I WAS REALLY SAD THAT MARY MARY WENT WITH THEM. I THOUGHT SHE LIKED ME.
"I WANDERED AROUND FOR A LONG TIME. IT WAS COLD AND SCARY. I DIDN'T HAVE ANY OF MY THINGS. EVEN MY NEW FRIENDS COULDN'T CHEER ME UP.
"SO I DECIDED TO LOOK FOR YOU."
LISTEN, JERRY--
GARY. OH, OR KENNETH MAYBE. I HAVEN'T DECI--
GARY, LISTEN. I'D LOVE TO TALK, BUT I'M IN THE MIDDLE OF SOMETHING RIGHT NOW. KIND OF IMPORTANT.
I'M HOLDING A WAKE.
FOR WHO?
FOR MY MONEY.

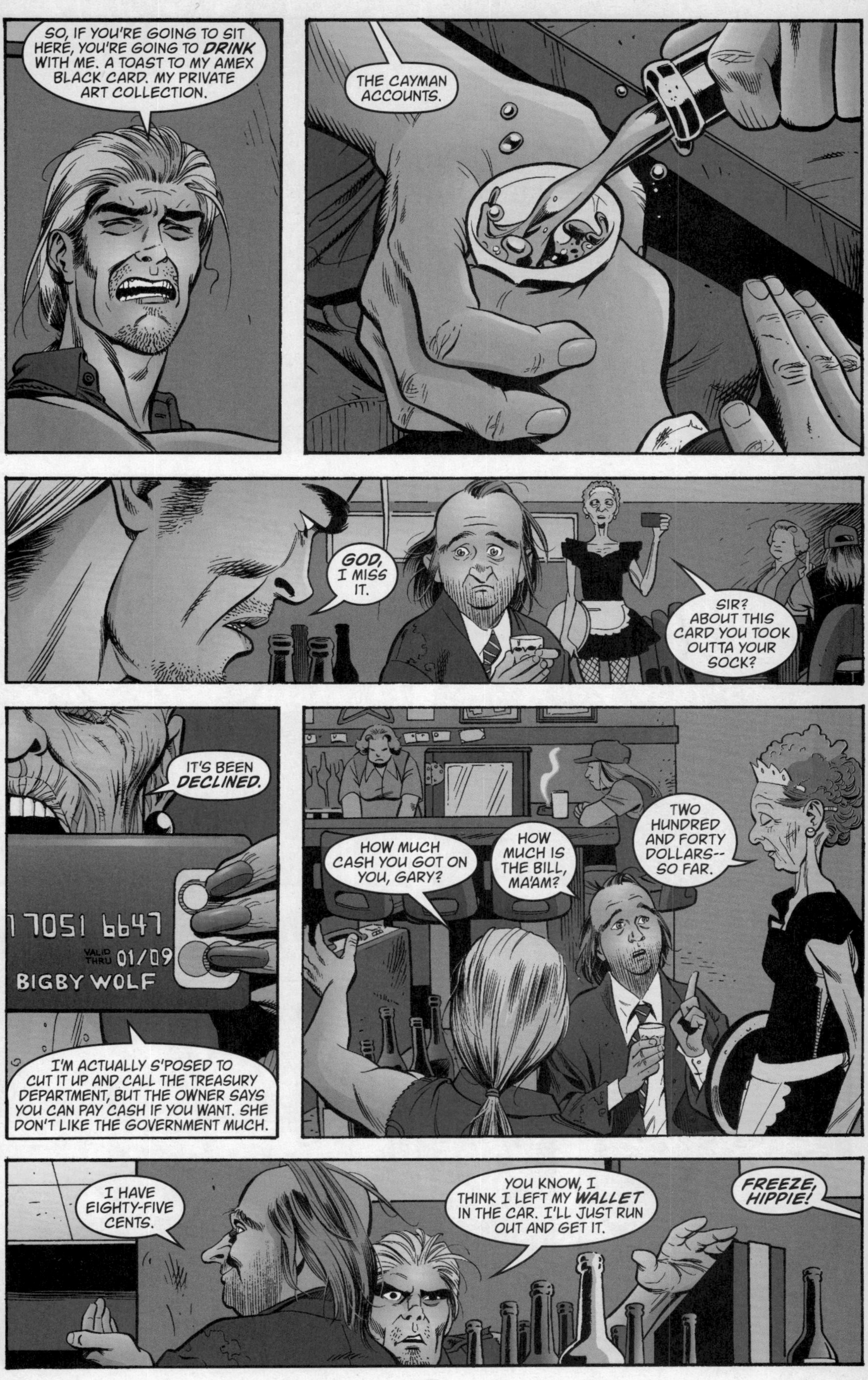
SO, IF YOU'RE GOING TO SIT HERE, YOU'RE GOING TO DRINK WITH ME. A TOAST TO MY AMEX BLACK CARD. MY PRIVATE ART COLLECTION.
THE CAYMAN ACCOUNTS.
GOD, I MISS IT.
SIR? ABOUT THIS CARD YOU TOOK OUTTA YOUR SOCK?
IT'S BEEN DECLINED.
17051 6647
VALID THRU 01/09
BIGBY WOLF
I'M ACTUALLY S'POSED TO CUT IT UP AND CALL THE TREASURY DEPARTMENT, BUT THE OWNER SAYS YOU CAN PAY CASH IF YOU WANT. SHE DON'T LIKE THE GOVERNMENT MUCH.
HOW MUCH CASH YOU GOT ON YOU, GARY?
HOW MUCH IS THE BILL, MA'AM?
TWO HUNDRED AND FORTY DOLLARS-- SO FAR.
I HAVE EIGHTY-FIVE CENTS.
YOU KNOW, I THINK I LEFT MY WALLET IN THE CAR. I'LL JUST RUN OUT AND GET IT.
FREEZE, HIPPIE!

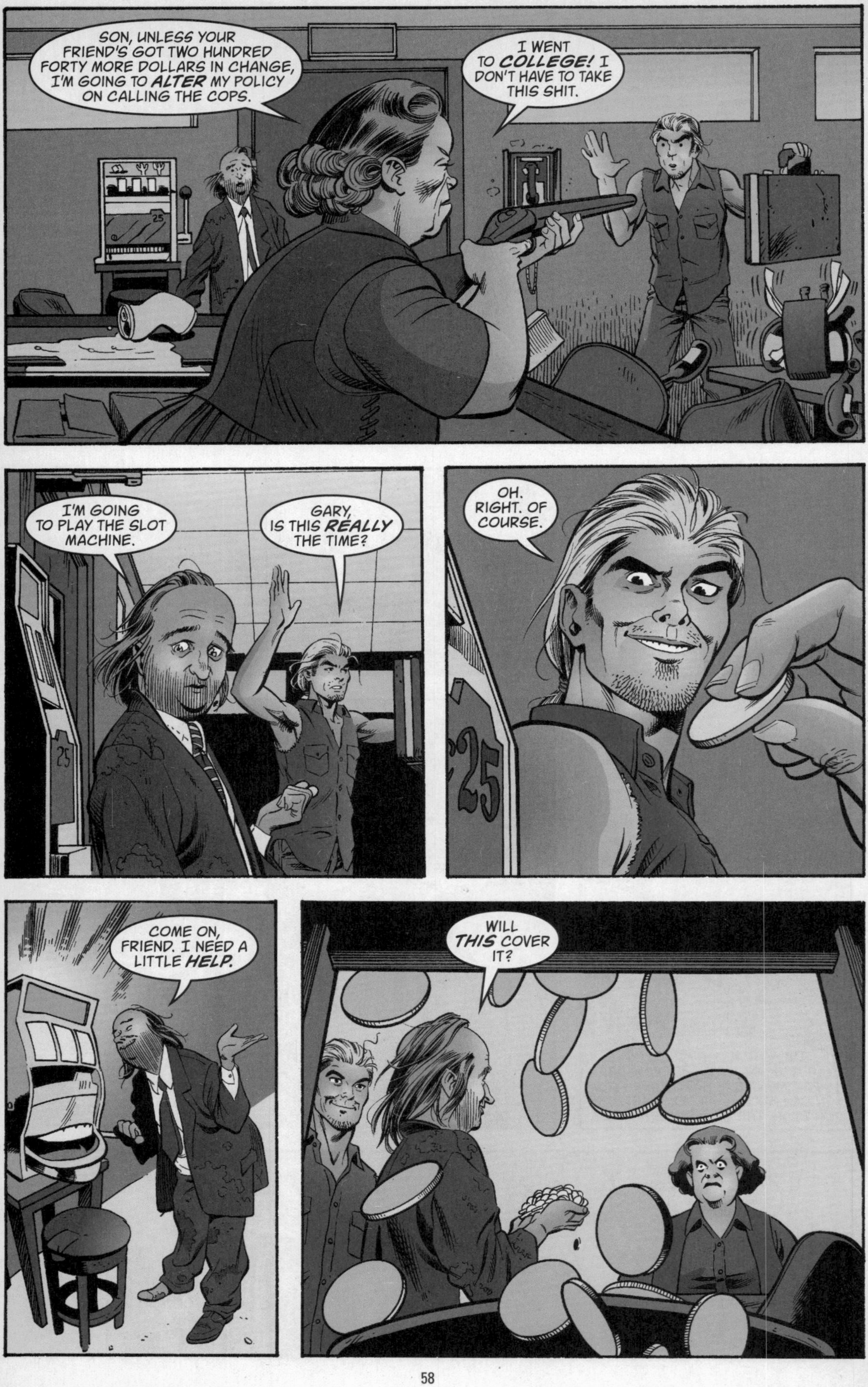
SON, UNLESS YOUR FRIEND'S GOT TWO HUNDRED FORTY MORE DOLLARS IN CHANGE, I'M GOING TO ALTER MY POLICY ON CALLING THE COPS.
I WENT TO COLLEGE! I DON'T HAVE TO TAKE THIS SHIT.
I'M GOING TO PLAY THE SLOT MACHINE.
GARY, IS THIS REALLY THE TIME?
OH. RIGHT. OF COURSE.
COME ON, FRIEND. I NEED A LITTLE HELP.
WILL THIS COVER IT?

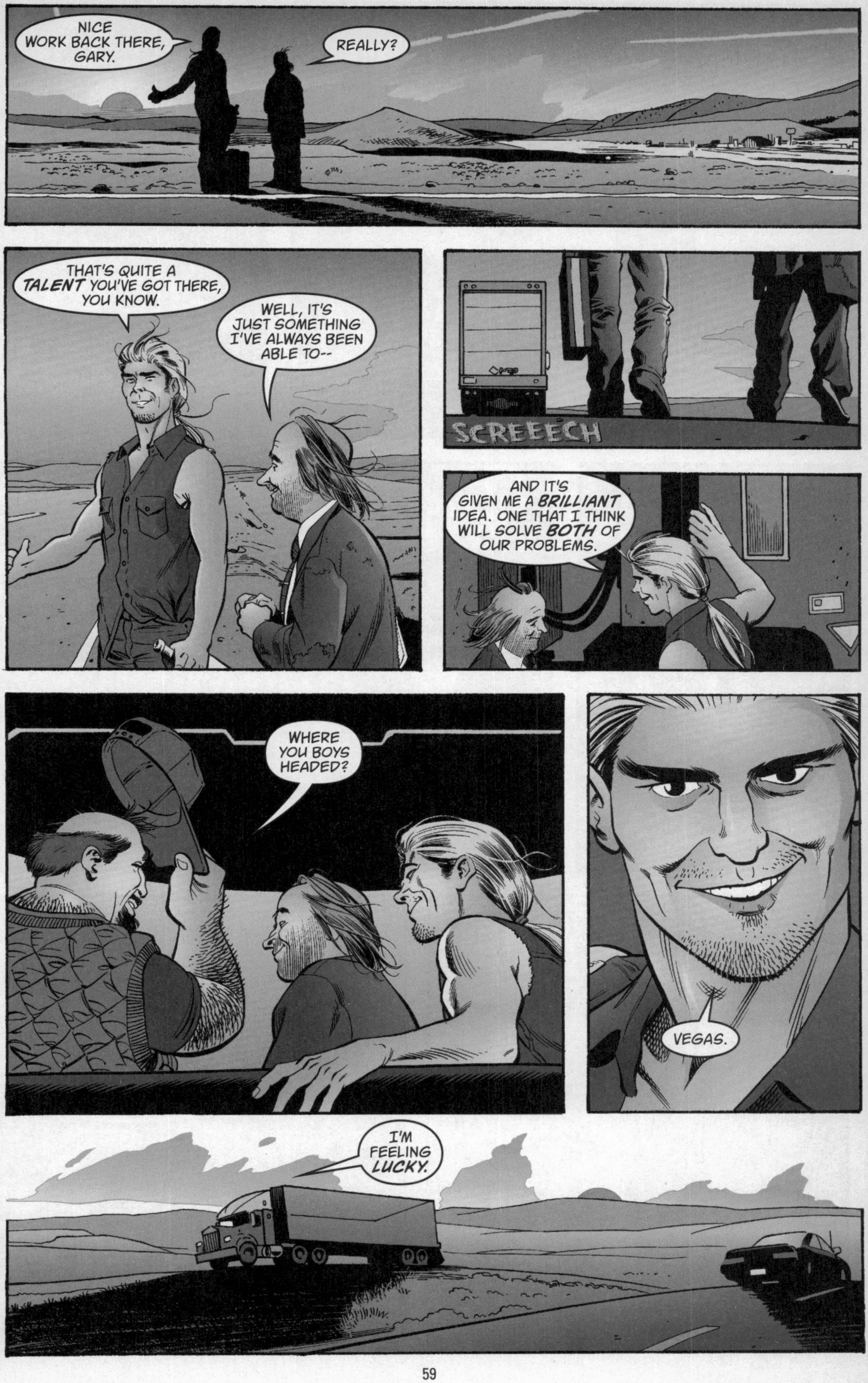
NICE WORK BACK THERE, GARY.
REALLY?
THAT'S QUITE A TALENT YOU'VE GOT THERE, YOU KNOW.
WELL, IT'S JUST SOMETHING I'VE ALWAYS BEEN ABLE TO--
SCREEECH
AND IT'S GIVEN ME A BRILLIANT IDEA. ONE THAT I THINK WILL SOLVE BOTH OF OUR PROBLEMS.
WHERE YOU BOYS HEADED?
VEGAS.
I'M FEELING LUCKY.

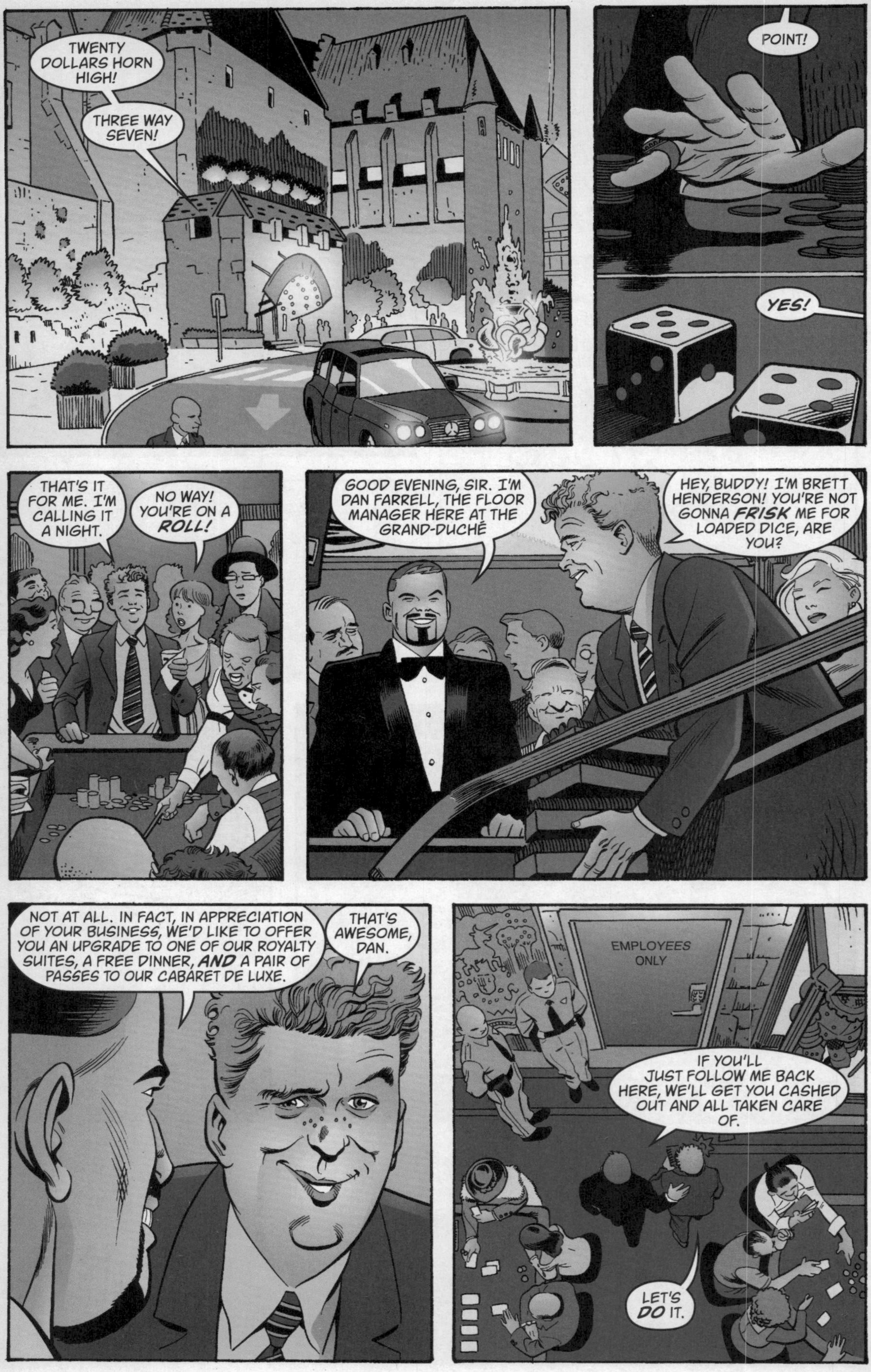
TWENTY DOLLARS HORN HIGH!
THREE WAY SEVEN!
POINT!
YES!
THAT'S IT FOR ME. I'M CALLING IT A NIGHT.
NO WAY! YOU'RE ON A ROLL!
GOOD EVENING, SIR. I'M DAN FARRELL, THE FLOOR MANAGER HERE AT THE GRAND-DUCHÉ
HEY, BUDDY! I'M BRETT HENDERSON! YOU'RE NOT GONNA FRISK ME FOR LOADED DICE, ARE YOU?
NOT AT ALL. IN FACT, IN APPRECIATION OF YOUR BUSINESS, WE'D LIKE TO OFFER YOU AN UPGRADE TO ONE OF OUR ROYALTY SUITES, A FREE DINNER, AND A PAIR OF PASSES TO OUR CABARET DE LUXE.
THAT'S AWESOME, DAN.
EMPLOYEES ONLY
IF YOU'LL JUST FOLLOW ME BACK HERE, WE'LL GET YOU CASHED OUT AND ALL TAKEN CARE OF.
LET'S DO IT.

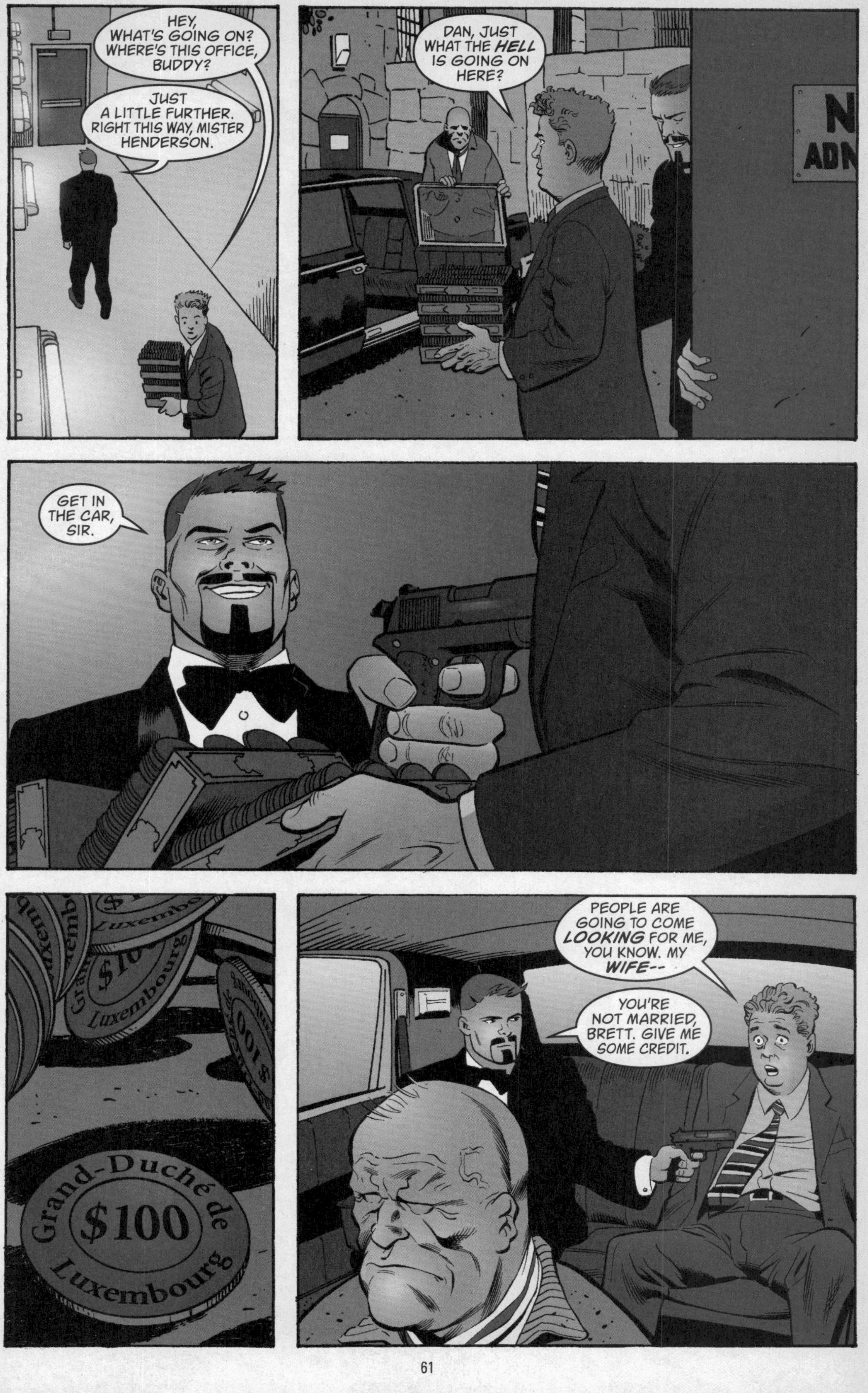
HEY, WHAT'S GOING ON? WHERE'S THIS OFFICE, BUDDY?
JUST A LITTLE FURTHER. RIGHT THIS WAY, MISTER HENDERSON.
DAN, JUST WHAT THE HELL IS GOING ON HERE?
GET IN THE CAR, SIR.
Grand-Duché de Luxembourg
$100
PEOPLE ARE GOING TO COME LOOKING FOR ME, YOU KNOW. MY WIFE--
YOU'RE NOT MARRIED, BRETT. GIVE ME SOME CREDIT.

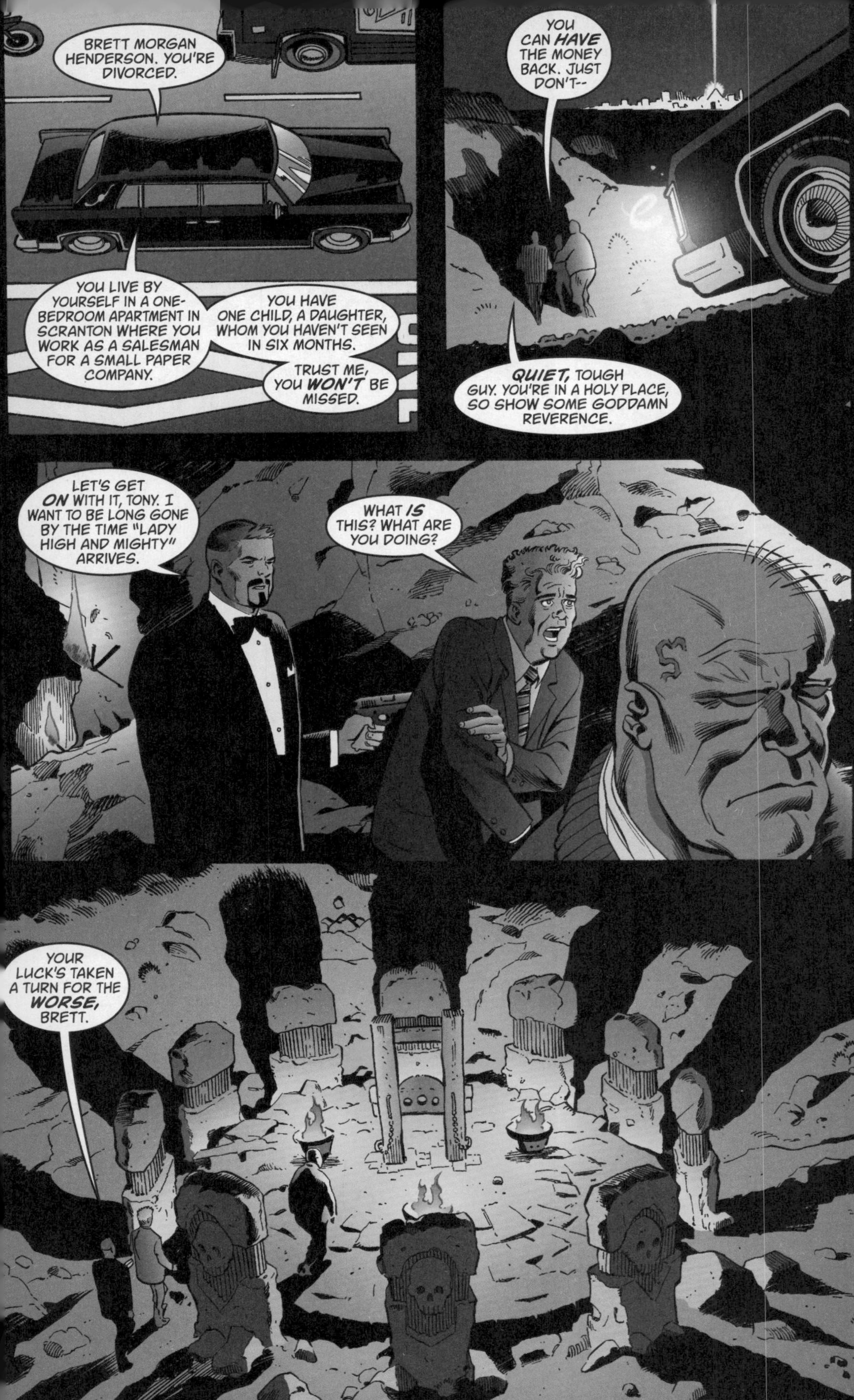
BRETT MORGAN HENDERSON. YOU'RE DIVORCED.
YOU LIVE BY YOURSELF IN A ONE-BEDROOM APARTMENT IN SCRANTON WHERE YOU WORK AS A SALESMAN FOR A SMALL PAPER COMPANY.
YOU HAVE ONE CHILD, A DAUGHTER, WHOM YOU HAVEN'T SEEN IN SIX MONTHS.
TRUST ME, YOU WON'T BE MISSED.
YOU CAN HAVE THE MONEY BACK. JUST DON'T--
QUIET, TOUGH GUY. YOU'RE IN A HOLY PLACE, SO SHOW SOME GODDAMN REVERENCE.
LET'S GET ON WITH IT, TONY. I WANT TO BE LONG GONE BY THE TIME "LADY HIGH AND MIGHTY" ARRIVES.
WHAT IS THIS? WHAT ARE YOU DOING?
YOUR LUCK'S TAKEN A TURN FOR THE WORSE, BRETT.

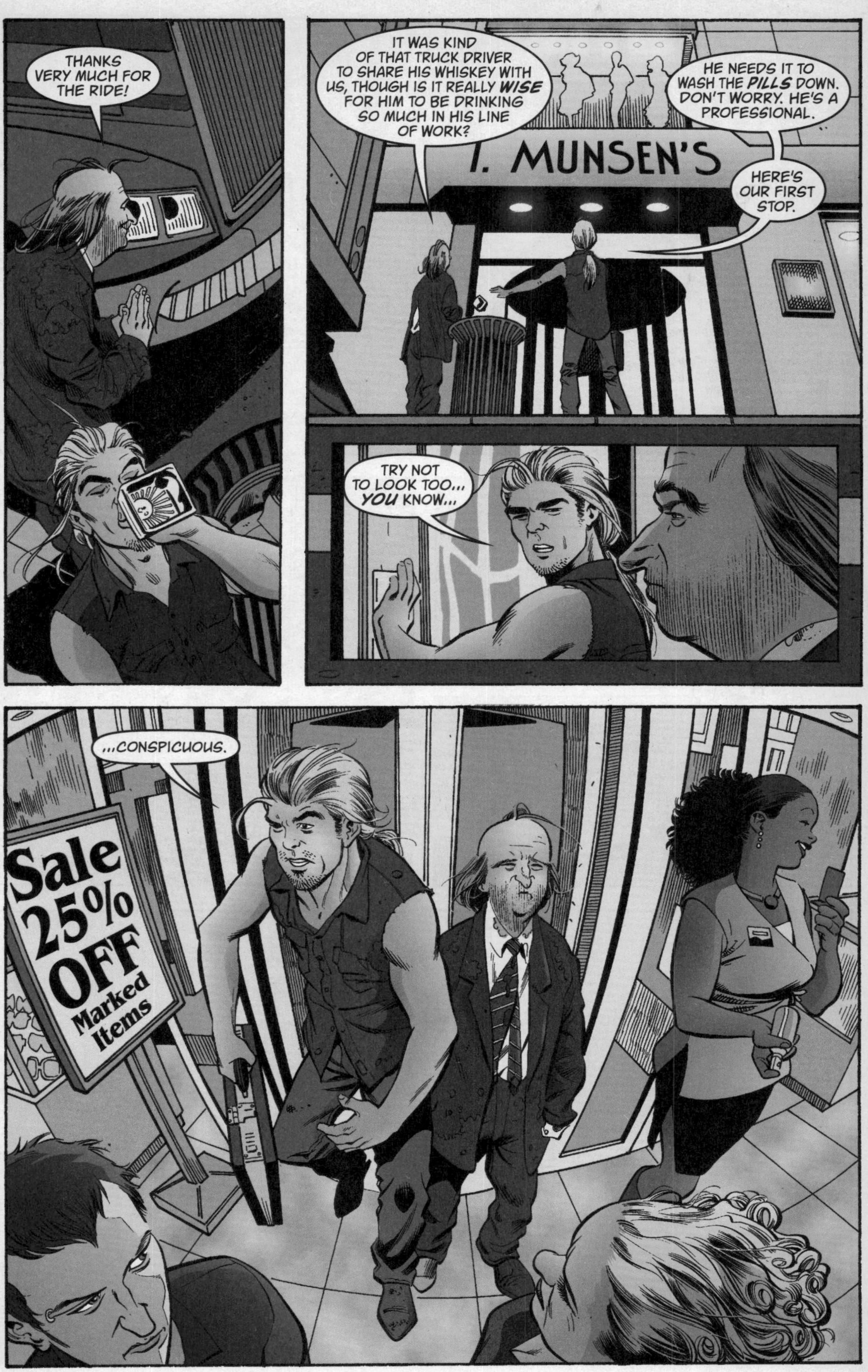
THANKS VERY MUCH FOR THE RIDE!
IT WAS KIND OF THAT TRUCK DRIVER TO SHARE HIS WHISKEY WITH US, THOUGH IS IT REALLY WISE FOR HIM TO BE DRINKING SO MUCH IN HIS LINE OF WORK?
HE NEEDS IT TO WASH THE PILLS DOWN. DON'T WORRY. HE'S A PROFESSIONAL.
HERE'S OUR FIRST STOP.
1. MUNSEN'S
TRY NOT TO LOOK TOO... YOU KNOW...
...CONSPICUOUS.
Sale 25% OFF Marked Items

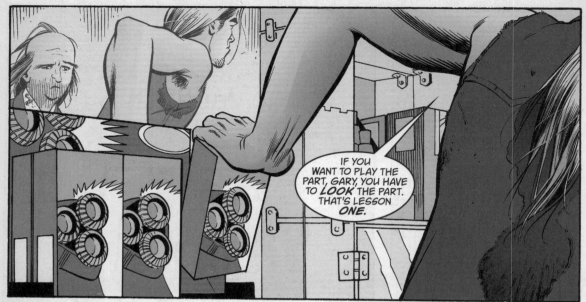

IF YOU WANT TO PLAY THE PART, GARY, YOU HAVE TO *LOOK* THE PART. THAT'S LESSON *ONE*.

LESSON *TWO* IS THAT ELECTRIC RAZORS DON'T WORK FOR *SHIT*. BLADES ARE MUCH BETTER.

UM, SHOULD YOU REALLY BE USING THAT?

LESSON *THREE*: A GOOD SUIT PREVENTS PEOPLE FROM QUESTIONING YOUR MOTIVES. THIS ISN'T SAVILE ROW, BUT IT'LL DO.

JACK, HAVE YOU SEEN HOW MUCH THESE *COST?* WE ONLY HAVE SIX DOLLARS IN QUARTERS BETWEEN US.

HOW ARE WE GOING TO *PAY* FOR THEM?

WHO SAID ANYTHING ABOUT PAYING, GARY?

BUT--THAT'S *STEALING*.

SO WHAT? TRY TO ACT NATURAL.

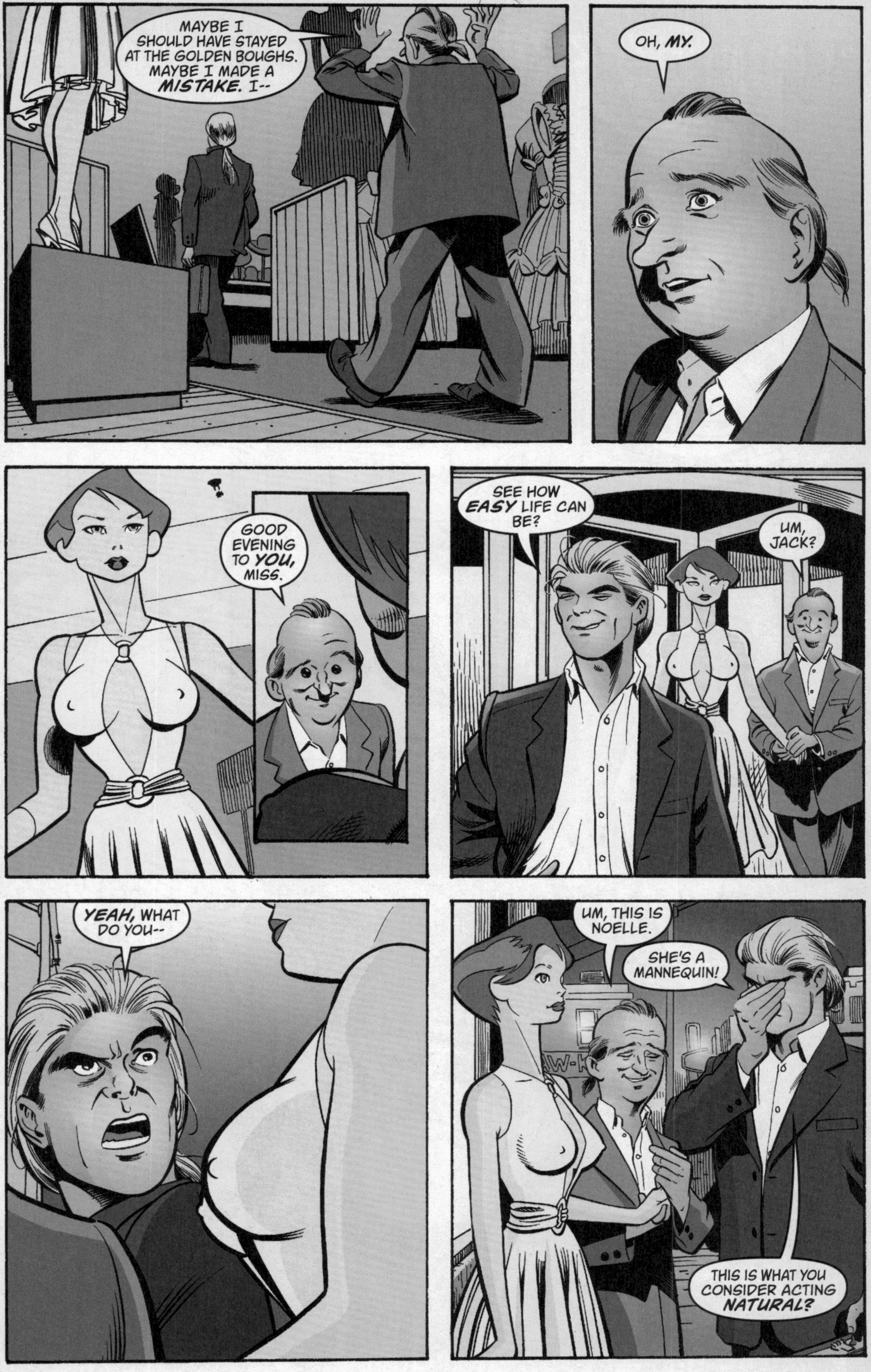

MAYBE I SHOULD HAVE STAYED AT THE GOLDEN BOUGHS. MAYBE I MADE A MISTAKE. I--
OH, MY.
GOOD EVENING TO YOU, MISS.
SEE HOW EASY LIFE CAN BE?
UM, JACK?
YEAH, WHAT DO YOU--
UM, THIS IS NOELLE.
SHE'S A MANNEQUIN!
THIS IS WHAT YOU CONSIDER ACTING NATURAL?

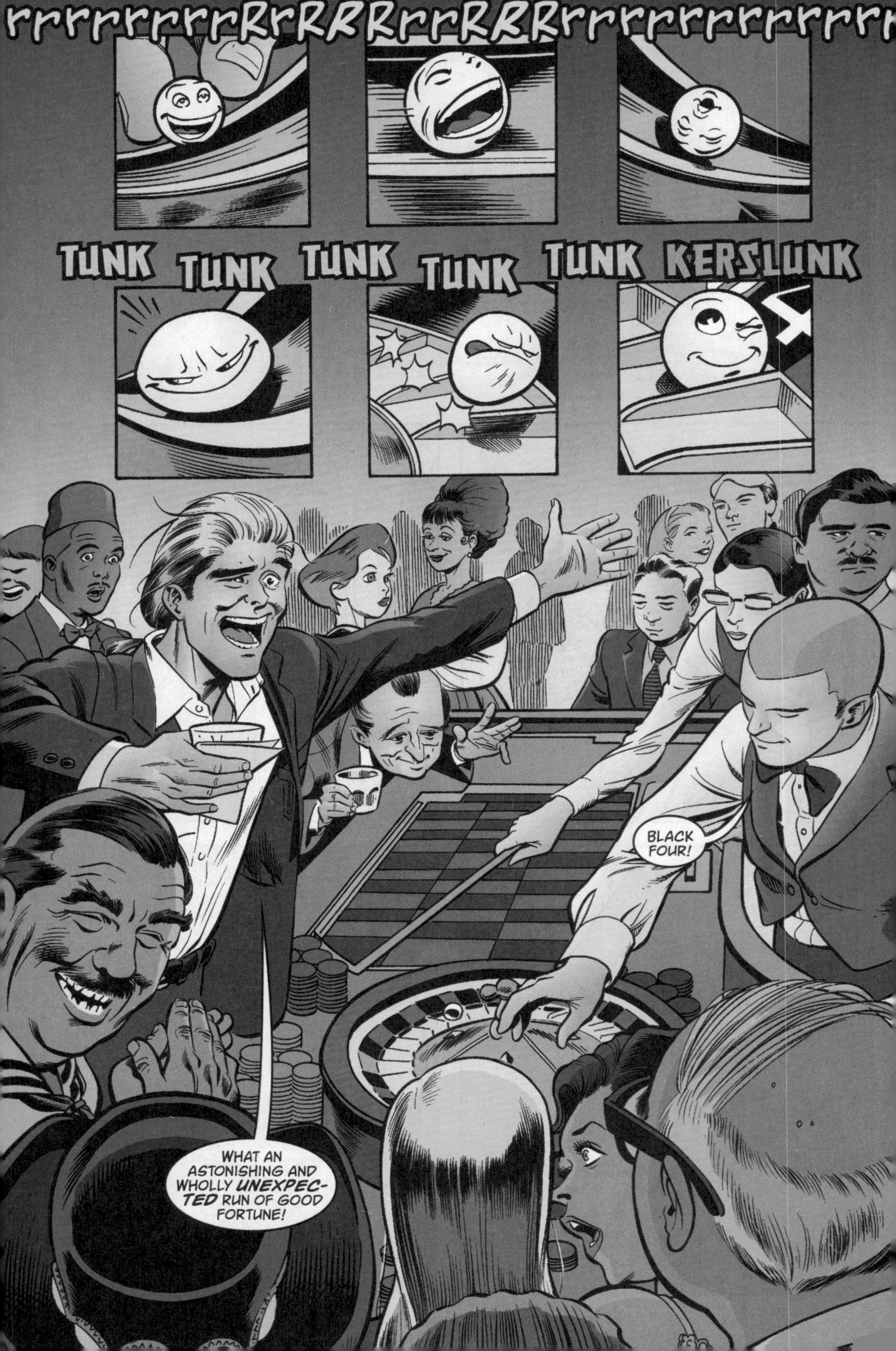
rrrrrrrrRrRRRrrrRRRrrrrrrrrrrrrrr
TUNK TUNK TUNK TUNK TUNK KERSLUNK
BLACK FOUR!
WHAT AN ASTONISHING AND WHOLLY *UNEXPECTED* RUN OF GOOD FORTUNE!

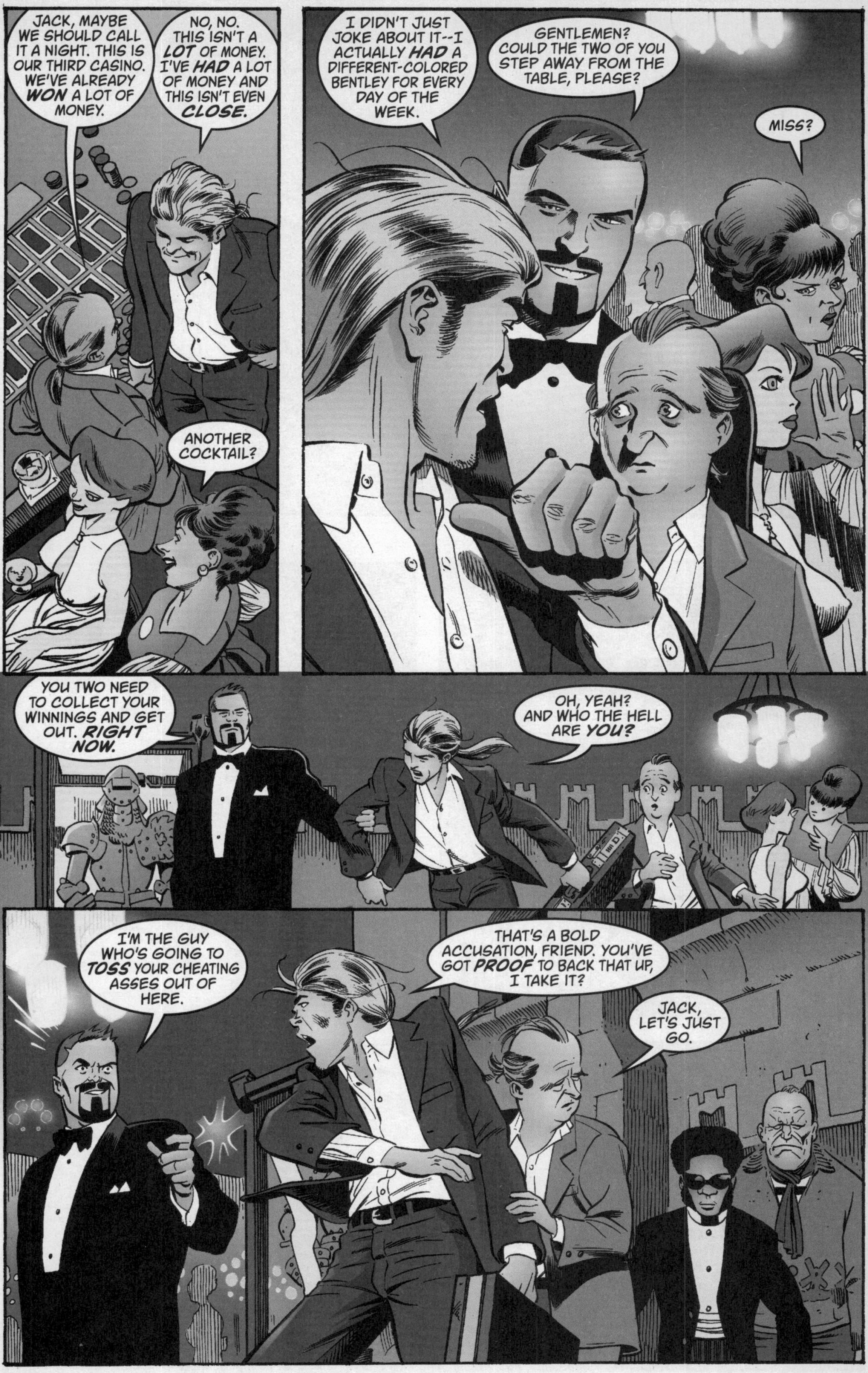
JACK, MAYBE WE SHOULD CALL IT A NIGHT. THIS IS OUR THIRD CASINO. WE'VE ALREADY WON A LOT OF MONEY.
NO, NO. THIS ISN'T A LOT OF MONEY. I'VE HAD A LOT OF MONEY AND THIS ISN'T EVEN CLOSE.
ANOTHER COCKTAIL?
I DIDN'T JUST JOKE ABOUT IT--I ACTUALLY HAD A DIFFERENT-COLORED BENTLEY FOR EVERY DAY OF THE WEEK.
GENTLEMEN? COULD THE TWO OF YOU STEP AWAY FROM THE TABLE, PLEASE?
MISS?
YOU TWO NEED TO COLLECT YOUR WINNINGS AND GET OUT. RIGHT NOW.
OH, YEAH? AND WHO THE HELL ARE YOU?
I'M THE GUY WHO'S GOING TO TOSS YOUR CHEATING ASSES OUT OF HERE.
THAT'S A BOLD ACCUSATION, FRIEND. YOU'VE GOT PROOF TO BACK THAT UP, I TAKE IT?
JACK, LET'S JUST GO.

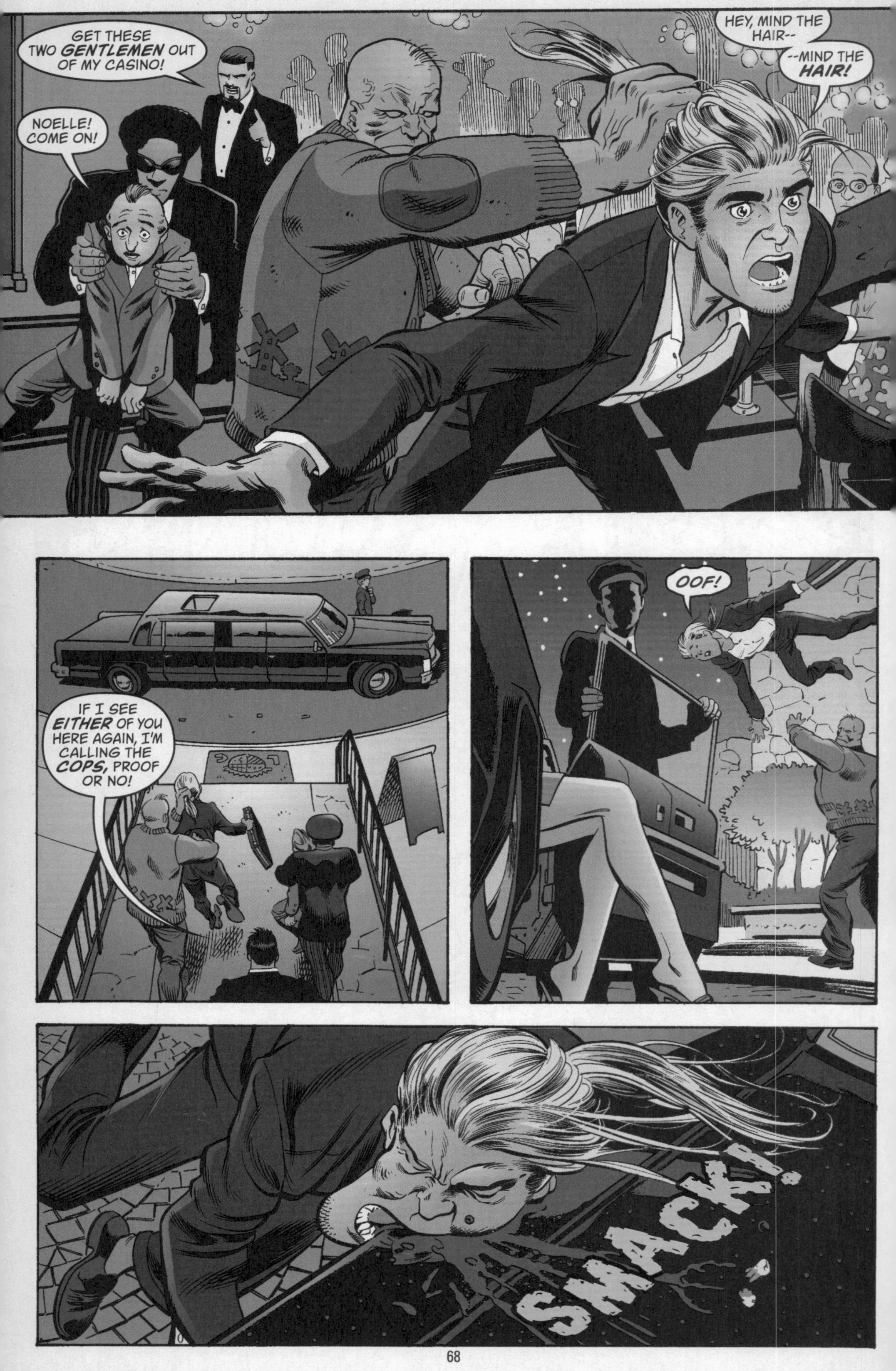
GET THESE TWO GENTLEMEN OUT OF MY CASINO!
NOELLE! COME ON!
HEY, MIND THE HAIR--
--MIND THE HAIR!
IF I SEE EITHER OF YOU HERE AGAIN, I'M CALLING THE COPS, PROOF OR NO!
OOF!
SMACK!

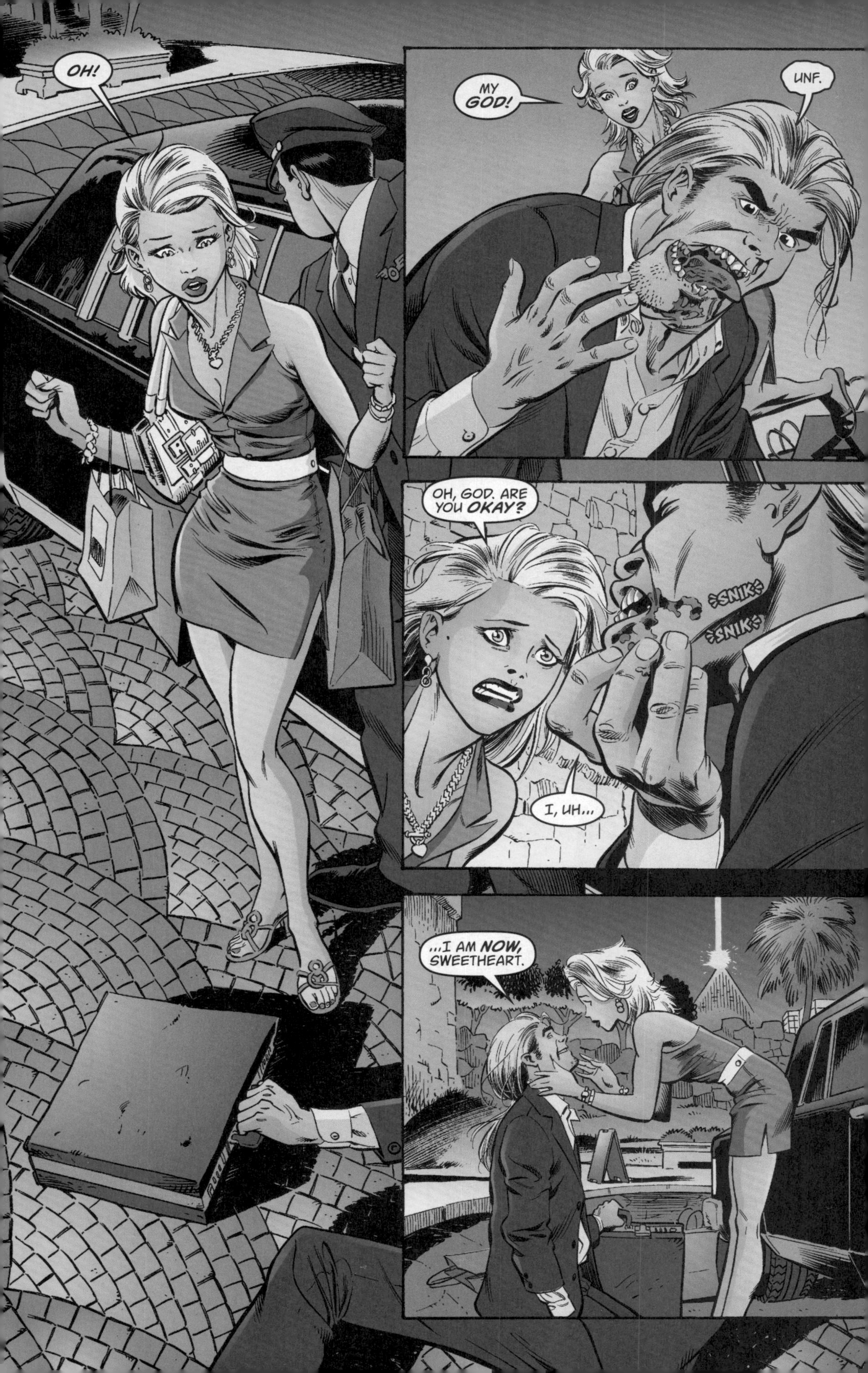
OH!
MY GOD!
UNF.
OH, GOD. ARE YOU OKAY?
SNIK
SNIK
I, UH...
...I AM NOW, SWEETHEART.

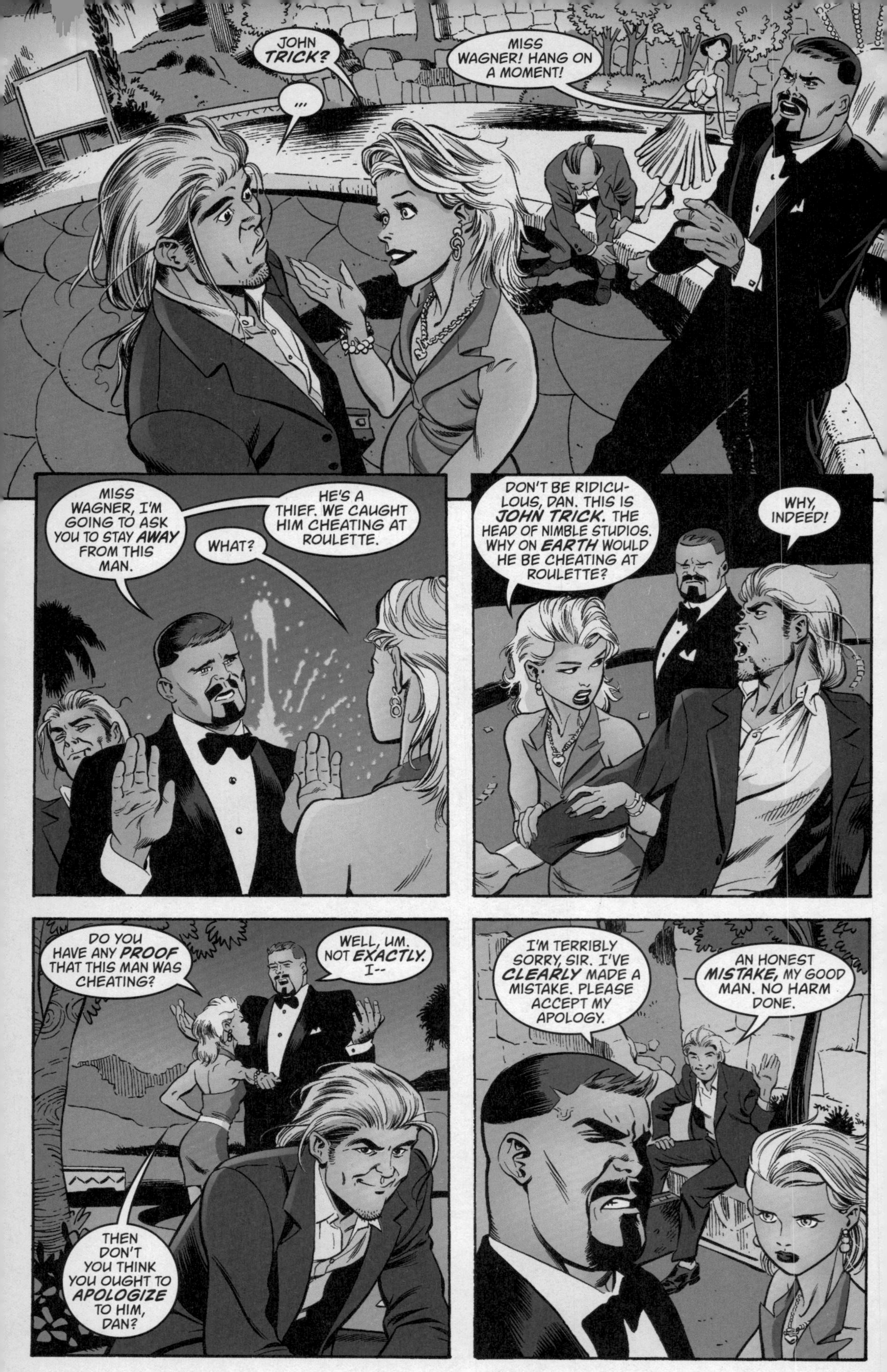
JOHN TRICK?
...
MISS WAGNER! HANG ON A MOMENT!
MISS WAGNER, I'M GOING TO ASK YOU TO STAY AWAY FROM THIS MAN.
WHAT?
HE'S A THIEF. WE CAUGHT HIM CHEATING AT ROULETTE.
DON'T BE RIDICULOUS, DAN. THIS IS JOHN TRICK. THE HEAD OF NIMBLE STUDIOS. WHY ON EARTH WOULD HE BE CHEATING AT ROULETTE?
WHY, INDEED!
DO YOU HAVE ANY PROOF THAT THIS MAN WAS CHEATING?
WELL, UM. NOT EXACTLY. I--
THEN DON'T YOU THINK YOU OUGHT TO APOLOGIZE TO HIM, DAN?
I'M TERRIBLY SORRY, SIR. I'VE CLEARLY MADE A MISTAKE. PLEASE ACCEPT MY APOLOGY.
AN HONEST MISTAKE, MY GOOD MAN. NO HARM DONE.

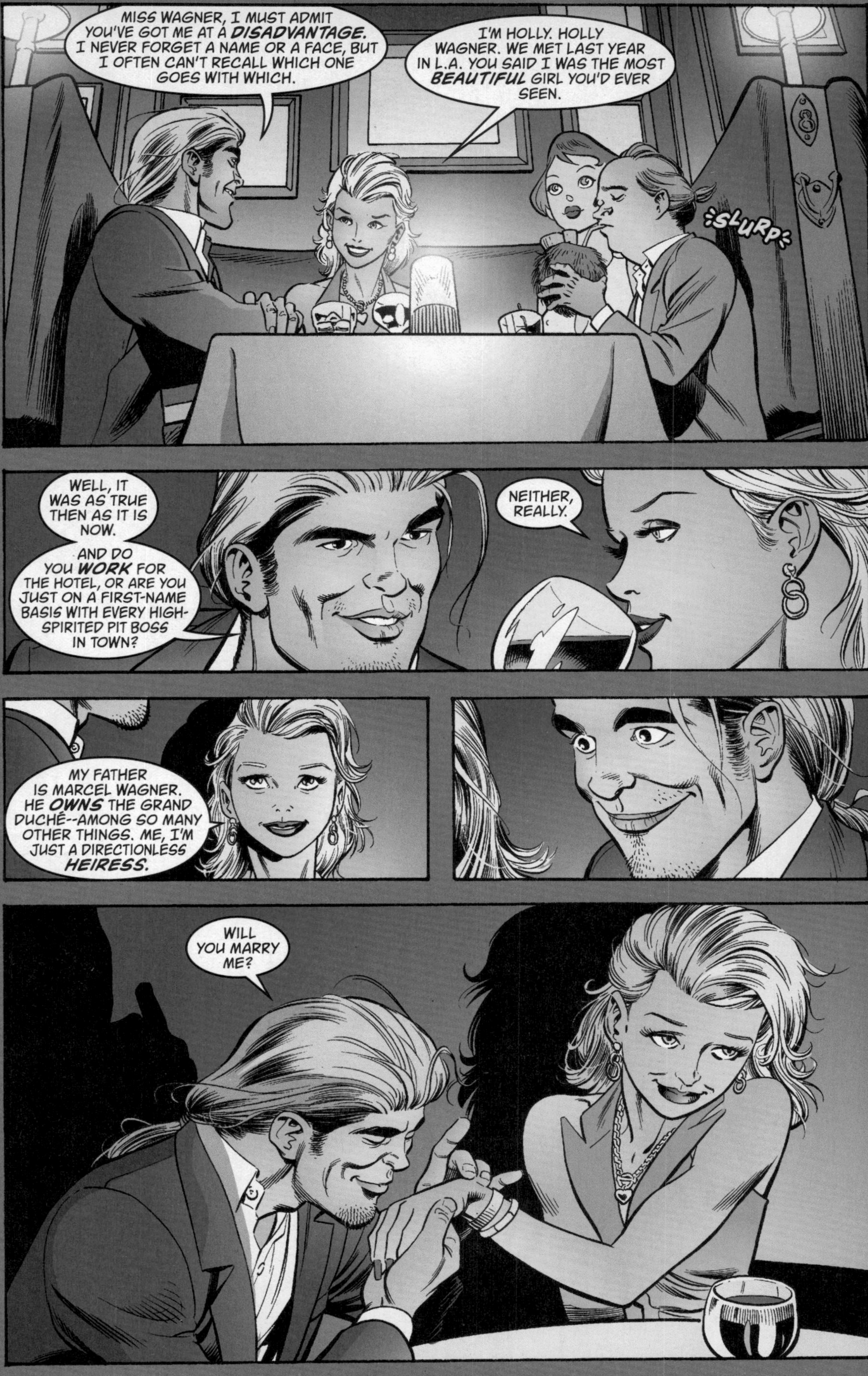
MISS WAGNER, I MUST ADMIT YOU'VE GOT ME AT A DISADVANTAGE. I NEVER FORGET A NAME OR A FACE, BUT I OFTEN CAN'T RECALL WHICH ONE GOES WITH WHICH.
I'M HOLLY. HOLLY WAGNER. WE MET LAST YEAR IN L.A. YOU SAID I WAS THE MOST BEAUTIFUL GIRL YOU'D EVER SEEN.
SLURP
WELL, IT WAS AS TRUE THEN AS IT IS NOW.
AND DO YOU WORK FOR THE HOTEL, OR ARE YOU JUST ON A FIRST-NAME BASIS WITH EVERY HIGH-SPIRITED PIT BOSS IN TOWN?
NEITHER, REALLY.
MY FATHER IS MARCEL WAGNER. HE OWNS THE GRAND DUCHÉ--AMONG SO MANY OTHER THINGS. ME, I'M JUST A DIRECTIONLESS HEIRESS.
WILL YOU MARRY ME?

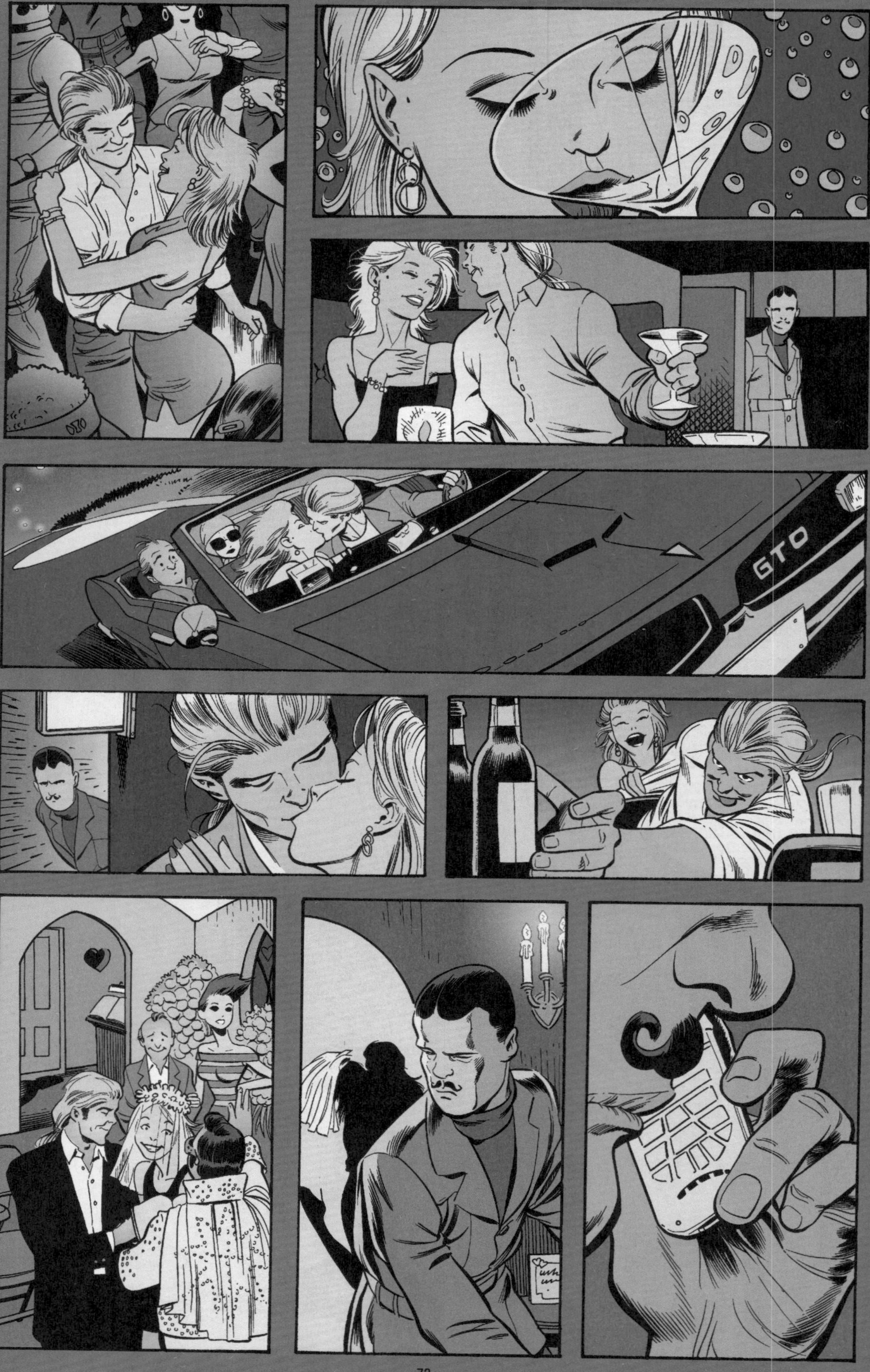
GTO

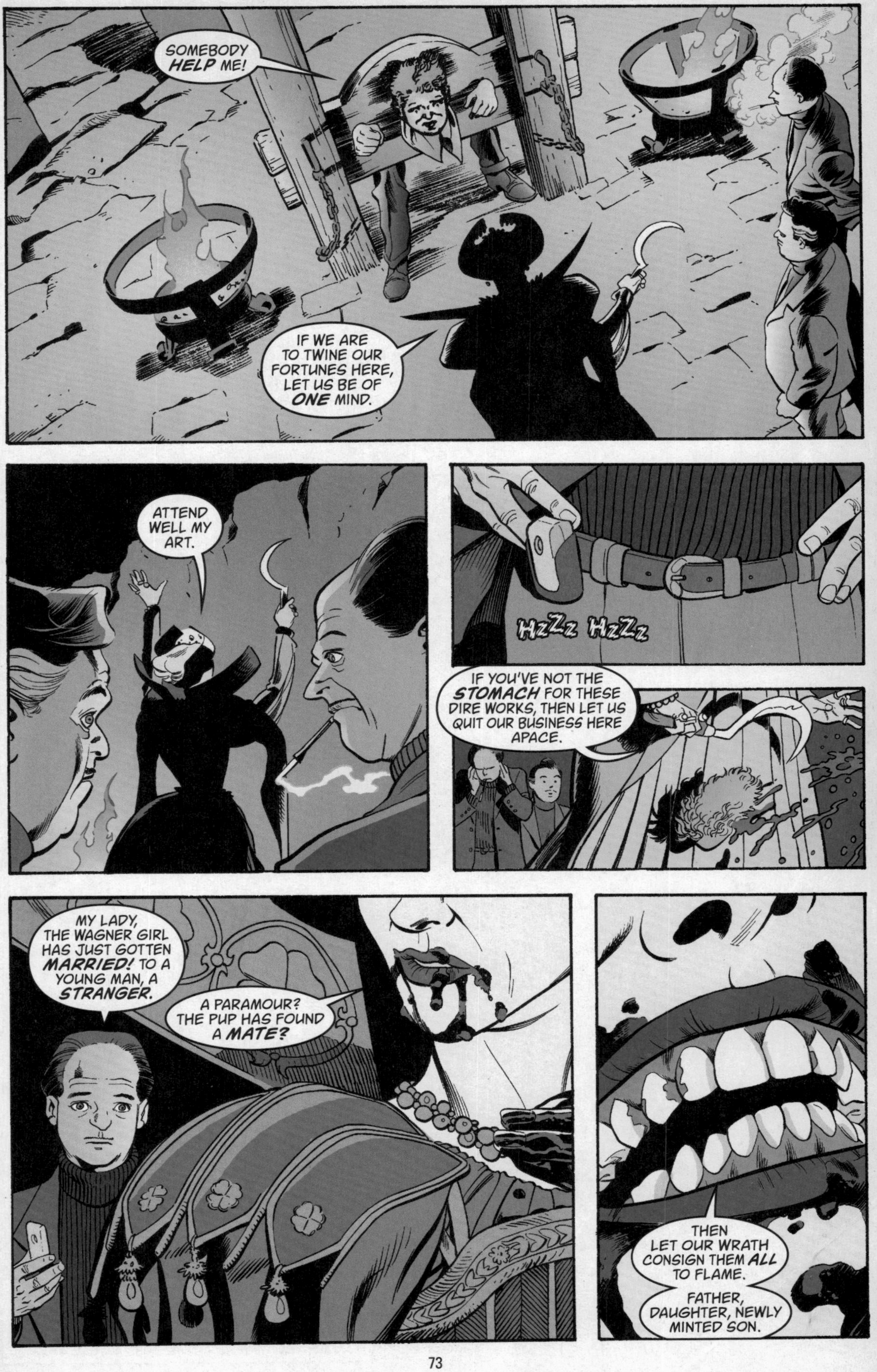
SOMEBODY **HELP** ME!
IF WE ARE TO TWINE OUR FORTUNES HERE, LET US BE OF **ONE** MIND.
ATTEND WELL MY ART.
HzZz HzZz
IF YOU'VE NOT THE **STOMACH** FOR THESE DIRE WORKS, THEN LET US QUIT OUR BUSINESS HERE APACE.
MY LADY, THE WAGNER GIRL HAS JUST GOTTEN **MARRIED!** TO A YOUNG MAN, A **STRANGER**.
A PARAMOUR? THE PUP HAS FOUND A **MATE?**
THEN LET OUR WRATH CONSIGN THEM **ALL** TO FLAME.
FATHER, DAUGHTER, NEWLY MINTED SON.

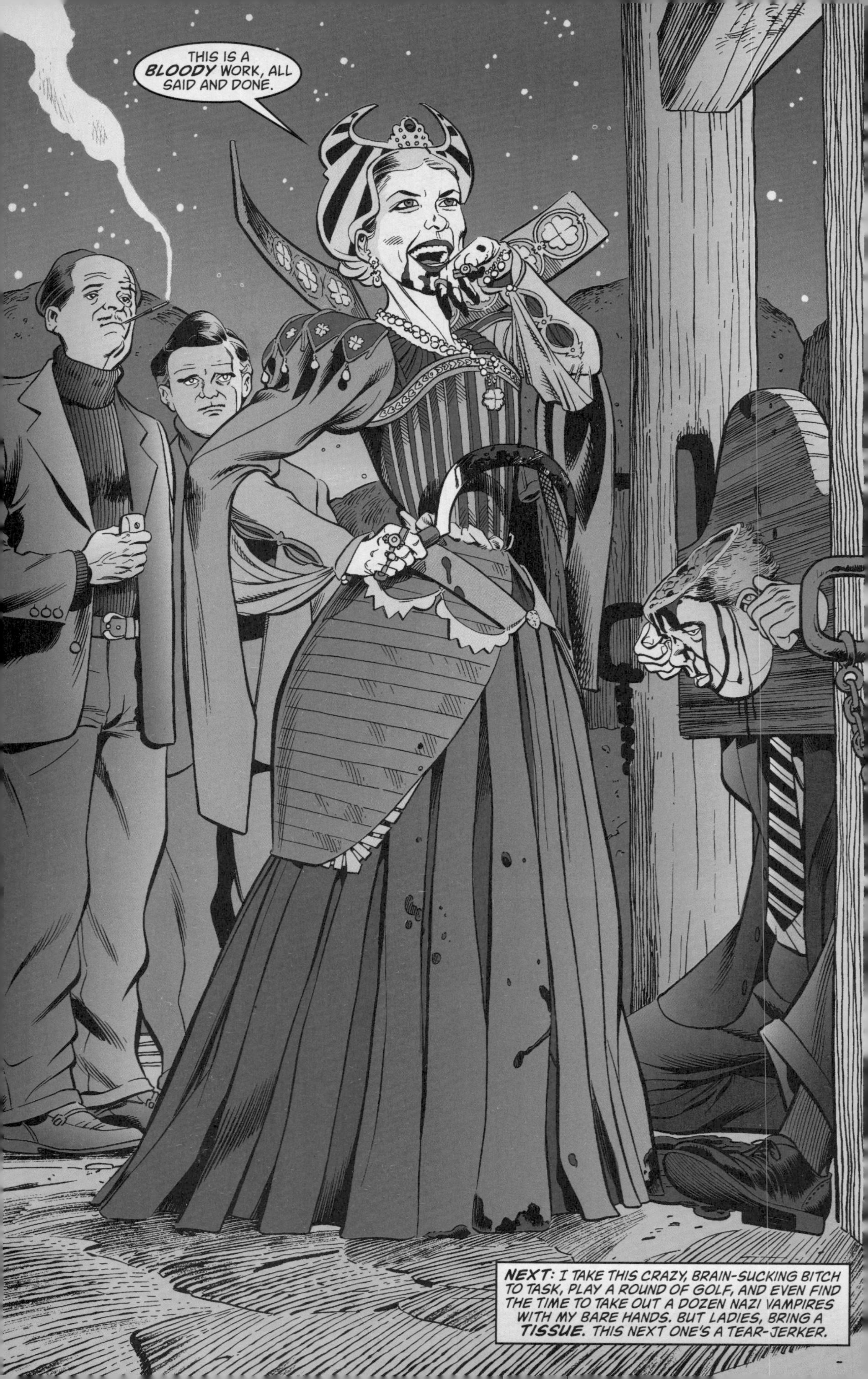
THIS IS A BLOODY WORK, ALL SAID AND DONE.
NEXT: I TAKE THIS CRAZY, BRAIN-SUCKING BITCH TO TASK, PLAY A ROUND OF GOLF, AND EVEN FIND THE TIME TO TAKE OUT A DOZEN NAZI VAMPIRES WITH MY BARE HANDS. BUT LADIES, BRING A TISSUE. THIS NEXT ONE'S A TEAR-JERKER.

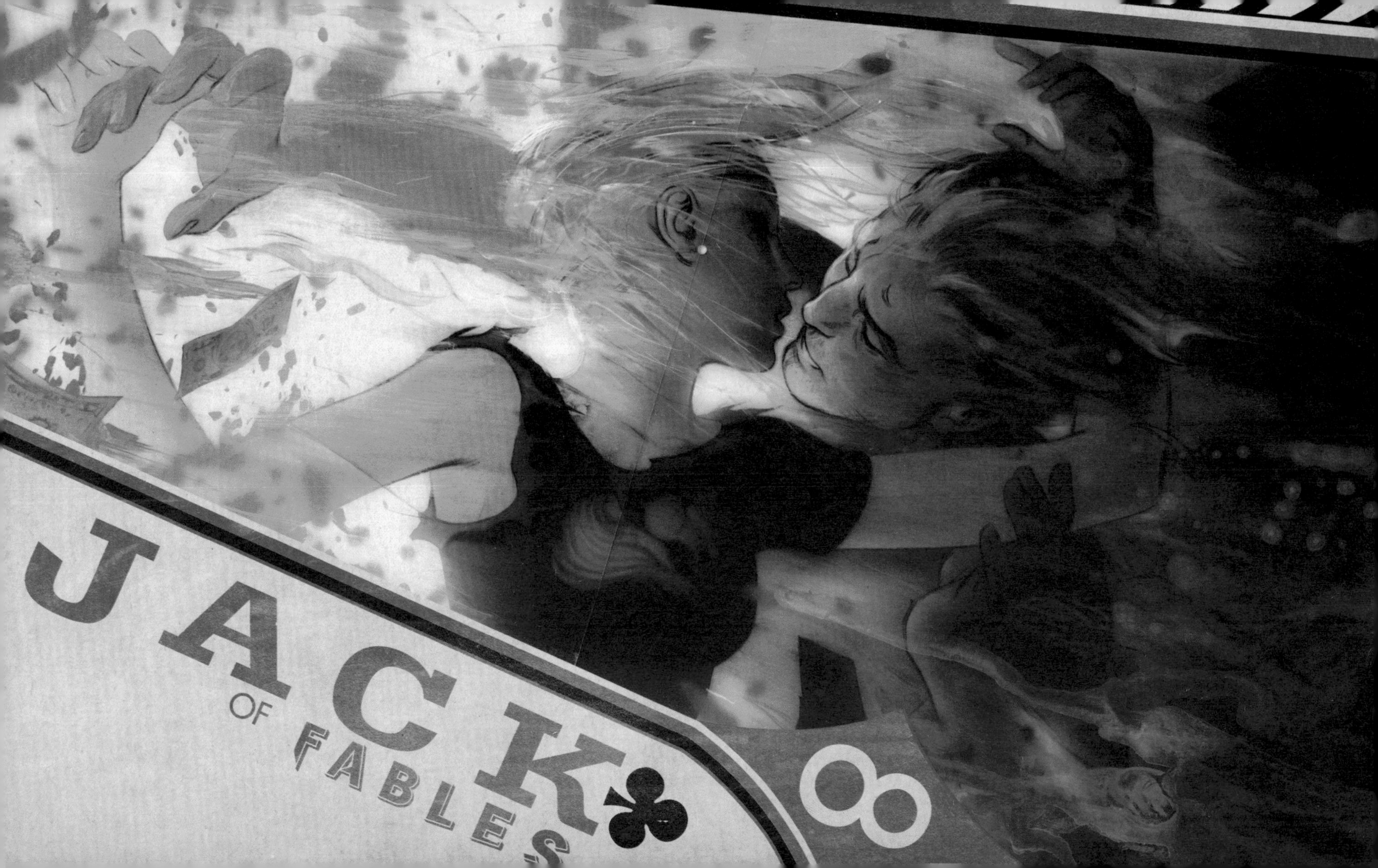
JACK OF FABLES
8

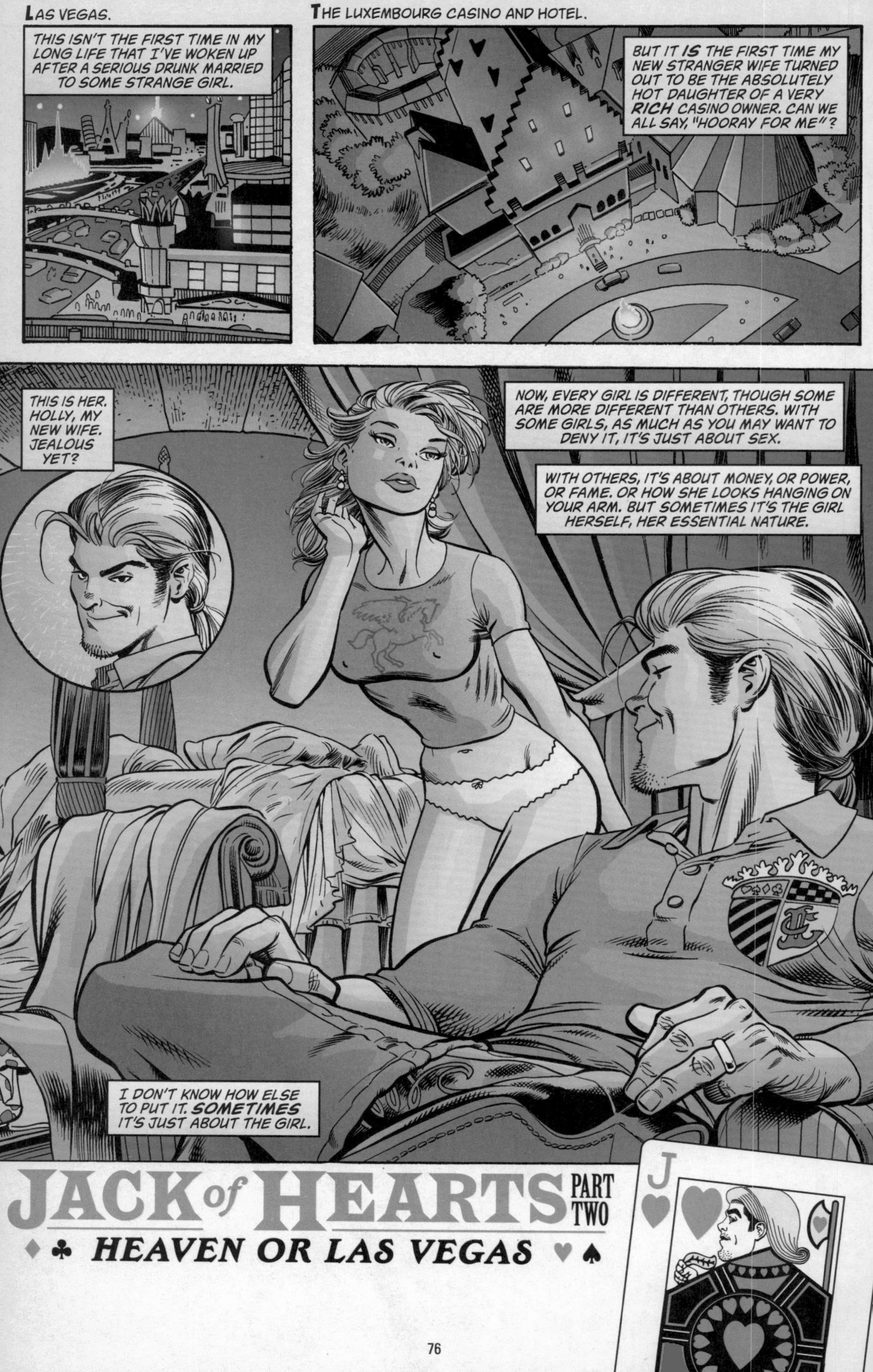
LAS VEGAS.
THIS ISN'T THE FIRST TIME IN MY LONG LIFE THAT I'VE WOKEN UP AFTER A SERIOUS DRUNK MARRIED TO SOME STRANGE GIRL.
THE LUXEMBOURG CASINO AND HOTEL.
BUT IT IS THE FIRST TIME MY NEW STRANGER WIFE TURNED OUT TO BE THE ABSOLUTELY HOT DAUGHTER OF A VERY RICH CASINO OWNER. CAN WE ALL SAY, "HOORAY FOR ME"?
THIS IS HER. HOLLY, MY NEW WIFE. JEALOUS YET?
NOW, EVERY GIRL IS DIFFERENT, THOUGH SOME ARE MORE DIFFERENT THAN OTHERS. WITH SOME GIRLS, AS MUCH AS YOU MAY WANT TO DENY IT, IT'S JUST ABOUT SEX.
WITH OTHERS, IT'S ABOUT MONEY, OR POWER, OR FAME. OR HOW SHE LOOKS HANGING ON YOUR ARM. BUT SOMETIMES IT'S THE GIRL HERSELF, HER ESSENTIAL NATURE.
I DON'T KNOW HOW ELSE TO PUT IT. SOMETIMES IT'S JUST ABOUT THE GIRL.
JACK of HEARTS PART TWO
HEAVEN OR LAS VEGAS
J

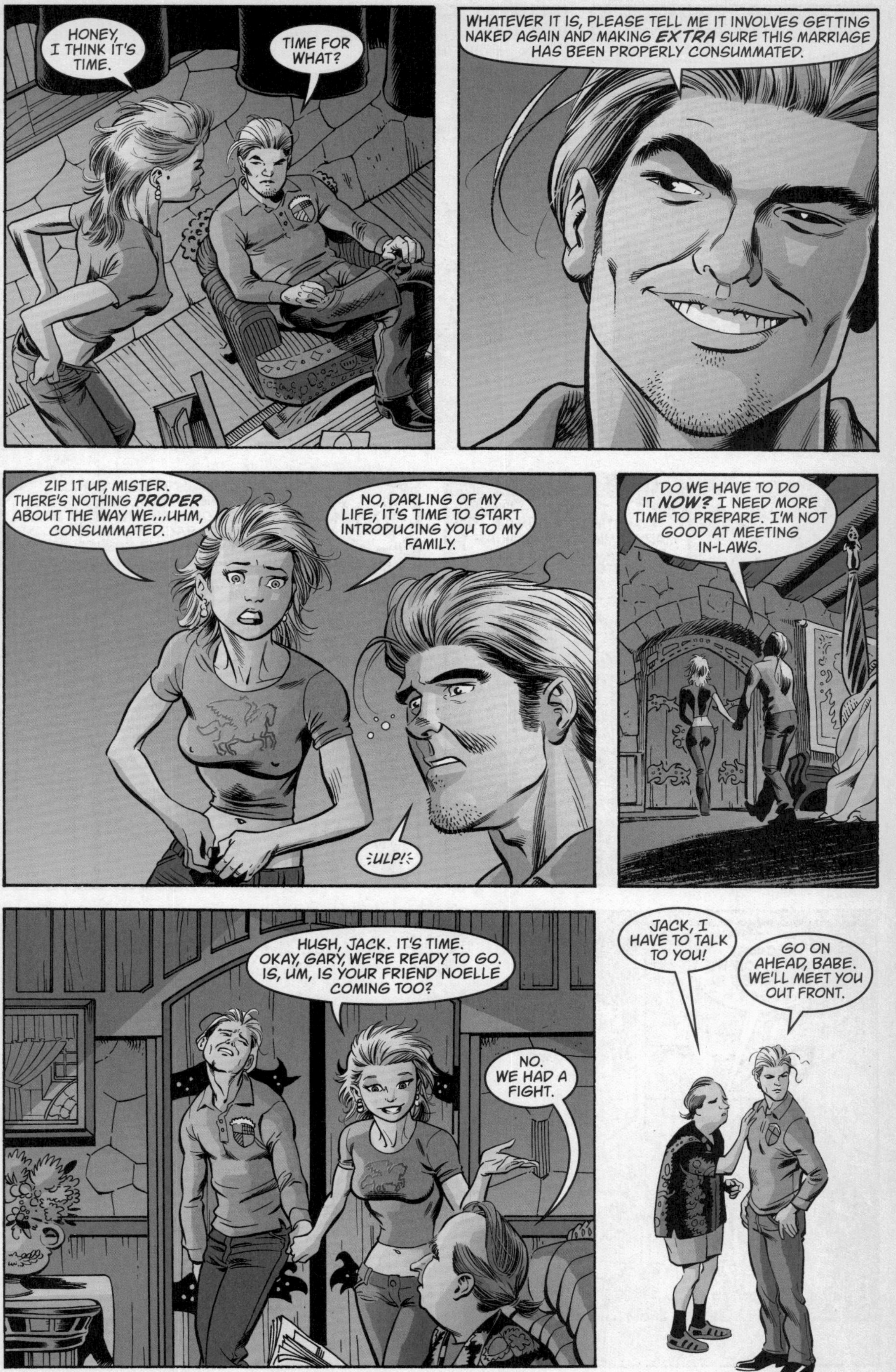
HONEY, I THINK IT'S TIME.
TIME FOR WHAT?
WHATEVER IT IS, PLEASE TELL ME IT INVOLVES GETTING NAKED AGAIN AND MAKING EXTRA SURE THIS MARRIAGE HAS BEEN PROPERLY CONSUMMATED.
ZIP IT UP, MISTER. THERE'S NOTHING PROPER ABOUT THE WAY WE...UHM, CONSUMMATED.
NO, DARLING OF MY LIFE, IT'S TIME TO START INTRODUCING YOU TO MY FAMILY.
ULP!
DO WE HAVE TO DO IT NOW? I NEED MORE TIME TO PREPARE. I'M NOT GOOD AT MEETING IN-LAWS.
HUSH, JACK. IT'S TIME. OKAY, GARY, WE'RE READY TO GO. IS, UM, IS YOUR FRIEND NOELLE COMING TOO?
NO. WE HAD A FIGHT.
JACK, I HAVE TO TALK TO YOU!
GO ON AHEAD, BABE. WE'LL MEET YOU OUT FRONT.

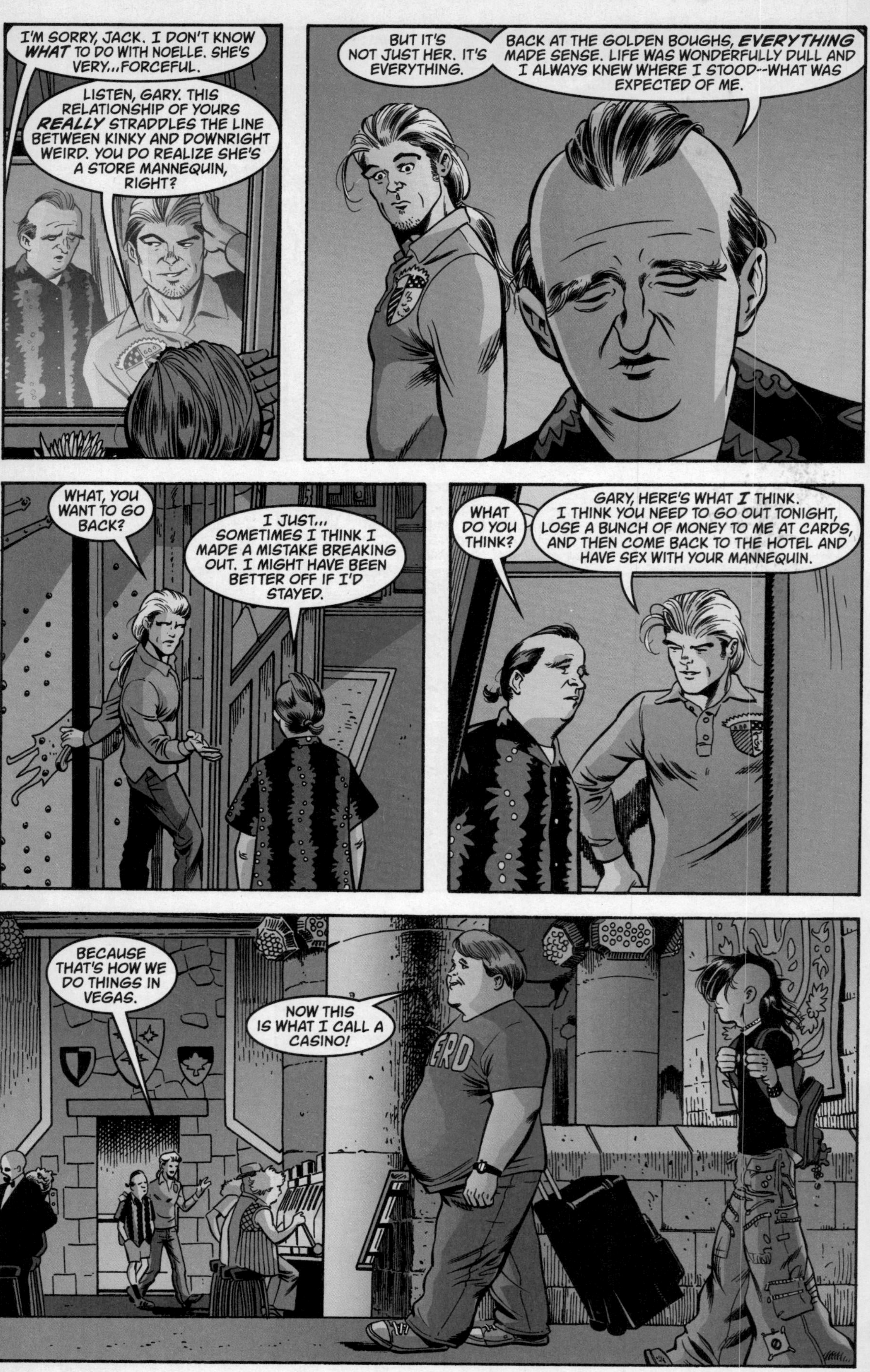
I'M SORRY, JACK. I DON'T KNOW WHAT TO DO WITH NOELLE. SHE'S VERY...FORCEFUL.
LISTEN, GARY. THIS RELATIONSHIP OF YOURS REALLY STRADDLES THE LINE BETWEEN KINKY AND DOWNRIGHT WEIRD. YOU DO REALIZE SHE'S A STORE MANNEQUIN, RIGHT?
BUT IT'S NOT JUST HER. IT'S EVERYTHING.
BACK AT THE GOLDEN BOUGHS, EVERYTHING MADE SENSE. LIFE WAS WONDERFULLY DULL AND I ALWAYS KNEW WHERE I STOOD--WHAT WAS EXPECTED OF ME.
WHAT, YOU WANT TO GO BACK?
I JUST... SOMETIMES I THINK I MADE A MISTAKE BREAKING OUT. I MIGHT HAVE BEEN BETTER OFF IF I'D STAYED.
WHAT DO YOU THINK?
GARY, HERE'S WHAT I THINK. I THINK YOU NEED TO GO OUT TONIGHT, LOSE A BUNCH OF MONEY TO ME AT CARDS, AND THEN COME BACK TO THE HOTEL AND HAVE SEX WITH YOUR MANNEQUIN.
BECAUSE THAT'S HOW WE DO THINGS IN VEGAS.
NOW THIS IS WHAT I CALL A CASINO!
ERD

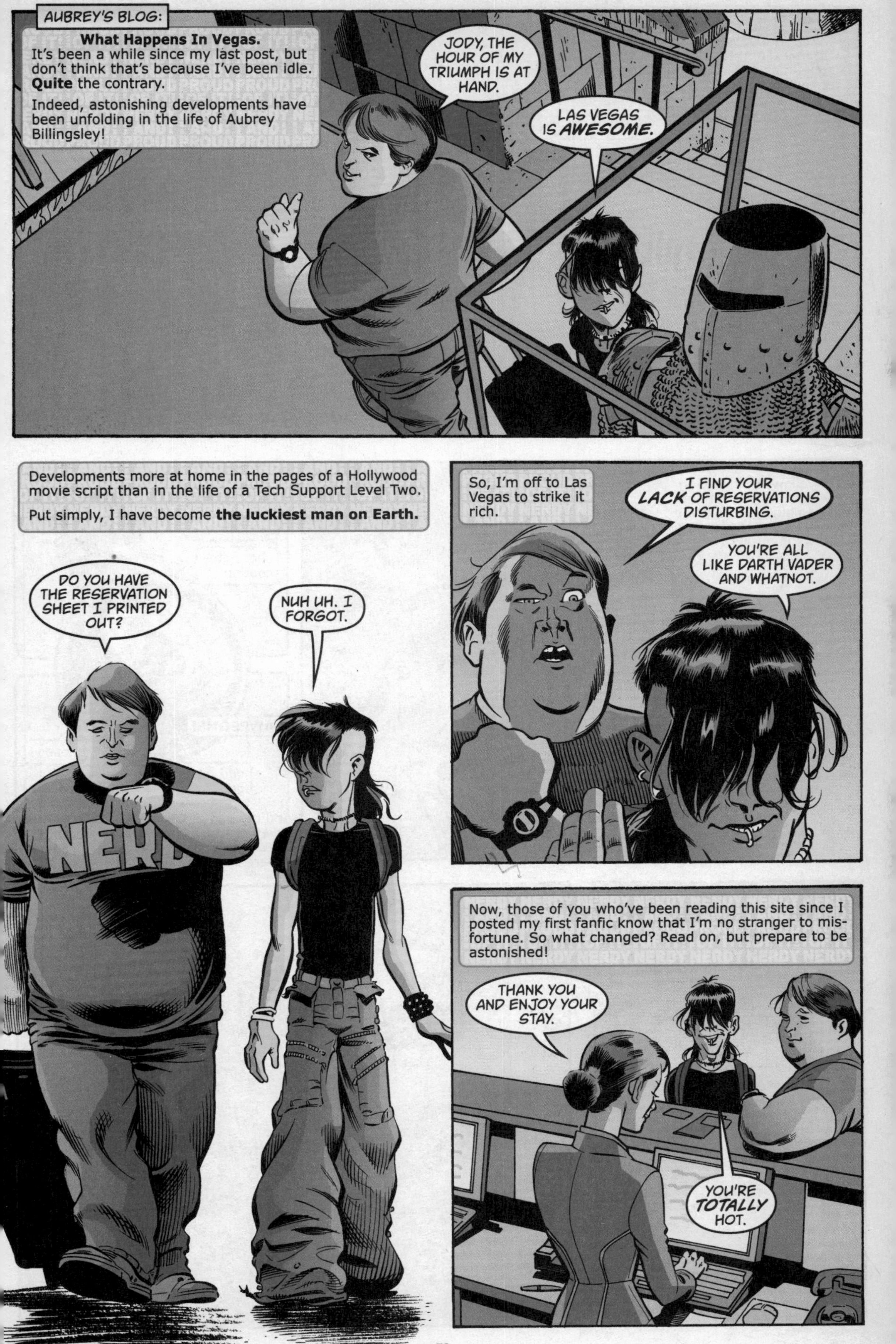
AUBREY'S BLOG:
What Happens In Vegas.
It's been a while since my last post, but don't think that's because I've been idle. **Quite** the contrary.
Indeed, astonishing developments have been unfolding in the life of Aubrey Billingsley!
JODY, THE HOUR OF MY TRIUMPH IS AT HAND.
LAS VEGAS IS *AWESOME.*
Developments more at home in the pages of a Hollywood movie script than in the life of a Tech Support Level Two.
Put simply, I have become **the luckiest man on Earth.**
DO YOU HAVE THE RESERVATION SHEET I PRINTED OUT?
NUH UH. I FORGOT.
NERD
So, I'm off to Las Vegas to strike it rich.
I FIND YOUR *LACK* OF RESERVATIONS DISTURBING.
YOU'RE ALL LIKE DARTH VADER AND WHATNOT.
Now, those of you who've been reading this site since I posted my first fanfic know that I'm no stranger to misfortune. So what changed? Read on, but prepare to be astonished!
THANK YOU AND ENJOY YOUR STAY.
YOU'RE *TOTALLY* HOT.

Willows, California.

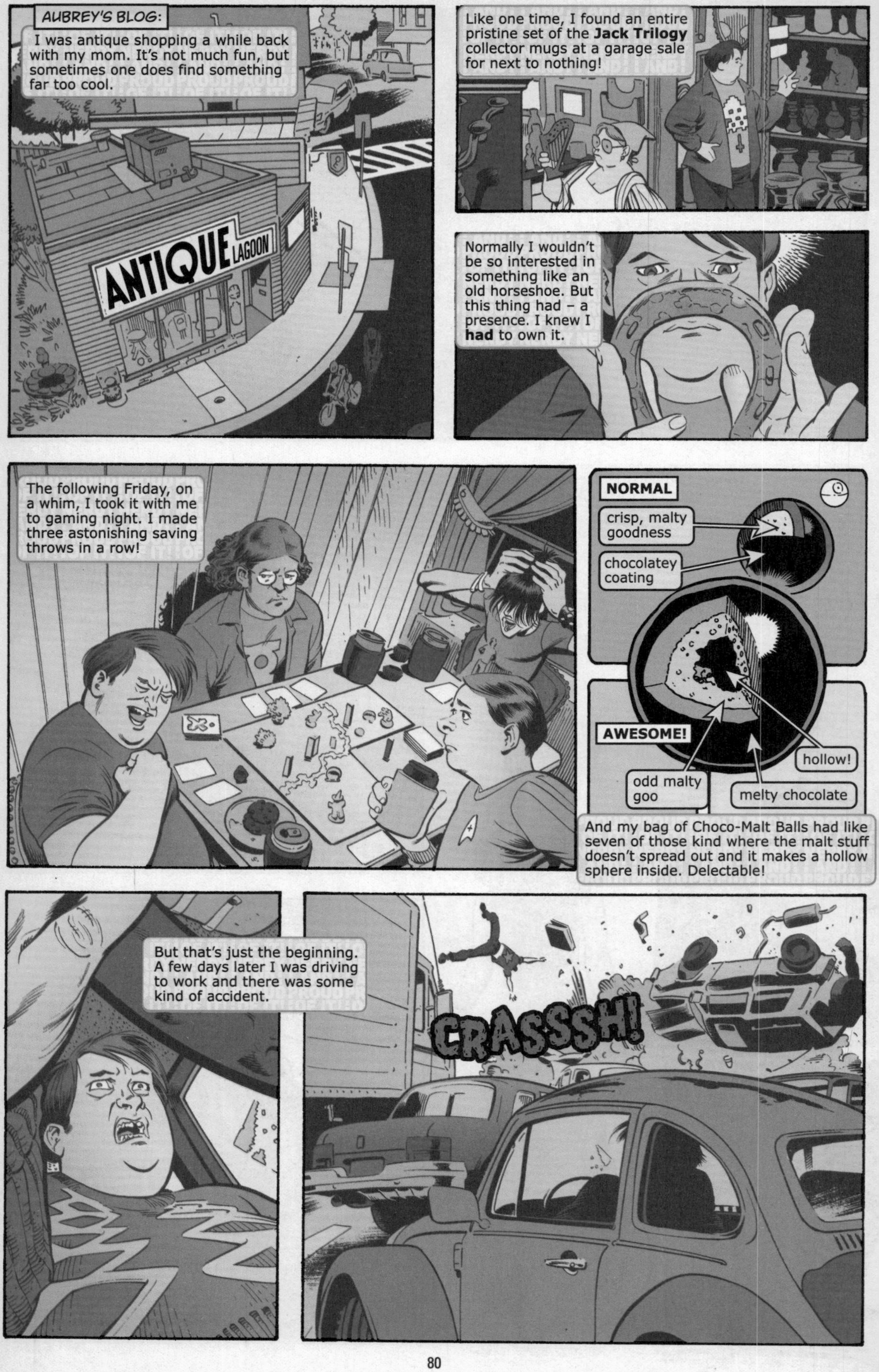

AUBREY'S BLOG:
I was antique shopping a while back with my mom. It's not much fun, but sometimes one does find something far too cool.
ANTIQUE LAGOON
Like one time, I found an entire pristine set of the **Jack Trilogy** collector mugs at a garage sale for next to nothing!
Normally I wouldn't be so interested in something like an old horseshoe. But this thing had – a presence. I knew I **had** to own it.
The following Friday, on a whim, I took it with me to gaming night. I made three astonishing saving throws in a row!
NORMAL
crisp, malty goodness
chocolatey coating
AWESOME!
odd malty goo
hollow!
melty chocolate
And my bag of Choco-Malt Balls had like seven of those kind where the malt stuff doesn't spread out and it makes a hollow sphere inside. Delectable!
But that's just the beginning. A few days later I was driving to work and there was some kind of accident.
CRASSSH!

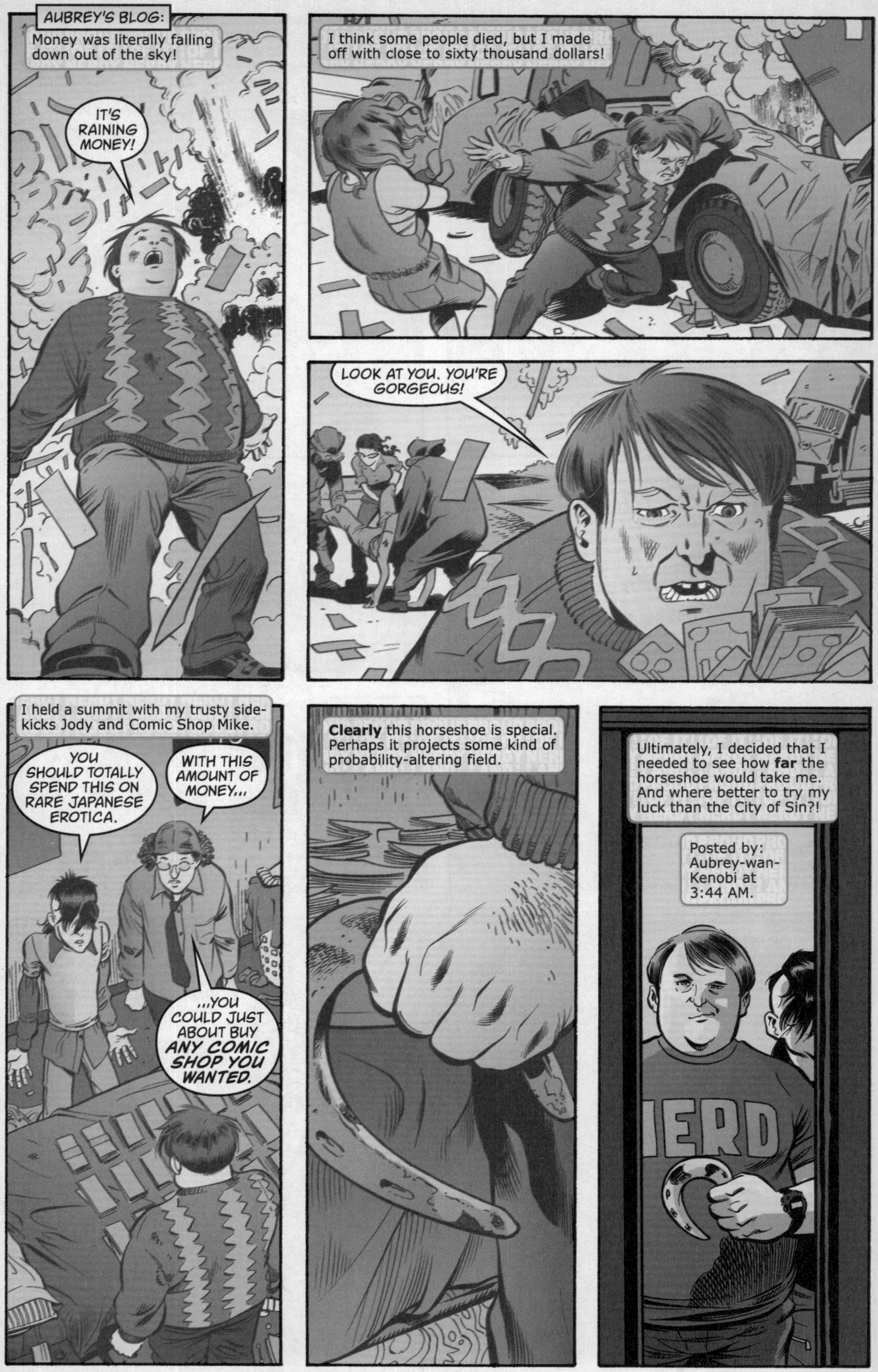
AUBREY'S BLOG:
Money was literally falling down out of the sky!
IT'S RAINING MONEY!
I think some people died, but I made off with close to sixty thousand dollars!
LOOK AT YOU. YOU'RE GORGEOUS!
I held a summit with my trusty side-kicks Jody and Comic Shop Mike.
YOU SHOULD TOTALLY SPEND THIS ON RARE JAPANESE EROTICA.
WITH THIS AMOUNT OF MONEY...
...YOU COULD JUST ABOUT BUY ANY COMIC SHOP YOU WANTED.
Clearly this horseshoe is special. Perhaps it projects some kind of probability-altering field.
Ultimately, I decided that I needed to see how far the horseshoe would take me. And where better to try my luck than the City of Sin?!
Posted by: Aubrey-wan-Kenobi at 3:44 AM.

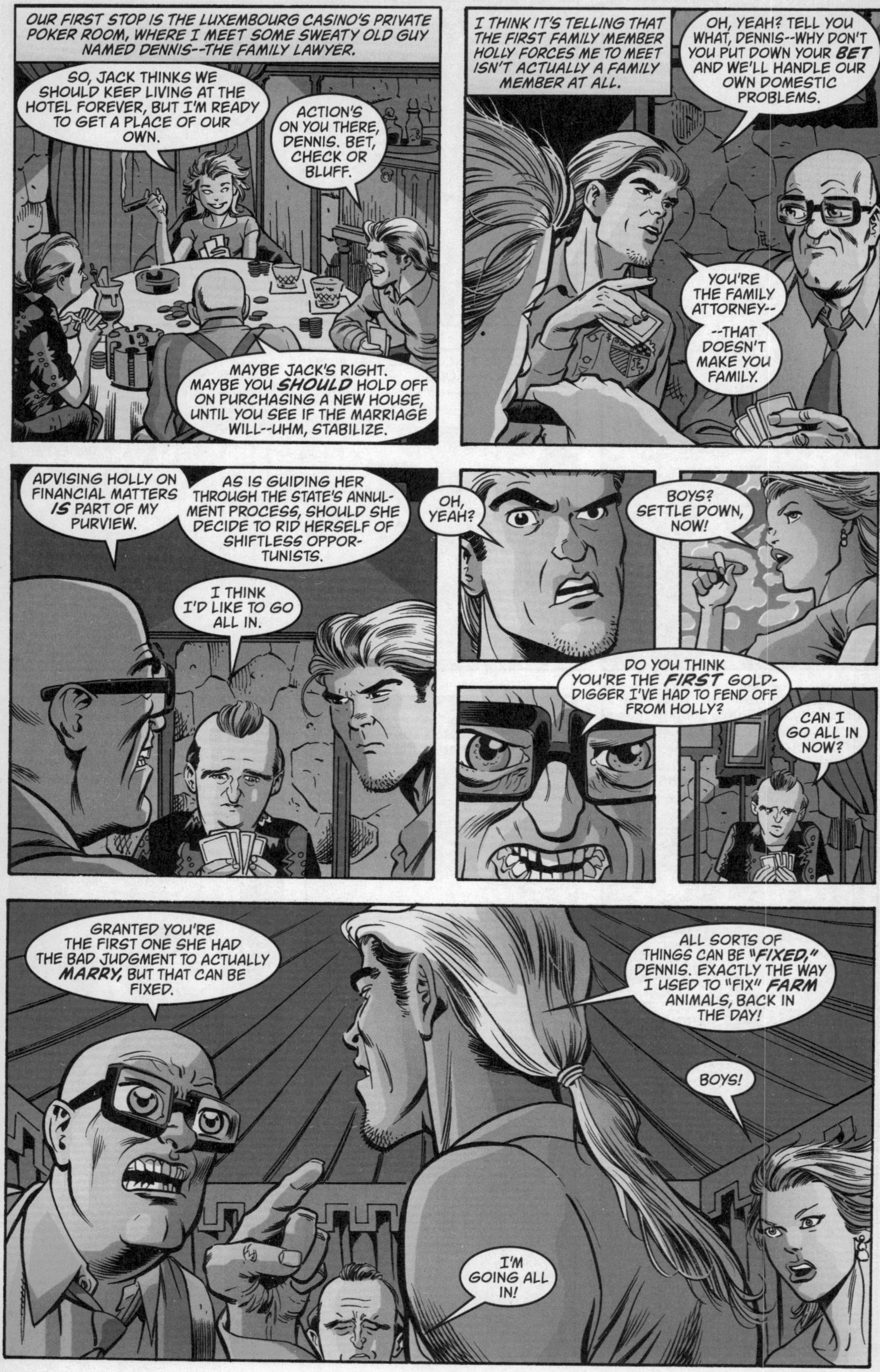
OUR FIRST STOP IS THE LUXEMBOURG CASINO'S PRIVATE POKER ROOM, WHERE I MEET SOME SWEATY OLD GUY NAMED DENNIS--THE FAMILY LAWYER.
SO, JACK THINKS WE SHOULD KEEP LIVING AT THE HOTEL FOREVER, BUT I'M READY TO GET A PLACE OF OUR OWN.
ACTION'S ON YOU THERE, DENNIS. BET, CHECK OR BLUFF.
MAYBE JACK'S RIGHT. MAYBE YOU SHOULD HOLD OFF ON PURCHASING A NEW HOUSE, UNTIL YOU SEE IF THE MARRIAGE WILL--UHM, STABILIZE.
I THINK IT'S TELLING THAT THE FIRST FAMILY MEMBER HOLLY FORCES ME TO MEET ISN'T ACTUALLY A FAMILY MEMBER AT ALL.
OH, YEAH? TELL YOU WHAT, DENNIS--WHY DON'T YOU PUT DOWN YOUR BET AND WE'LL HANDLE OUR OWN DOMESTIC PROBLEMS.
YOU'RE THE FAMILY ATTORNEY--
--THAT DOESN'T MAKE YOU FAMILY.
ADVISING HOLLY ON FINANCIAL MATTERS IS PART OF MY PURVIEW.
AS IS GUIDING HER THROUGH THE STATE'S ANNULMENT PROCESS, SHOULD SHE DECIDE TO RID HERSELF OF SHIFTLESS OPPORTUNISTS.
I THINK I'D LIKE TO GO ALL IN.
OH, YEAH?
BOYS? SETTLE DOWN, NOW!
DO YOU THINK YOU'RE THE FIRST GOLD-DIGGER I'VE HAD TO FEND OFF FROM HOLLY?
CAN I GO ALL IN NOW?
GRANTED YOU'RE THE FIRST ONE SHE HAD THE BAD JUDGMENT TO ACTUALLY MARRY, BUT THAT CAN BE FIXED.
ALL SORTS OF THINGS CAN BE "FIXED," DENNIS. EXACTLY THE WAY I USED TO "FIX" FARM ANIMALS, BACK IN THE DAY!
BOYS!
I'M GOING ALL IN!

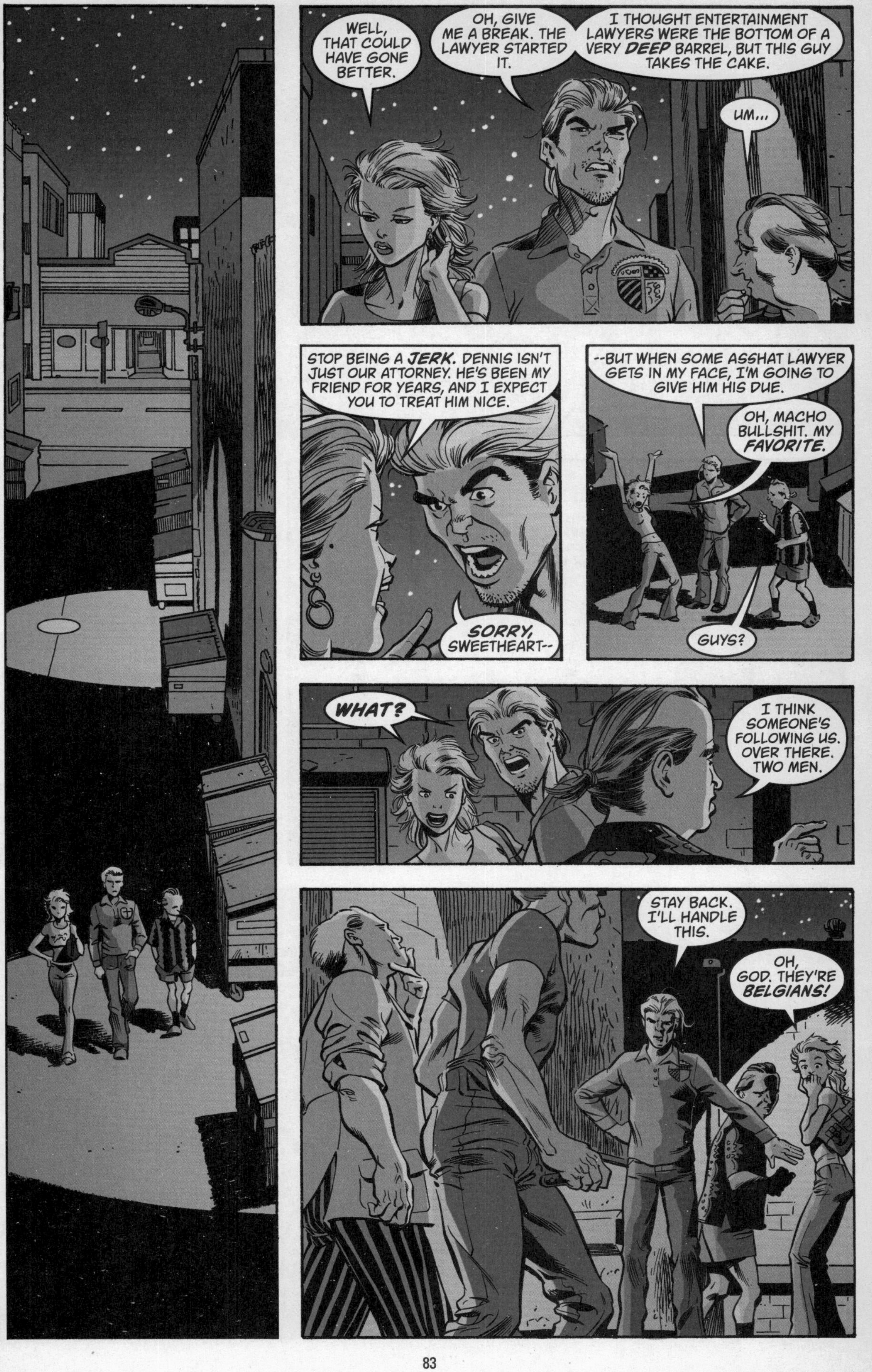

WELL, THAT COULD HAVE GONE BETTER.
OH, GIVE ME A BREAK. THE LAWYER STARTED IT.
I THOUGHT ENTERTAINMENT LAWYERS WERE THE BOTTOM OF A VERY DEEP BARREL, BUT THIS GUY TAKES THE CAKE.
UM...
STOP BEING A JERK. DENNIS ISN'T JUST OUR ATTORNEY. HE'S BEEN MY FRIEND FOR YEARS, AND I EXPECT YOU TO TREAT HIM NICE.
SORRY, SWEETHEART--
--BUT WHEN SOME ASSHAT LAWYER GETS IN MY FACE, I'M GOING TO GIVE HIM HIS DUE.
OH, MACHO BULLSHIT. MY FAVORITE.
GUYS?
WHAT?
I THINK SOMEONE'S FOLLOWING US. OVER THERE. TWO MEN.
STAY BACK. I'LL HANDLE THIS.
OH, GOD. THEY'RE BELGIANS!

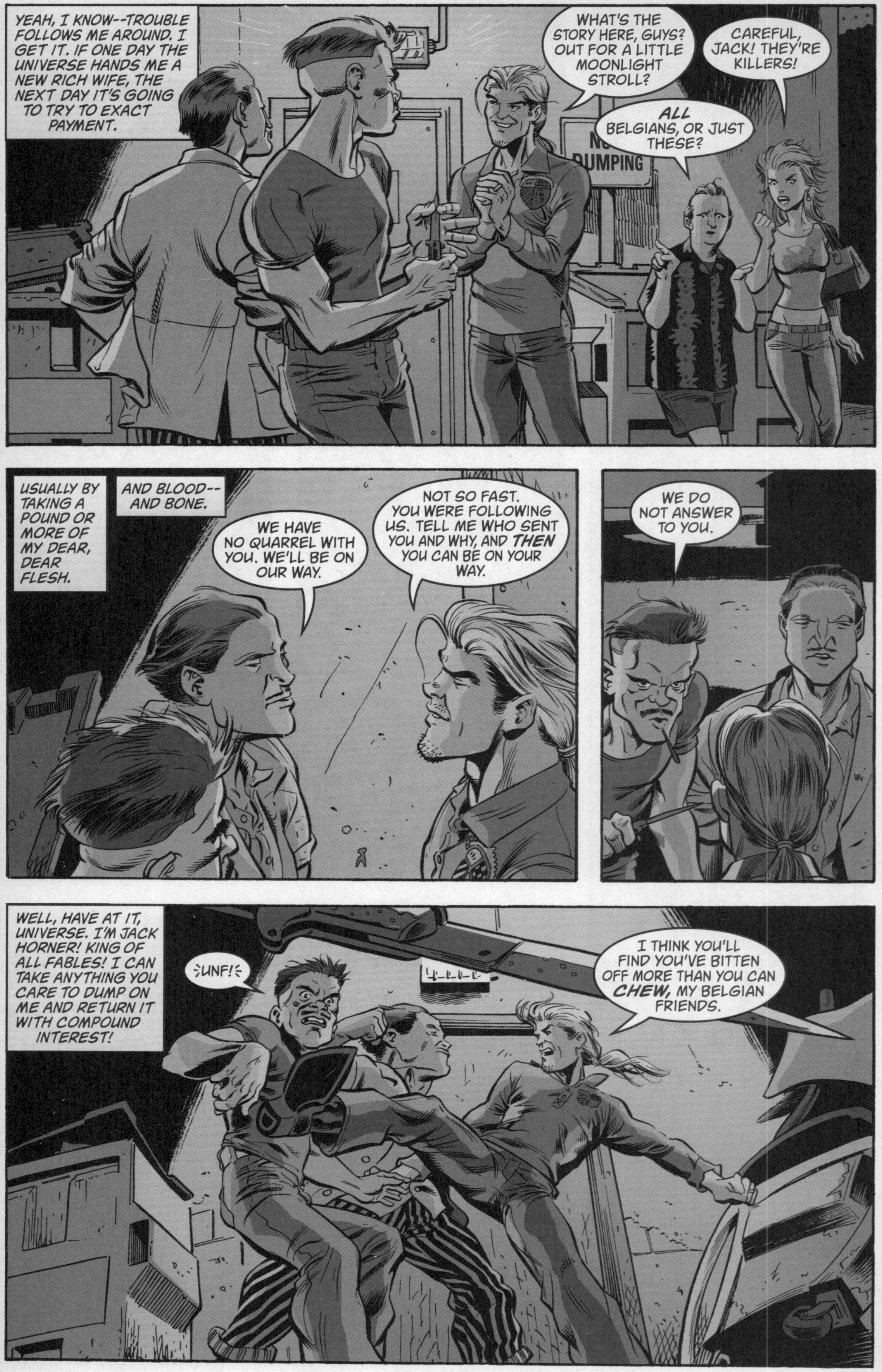

YEAH, I KNOW--TROUBLE FOLLOWS ME AROUND. I GET IT. IF ONE DAY THE UNIVERSE HANDS ME A NEW RICH WIFE, THE NEXT DAY IT'S GOING TO TRY TO EXACT PAYMENT.
WHAT'S THE STORY HERE, GUYS? OUT FOR A LITTLE MOONLIGHT STROLL?
CAREFUL, JACK! THEY'RE KILLERS!
ALL BELGIANS, OR JUST THESE?
NO DUMPING
USUALLY BY TAKING A POUND OR MORE OF MY DEAR, DEAR FLESH.
AND BLOOD--AND BONE.
WE HAVE NO QUARREL WITH YOU. WE'LL BE ON OUR WAY.
NOT SO FAST. YOU WERE FOLLOWING US. TELL ME WHO SENT YOU AND WHY, AND THEN YOU CAN BE ON YOUR WAY.
WE DO NOT ANSWER TO YOU.
WELL, HAVE AT IT, UNIVERSE. I'M JACK HORNER! KING OF ALL FABLES! I CAN TAKE ANYTHING YOU CARE TO DUMP ON ME AND RETURN IT WITH COMPOUND INTEREST!
UNF!
I THINK YOU'LL FIND YOU'VE BITTEN OFF MORE THAN YOU CAN CHEW, MY BELGIAN FRIENDS.

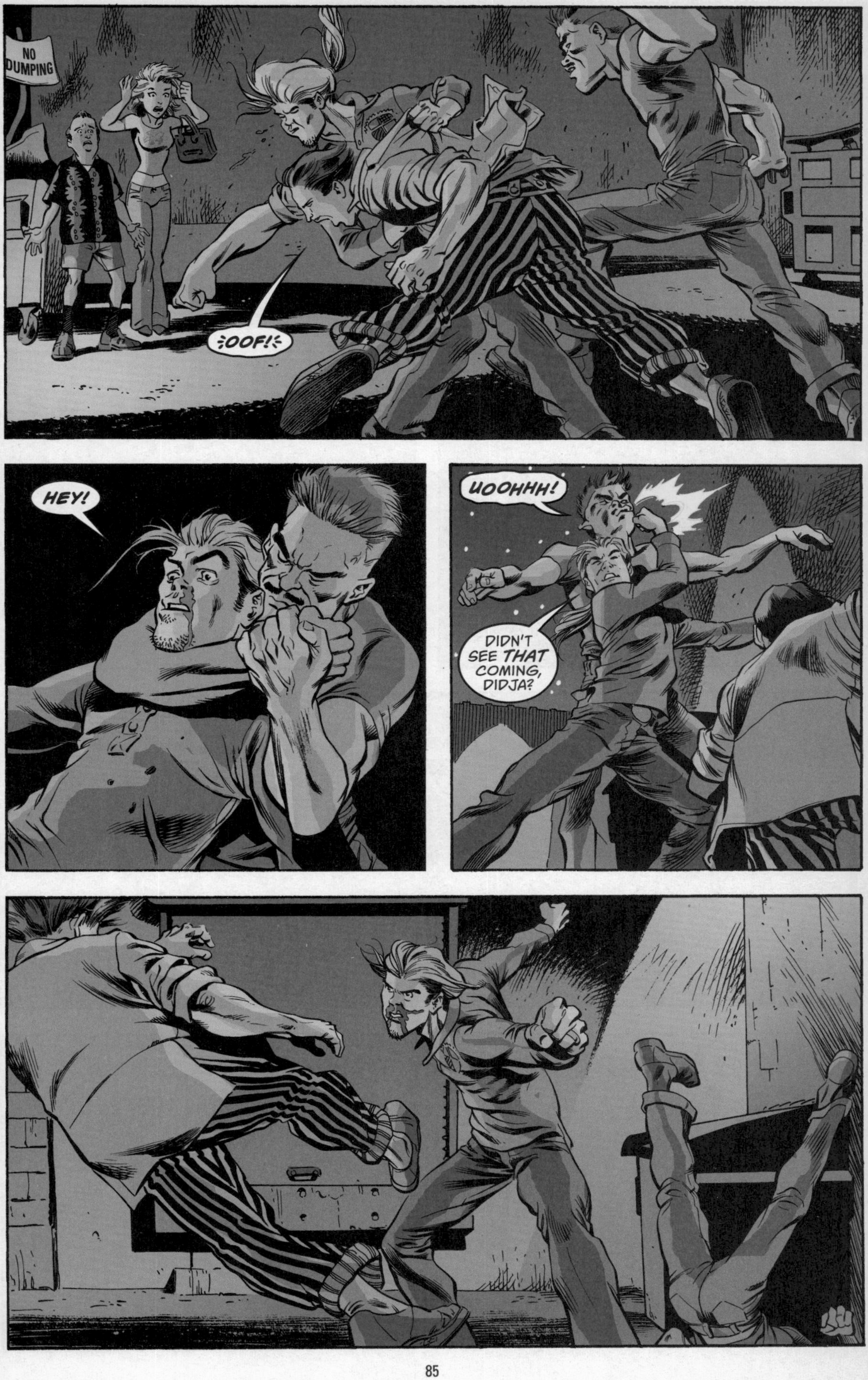
NO DUMPING
OOF!
HEY!
UOOHHH!
DIDN'T SEE *THAT* COMING, DIDJA?

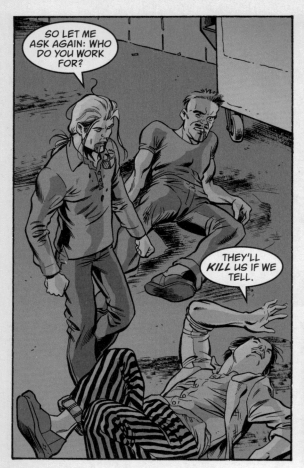

SO LET ME ASK AGAIN: WHO DO YOU WORK FOR?

THEY'LL **KILL** US IF WE TELL.

MAYBE, BUT THAT'S IN THE UNCERTAIN **FUTURE.** I'M GOING TO KILL YOU IF YOU **DON'T** TELL AND THAT'S VERY MUCH IN THE VERY CERTAIN **PRESENT.**

THE LAMBERTS. IT WAS THE **LAMBERTS.**

JACK--YOU HIT HIM SO HARD HE KIND OF--HE FLEW BACKWARDS!

YEAH, THAT WAS COOL.

SWEETIE, YOU LOOK HURT. LET'S GET YOU TO A HOSPITAL.

I'M FINE.

LET ME JUST MAKE IT CLEAR TO THEM THAT WE'RE NOT TO BE DISTURBED FURTHER, AND WE'LL BE ON OUR WAY.

BELGIANS?

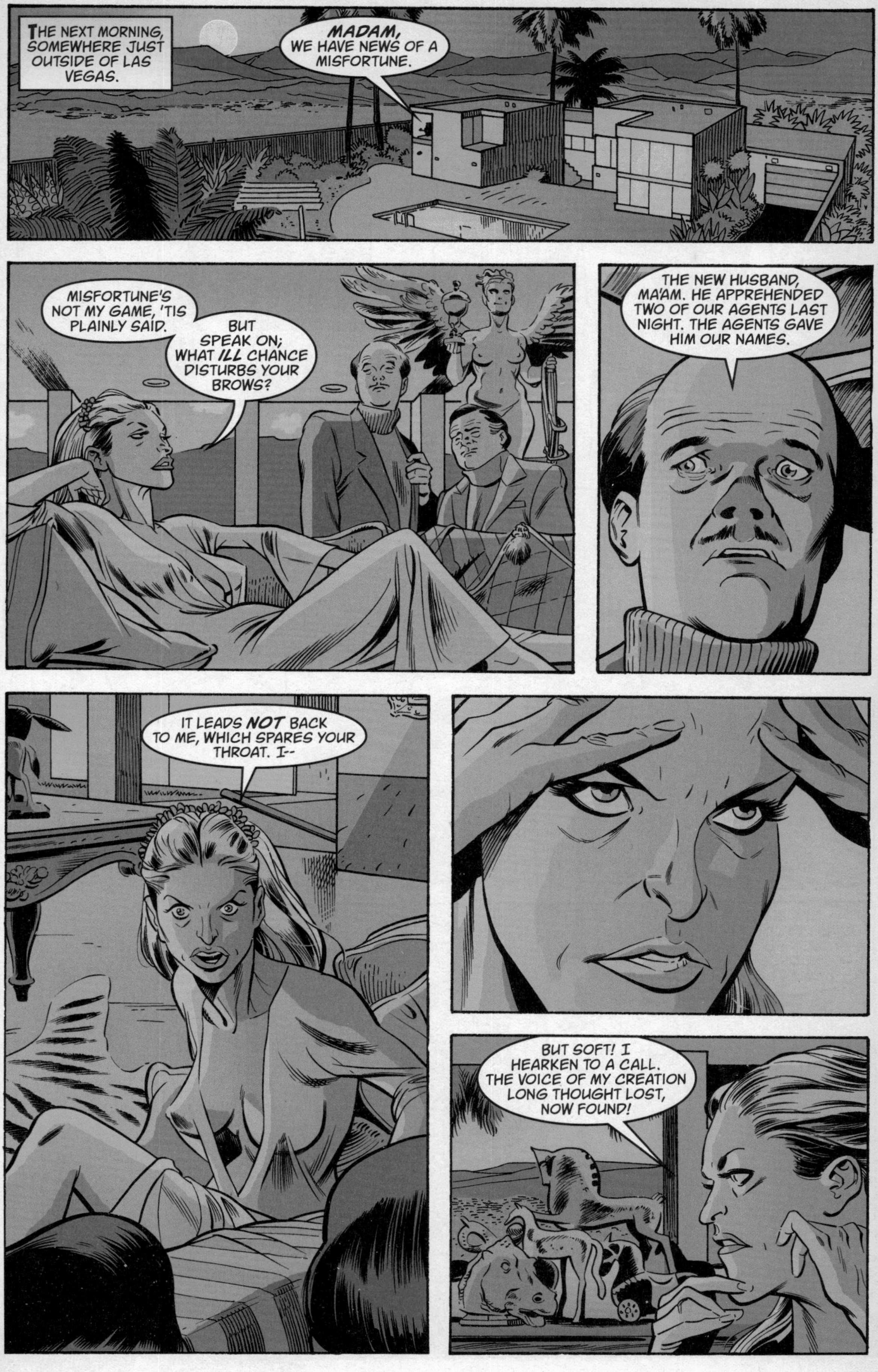
THE NEXT MORNING, SOMEWHERE JUST OUTSIDE OF LAS VEGAS.
MADAM, WE HAVE NEWS OF A MISFORTUNE.
MISFORTUNE'S NOT MY GAME, 'TIS PLAINLY SAID.
BUT SPEAK ON; WHAT ILL CHANCE DISTURBS YOUR BROWS?
THE NEW HUSBAND, MA'AM. HE APPREHENDED TWO OF OUR AGENTS LAST NIGHT. THE AGENTS GAVE HIM OUR NAMES.
IT LEADS NOT BACK TO ME, WHICH SPARES YOUR THROAT. I--
BUT SOFT! I HEARKEN TO A CALL. THE VOICE OF MY CREATION LONG THOUGHT LOST, NOW FOUND!

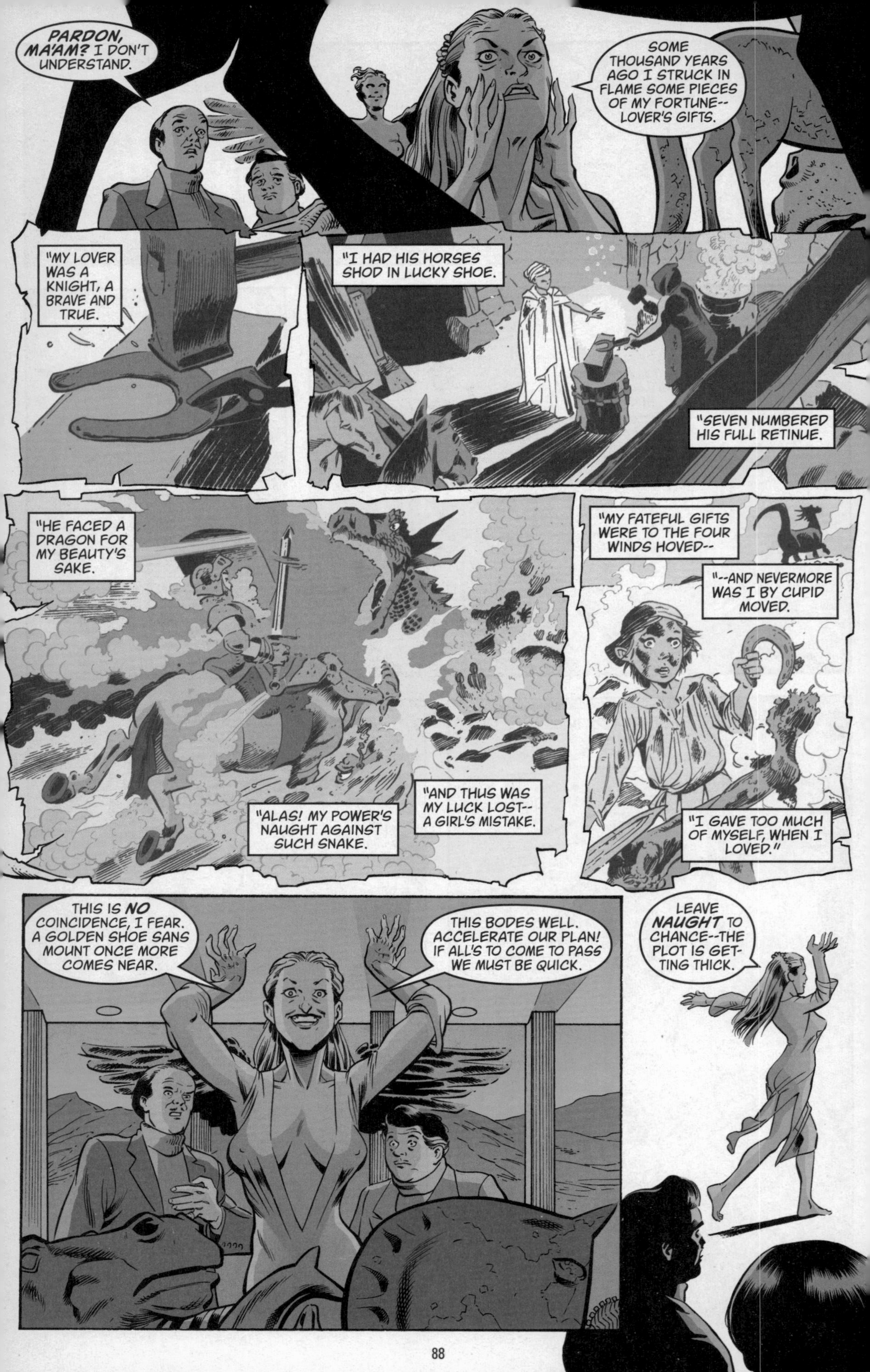

PARDON, MA'AM? I DON'T UNDERSTAND.
SOME THOUSAND YEARS AGO I STRUCK IN FLAME SOME PIECES OF MY FORTUNE--LOVER'S GIFTS.
"MY LOVER WAS A KNIGHT, A BRAVE AND TRUE.
"I HAD HIS HORSES SHOD IN LUCKY SHOE.
"SEVEN NUMBERED HIS FULL RETINUE.
"HE FACED A DRAGON FOR MY BEAUTY'S SAKE.
"ALAS! MY POWER'S NAUGHT AGAINST SUCH SNAKE.
"AND THUS WAS MY LUCK LOST--A GIRL'S MISTAKE.
"MY FATEFUL GIFTS WERE TO THE FOUR WINDS HOVED--
"--AND NEVERMORE WAS I BY CUPID MOVED.
"I GAVE TOO MUCH OF MYSELF, WHEN I LOVED."
THIS IS NO COINCIDENCE, I FEAR. A GOLDEN SHOE SANS MOUNT ONCE MORE COMES NEAR.
THIS BODES WELL. ACCELERATE OUR PLAN! IF ALL'S TO COME TO PASS WE MUST BE QUICK.
LEAVE NAUGHT TO CHANCE--THE PLOT IS GETTING THICK.

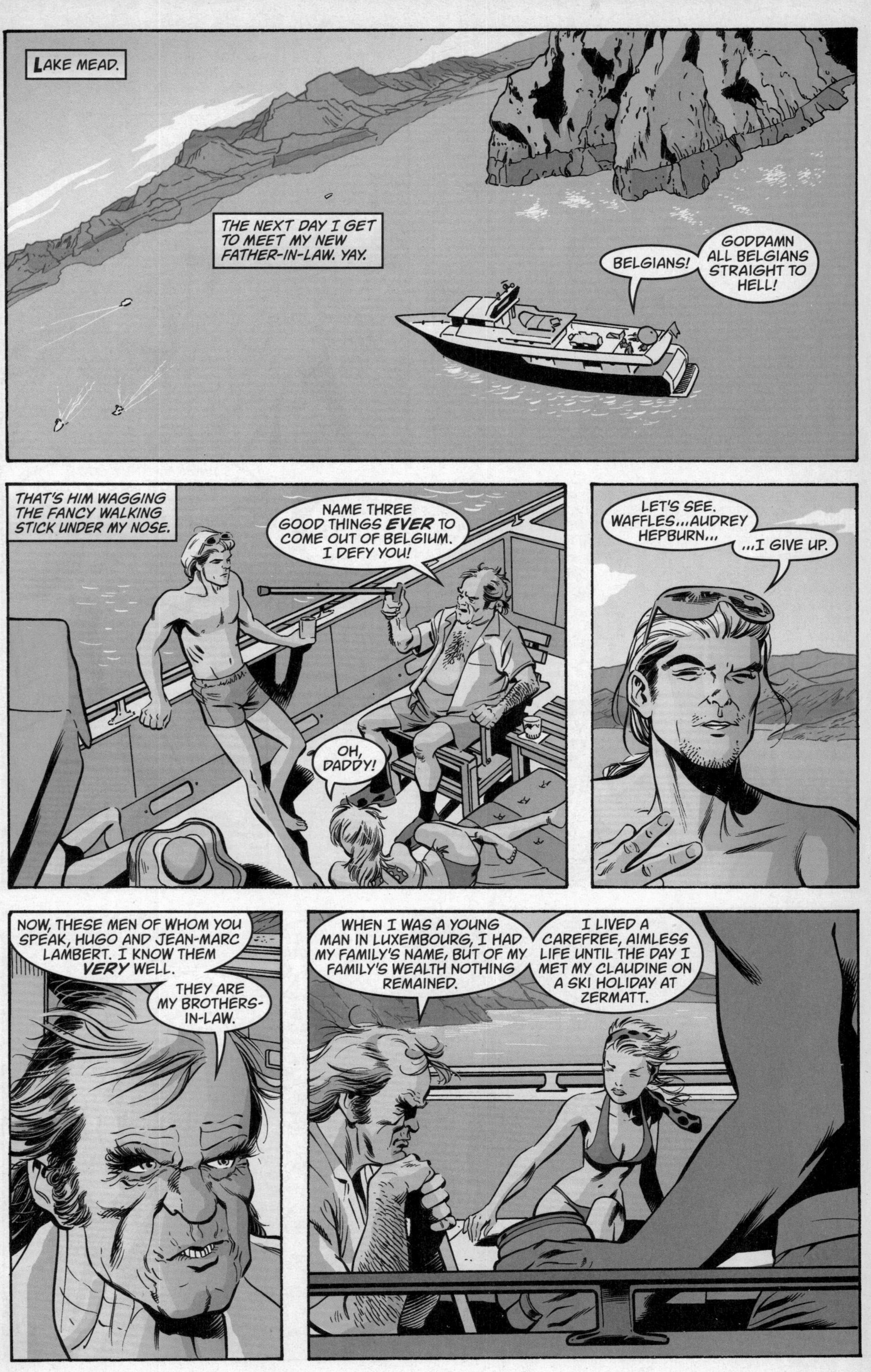
LAKE MEAD.
THE NEXT DAY I GET TO MEET MY NEW FATHER-IN-LAW. YAY.
BELGIANS!
GODDAMN ALL BELGIANS STRAIGHT TO HELL!
THAT'S HIM WAGGING THE FANCY WALKING STICK UNDER MY NOSE.
NAME THREE GOOD THINGS EVER TO COME OUT OF BELGIUM. I DEFY YOU!
OH, DADDY!
LET'S SEE. WAFFLES...AUDREY HEPBURN...
...I GIVE UP.
NOW, THESE MEN OF WHOM YOU SPEAK, HUGO AND JEAN-MARC LAMBERT. I KNOW THEM VERY WELL.
THEY ARE MY BROTHERS-IN-LAW.
WHEN I WAS A YOUNG MAN IN LUXEMBOURG, I HAD MY FAMILY'S NAME, BUT OF MY FAMILY'S WEALTH NOTHING REMAINED.
I LIVED A CAREFREE, AIMLESS LIFE UNTIL THE DAY I MET MY CLAUDINE ON A SKI HOLIDAY AT ZERMATT.

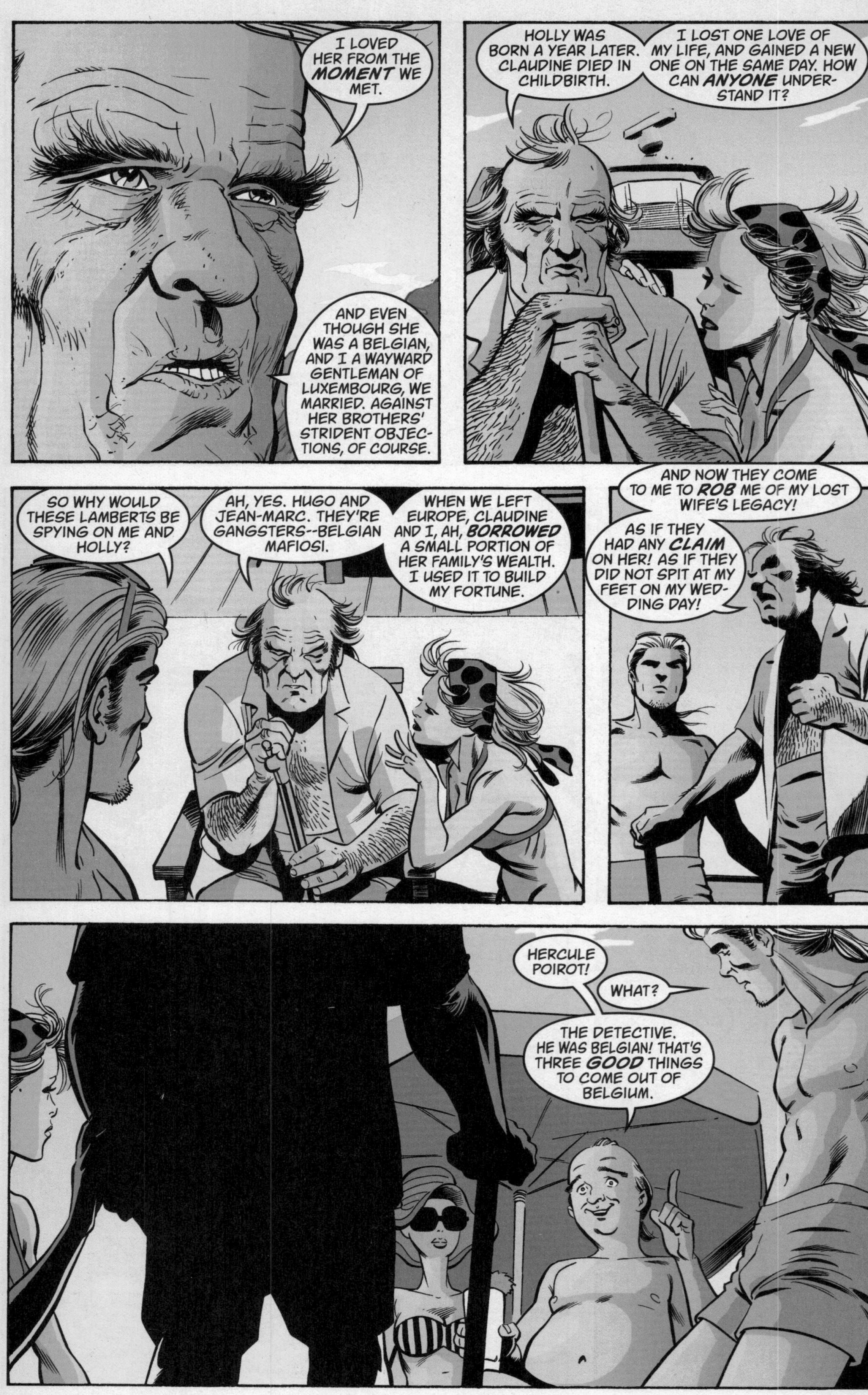

I LOVED HER FROM THE MOMENT WE MET.
AND EVEN THOUGH SHE WAS A BELGIAN, AND I A WAYWARD GENTLEMAN OF LUXEMBOURG, WE MARRIED. AGAINST HER BROTHERS' STRIDENT OBJECTIONS, OF COURSE.
HOLLY WAS BORN A YEAR LATER. CLAUDINE DIED IN CHILDBIRTH.
I LOST ONE LOVE OF MY LIFE, AND GAINED A NEW ONE ON THE SAME DAY. HOW CAN ANYONE UNDERSTAND IT?
SO WHY WOULD THESE LAMBERTS BE SPYING ON ME AND HOLLY?
AH, YES. HUGO AND JEAN-MARC. THEY'RE GANGSTERS--BELGIAN MAFIOSI.
WHEN WE LEFT EUROPE, CLAUDINE AND I, AH, BORROWED A SMALL PORTION OF HER FAMILY'S WEALTH. I USED IT TO BUILD MY FORTUNE.
AND NOW THEY COME TO ME TO ROB ME OF MY LOST WIFE'S LEGACY!
AS IF THEY HAD ANY CLAIM ON HER! AS IF THEY DID NOT SPIT AT MY FEET ON MY WEDDING DAY!
HERCULE POIROT!
WHAT?
THE DETECTIVE. HE WAS BELGIAN! THAT'S THREE GOOD THINGS TO COME OUT OF BELGIUM.

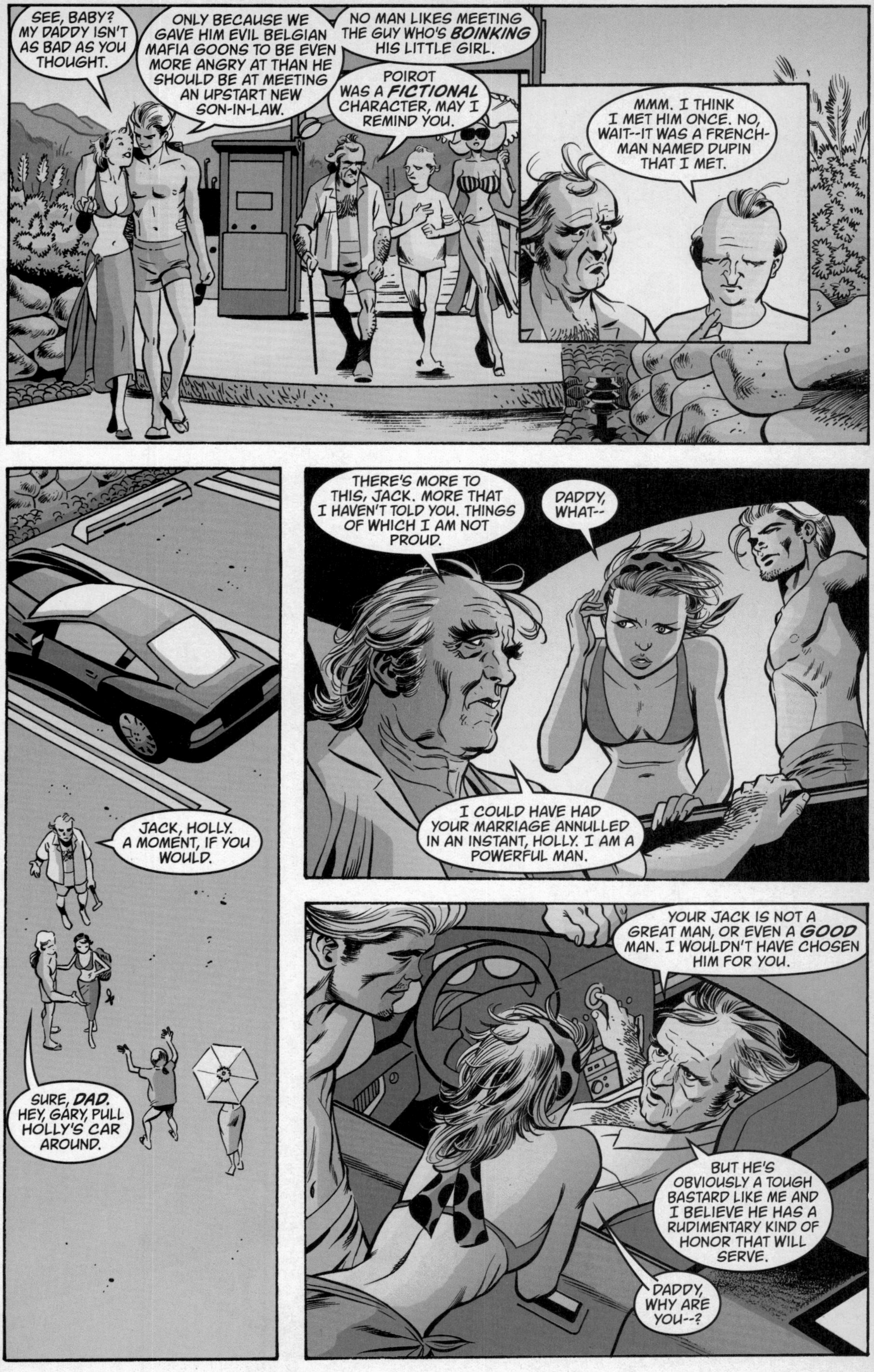

SEE, BABY? MY DADDY ISN'T AS BAD AS YOU THOUGHT.
ONLY BECAUSE WE GAVE HIM EVIL BELGIAN MAFIA GOONS TO BE EVEN MORE ANGRY AT THAN HE SHOULD BE AT MEETING AN UPSTART NEW SON-IN-LAW.
NO MAN LIKES MEETING THE GUY WHO'S BOINKING HIS LITTLE GIRL.
POIROT WAS A FICTIONAL CHARACTER, MAY I REMIND YOU.
MMM. I THINK I MET HIM ONCE. NO, WAIT--IT WAS A FRENCH-MAN NAMED DUPIN THAT I MET.
JACK, HOLLY. A MOMENT, IF YOU WOULD.
SURE, DAD. HEY, GARY, PULL HOLLY'S CAR AROUND.
THERE'S MORE TO THIS, JACK. MORE THAT I HAVEN'T TOLD YOU. THINGS OF WHICH I AM NOT PROUD.
DADDY, WHAT--
I COULD HAVE HAD YOUR MARRIAGE ANNULLED IN AN INSTANT, HOLLY. I AM A POWERFUL MAN.
YOUR JACK IS NOT A GREAT MAN, OR EVEN A GOOD MAN. I WOULDN'T HAVE CHOSEN HIM FOR YOU.
BUT HE'S OBVIOUSLY A TOUGH BASTARD LIKE ME AND I BELIEVE HE HAS A RUDIMENTARY KIND OF HONOR THAT WILL SERVE.
DADDY, WHY ARE YOU--?

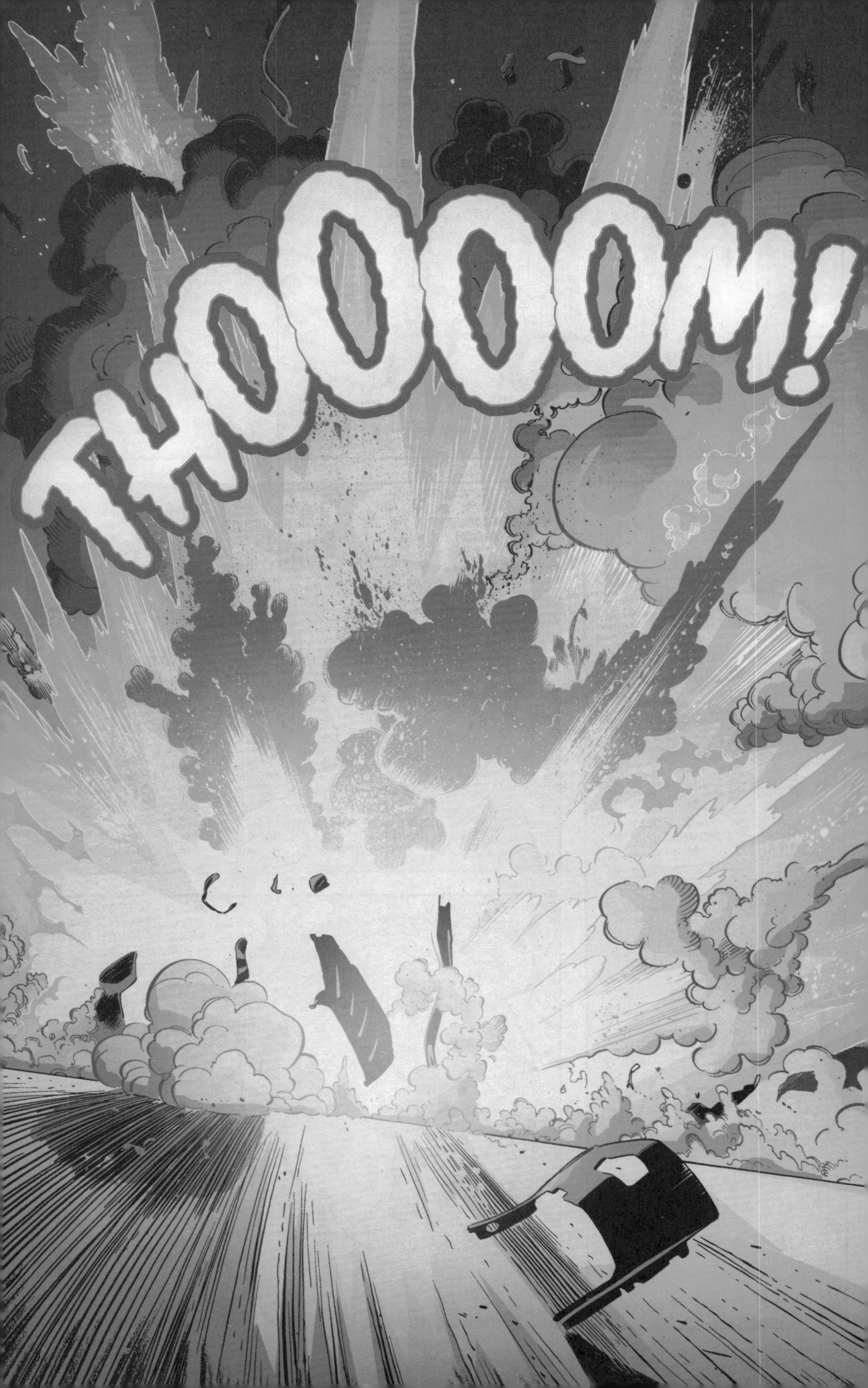
THOOOOM!

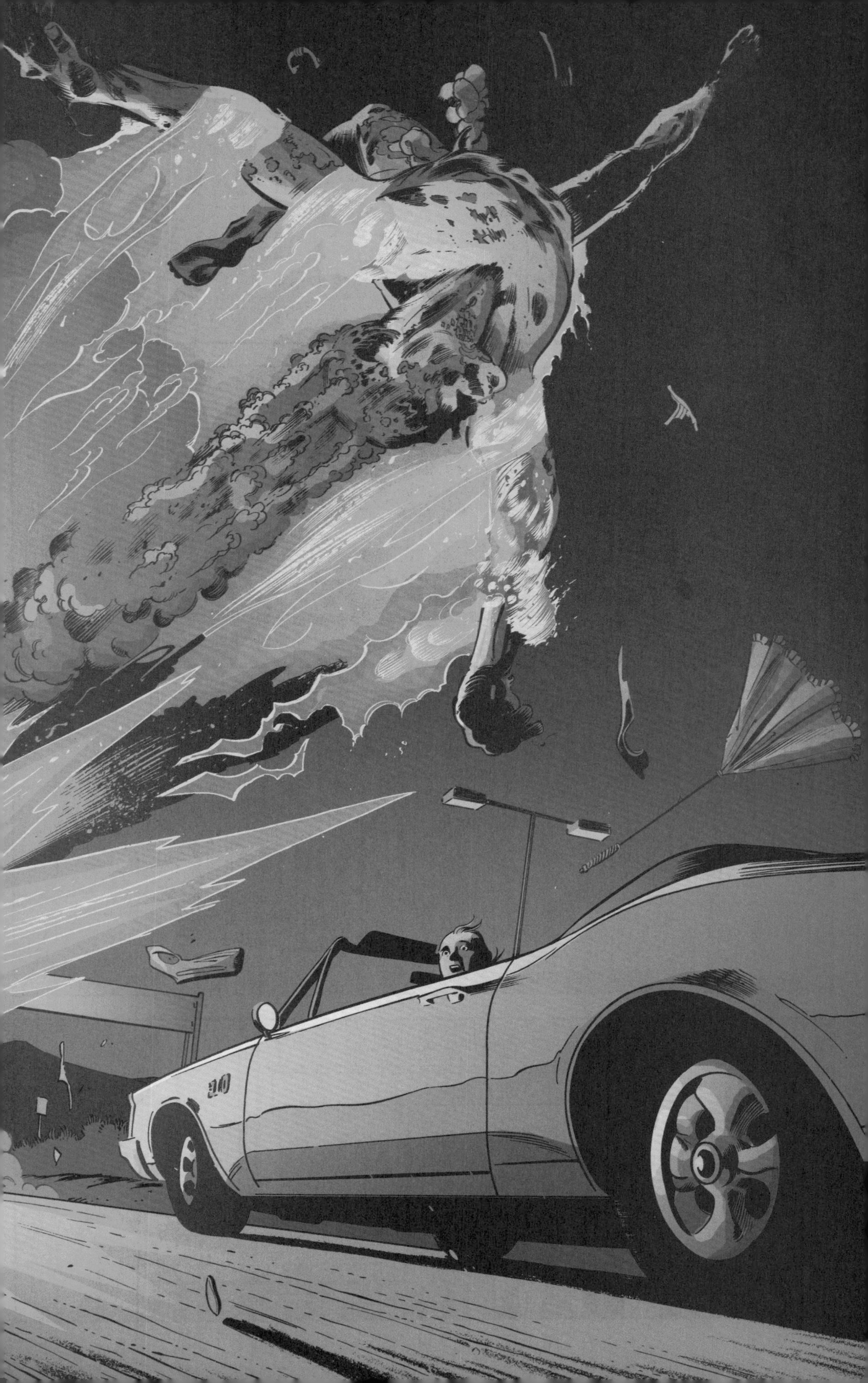

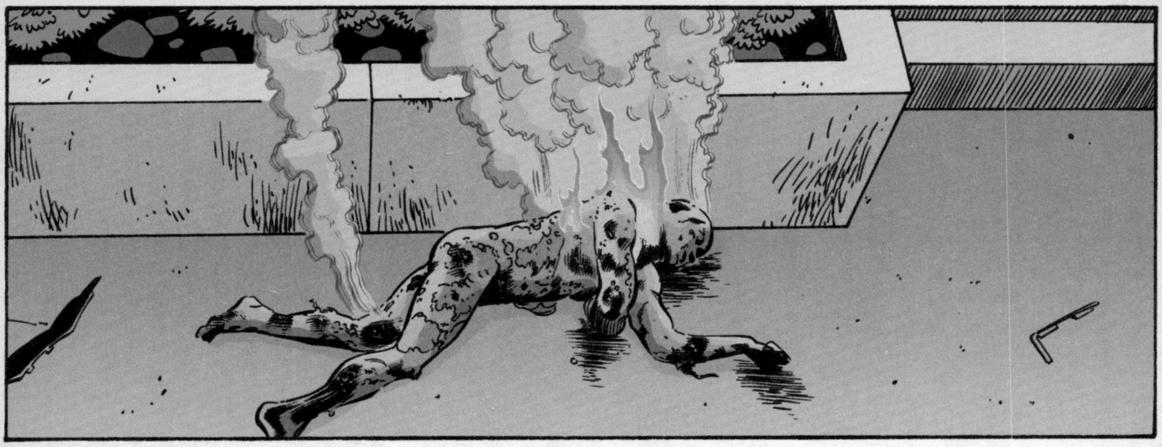

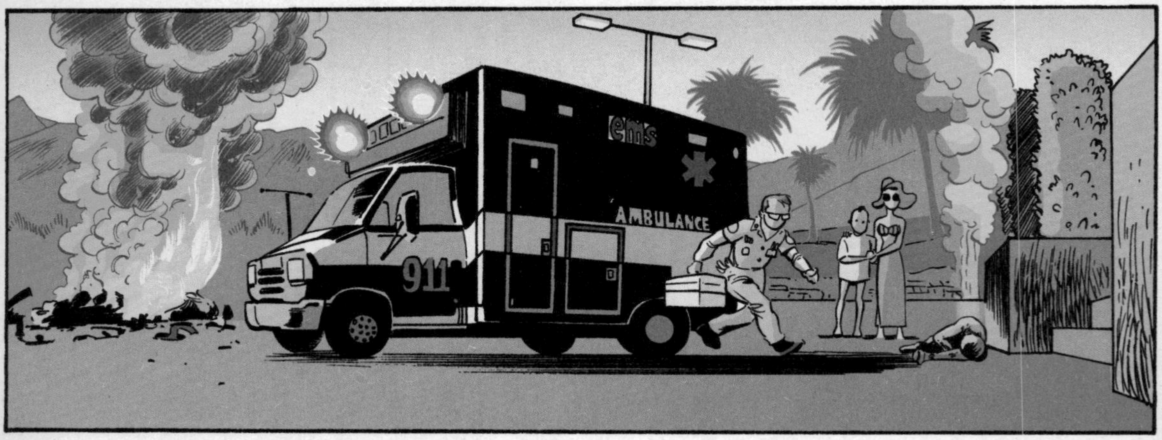
ems
AMBULANCE
911

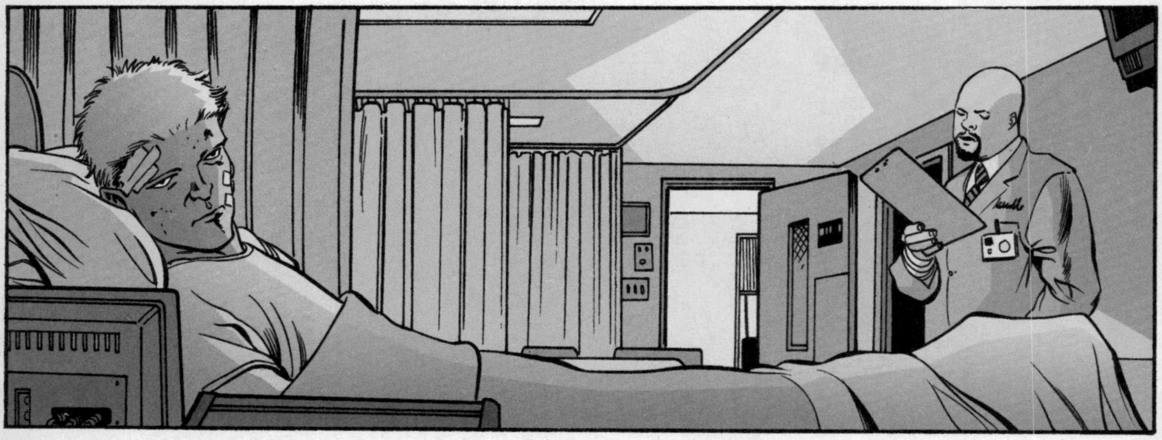

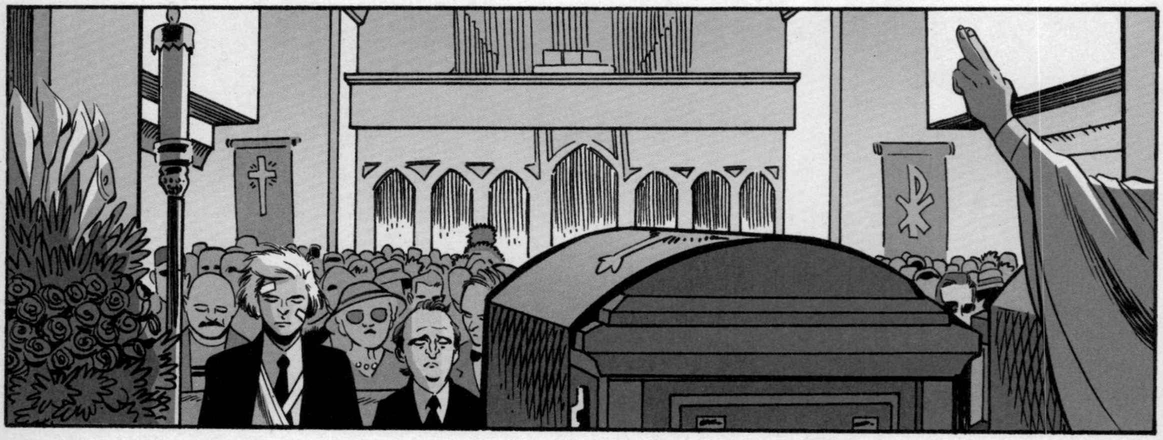

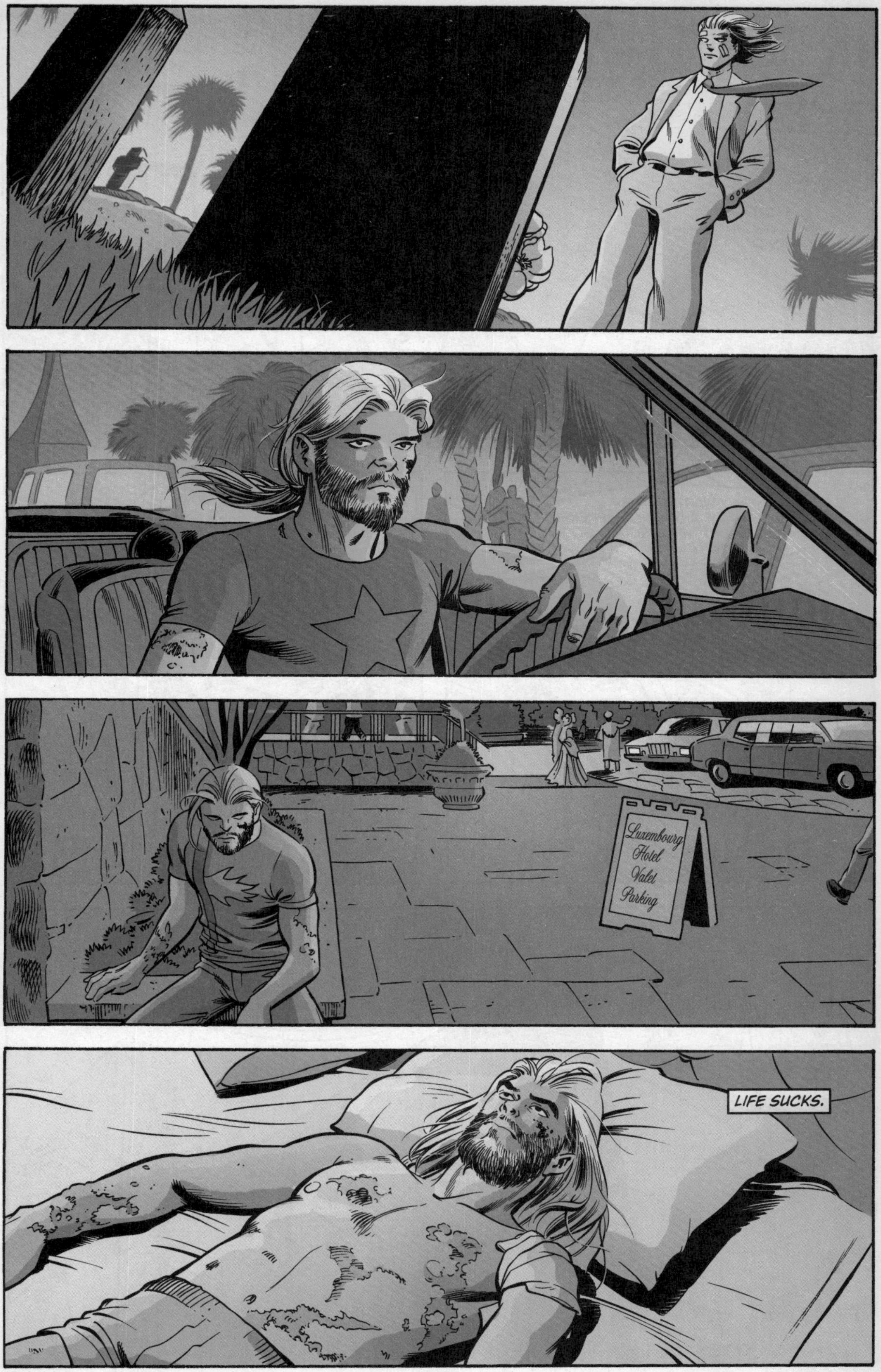
Luxembourg Hotel Valet Parking
LIFE SUCKS.

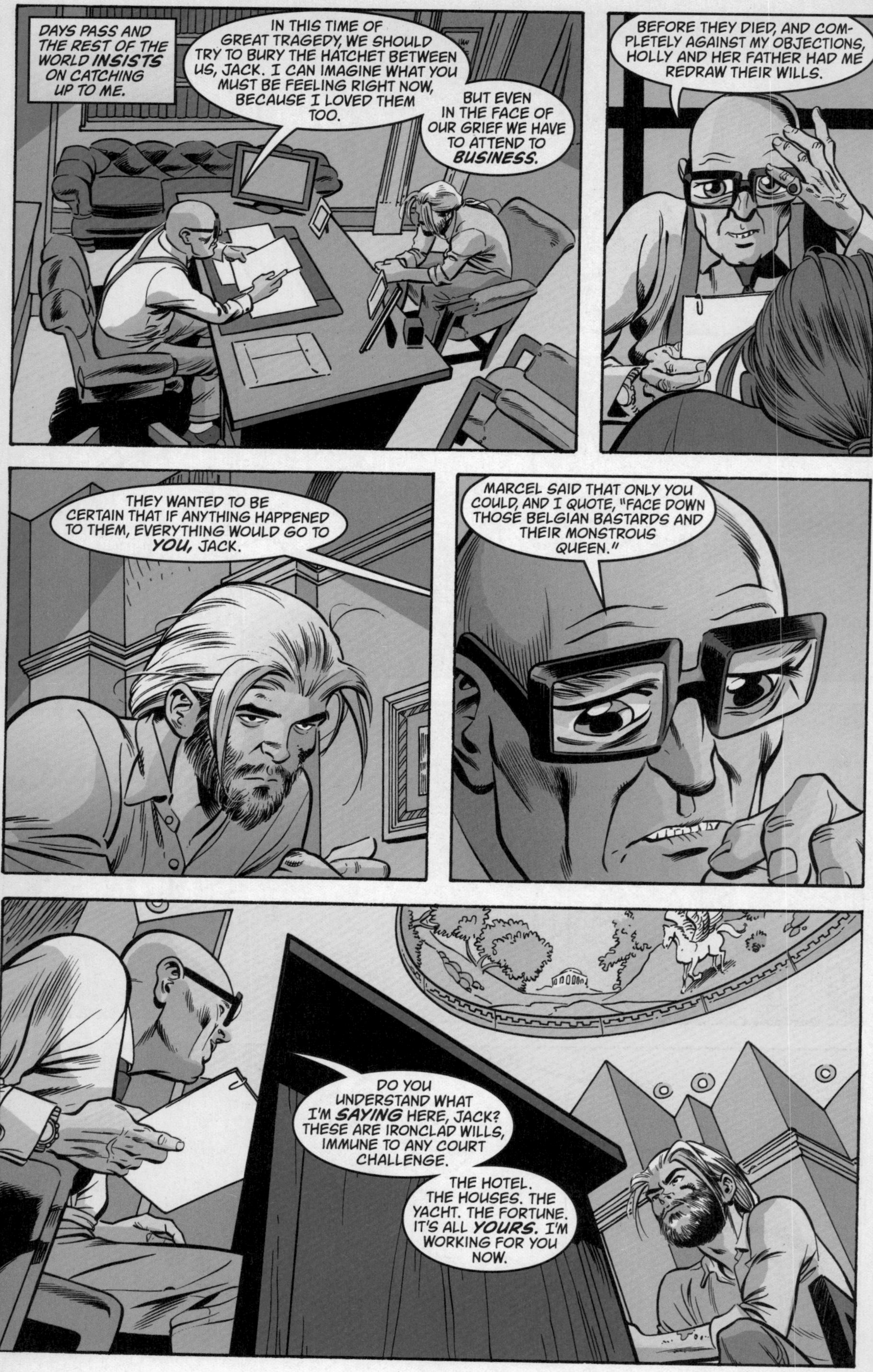
DAYS PASS AND THE REST OF THE WORLD INSISTS ON CATCHING UP TO ME.
IN THIS TIME OF GREAT TRAGEDY, WE SHOULD TRY TO BURY THE HATCHET BETWEEN US, JACK. I CAN IMAGINE WHAT YOU MUST BE FEELING RIGHT NOW, BECAUSE I LOVED THEM TOO.
BUT EVEN IN THE FACE OF OUR GRIEF WE HAVE TO ATTEND TO BUSINESS.
BEFORE THEY DIED, AND COMPLETELY AGAINST MY OBJECTIONS, HOLLY AND HER FATHER HAD ME REDRAW THEIR WILLS.
THEY WANTED TO BE CERTAIN THAT IF ANYTHING HAPPENED TO THEM, EVERYTHING WOULD GO TO YOU, JACK.
MARCEL SAID THAT ONLY YOU COULD, AND I QUOTE, "FACE DOWN THOSE BELGIAN BASTARDS AND THEIR MONSTROUS QUEEN."
DO YOU UNDERSTAND WHAT I'M SAYING HERE, JACK? THESE ARE IRONCLAD WILLS, IMMUNE TO ANY COURT CHALLENGE.
THE HOTEL. THE HOUSES. THE YACHT. THE FORTUNE. IT'S ALL YOURS. I'M WORKING FOR YOU NOW.

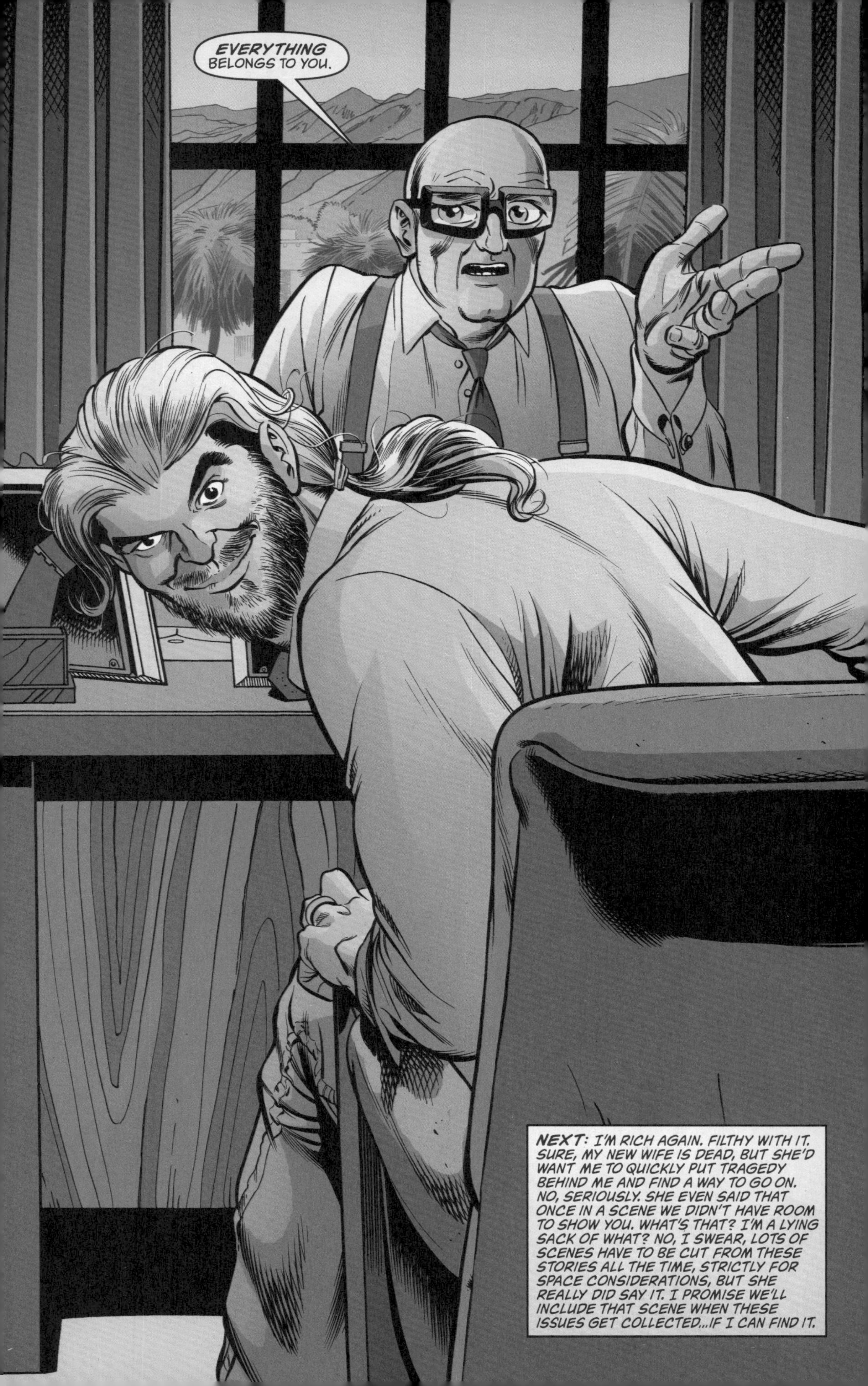
EVERYTHING BELONGS TO YOU.
NEXT: I'M RICH AGAIN. FILTHY WITH IT. SURE, MY NEW WIFE IS DEAD, BUT SHE'D WANT ME TO QUICKLY PUT TRAGEDY BEHIND ME AND FIND A WAY TO GO ON. NO, SERIOUSLY. SHE EVEN SAID THAT ONCE IN A SCENE WE DIDN'T HAVE ROOM TO SHOW YOU. WHAT'S THAT? I'M A LYING SACK OF WHAT? NO, I SWEAR, LOTS OF SCENES HAVE TO BE CUT FROM THESE STORIES ALL THE TIME, STRICTLY FOR SPACE CONSIDERATIONS, BUT SHE REALLY DID SAY IT. I PROMISE WE'LL INCLUDE THAT SCENE WHEN THESE ISSUES GET COLLECTED...IF I CAN FIND IT.

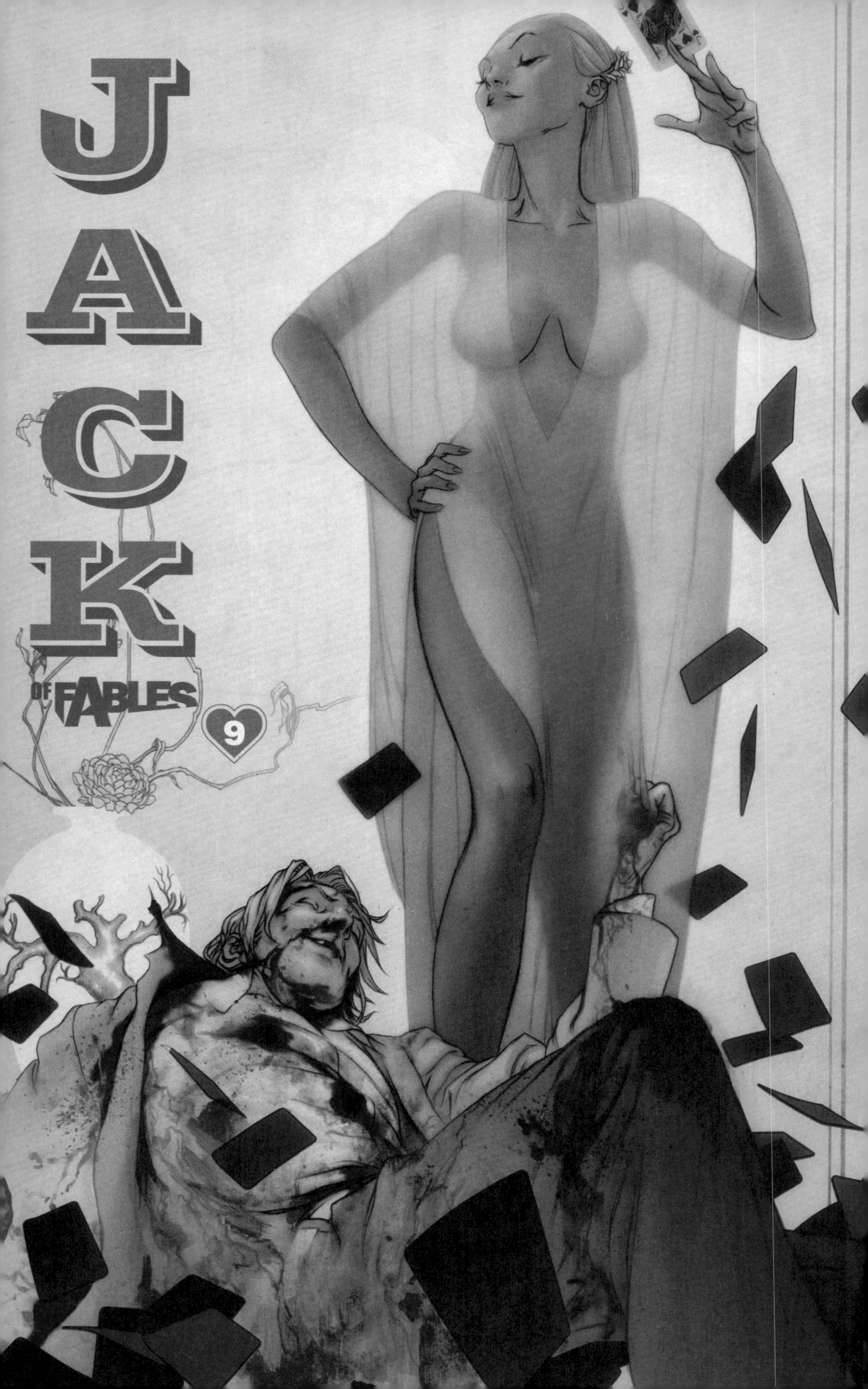
JACK
OF FABLES
9

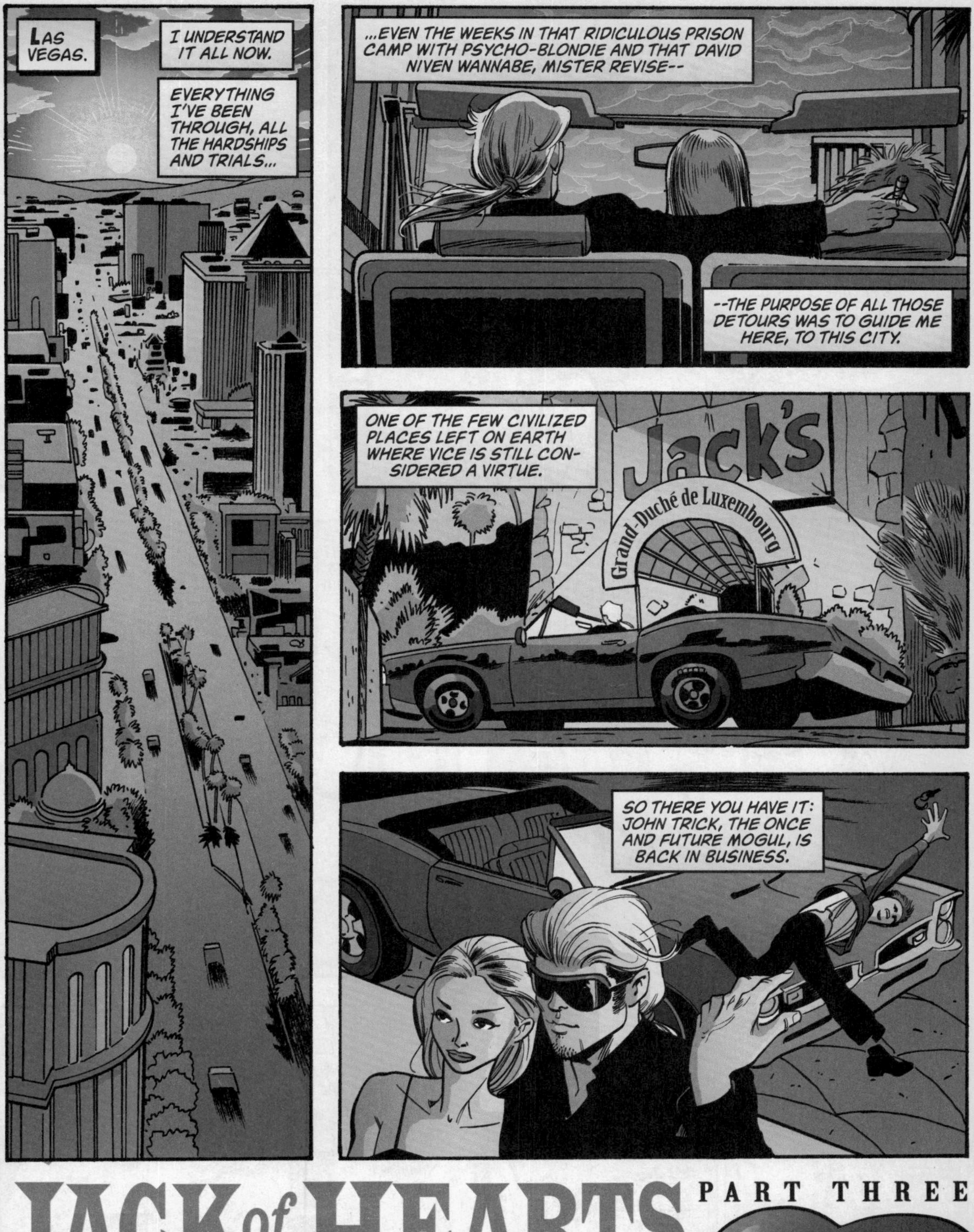
LAS VEGAS.
I UNDERSTAND IT ALL NOW.
EVERYTHING I'VE BEEN THROUGH, ALL THE HARDSHIPS AND TRIALS...
...EVEN THE WEEKS IN THAT RIDICULOUS PRISON CAMP WITH PSYCHO-BLONDIE AND THAT DAVID NIVEN WANNABE, MISTER REVISE--
--THE PURPOSE OF ALL THOSE DETOURS WAS TO GUIDE ME HERE, TO THIS CITY.
ONE OF THE FEW CIVILIZED PLACES LEFT ON EARTH WHERE VICE IS STILL CONSIDERED A VIRTUE.
Jack's
Grand-Duché de Luxembourg
SO THERE YOU HAVE IT: JOHN TRICK, THE ONCE AND FUTURE MOGUL, IS BACK IN BUSINESS.

JACK of HEARTS PART THREE

♦♣♥♠ LUCK BE A LADY ♦♣♥♠

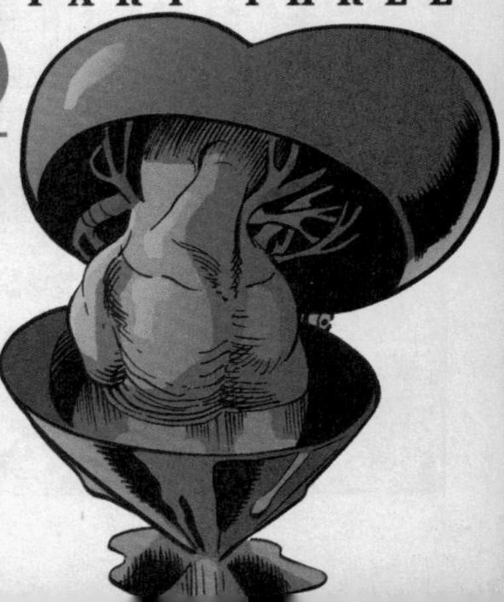

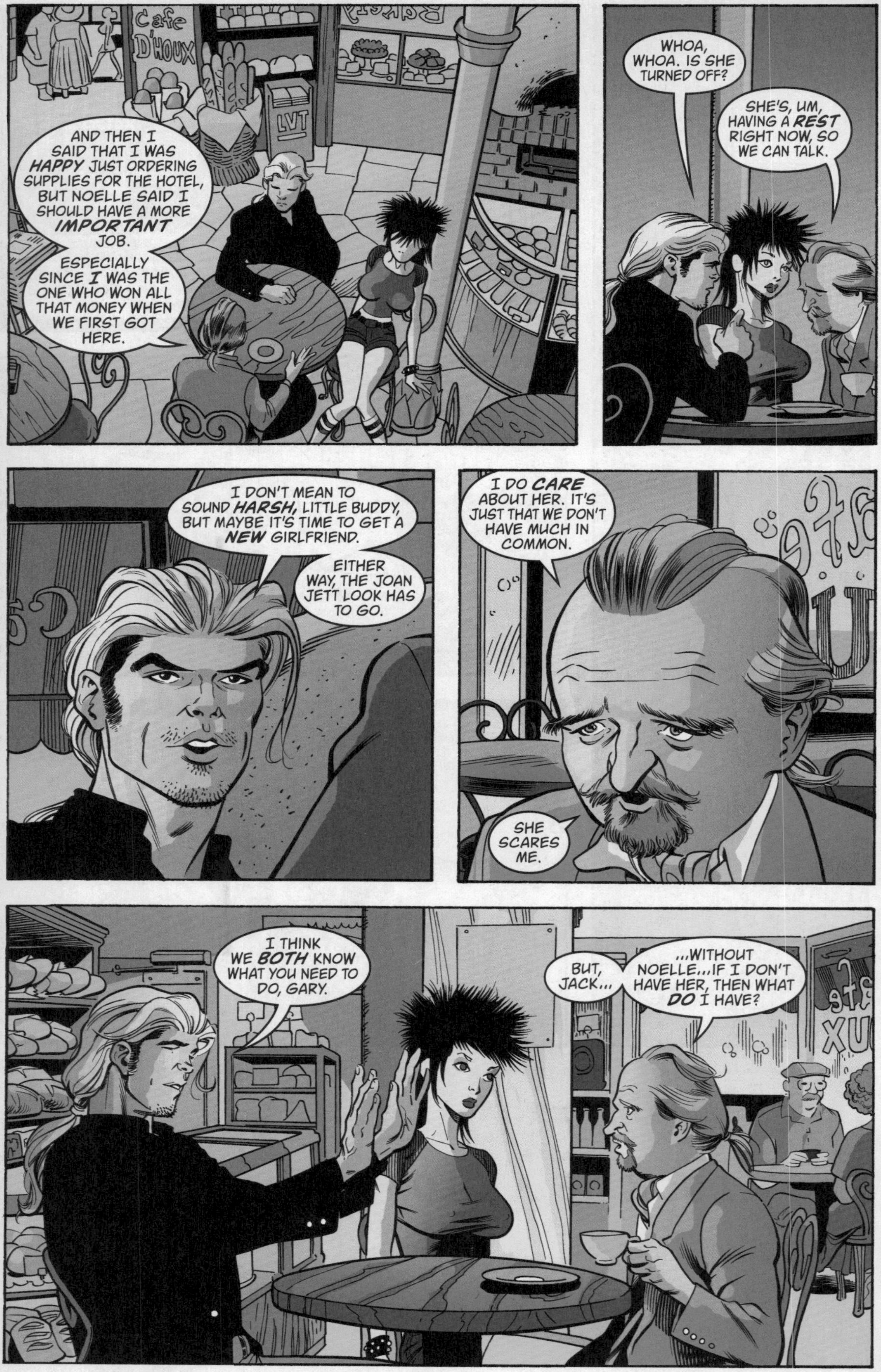
Cafe D'HOUX
AND THEN I SAID THAT I WAS HAPPY JUST ORDERING SUPPLIES FOR THE HOTEL, BUT NOELLE SAID I SHOULD HAVE A MORE IMPORTANT JOB.
ESPECIALLY SINCE I WAS THE ONE WHO WON ALL THAT MONEY WHEN WE FIRST GOT HERE.
WHOA, WHOA. IS SHE TURNED OFF?
SHE'S, UM, HAVING A REST RIGHT NOW, SO WE CAN TALK.
I DON'T MEAN TO SOUND HARSH, LITTLE BUDDY, BUT MAYBE IT'S TIME TO GET A NEW GIRLFRIEND.
EITHER WAY, THE JOAN JETT LOOK HAS TO GO.
I DO CARE ABOUT HER. IT'S JUST THAT WE DON'T HAVE MUCH IN COMMON.
SHE SCARES ME.
I THINK WE BOTH KNOW WHAT YOU NEED TO DO, GARY.
BUT, JACK...
...WITHOUT NOELLE...IF I DON'T HAVE HER, THEN WHAT DO I HAVE?

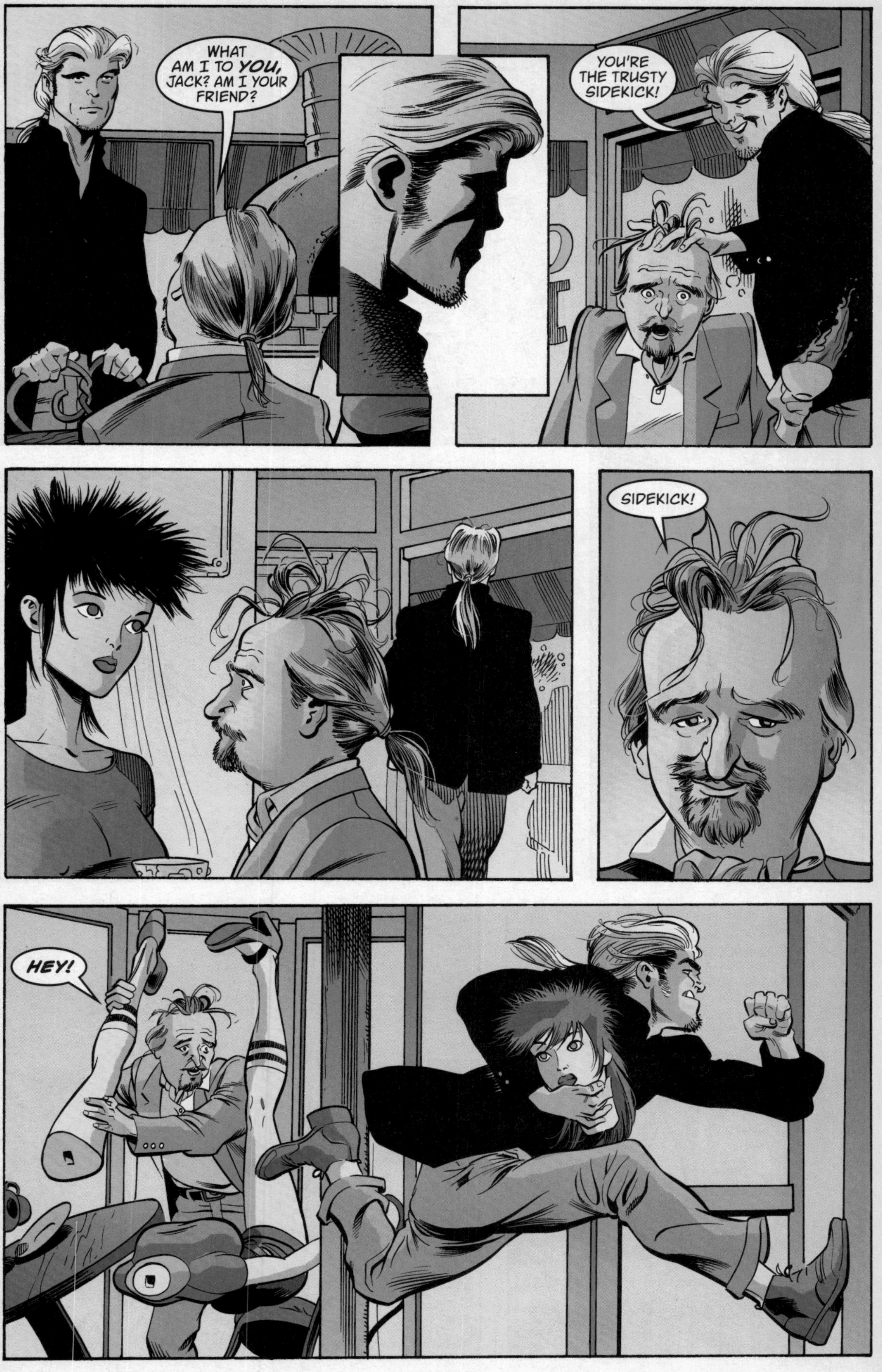
WHAT AM I TO YOU, JACK? AM I YOUR FRIEND?
YOU'RE THE TRUSTY SIDEKICK!
SIDEKICK!
HEY!

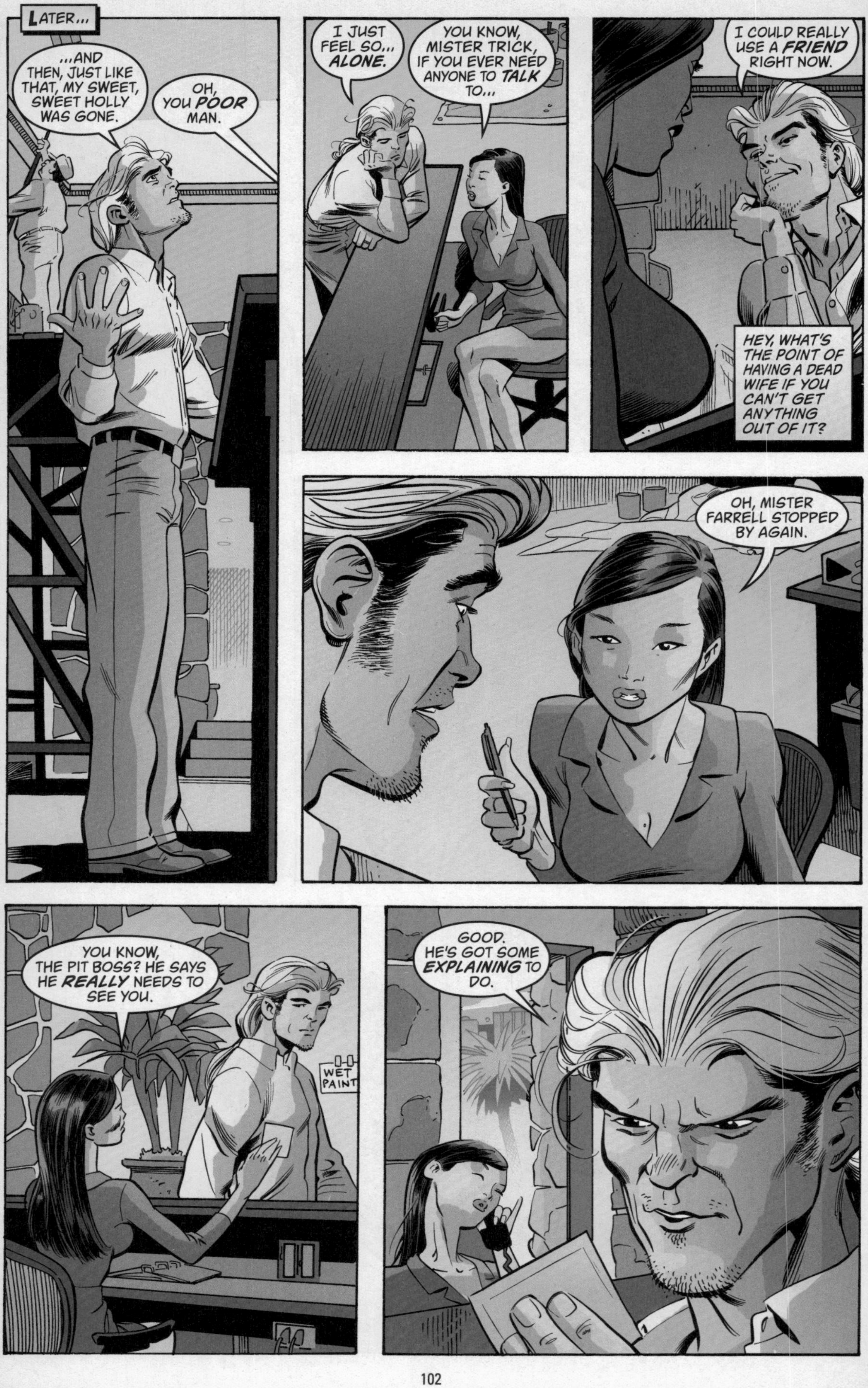
LATER...
...AND THEN, JUST LIKE THAT, MY SWEET, SWEET HOLLY WAS GONE.
OH, YOU POOR MAN.
I JUST FEEL SO... ALONE.
YOU KNOW, MISTER TRICK, IF YOU EVER NEED ANYONE TO TALK TO...
I COULD REALLY USE A FRIEND RIGHT NOW.
HEY, WHAT'S THE POINT OF HAVING A DEAD WIFE IF YOU CAN'T GET ANYTHING OUT OF IT?
OH, MISTER FARRELL STOPPED BY AGAIN.
YOU KNOW, THE PIT BOSS? HE SAYS HE REALLY NEEDS TO SEE YOU.
WET PAINT
GOOD. HE'S GOT SOME EXPLAINING TO DO.

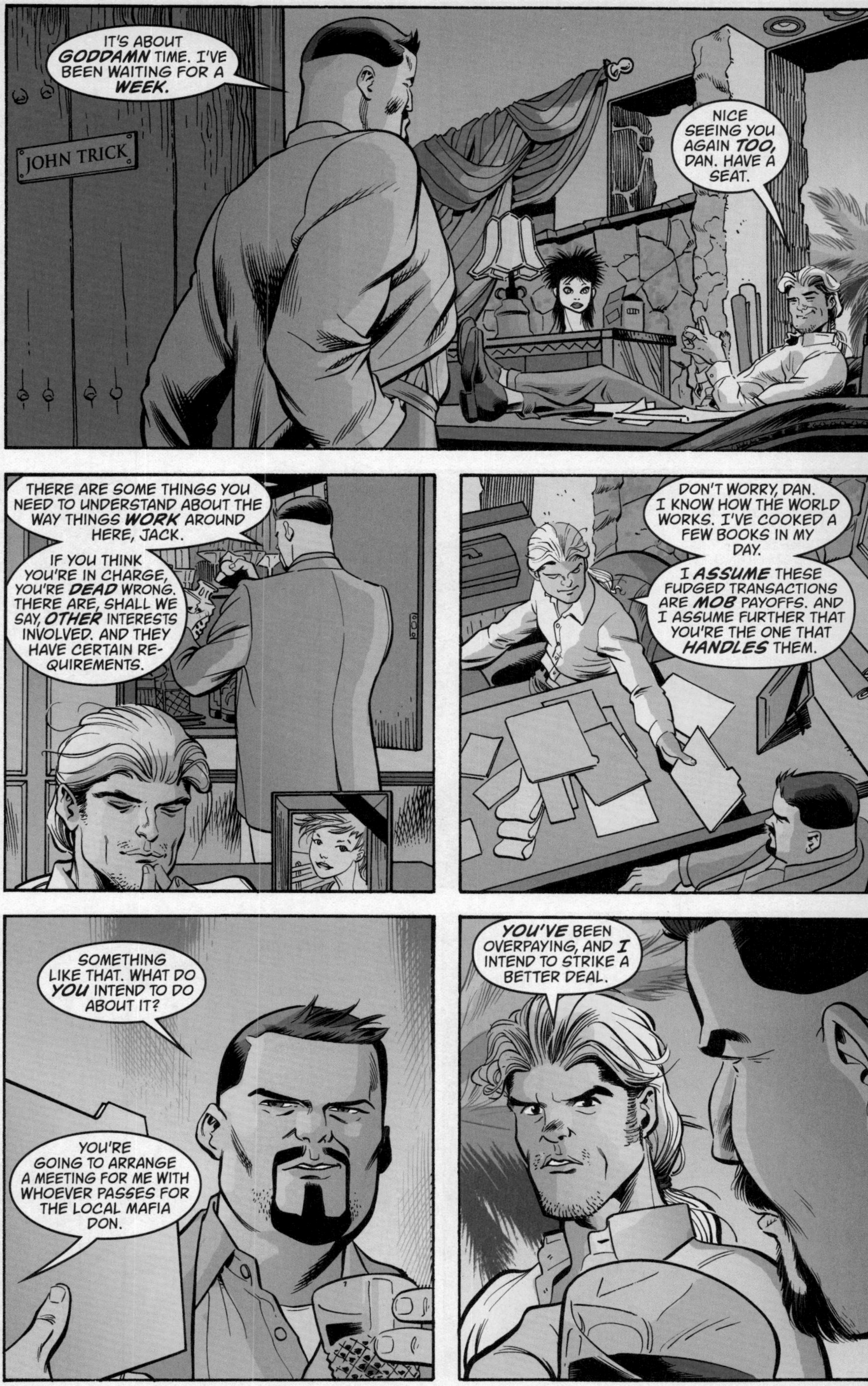
IT'S ABOUT GODDAMN TIME. I'VE BEEN WAITING FOR A WEEK.
JOHN TRICK
NICE SEEING YOU AGAIN TOO, DAN. HAVE A SEAT.
THERE ARE SOME THINGS YOU NEED TO UNDERSTAND ABOUT THE WAY THINGS WORK AROUND HERE, JACK.
IF YOU THINK YOU'RE IN CHARGE, YOU'RE DEAD WRONG. THERE ARE, SHALL WE SAY, OTHER INTERESTS INVOLVED. AND THEY HAVE CERTAIN RE-QUIREMENTS.
DON'T WORRY, DAN. I KNOW HOW THE WORLD WORKS. I'VE COOKED A FEW BOOKS IN MY DAY.
I ASSUME THESE FUDGED TRANSACTIONS ARE MOB PAYOFFS. AND I ASSUME FURTHER THAT YOU'RE THE ONE THAT HANDLES THEM.
SOMETHING LIKE THAT. WHAT DO YOU INTEND TO DO ABOUT IT?
YOU'RE GOING TO ARRANGE A MEETING FOR ME WITH WHOEVER PASSES FOR THE LOCAL MAFIA DON.
YOU'VE BEEN OVERPAYING, AND I INTEND TO STRIKE A BETTER DEAL.

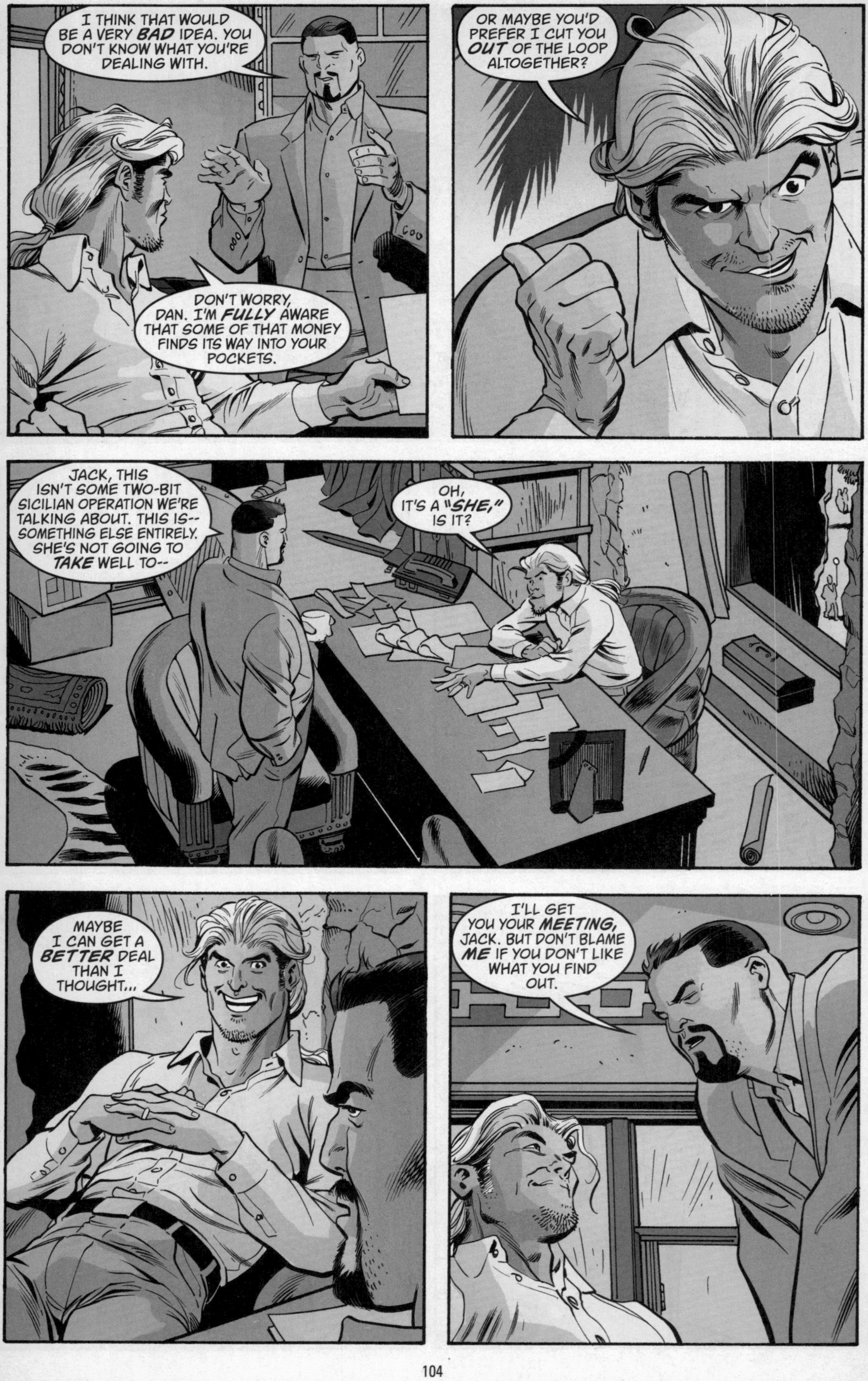

I THINK THAT WOULD BE A VERY BAD IDEA. YOU DON'T KNOW WHAT YOU'RE DEALING WITH.
DON'T WORRY, DAN. I'M FULLY AWARE THAT SOME OF THAT MONEY FINDS ITS WAY INTO YOUR POCKETS.
OR MAYBE YOU'D PREFER I CUT YOU OUT OF THE LOOP ALTOGETHER?
JACK, THIS ISN'T SOME TWO-BIT SICILIAN OPERATION WE'RE TALKING ABOUT. THIS IS-- SOMETHING ELSE ENTIRELY. SHE'S NOT GOING TO TAKE WELL TO--
OH, IT'S A "SHE," IS IT?
MAYBE I CAN GET A BETTER DEAL THAN I THOUGHT...
I'LL GET YOU YOUR MEETING, JACK. BUT DON'T BLAME ME IF YOU DON'T LIKE WHAT YOU FIND OUT.

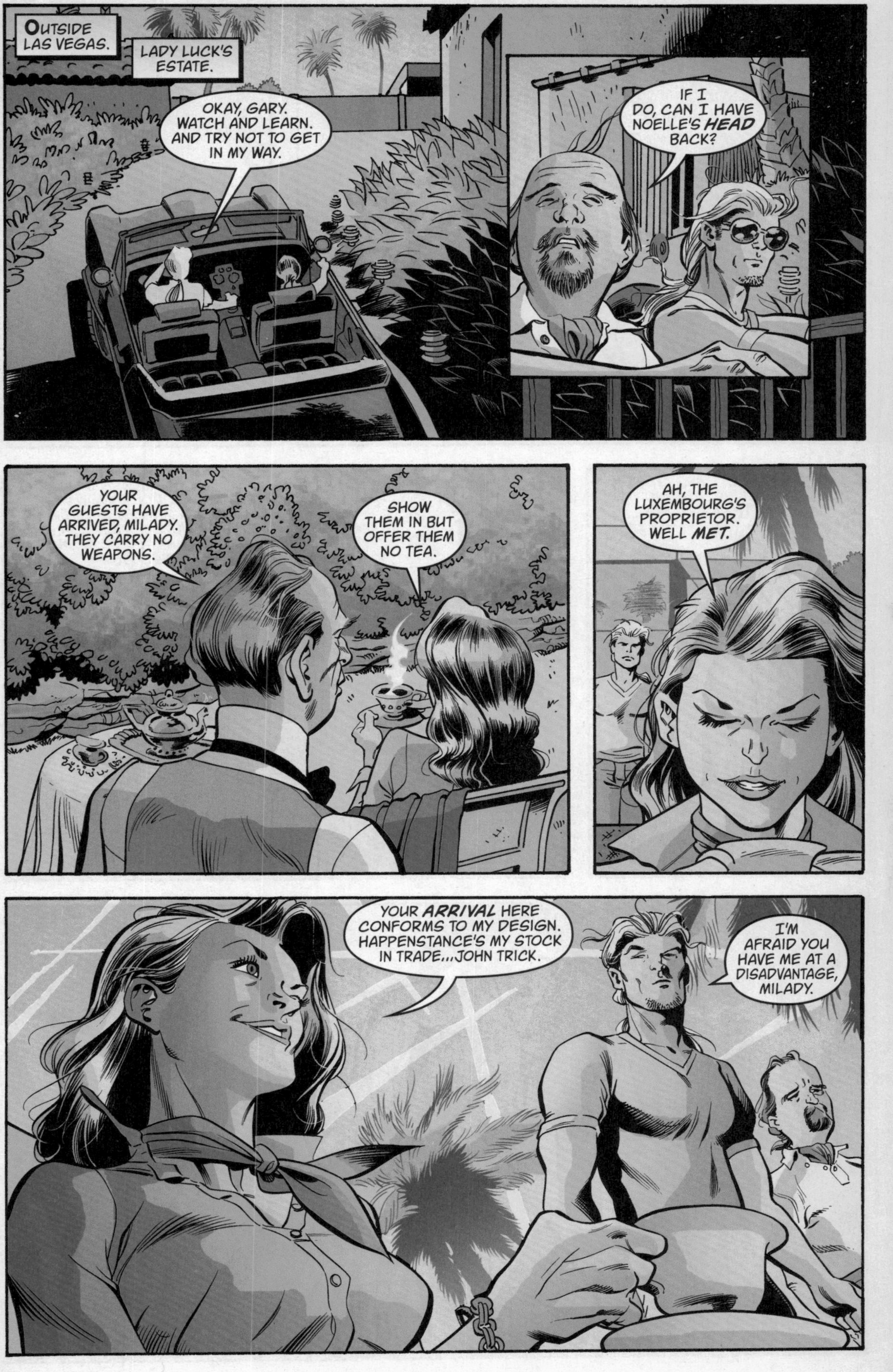
OUTSIDE LAS VEGAS.
LADY LUCK'S ESTATE.
OKAY, GARY. WATCH AND LEARN. AND TRY NOT TO GET IN MY WAY.
IF I DO, CAN I HAVE NOELLE'S HEAD BACK?
YOUR GUESTS HAVE ARRIVED, MILADY. THEY CARRY NO WEAPONS.
SHOW THEM IN BUT OFFER THEM NO TEA.
AH, THE LUXEMBOURG'S PROPRIETOR. WELL MET.
YOUR ARRIVAL HERE CONFORMS TO MY DESIGN. HAPPENSTANCE'S MY STOCK IN TRADE...JOHN TRICK.
I'M AFRAID YOU HAVE ME AT A DISADVANTAGE, MILADY.

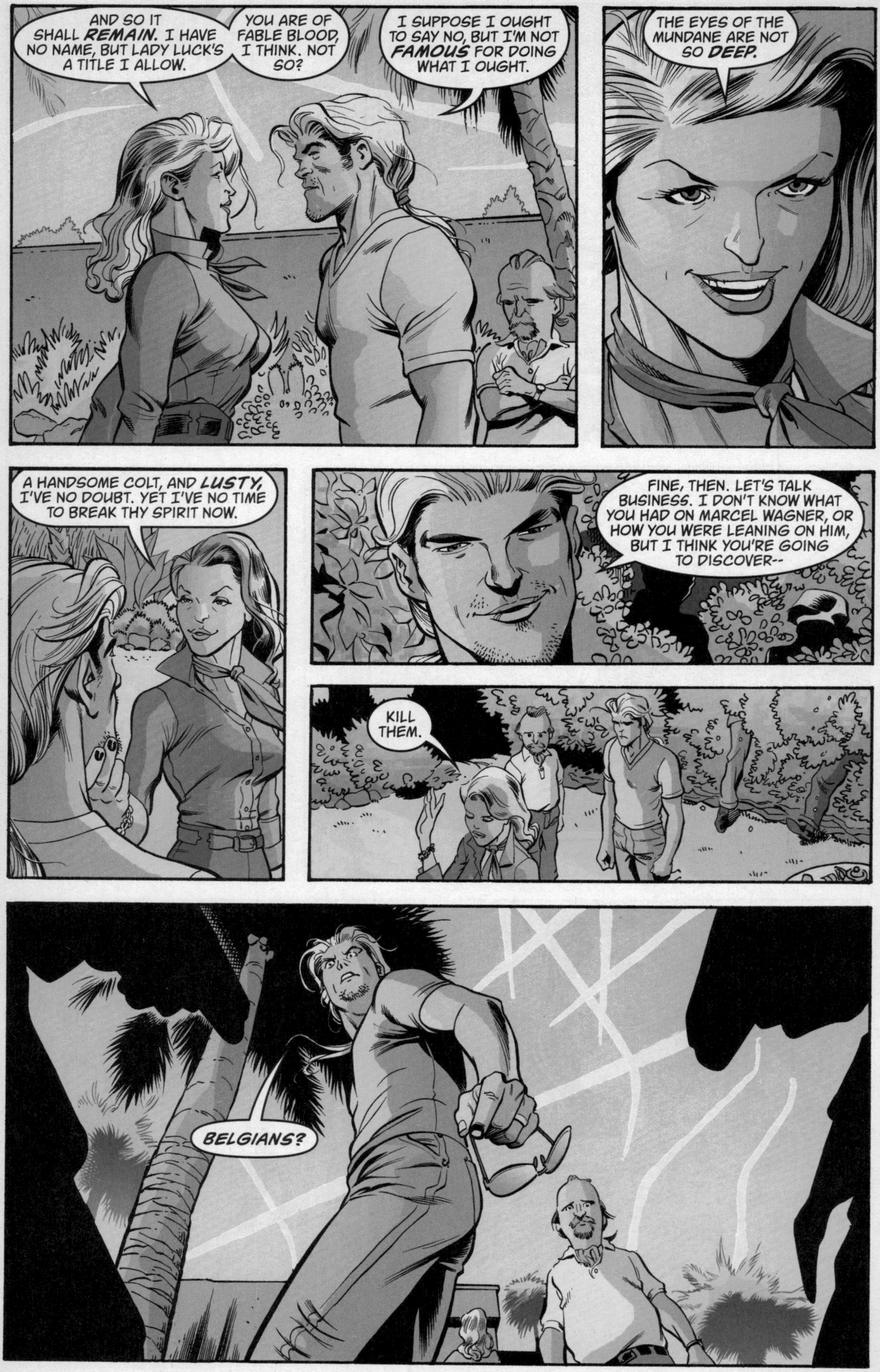
AND SO IT SHALL REMAIN. I HAVE NO NAME, BUT LADY LUCK'S A TITLE I ALLOW.
YOU ARE OF FABLE BLOOD, I THINK. NOT SO?
I SUPPOSE I OUGHT TO SAY NO, BUT I'M NOT FAMOUS FOR DOING WHAT I OUGHT.
THE EYES OF THE MUNDANE ARE NOT SO DEEP.
A HANDSOME COLT, AND LUSTY, I'VE NO DOUBT. YET I'VE NO TIME TO BREAK THY SPIRIT NOW.
FINE, THEN. LET'S TALK BUSINESS. I DON'T KNOW WHAT YOU HAD ON MARCEL WAGNER, OR HOW YOU WERE LEANING ON HIM, BUT I THINK YOU'RE GOING TO DISCOVER--
KILL THEM.
BELGIANS?

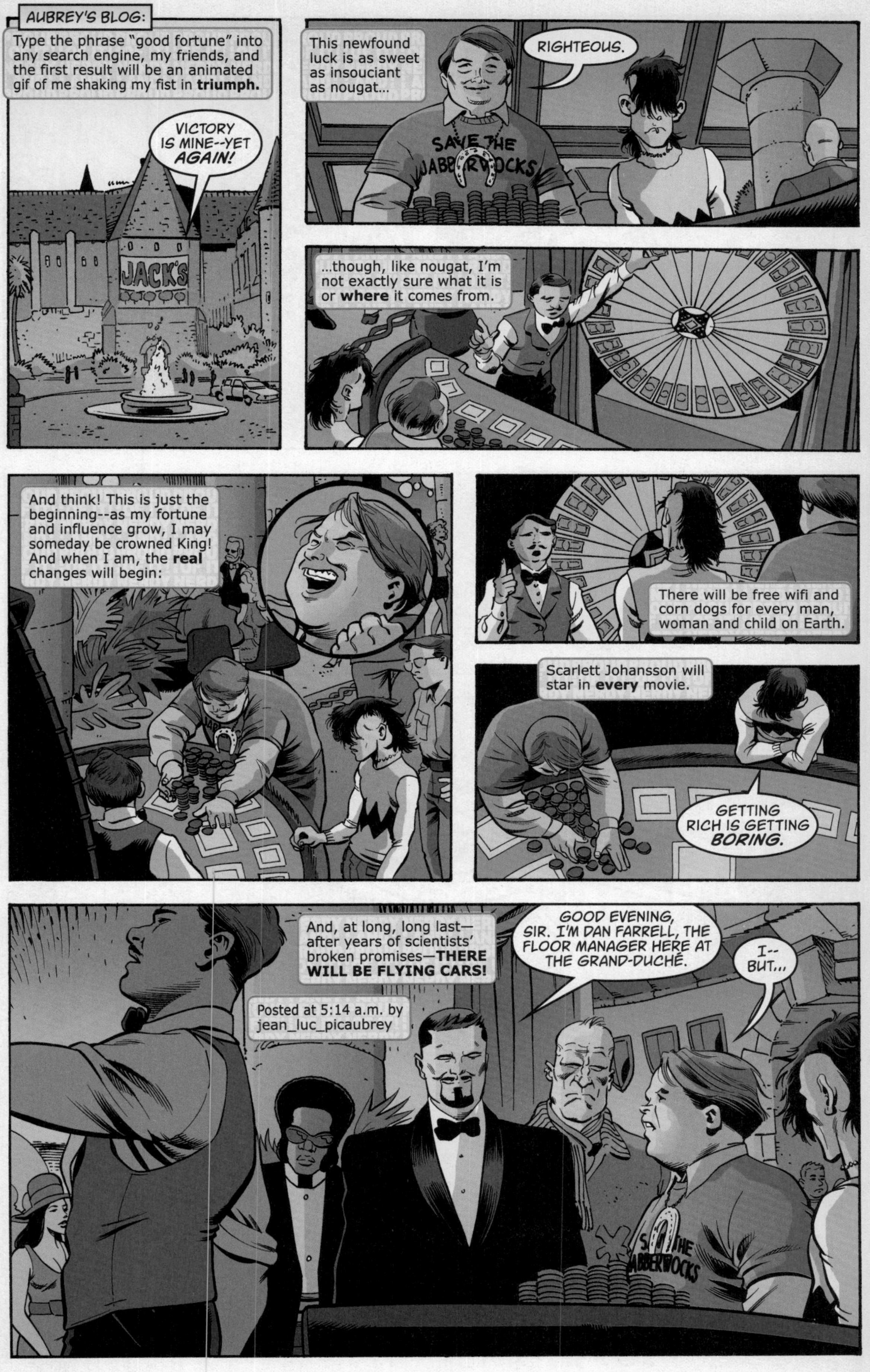
AUBREY'S BLOG:
Type the phrase "good fortune" into any search engine, my friends, and the first result will be an animated gif of me shaking my fist in **triumph.**
VICTORY IS MINE--YET AGAIN!
JACK'S
This newfound luck is as sweet as insouciant as nougat...
RIGHTEOUS.
SAVE THE JABBERWOCKS
...though, like nougat, I'm not exactly sure what it is or **where** it comes from.
And think! This is just the beginning--as my fortune and influence grow, I may someday be crowned King! And when I am, the **real** changes will begin:
There will be free wifi and corn dogs for every man, woman and child on Earth.
Scarlett Johansson will star in **every** movie.
GETTING RICH IS GETTING BORING.
And, at long, long last—after years of scientists' broken promises—**THERE WILL BE FLYING CARS!**
Posted at 5:14 a.m. by jean_luc_picaubrey
GOOD EVENING, SIR. I'M DAN FARRELL, THE FLOOR MANAGER HERE AT THE GRAND-DUCHÉ.
I-- BUT...

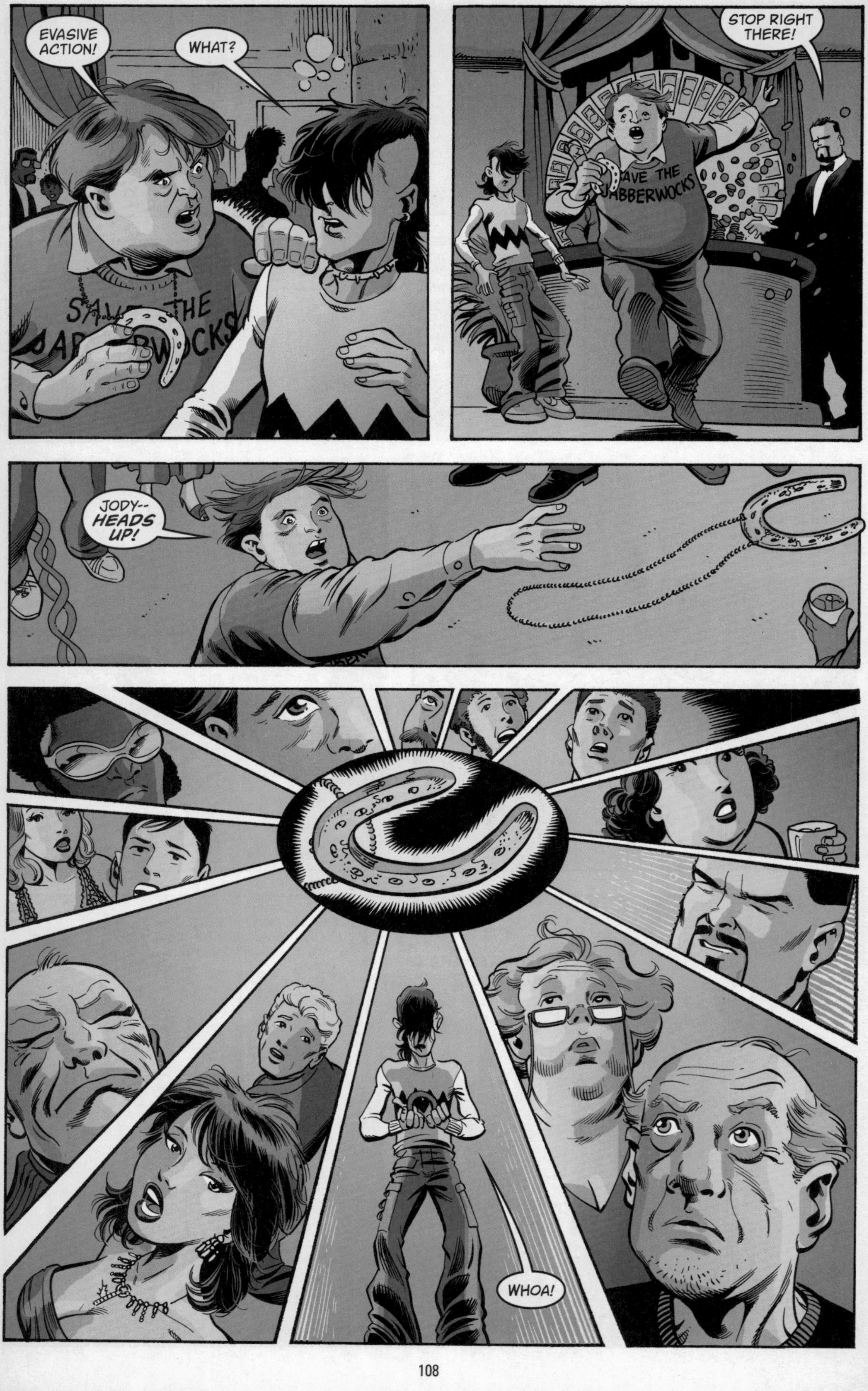
EVASIVE ACTION!
WHAT?
SAVE THE JABBERWOCKS
STOP RIGHT THERE!
SAVE THE JABBERWOCKS
JODY-- HEADS UP!
WHOA!

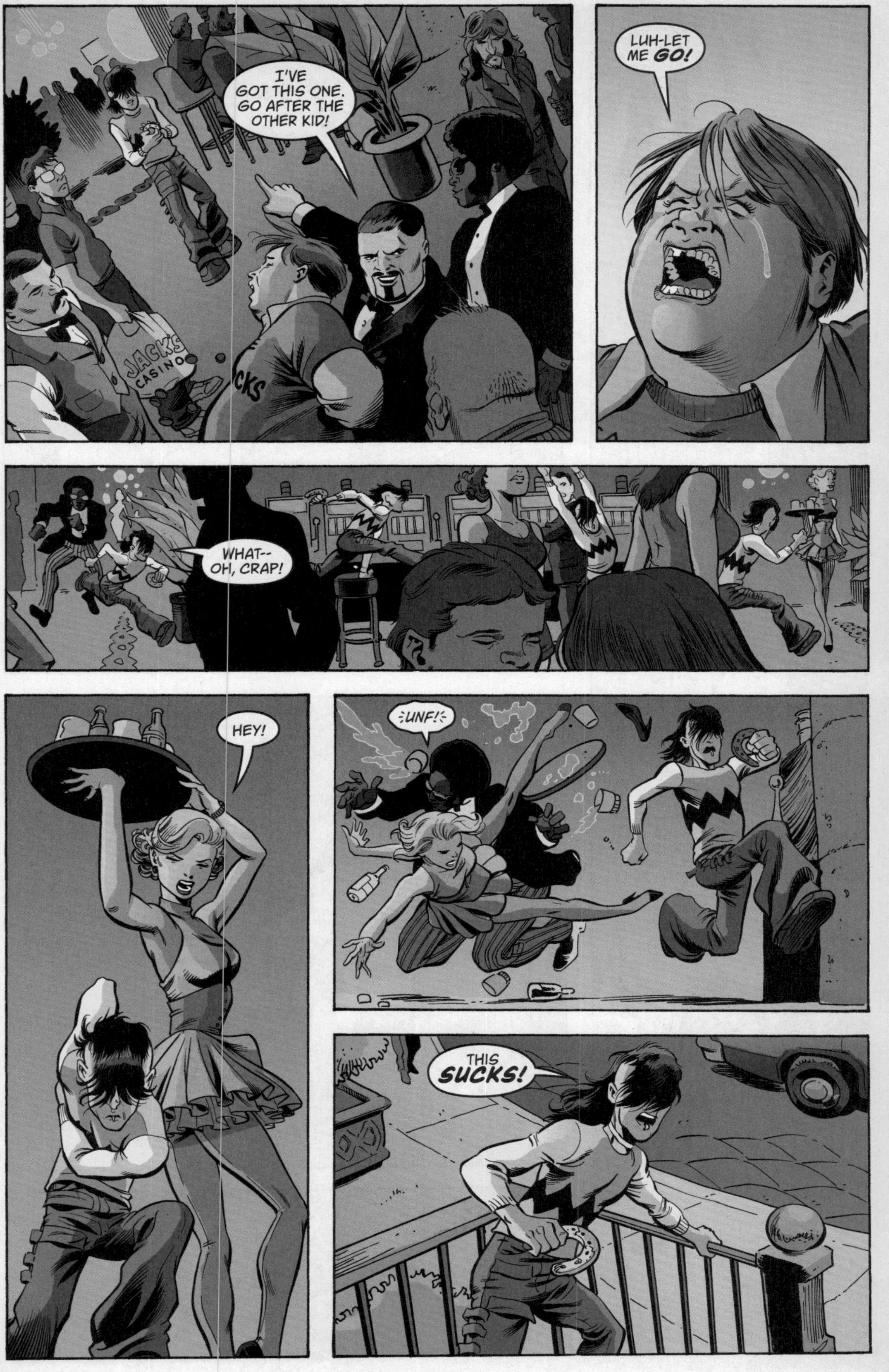

I'VE GOT THIS ONE. GO AFTER THE OTHER KID!
JACKS CASINO
LUH-LET ME **GO!**
WHAT-- OH, CRAP!
HEY!
UNF!
THIS **SUCKS!**

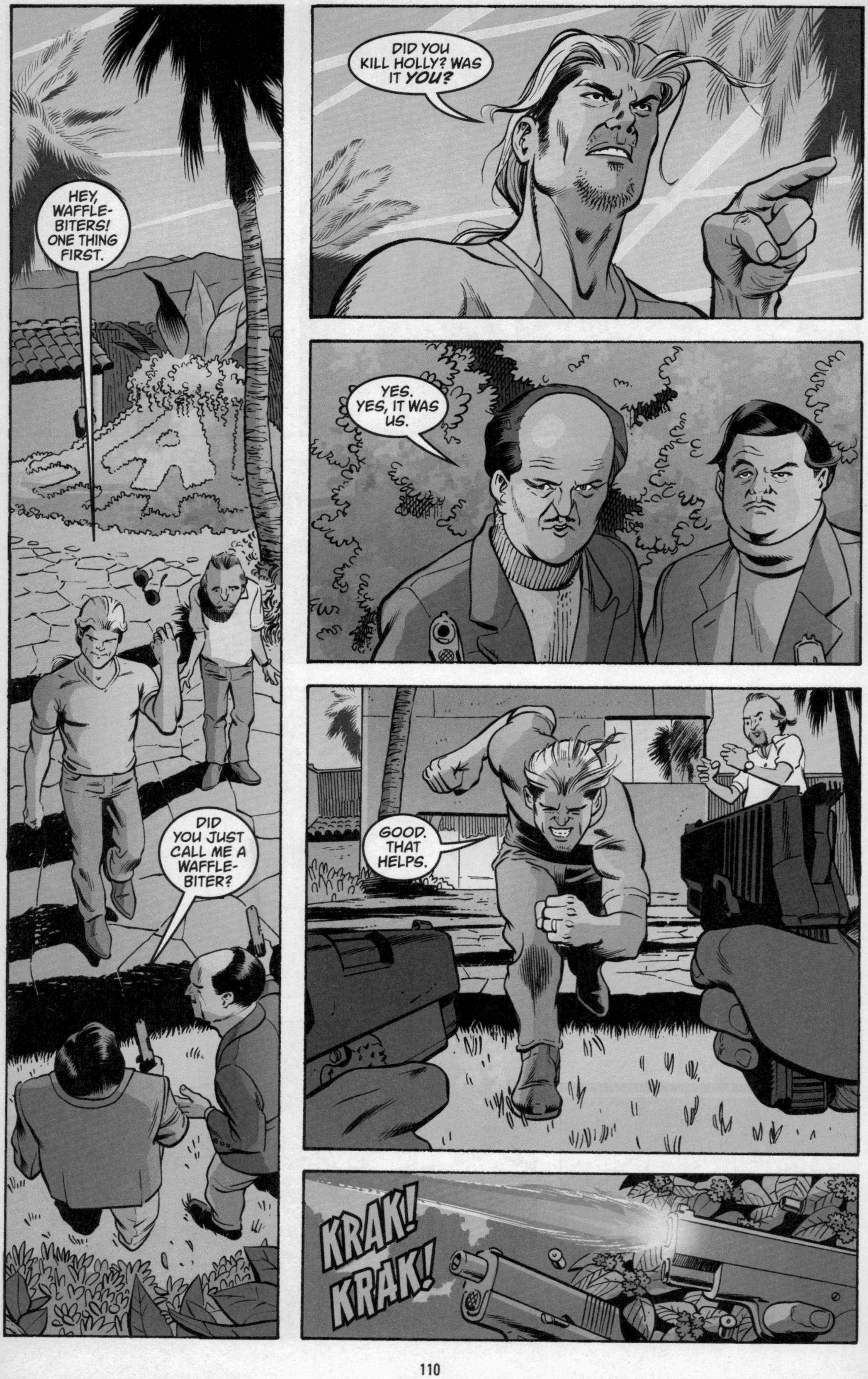
HEY, WAFFLE-BITERS! ONE THING FIRST.
DID YOU JUST CALL ME A WAFFLE-BITER?
DID YOU KILL HOLLY? WAS IT *YOU?*
YES. YES, IT WAS US.
GOOD. THAT HELPS.
KRAK! KRAK!

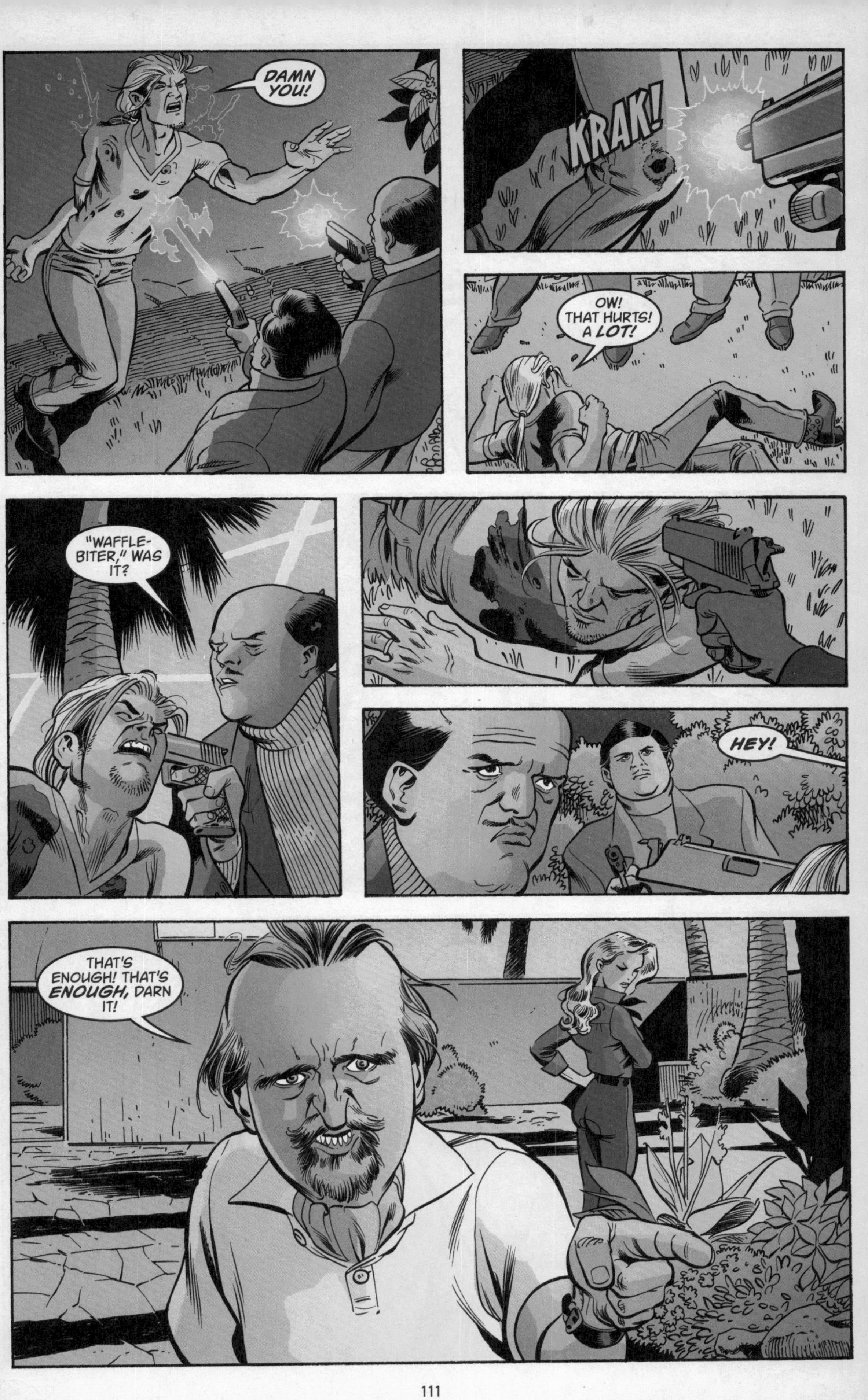
DAMN YOU!
KRAK!
OW! THAT HURTS! A *LOT*!
"WAFFLE-BITER," WAS IT?
HEY!
THAT'S ENOUGH! THAT'S *ENOUGH*, DARN IT!

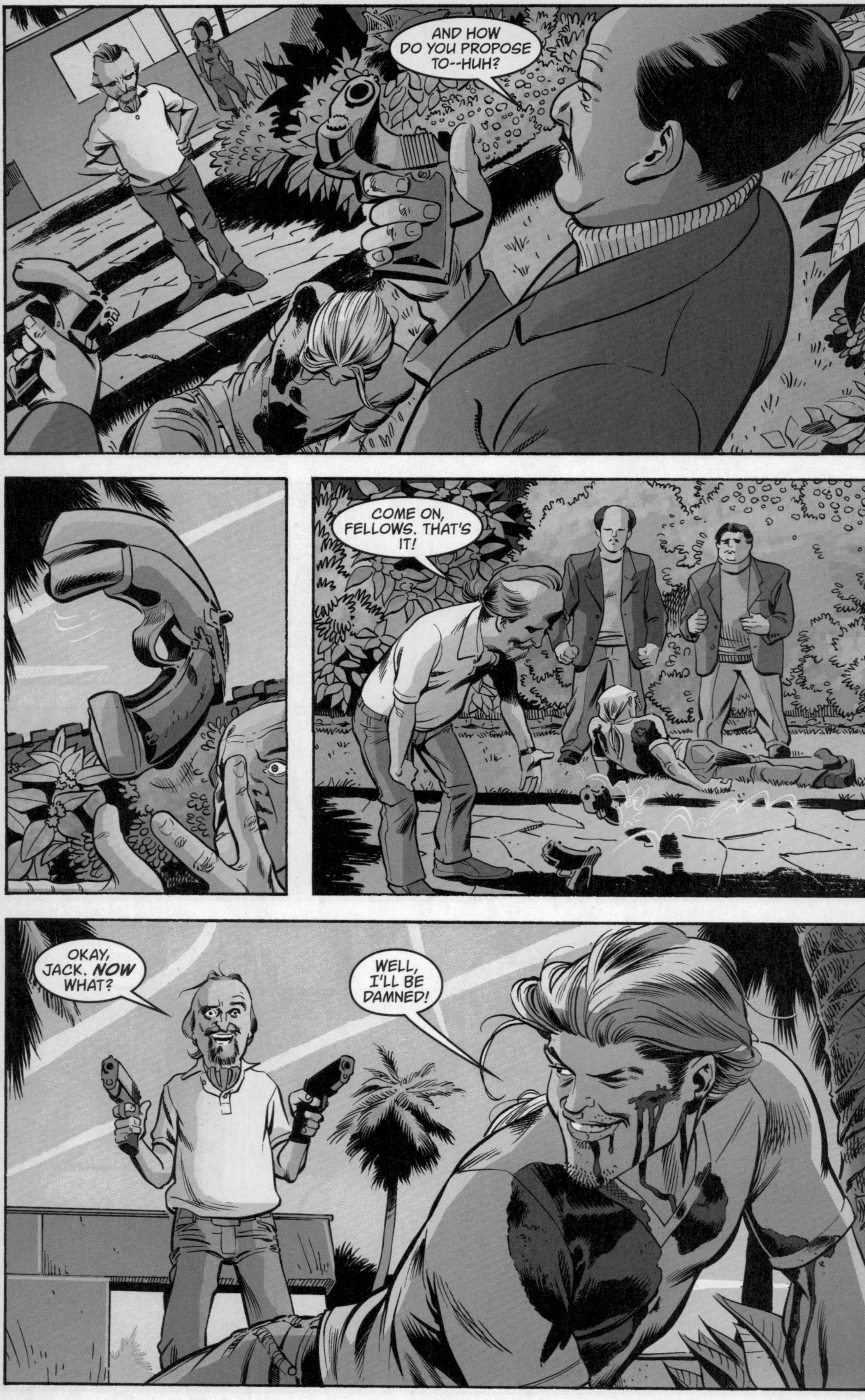
AND HOW DO YOU PROPOSE TO--HUH?
COME ON, FELLOWS. THAT'S IT!
OKAY, JACK. **NOW** WHAT?
WELL, I'LL BE DAMNED!

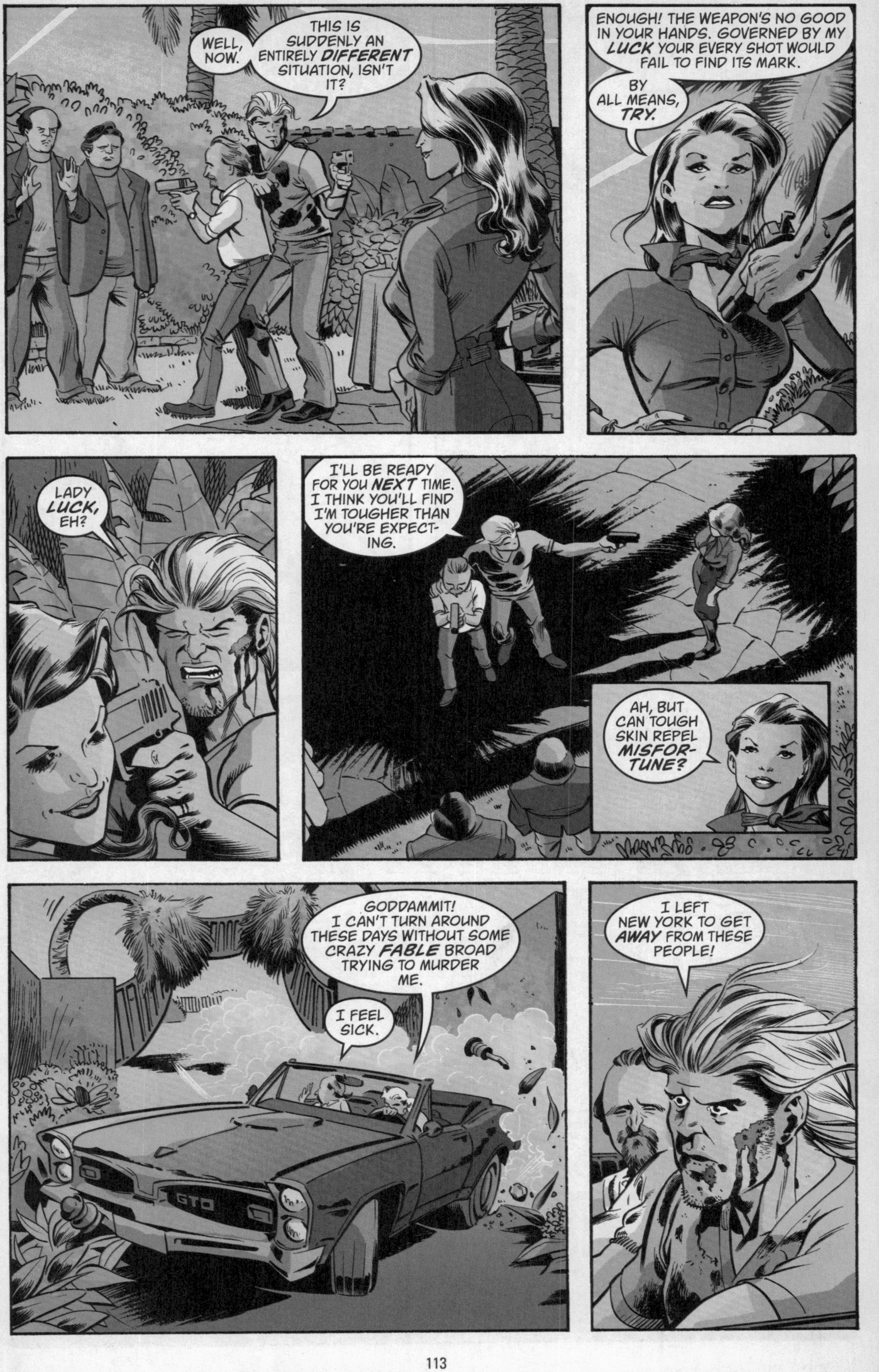
WELL, NOW.
THIS IS SUDDENLY AN ENTIRELY DIFFERENT SITUATION, ISN'T IT?
ENOUGH! THE WEAPON'S NO GOOD IN YOUR HANDS. GOVERNED BY MY LUCK YOUR EVERY SHOT WOULD FAIL TO FIND ITS MARK.
BY ALL MEANS, TRY.
LADY LUCK, EH?
I'LL BE READY FOR YOU NEXT TIME. I THINK YOU'LL FIND I'M TOUGHER THAN YOU'RE EXPECTING.
AH, BUT CAN TOUGH SKIN REPEL MISFORTUNE?
GODDAMMIT! I CAN'T TURN AROUND THESE DAYS WITHOUT SOME CRAZY FABLE BROAD TRYING TO MURDER ME.
I FEEL SICK.
GTO
I LEFT NEW YORK TO GET AWAY FROM THESE PEOPLE!

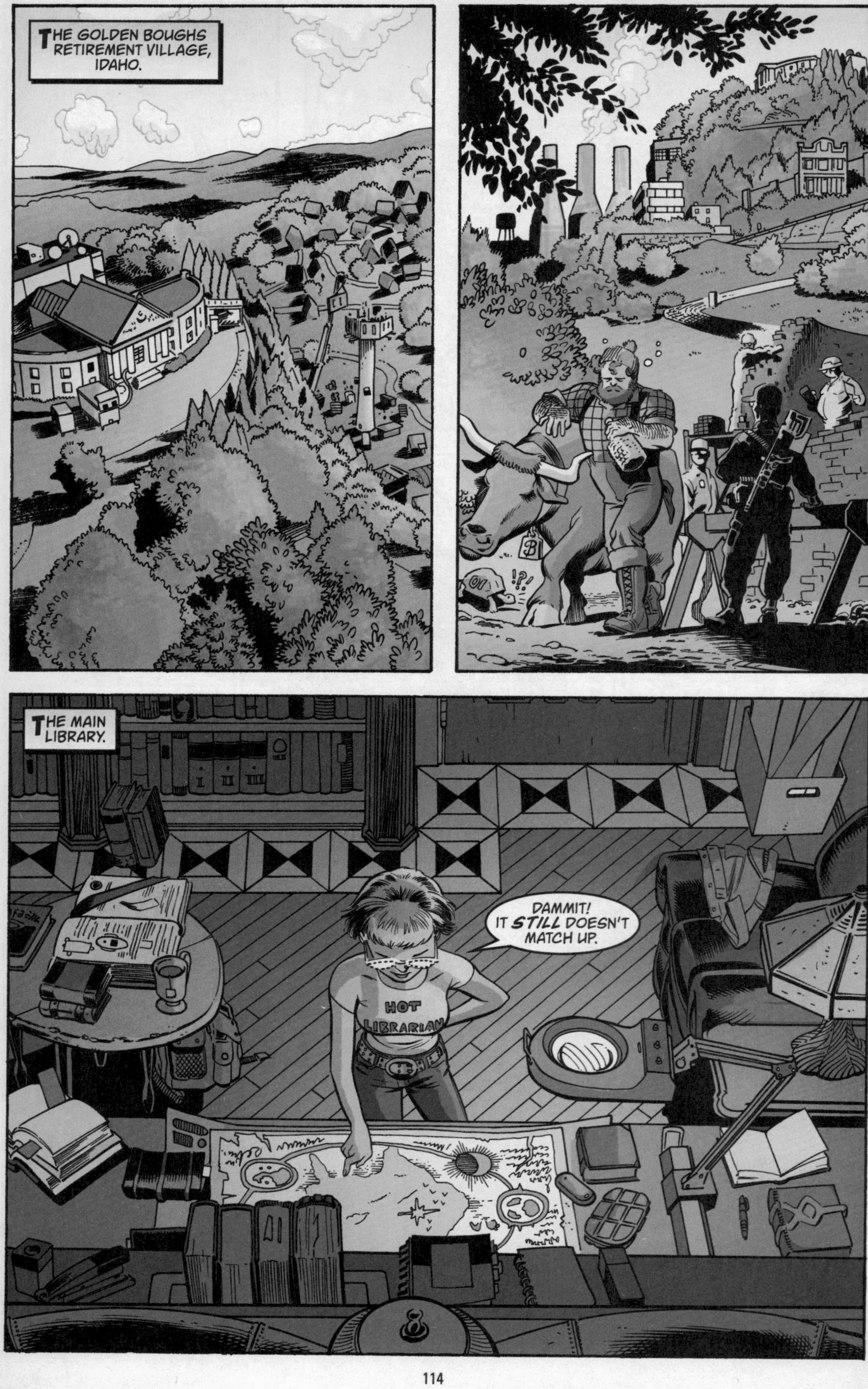
THE GOLDEN BOUGHS RETIREMENT VILLAGE, IDAHO.
!?!
THE MAIN LIBRARY.
DAMMIT! IT STILL DOESN'T MATCH UP.
HOT LIBRARIAN

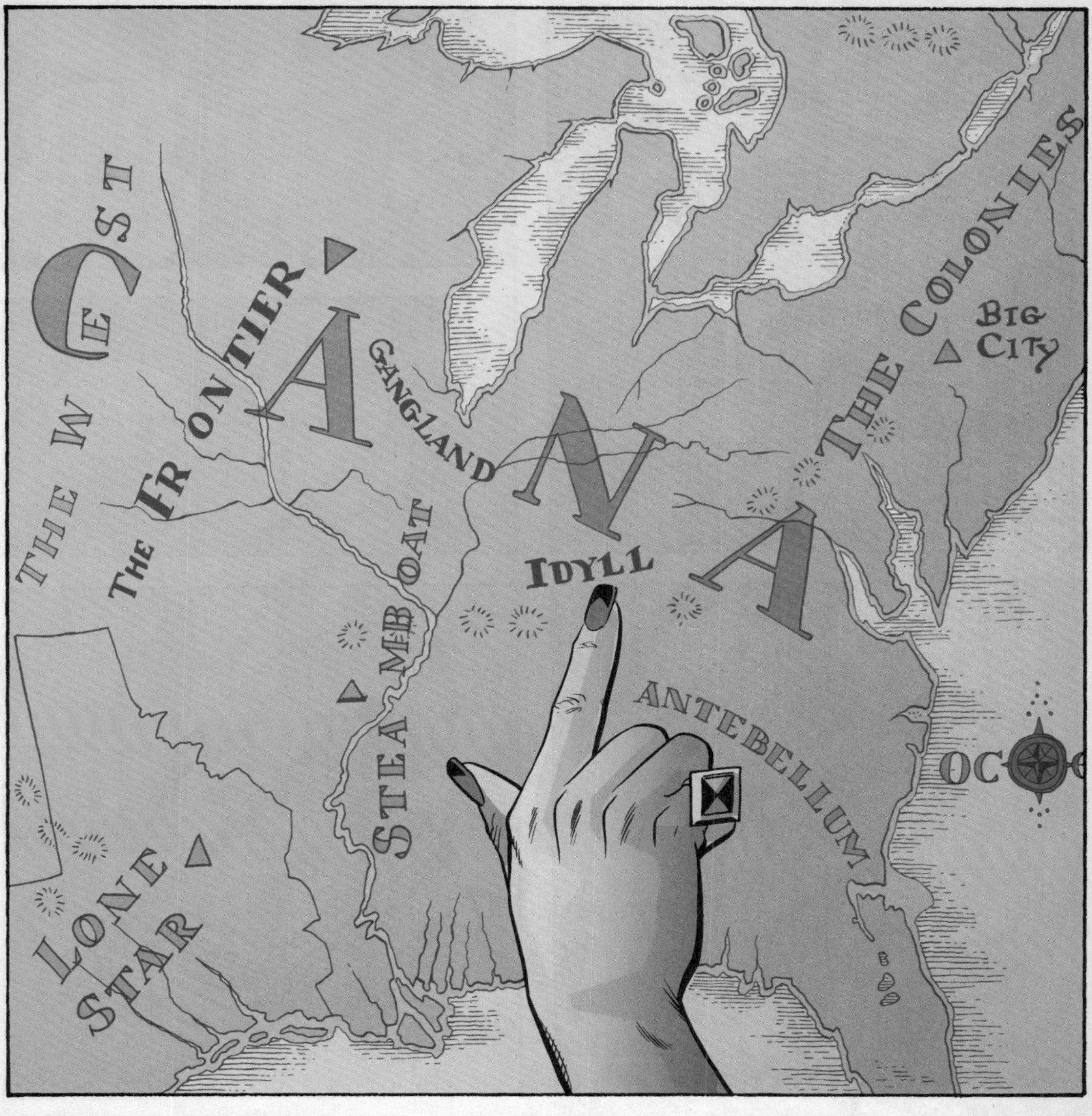
THE WEST
THE FRONTIER
GANGLAND
THE COLONIES
BIG CITY
STEAMBOAT
IDYLL
ANTEBELLUM
LONE STAR

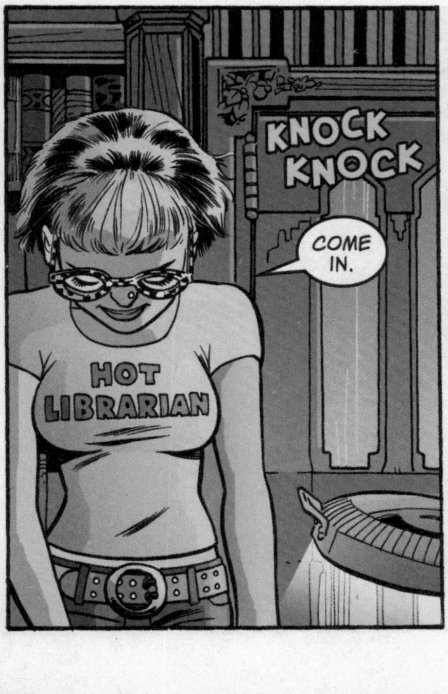
KNOCK KNOCK
COME IN.
HOT LIBRARIAN

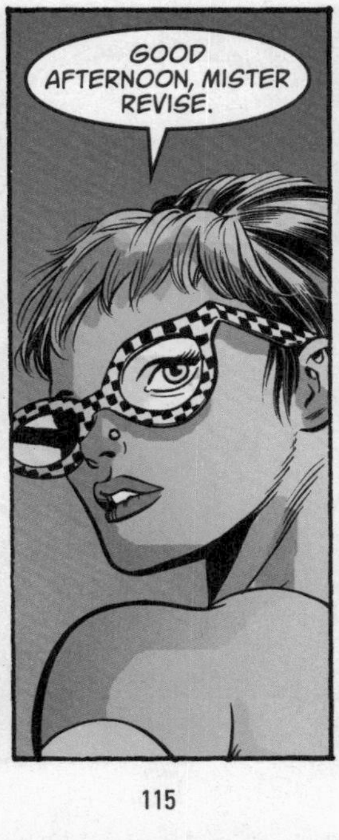
GOOD AFTERNOON, MISTER REVISE.

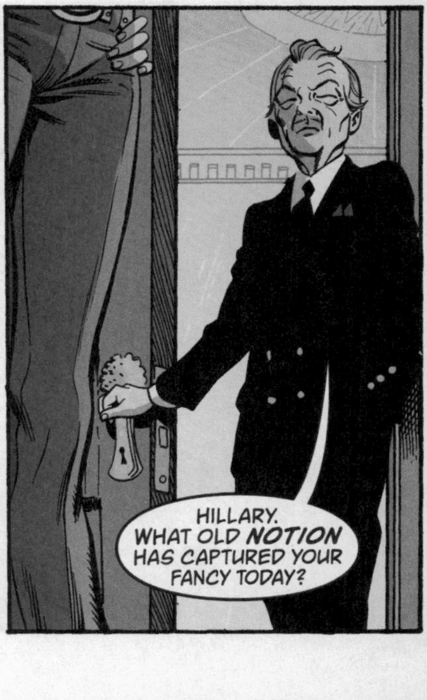
HILLARY. WHAT OLD *NOTION* HAS CAPTURED YOUR FANCY TODAY?

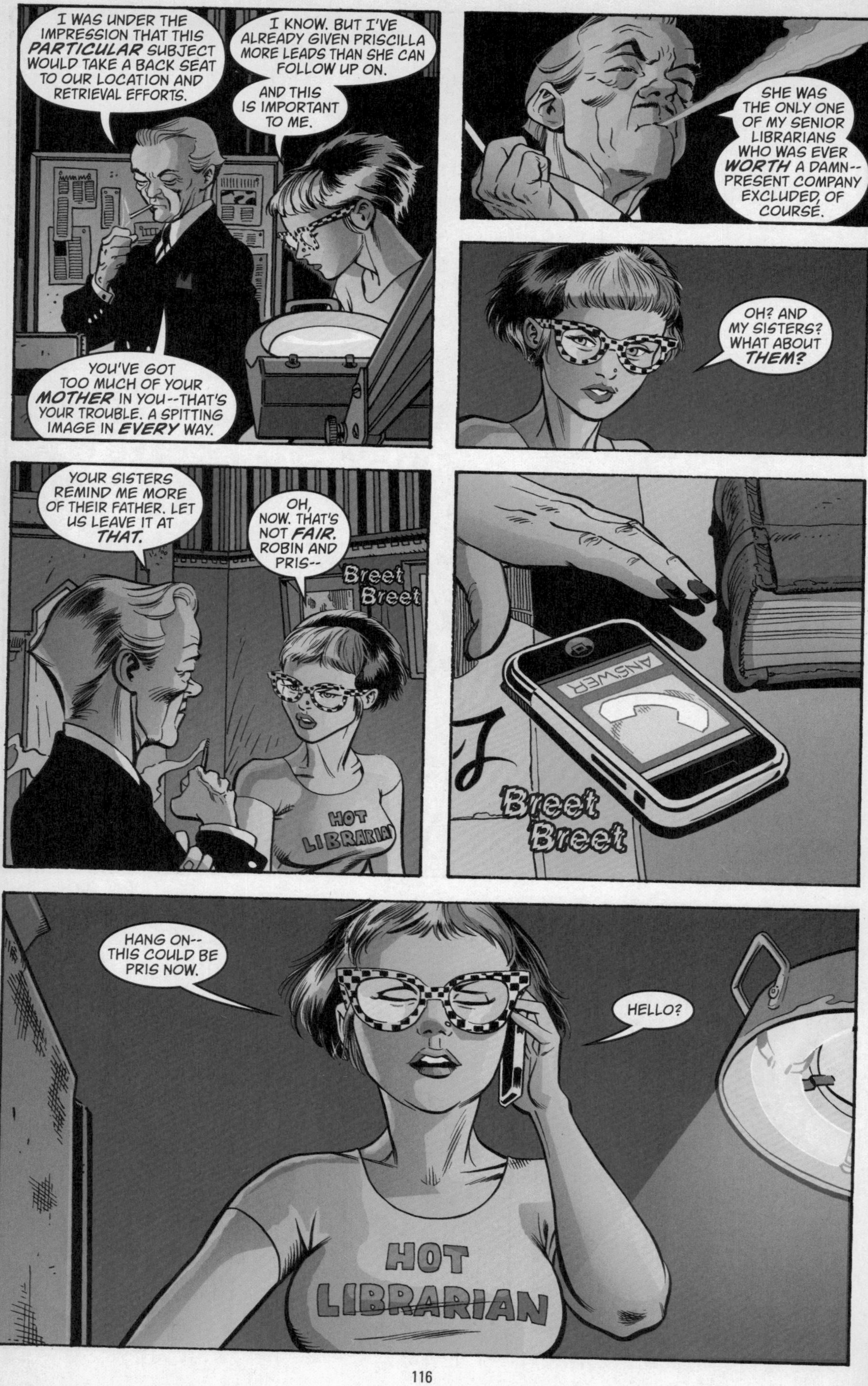
I WAS UNDER THE IMPRESSION THAT THIS PARTICULAR SUBJECT WOULD TAKE A BACK SEAT TO OUR LOCATION AND RETRIEVAL EFFORTS.
I KNOW. BUT I'VE ALREADY GIVEN PRISCILLA MORE LEADS THAN SHE CAN FOLLOW UP ON.
AND THIS IS IMPORTANT TO ME.
YOU'VE GOT TOO MUCH OF YOUR MOTHER IN YOU--THAT'S YOUR TROUBLE. A SPITTING IMAGE IN EVERY WAY.
SHE WAS THE ONLY ONE OF MY SENIOR LIBRARIANS WHO WAS EVER WORTH A DAMN--PRESENT COMPANY EXCLUDED, OF COURSE.
OH? AND MY SISTERS? WHAT ABOUT THEM?
YOUR SISTERS REMIND ME MORE OF THEIR FATHER. LET US LEAVE IT AT THAT.
OH, NOW. THAT'S NOT FAIR. ROBIN AND PRIS--
Breet Breet
HOT LIBRARIAN
ANSWER
Breet Breet
HANG ON--THIS COULD BE PRIS NOW.
HELLO?
HOT LIBRARIAN

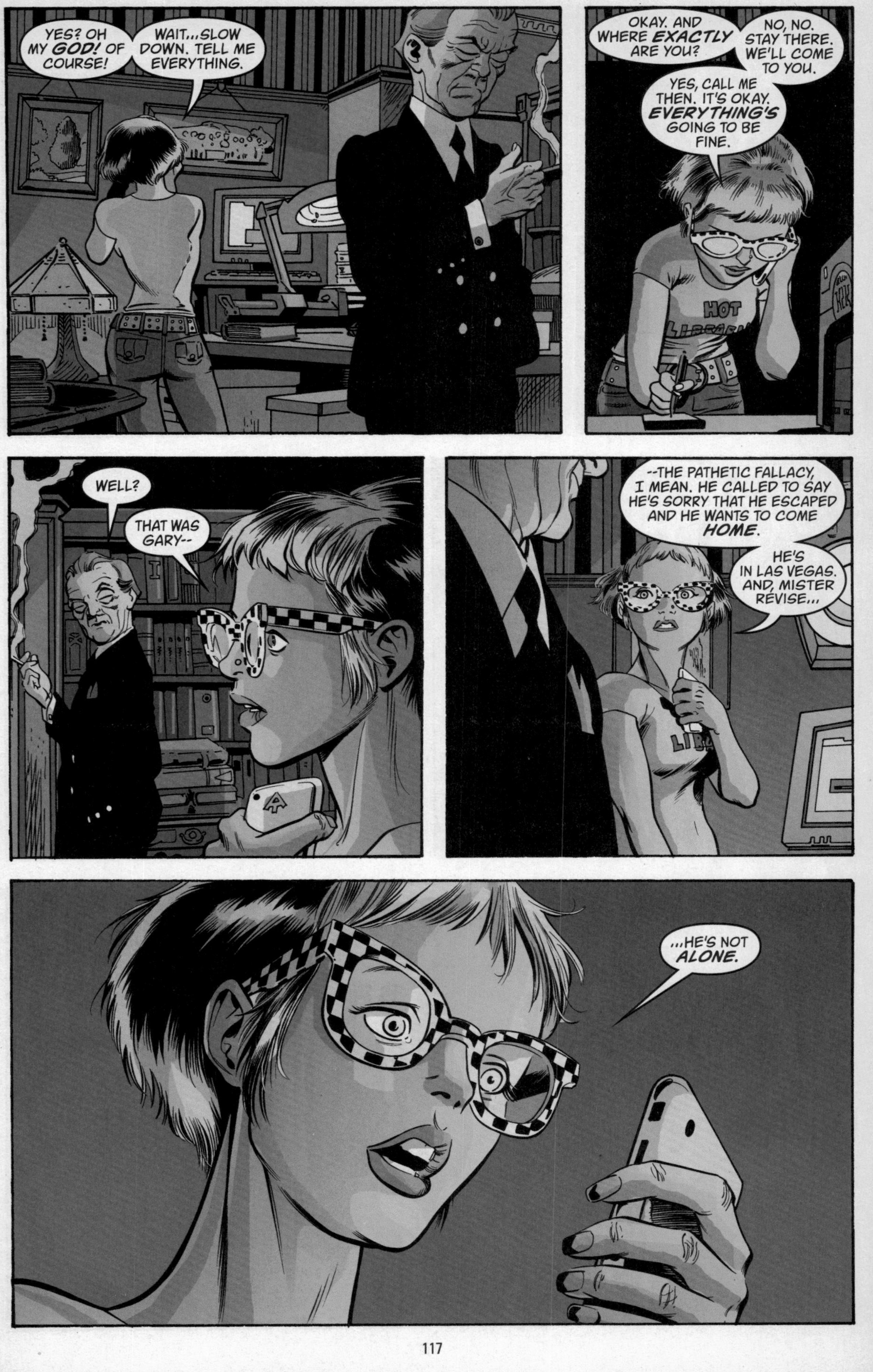
YES? OH MY GOD! OF COURSE!
WAIT...SLOW DOWN. TELL ME EVERYTHING.
OKAY. AND WHERE EXACTLY ARE YOU?
NO, NO. STAY THERE. WE'LL COME TO YOU.
YES, CALL ME THEN. IT'S OKAY. EVERYTHING'S GOING TO BE FINE.
HOT
WELL?
THAT WAS GARY--
--THE PATHETIC FALLACY, I MEAN. HE CALLED TO SAY HE'S SORRY THAT HE ESCAPED AND HE WANTS TO COME HOME.
HE'S IN LAS VEGAS. AND, MISTER REVISE...
...HE'S NOT ALONE.

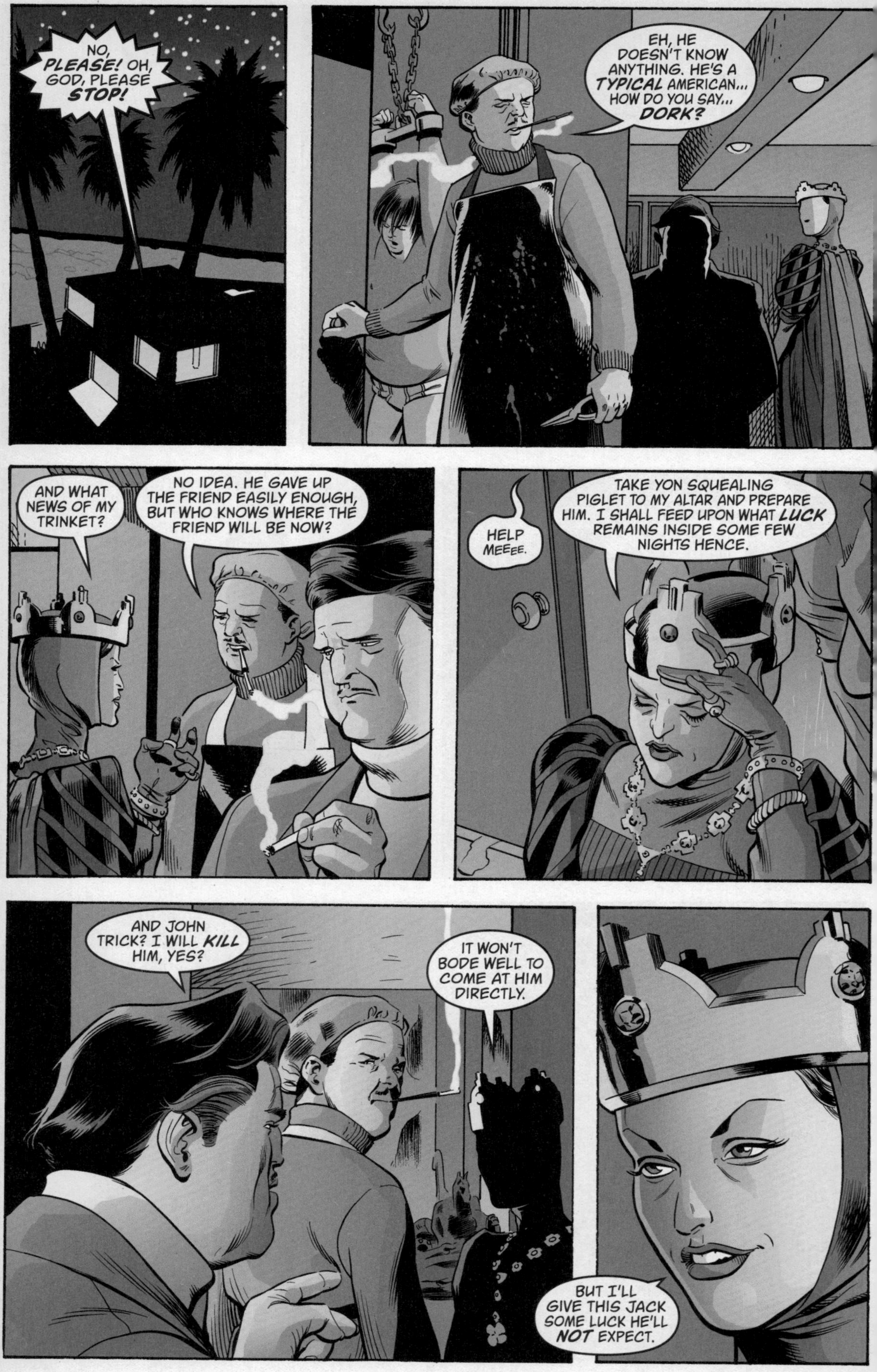
NO, PLEASE! OH, GOD, PLEASE STOP!
EH, HE DOESN'T KNOW ANYTHING. HE'S A TYPICAL AMERICAN... HOW DO YOU SAY... DORK?
AND WHAT NEWS OF MY TRINKET?
NO IDEA. HE GAVE UP THE FRIEND EASILY ENOUGH, BUT WHO KNOWS WHERE THE FRIEND WILL BE NOW?
HELP MEEEE.
TAKE YON SQUEALING PIGLET TO MY ALTAR AND PREPARE HIM. I SHALL FEED UPON WHAT LUCK REMAINS INSIDE SOME FEW NIGHTS HENCE.
AND JOHN TRICK? I WILL KILL HIM, YES?
IT WON'T BODE WELL TO COME AT HIM DIRECTLY.
BUT I'LL GIVE THIS JACK SOME LUCK HE'LL NOT EXPECT.

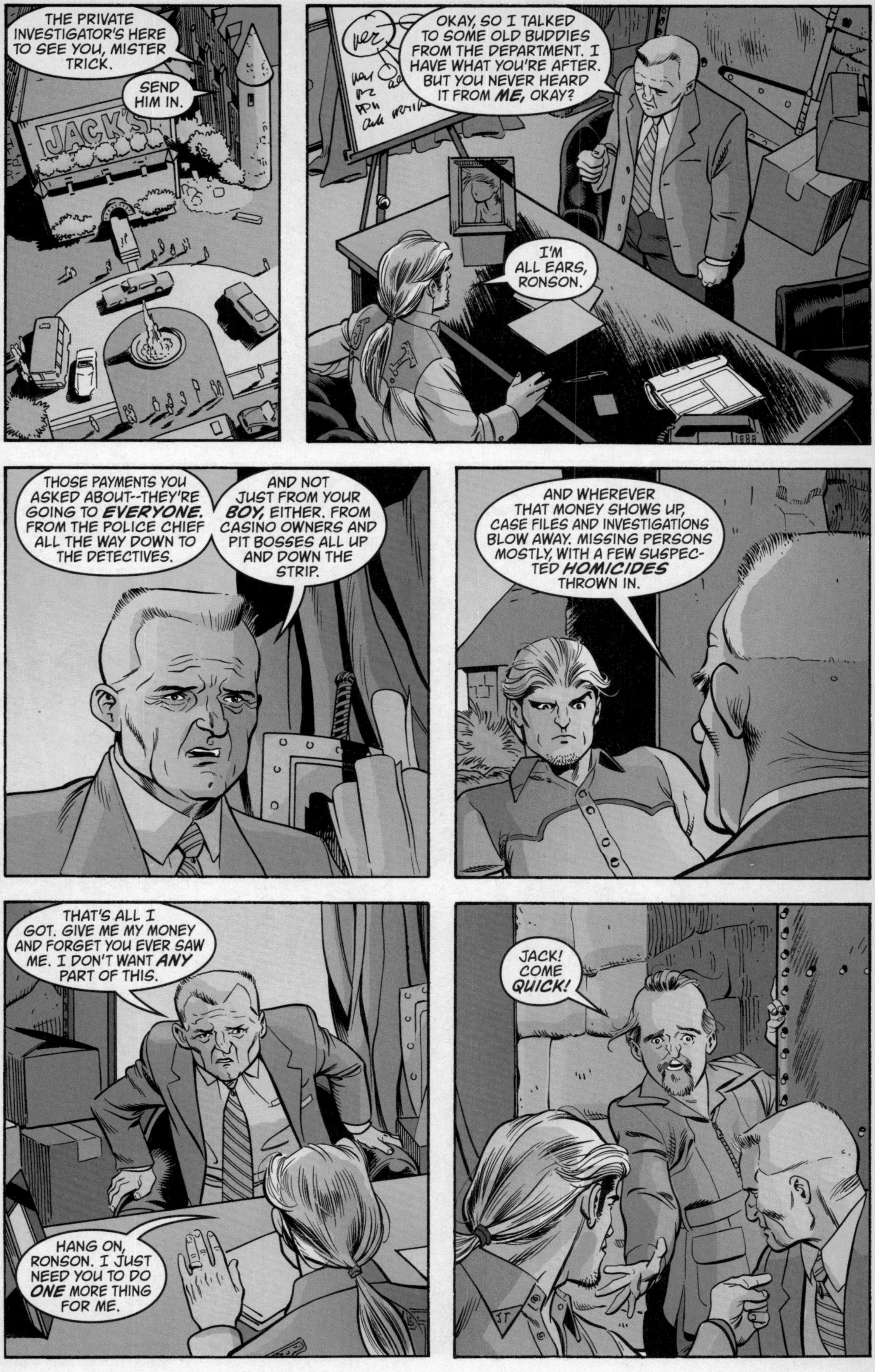
THE PRIVATE INVESTIGATOR'S HERE TO SEE YOU, MISTER TRICK.
SEND HIM IN.
JACK'S
OKAY, SO I TALKED TO SOME OLD BUDDIES FROM THE DEPARTMENT. I HAVE WHAT YOU'RE AFTER. BUT YOU NEVER HEARD IT FROM ME, OKAY?
I'M ALL EARS, RONSON.
THOSE PAYMENTS YOU ASKED ABOUT--THEY'RE GOING TO EVERYONE. FROM THE POLICE CHIEF ALL THE WAY DOWN TO THE DETECTIVES.
AND NOT JUST FROM YOUR BOY, EITHER. FROM CASINO OWNERS AND PIT BOSSES ALL UP AND DOWN THE STRIP.
AND WHEREVER THAT MONEY SHOWS UP, CASE FILES AND INVESTIGATIONS BLOW AWAY. MISSING PERSONS MOSTLY, WITH A FEW SUSPECTED HOMICIDES THROWN IN.
THAT'S ALL I GOT. GIVE ME MY MONEY AND FORGET YOU EVER SAW ME. I DON'T WANT ANY PART OF THIS.
HANG ON, RONSON. I JUST NEED YOU TO DO ONE MORE THING FOR ME.
JACK! COME QUICK!

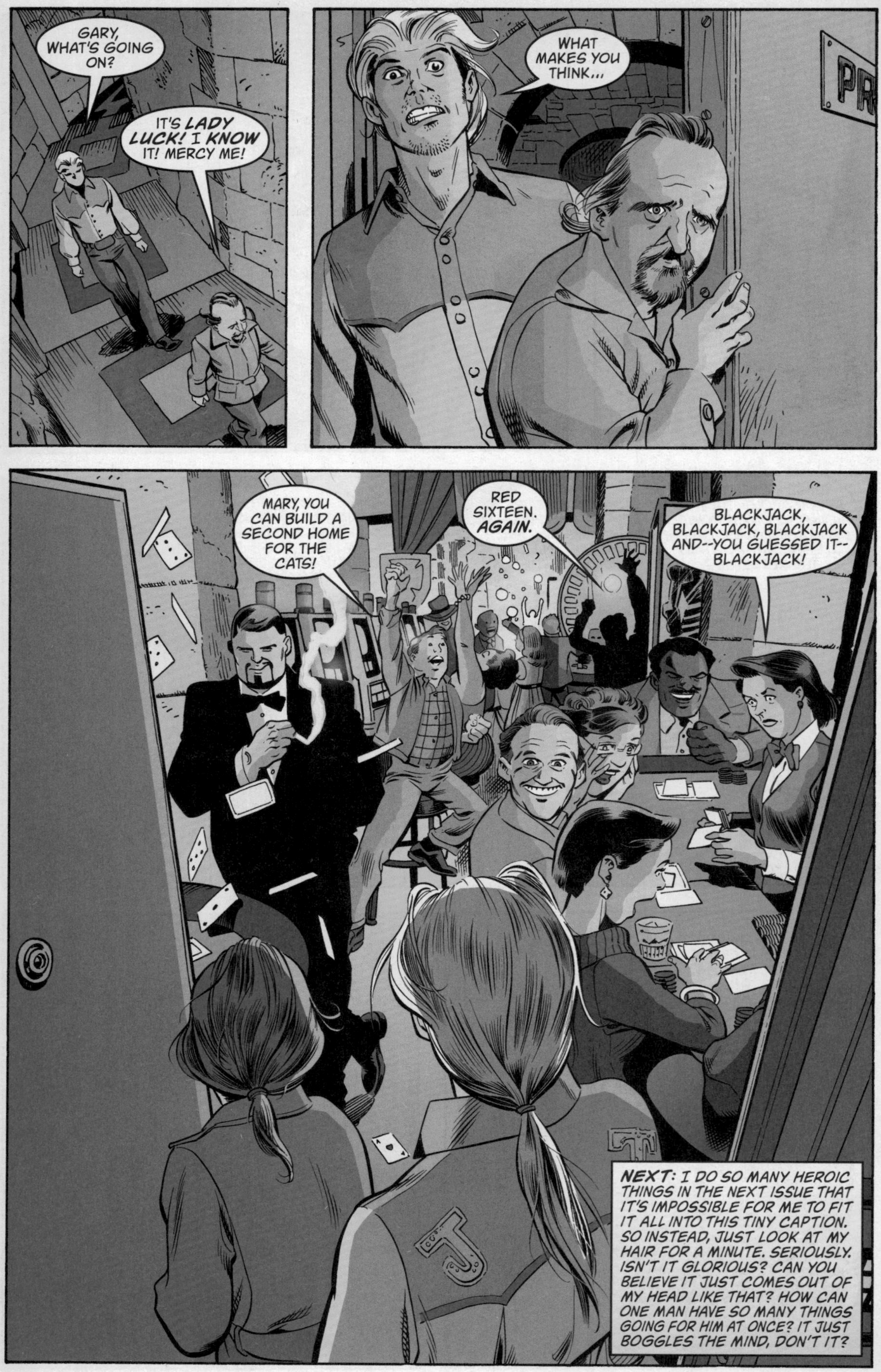
GARY, WHAT'S GOING ON?
IT'S LADY LUCK! I KNOW IT! MERCY ME!
WHAT MAKES YOU THINK...
MARY, YOU CAN BUILD A SECOND HOME FOR THE CATS!
RED SIXTEEN. AGAIN.
BLACKJACK, BLACKJACK, BLACKJACK AND--YOU GUESSED IT--BLACKJACK!
NEXT: I DO SO MANY HEROIC THINGS IN THE NEXT ISSUE THAT IT'S IMPOSSIBLE FOR ME TO FIT IT ALL INTO THIS TINY CAPTION. SO INSTEAD, JUST LOOK AT MY HAIR FOR A MINUTE. SERIOUSLY. ISN'T IT GLORIOUS? CAN YOU BELIEVE IT JUST COMES OUT OF MY HEAD LIKE THAT? HOW CAN ONE MAN HAVE SO MANY THINGS GOING FOR HIM AT ONCE? IT JUST BOGGLES THE MIND, DON'T IT?

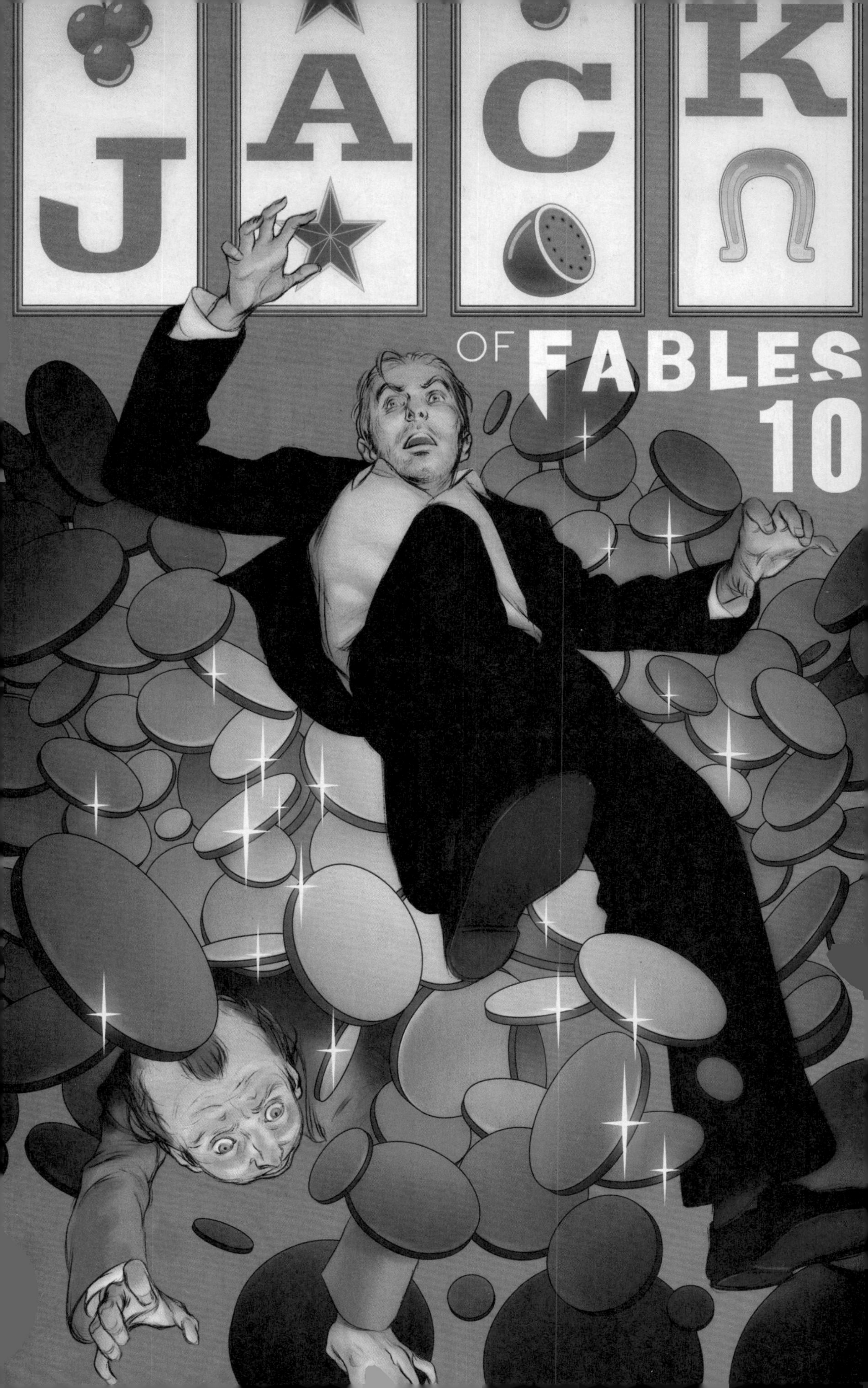

JACK
OF FABLES
10

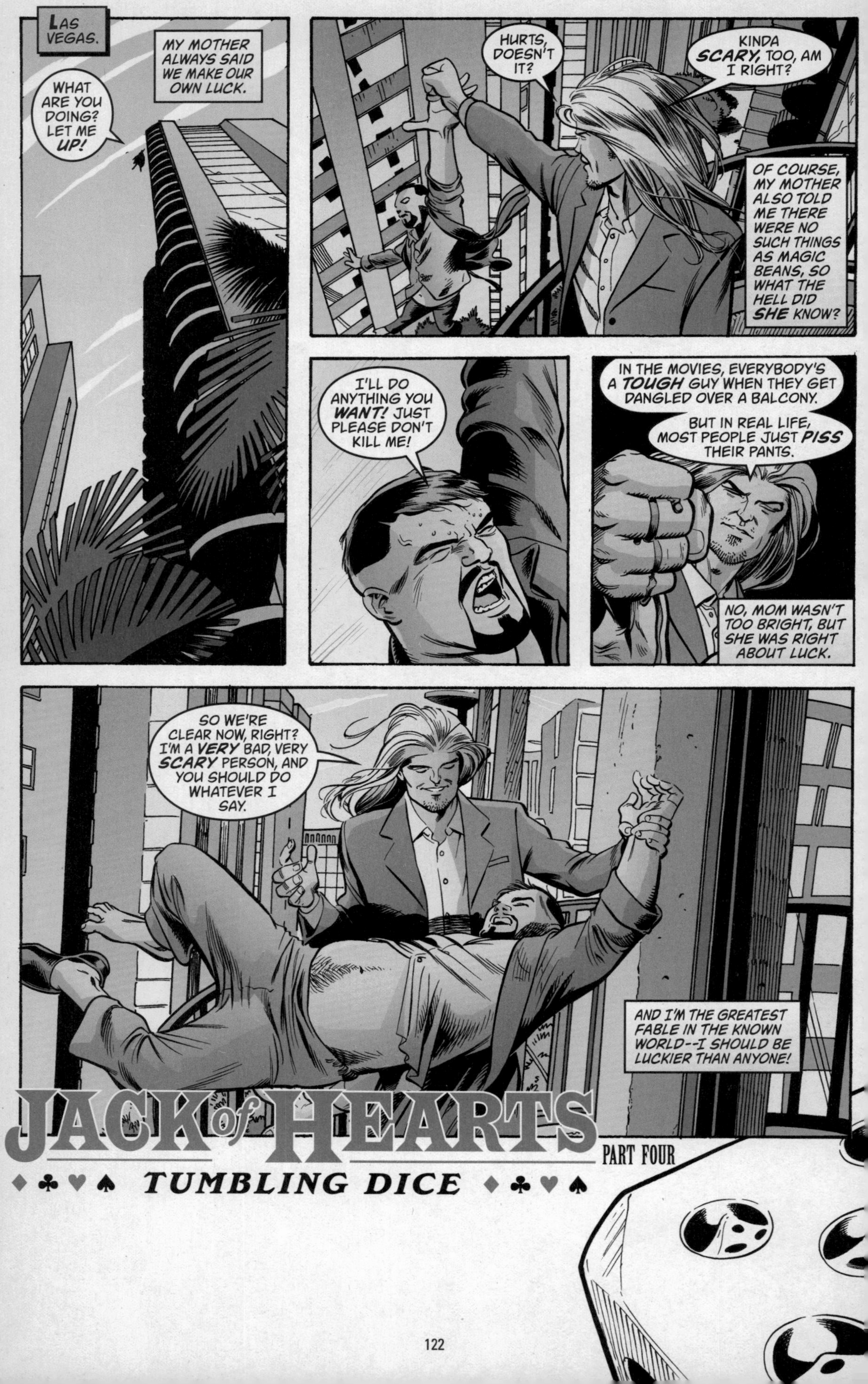
LAS VEGAS.
WHAT ARE YOU DOING? LET ME UP!
MY MOTHER ALWAYS SAID WE MAKE OUR OWN LUCK.
HURTS, DOESN'T IT?
KINDA SCARY, TOO, AM I RIGHT?
OF COURSE, MY MOTHER ALSO TOLD ME THERE WERE NO SUCH THINGS AS MAGIC BEANS, SO WHAT THE HELL DID SHE KNOW?
I'LL DO ANYTHING YOU WANT! JUST PLEASE DON'T KILL ME!
IN THE MOVIES, EVERYBODY'S A TOUGH GUY WHEN THEY GET DANGLED OVER A BALCONY.
BUT IN REAL LIFE, MOST PEOPLE JUST PISS THEIR PANTS.
NO, MOM WASN'T TOO BRIGHT, BUT SHE WAS RIGHT ABOUT LUCK.
SO WE'RE CLEAR NOW, RIGHT? I'M A VERY BAD, VERY SCARY PERSON, AND YOU SHOULD DO WHATEVER I SAY.
AND I'M THE GREATEST FABLE IN THE KNOWN WORLD--I SHOULD BE LUCKIER THAN ANYONE!
JACK of HEARTS
PART FOUR
TUMBLING DICE

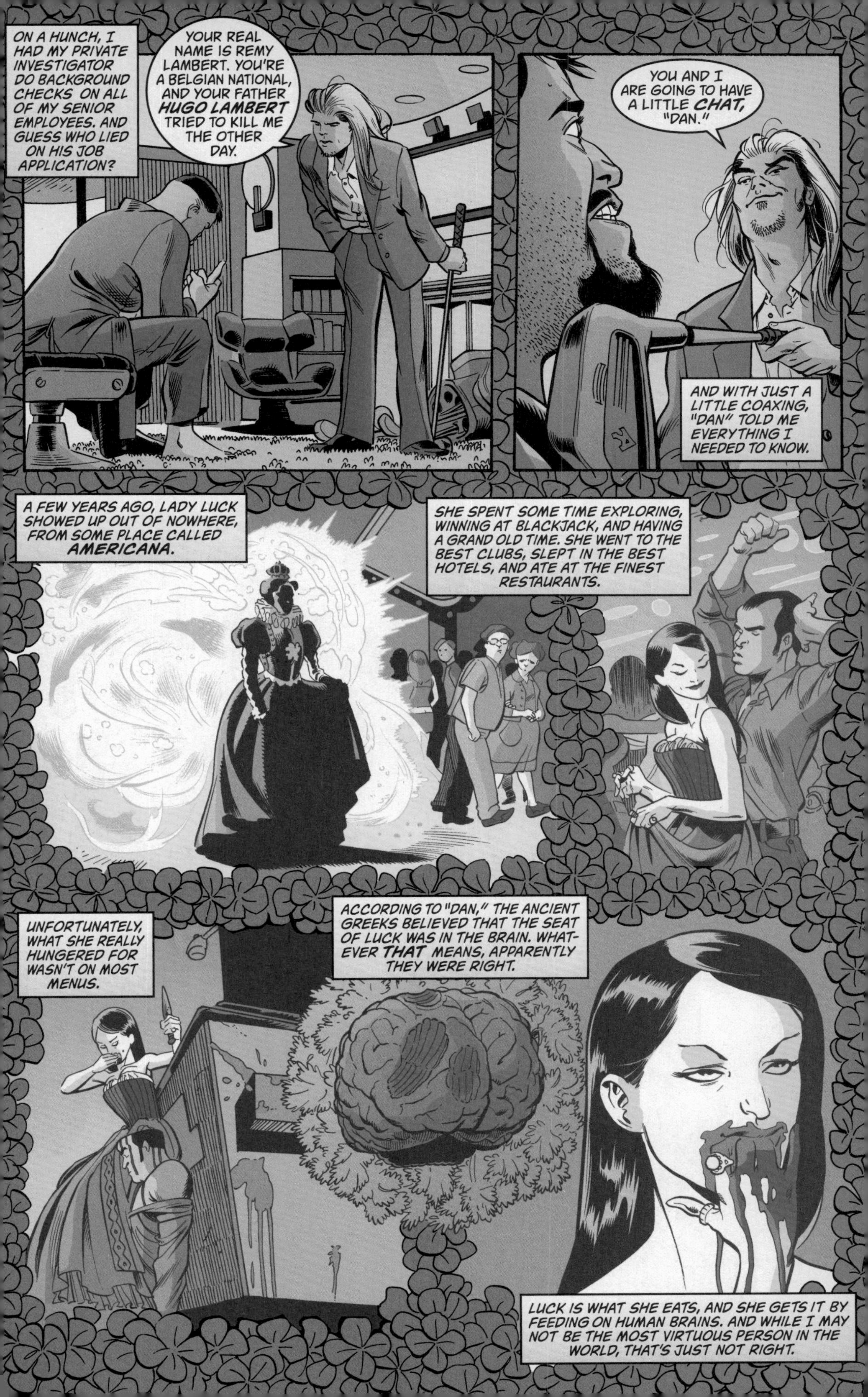

ON A HUNCH, I HAD MY PRIVATE INVESTIGATOR DO BACKGROUND CHECKS ON ALL OF MY SENIOR EMPLOYEES. AND GUESS WHO LIED ON HIS JOB APPLICATION?
YOUR REAL NAME IS REMY LAMBERT. YOU'RE A BELGIAN NATIONAL, AND YOUR FATHER HUGO LAMBERT TRIED TO KILL ME THE OTHER DAY.
YOU AND I ARE GOING TO HAVE A LITTLE CHAT, "DAN."
AND WITH JUST A LITTLE COAXING, "DAN" TOLD ME EVERYTHING I NEEDED TO KNOW.
A FEW YEARS AGO, LADY LUCK SHOWED UP OUT OF NOWHERE, FROM SOME PLACE CALLED AMERICANA.
SHE SPENT SOME TIME EXPLORING, WINNING AT BLACKJACK, AND HAVING A GRAND OLD TIME. SHE WENT TO THE BEST CLUBS, SLEPT IN THE BEST HOTELS, AND ATE AT THE FINEST RESTAURANTS.
UNFORTUNATELY, WHAT SHE REALLY HUNGERED FOR WASN'T ON MOST MENUS.
ACCORDING TO "DAN," THE ANCIENT GREEKS BELIEVED THAT THE SEAT OF LUCK WAS IN THE BRAIN. WHATEVER THAT MEANS, APPARENTLY THEY WERE RIGHT.
LUCK IS WHAT SHE EATS, AND SHE GETS IT BY FEEDING ON HUMAN BRAINS. AND WHILE I MAY NOT BE THE MOST VIRTUOUS PERSON IN THE WORLD, THAT'S JUST NOT RIGHT.

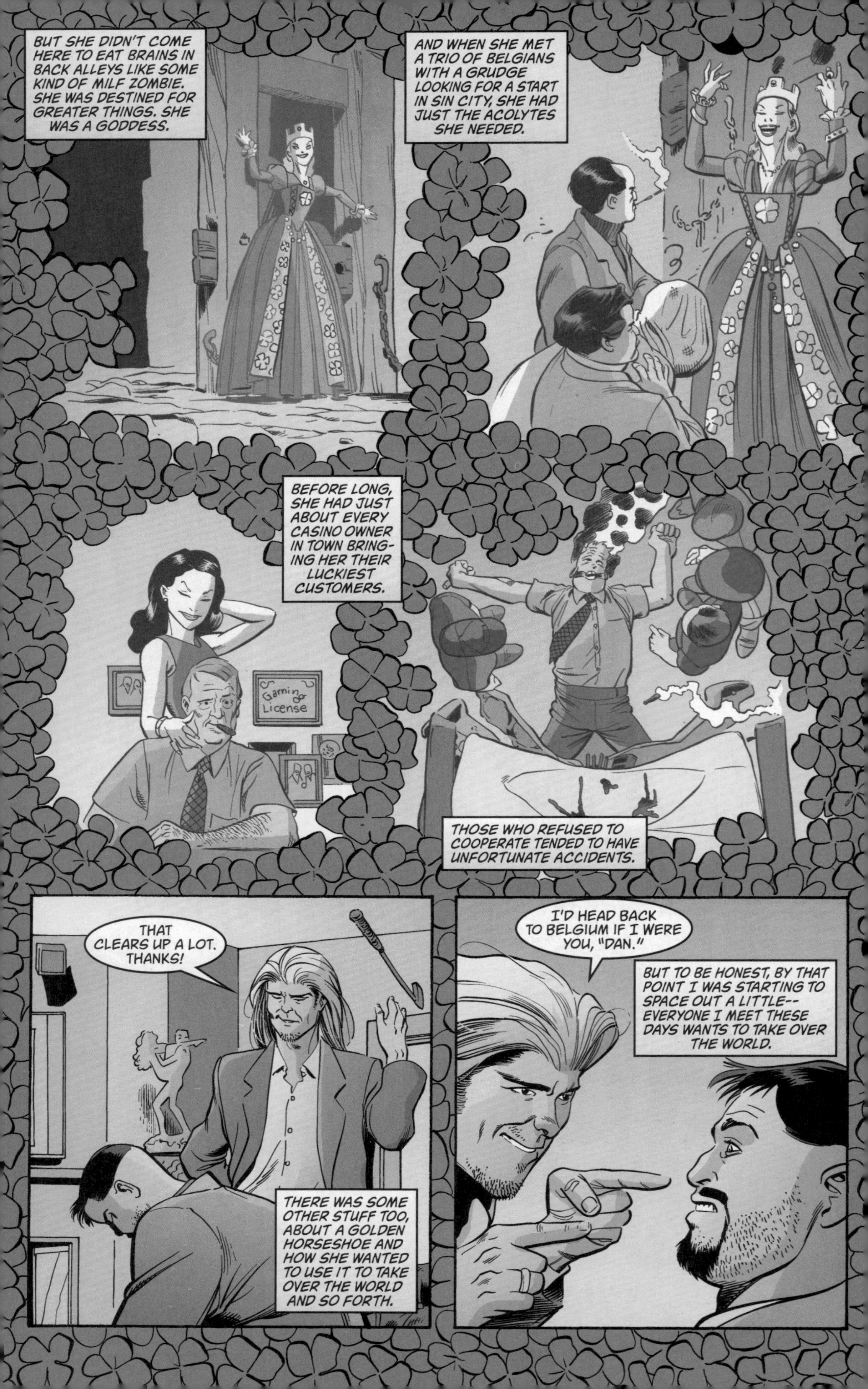
BUT SHE DIDN'T COME HERE TO EAT BRAINS IN BACK ALLEYS LIKE SOME KIND OF MILF ZOMBIE. SHE WAS DESTINED FOR GREATER THINGS. SHE WAS A GODDESS.
AND WHEN SHE MET A TRIO OF BELGIANS WITH A GRUDGE LOOKING FOR A START IN SIN CITY, SHE HAD JUST THE ACOLYTES SHE NEEDED.
BEFORE LONG, SHE HAD JUST ABOUT EVERY CASINO OWNER IN TOWN BRINGING HER THEIR LUCKIEST CUSTOMERS.
Gaming License
THOSE WHO REFUSED TO COOPERATE TENDED TO HAVE UNFORTUNATE ACCIDENTS.
THAT CLEARS UP A LOT. THANKS!
THERE WAS SOME OTHER STUFF TOO, ABOUT A GOLDEN HORSESHOE AND HOW SHE WANTED TO USE IT TO TAKE OVER THE WORLD AND SO FORTH.
I'D HEAD BACK TO BELGIUM IF I WERE YOU, "DAN."
BUT TO BE HONEST, BY THAT POINT I WAS STARTING TO SPACE OUT A LITTLE--EVERYONE I MEET THESE DAYS WANTS TO TAKE OVER THE WORLD.

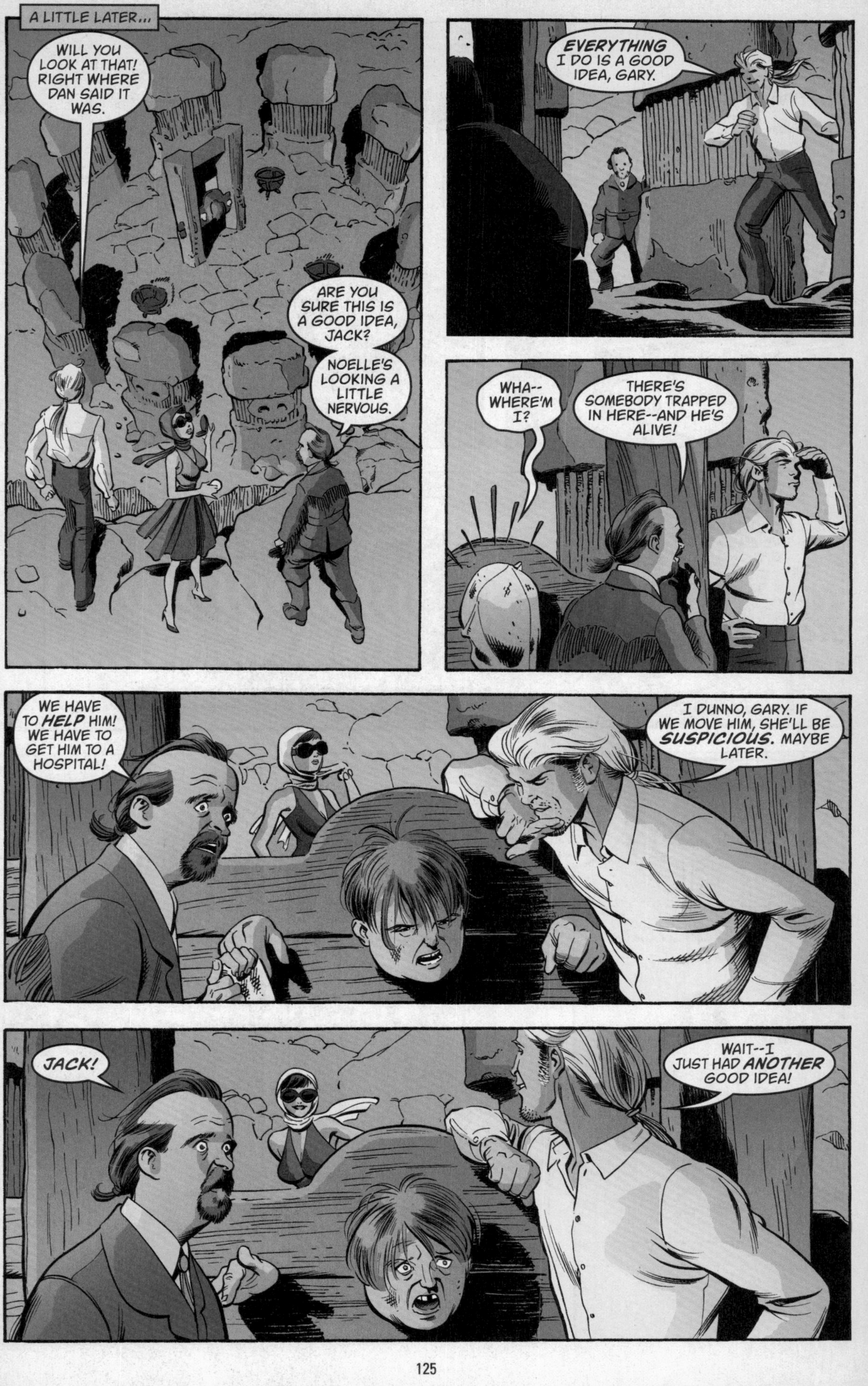

A LITTLE LATER...
WILL YOU LOOK AT THAT! RIGHT WHERE DAN SAID IT WAS.
ARE YOU SURE THIS IS A GOOD IDEA, JACK?
NOELLE'S LOOKING A LITTLE NERVOUS.
EVERYTHING I DO IS A GOOD IDEA, GARY.
WHA-- WHERE'M I?
THERE'S SOMEBODY TRAPPED IN HERE--AND HE'S ALIVE!
WE HAVE TO HELP HIM! WE HAVE TO GET HIM TO A HOSPITAL!
I DUNNO, GARY. IF WE MOVE HIM, SHE'LL BE SUSPICIOUS. MAYBE LATER.
JACK!
WAIT--I JUST HAD ANOTHER GOOD IDEA!

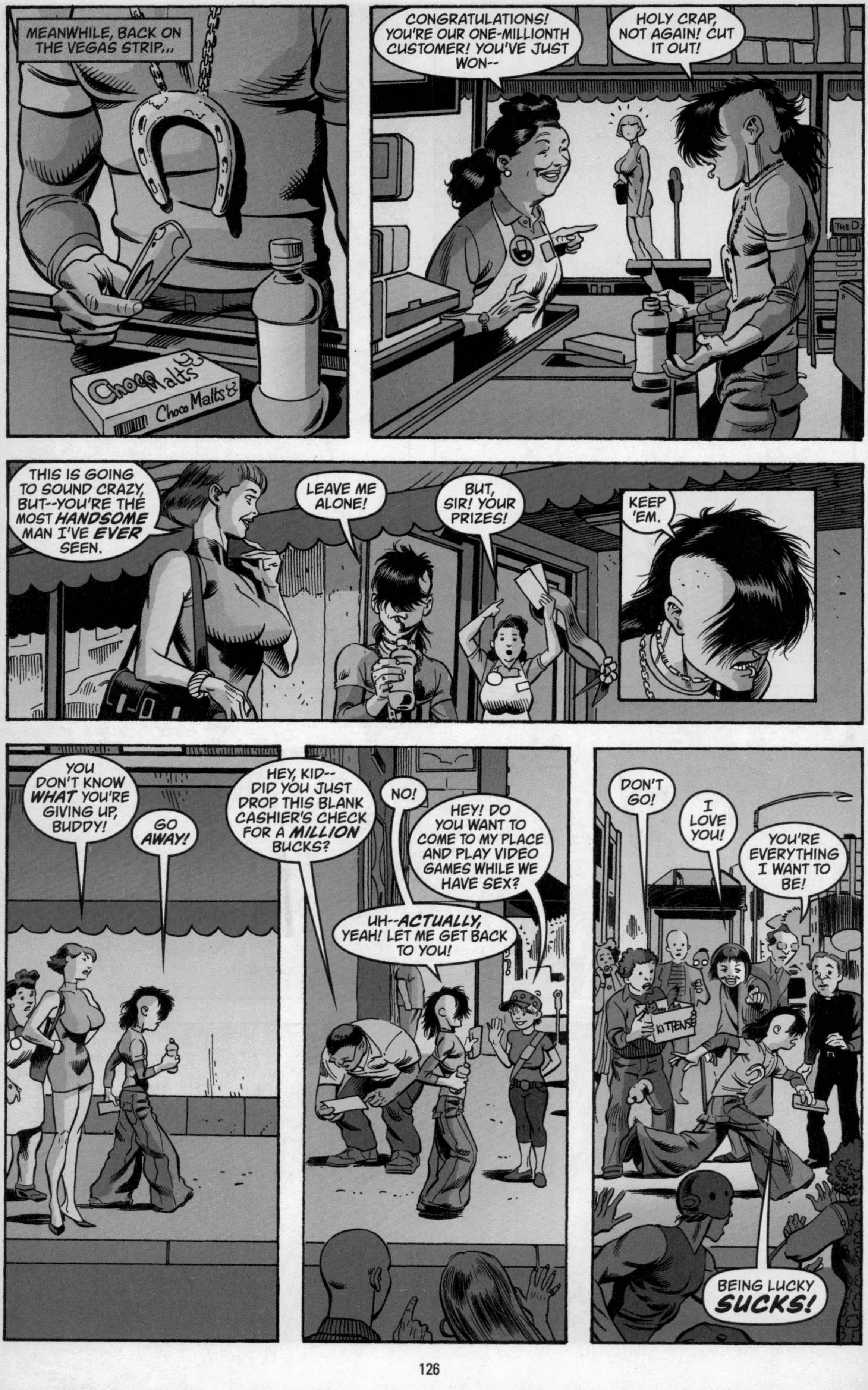

MEANWHILE, BACK ON THE VEGAS STRIP...
Choco Malts
Choco Malts
CONGRATULATIONS! YOU'RE OUR ONE-MILLIONTH CUSTOMER! YOU'VE JUST WON--
HOLY CRAP, NOT AGAIN! CUT IT OUT!
THIS IS GOING TO SOUND CRAZY, BUT--YOU'RE THE MOST **HANDSOME** MAN I'VE **EVER** SEEN.
LEAVE ME ALONE!
BUT, SIR! YOUR PRIZES!
KEEP 'EM.
YOU DON'T KNOW **WHAT** YOU'RE GIVING UP, BUDDY!
GO **AWAY!**
HEY, KID-- DID YOU JUST DROP THIS BLANK CASHIER'S CHECK FOR A **MILLION** BUCKS?
NO!
HEY! DO YOU WANT TO COME TO MY PLACE AND PLAY VIDEO GAMES WHILE WE HAVE SEX?
UH--**ACTUALLY,** YEAH! LET ME GET BACK TO YOU!
DON'T GO!
I LOVE YOU!
YOU'RE EVERYTHING I WANT TO BE!
KITTENS
BEING LUCKY **SUCKS!**

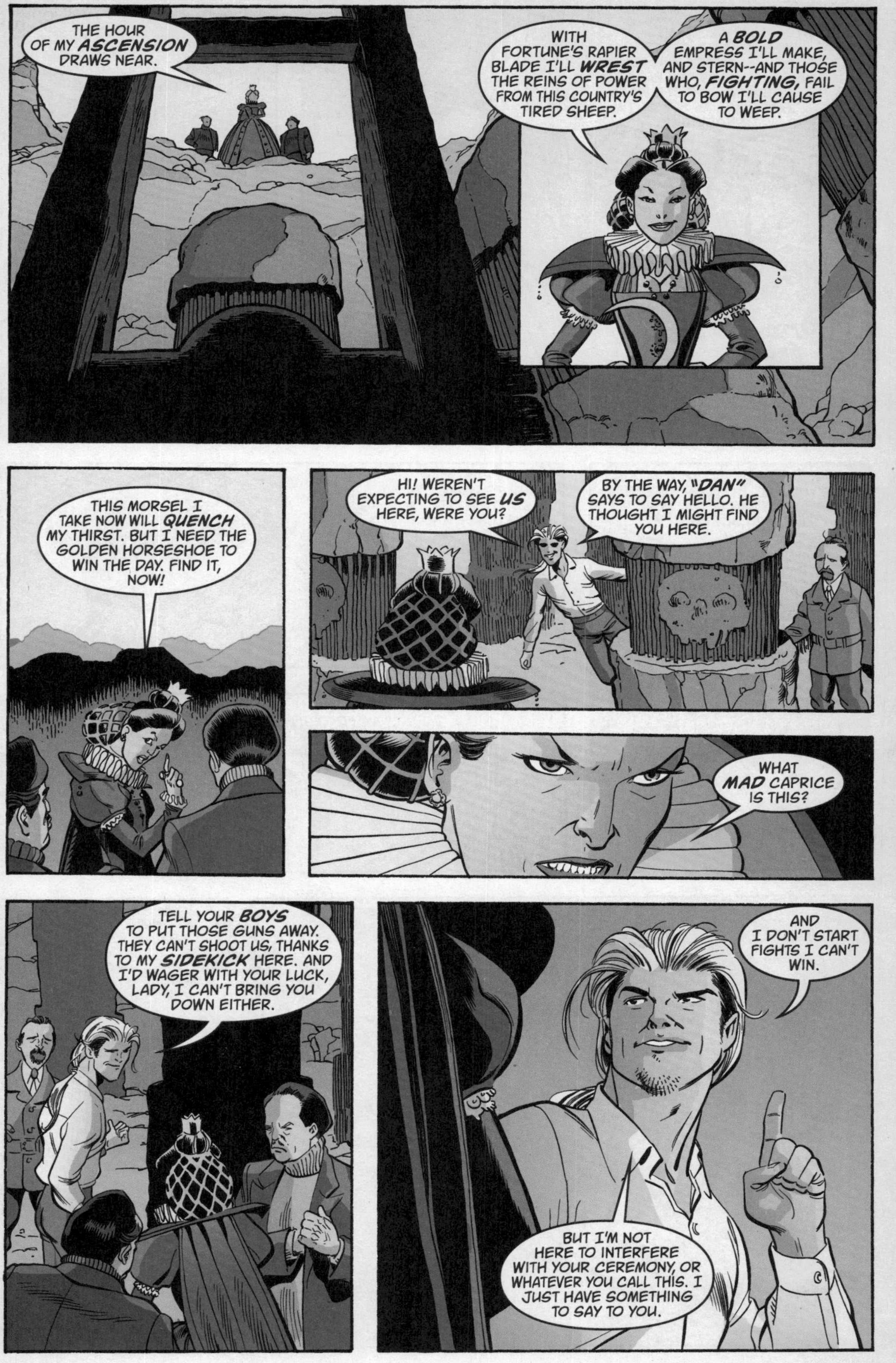
THE HOUR OF MY ASCENSION DRAWS NEAR.
WITH FORTUNE'S RAPIER BLADE I'LL WREST THE REINS OF POWER FROM THIS COUNTRY'S TIRED SHEEP.
A BOLD EMPRESS I'LL MAKE, AND STERN--AND THOSE WHO, FIGHTING, FAIL TO BOW I'LL CAUSE TO WEEP.
THIS MORSEL I TAKE NOW WILL QUENCH MY THIRST. BUT I NEED THE GOLDEN HORSESHOE TO WIN THE DAY. FIND IT, NOW!
HI! WEREN'T EXPECTING TO SEE US HERE, WERE YOU?
BY THE WAY, "DAN" SAYS TO SAY HELLO. HE THOUGHT I MIGHT FIND YOU HERE.
WHAT MAD CAPRICE IS THIS?
TELL YOUR BOYS TO PUT THOSE GUNS AWAY. THEY CAN'T SHOOT US, THANKS TO MY SIDEKICK HERE. AND I'D WAGER WITH YOUR LUCK, LADY, I CAN'T BRING YOU DOWN EITHER.
AND I DON'T START FIGHTS I CAN'T WIN.
BUT I'M NOT HERE TO INTERFERE WITH YOUR CEREMONY, OR WHATEVER YOU CALL THIS. I JUST HAVE SOMETHING TO SAY TO YOU.

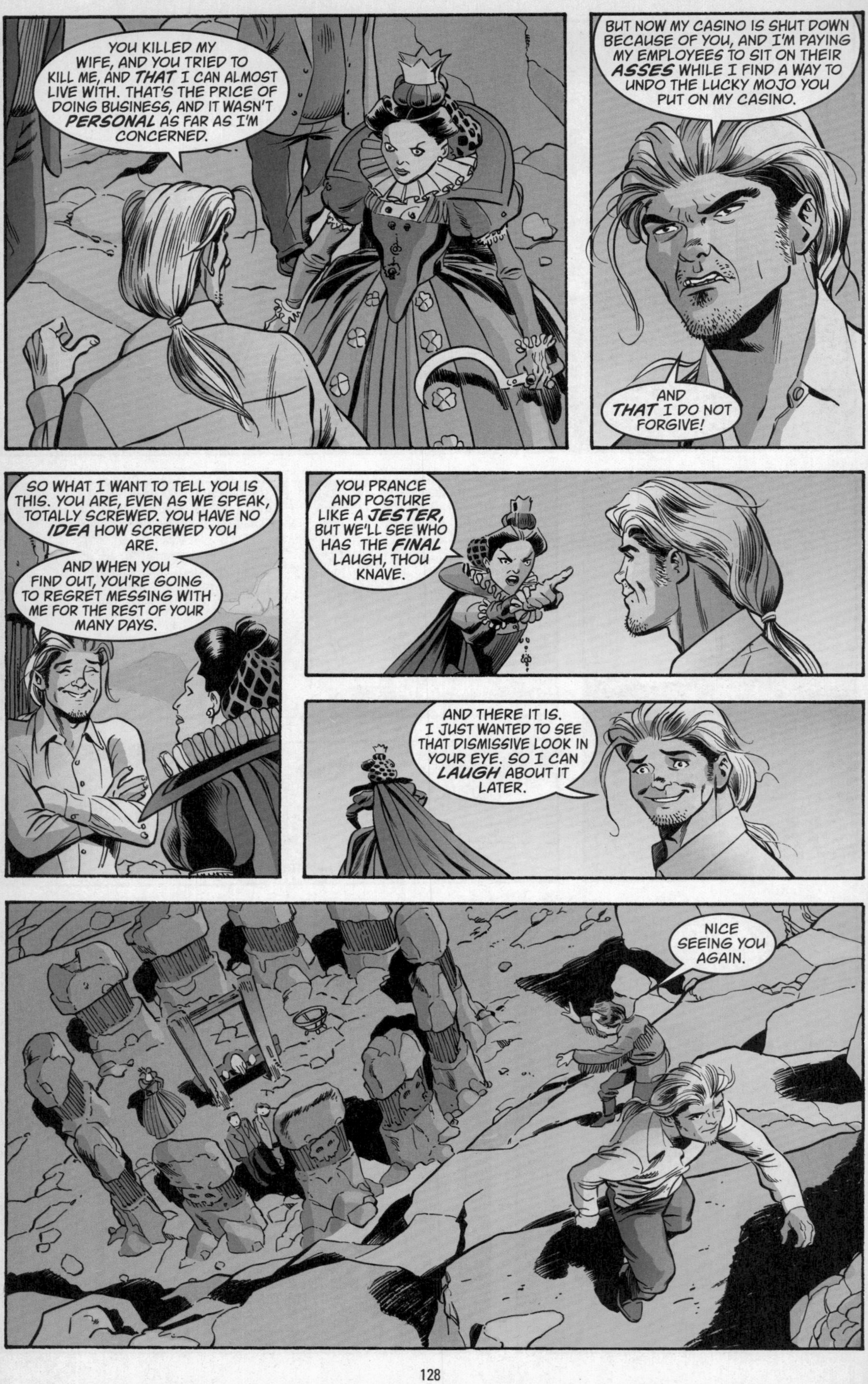
YOU KILLED MY WIFE, AND YOU TRIED TO KILL ME, AND THAT I CAN ALMOST LIVE WITH. THAT'S THE PRICE OF DOING BUSINESS, AND IT WASN'T PERSONAL AS FAR AS I'M CONCERNED.
BUT NOW MY CASINO IS SHUT DOWN BECAUSE OF YOU, AND I'M PAYING MY EMPLOYEES TO SIT ON THEIR ASSES WHILE I FIND A WAY TO UNDO THE LUCKY MOJO YOU PUT ON MY CASINO.
AND THAT I DO NOT FORGIVE!
SO WHAT I WANT TO TELL YOU IS THIS. YOU ARE, EVEN AS WE SPEAK, TOTALLY SCREWED. YOU HAVE NO IDEA HOW SCREWED YOU ARE.
AND WHEN YOU FIND OUT, YOU'RE GOING TO REGRET MESSING WITH ME FOR THE REST OF YOUR MANY DAYS.
YOU PRANCE AND POSTURE LIKE A JESTER, BUT WE'LL SEE WHO HAS THE FINAL LAUGH, THOU KNAVE.
AND THERE IT IS. I JUST WANTED TO SEE THAT DISMISSIVE LOOK IN YOUR EYE. SO I CAN LAUGH ABOUT IT LATER.
NICE SEEING YOU AGAIN.

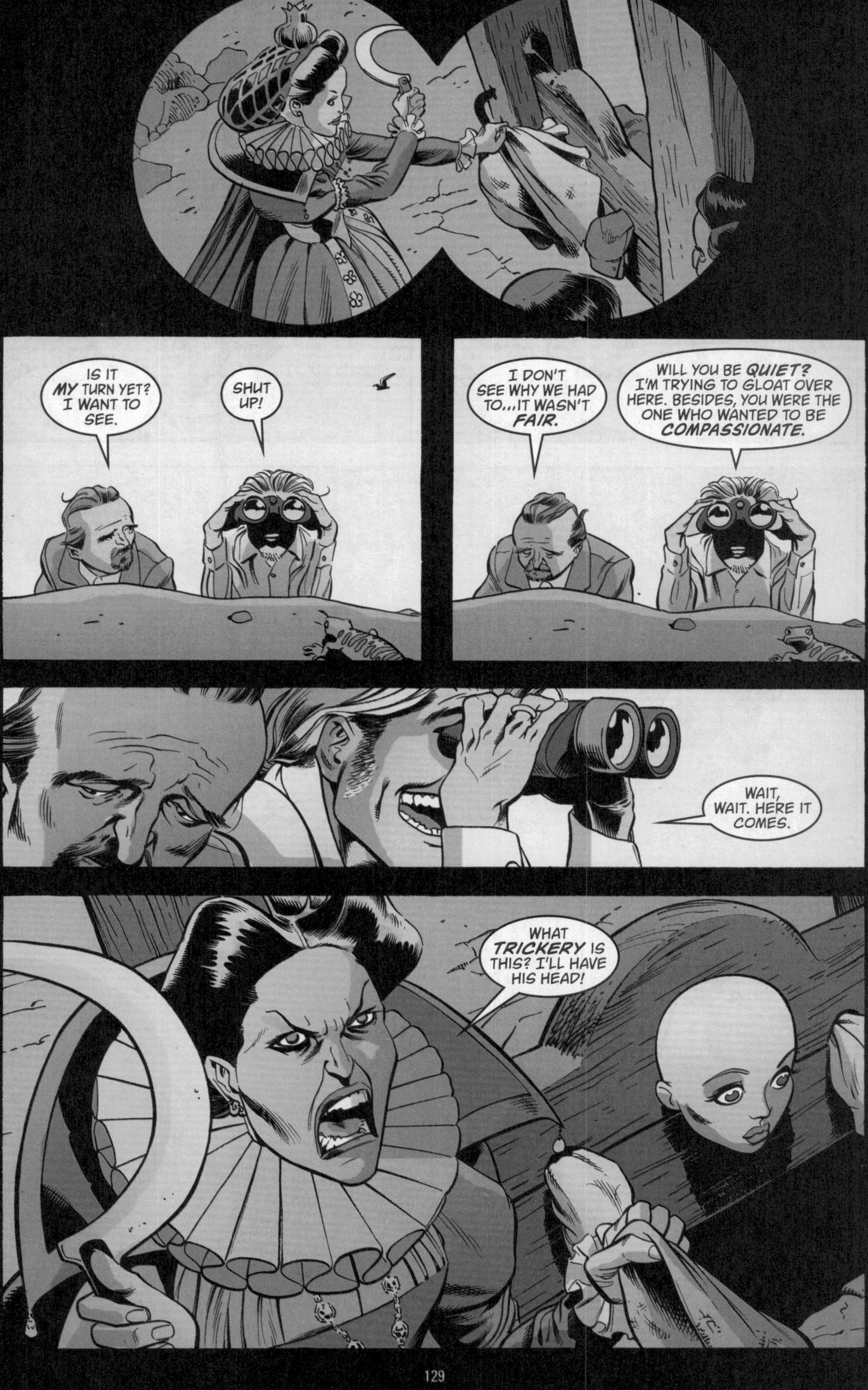
IS IT MY TURN YET? I WANT TO SEE.
SHUT UP!
I DON'T SEE WHY WE HAD TO...IT WASN'T FAIR.
WILL YOU BE QUIET? I'M TRYING TO GLOAT OVER HERE. BESIDES, YOU WERE THE ONE WHO WANTED TO BE COMPASSIONATE.
WAIT, WAIT. HERE IT COMES.
WHAT TRICKERY IS THIS? I'LL HAVE HIS HEAD!

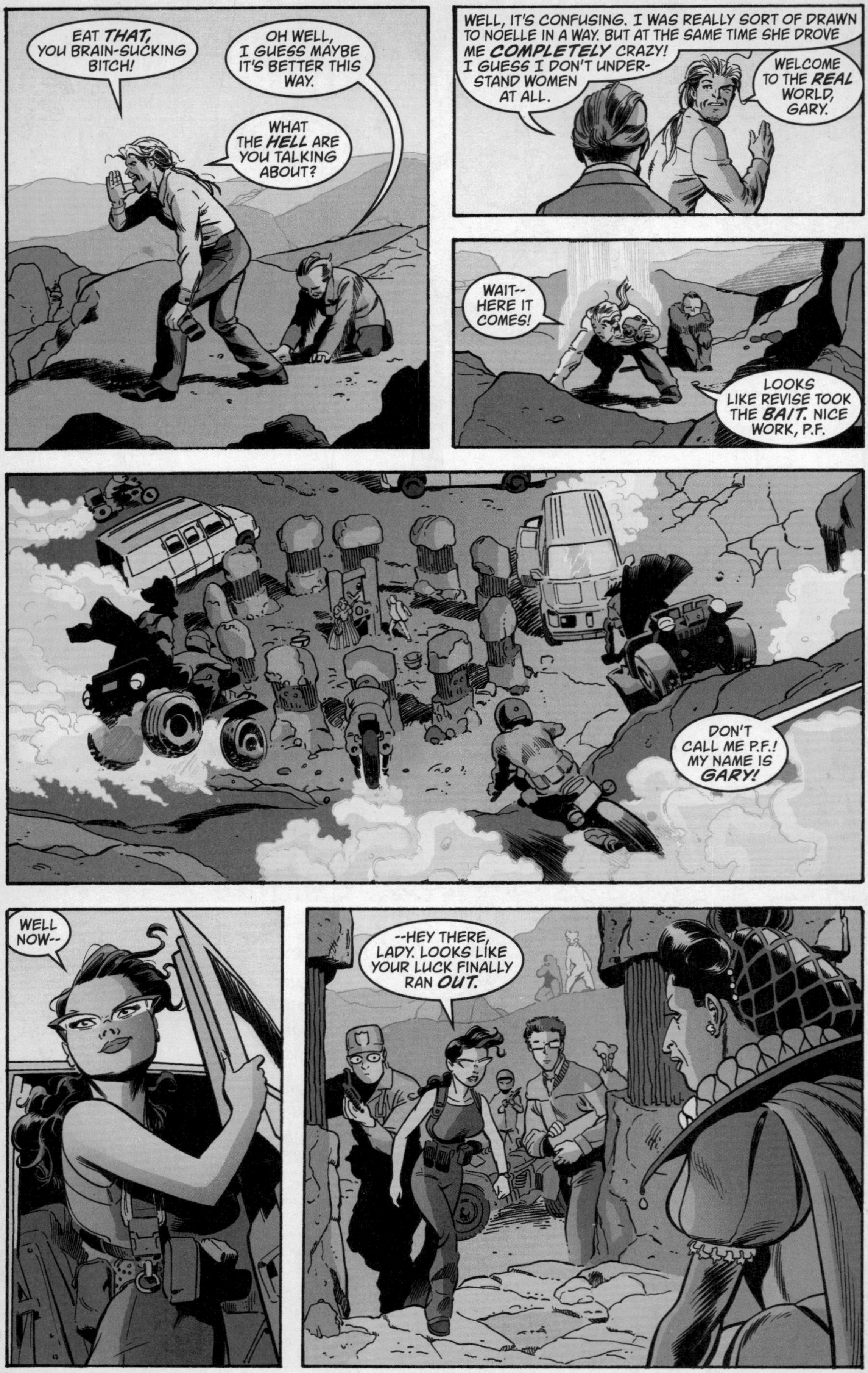
EAT THAT, YOU BRAIN-SUCKING BITCH!
OH WELL, I GUESS MAYBE IT'S BETTER THIS WAY.
WHAT THE HELL ARE YOU TALKING ABOUT?
WELL, IT'S CONFUSING. I WAS REALLY SORT OF DRAWN TO NOELLE IN A WAY. BUT AT THE SAME TIME SHE DROVE ME COMPLETELY CRAZY! I GUESS I DON'T UNDERSTAND WOMEN AT ALL.
WELCOME TO THE REAL WORLD, GARY.
WAIT-- HERE IT COMES!
LOOKS LIKE REVISE TOOK THE BAIT. NICE WORK, P.F.
DON'T CALL ME P.F.! MY NAME IS GARY!
WELL NOW--
--HEY THERE, LADY. LOOKS LIKE YOUR LUCK FINALLY RAN OUT.

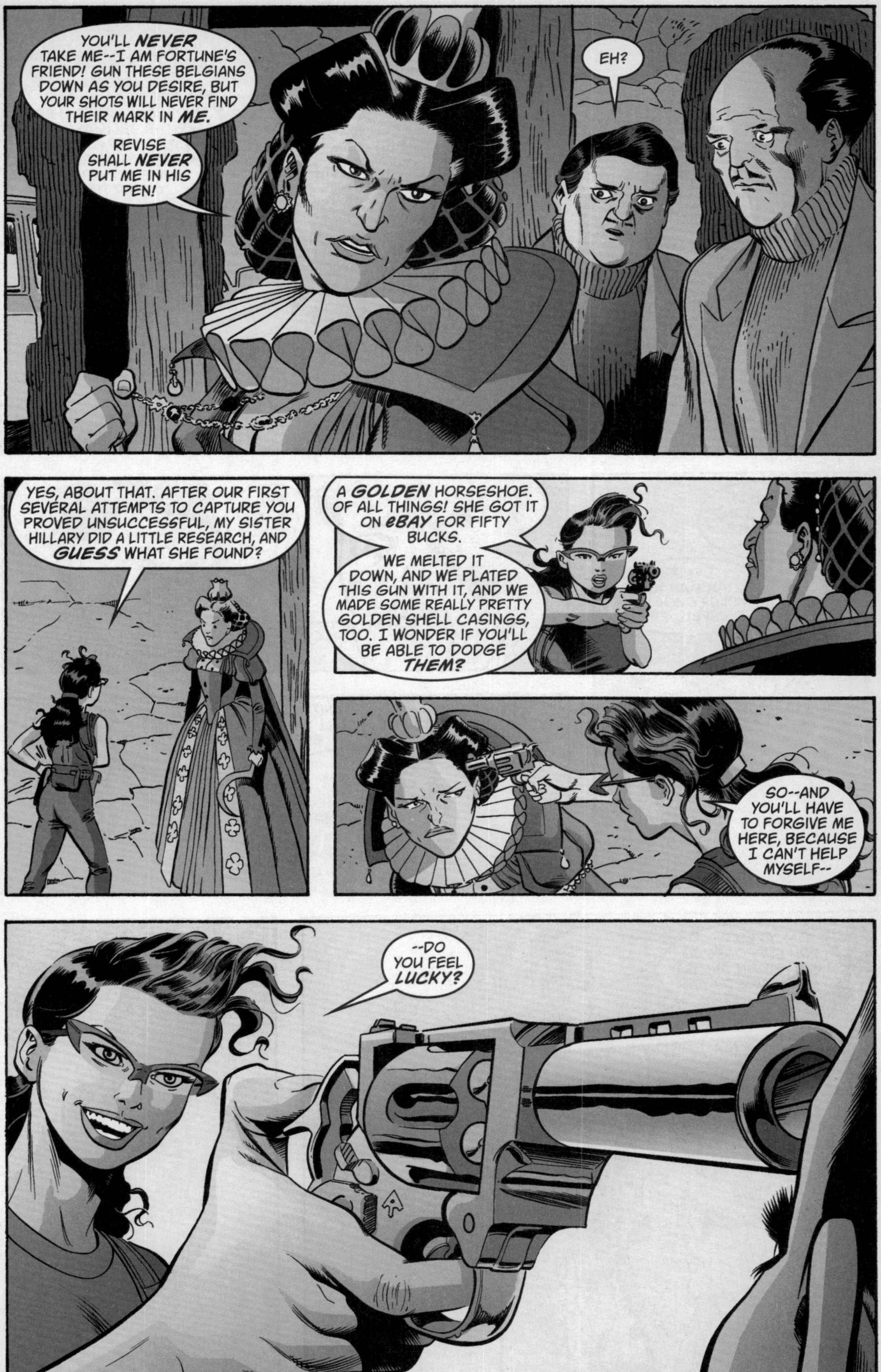
YOU'LL NEVER TAKE ME--I AM FORTUNE'S FRIEND! GUN THESE BELGIANS DOWN AS YOU DESIRE, BUT YOUR SHOTS WILL NEVER FIND THEIR MARK IN ME.
REVISE SHALL NEVER PUT ME IN HIS PEN!
EH?
YES, ABOUT THAT. AFTER OUR FIRST SEVERAL ATTEMPTS TO CAPTURE YOU PROVED UNSUCCESSFUL, MY SISTER HILLARY DID A LITTLE RESEARCH, AND GUESS WHAT SHE FOUND?
A GOLDEN HORSESHOE. OF ALL THINGS! SHE GOT IT ON eBAY FOR FIFTY BUCKS.
WE MELTED IT DOWN, AND WE PLATED THIS GUN WITH IT, AND WE MADE SOME REALLY PRETTY GOLDEN SHELL CASINGS, TOO. I WONDER IF YOU'LL BE ABLE TO DODGE THEM?
SO--AND YOU'LL HAVE TO FORGIVE ME HERE, BECAUSE I CAN'T HELP MYSELF--
--DO YOU FEEL LUCKY?

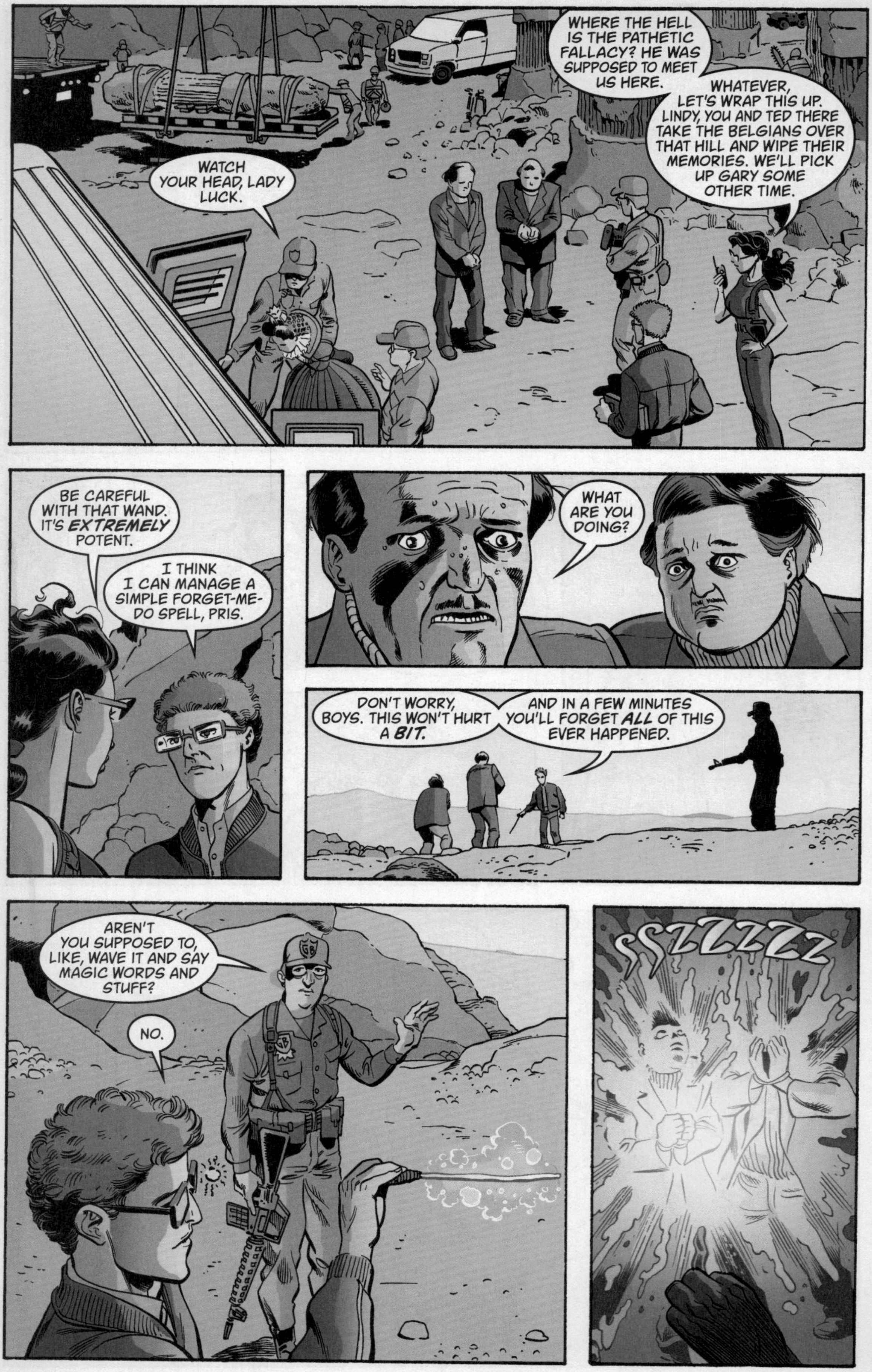
WHERE THE HELL IS THE PATHETIC FALLACY? HE WAS SUPPOSED TO MEET US HERE.
WHATEVER, LET'S WRAP THIS UP. LINDY, YOU AND TED THERE TAKE THE BELGIANS OVER THAT HILL AND WIPE THEIR MEMORIES. WE'LL PICK UP GARY SOME OTHER TIME.
WATCH YOUR HEAD, LADY LUCK.
BE CAREFUL WITH THAT WAND. IT'S ***EXTREMELY*** POTENT.
I THINK I CAN MANAGE A SIMPLE FORGET-ME-DO SPELL, PRIS.
WHAT ARE YOU DOING?
DON'T WORRY, BOYS. THIS WON'T HURT A ***BIT.***
AND IN A FEW MINUTES YOU'LL FORGET ***ALL*** OF THIS EVER HAPPENED.
AREN'T YOU SUPPOSED TO, LIKE, WAVE IT AND SAY MAGIC WORDS AND STUFF?
NO.
SSZZZZZ

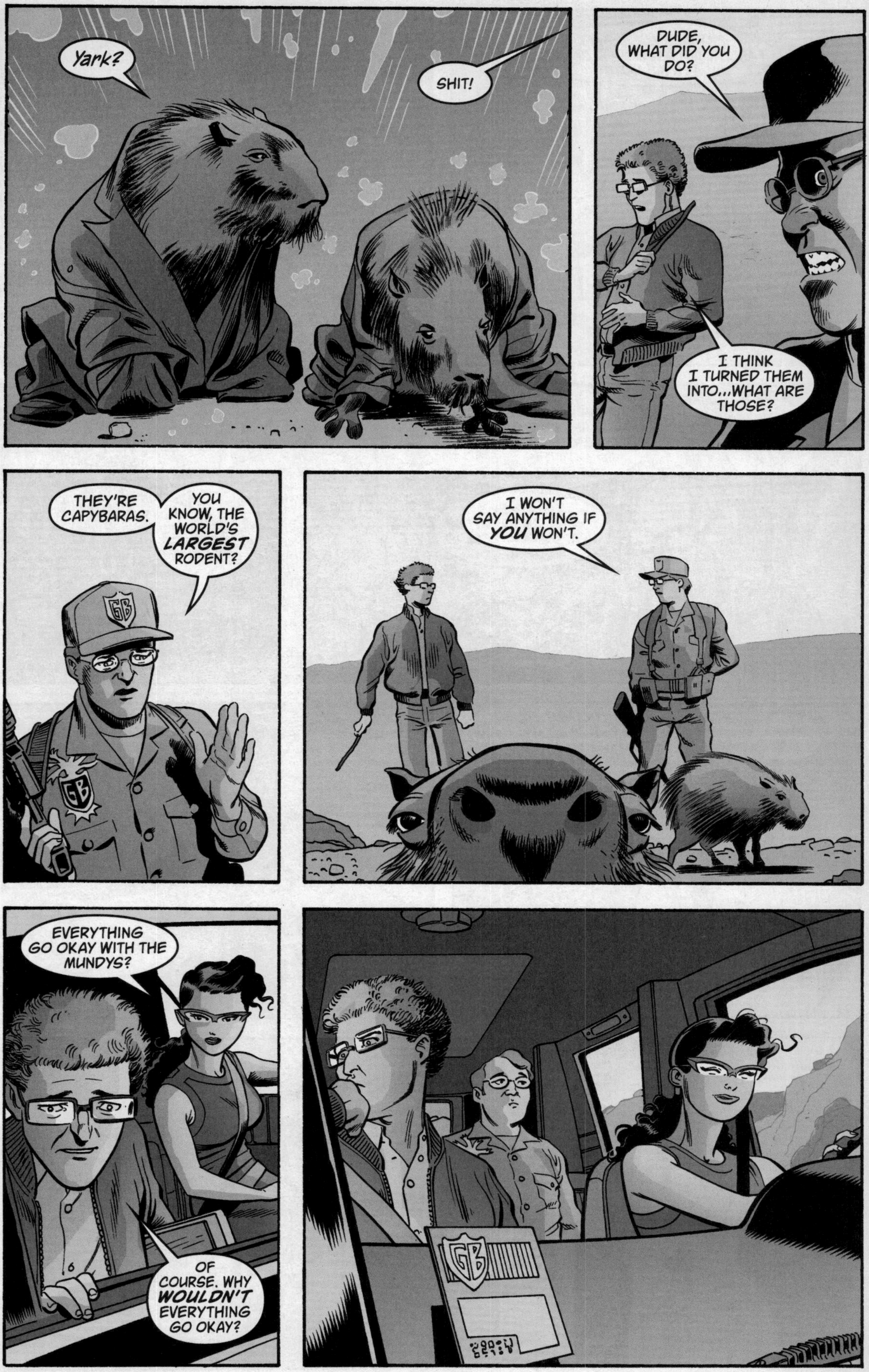
Yark?
SHIT!
DUDE, WHAT DID YOU DO?
I THINK I TURNED THEM INTO...WHAT ARE THOSE?
THEY'RE CAPYBARAS.
YOU KNOW, THE WORLD'S *LARGEST* RODENT?
I WON'T SAY ANYTHING IF *YOU* WON'T.
EVERYTHING GO OKAY WITH THE MUNDYS?
OF COURSE. WHY *WOULDN'T* EVERYTHING GO OKAY?

HA! I WIN!

IF THOSE *UPTIGHT* FABLETOWN ASSHOLES COULD SEE ME NOW!

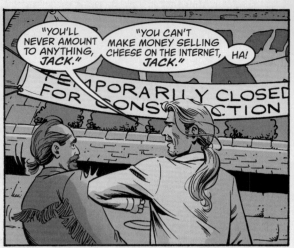

"YOU'LL NEVER AMOUNT TO ANYTHING, *JACK.*"

"YOU CAN'T MAKE MONEY SELLING CHEESE ON THE INTERNET, *JACK.*" HA!

TEMPORARILY CLOSED FOR CONSTRUCTION

HELLO, JACK. WE NEED TO TALK.

NOT NOW, DENNIS. I HAVE SOME IMPORTANT *CELEBRATING* TO ATTEND TO, AND WE NEED TO GET THIS CASINO OPENED, *ASAP.*

I THOUGHT YOU'D LIKE TO *KNOW* THAT DAN FARRELL IS DEAD.

WHA-- DEAD?

MURDERED, TO BE PRECISE. THE MAID FOUND HIM IN HIS LIVING ROOM WITH A *CRUSHED* SKULL.

THE POLICE DISCOVERED THE MURDER WEAPON IN A DUMPSTER OUTSIDE FARRELL'S BUILDING.

A GOLF CLUB-- A FIVE IRON, I BELIEVE. AND IT'S LITERALLY COVERED IN *YOUR* FINGER-PRINTS, JOHN, OR JACK, OR WHATEVER YOU'RE CALLING YOURSELF TODAY.

AS YOUR ATTORNEY, I CAN ASSURE YOU THAT YOU ARE IN A *GREAT* DEAL OF TROUBLE.

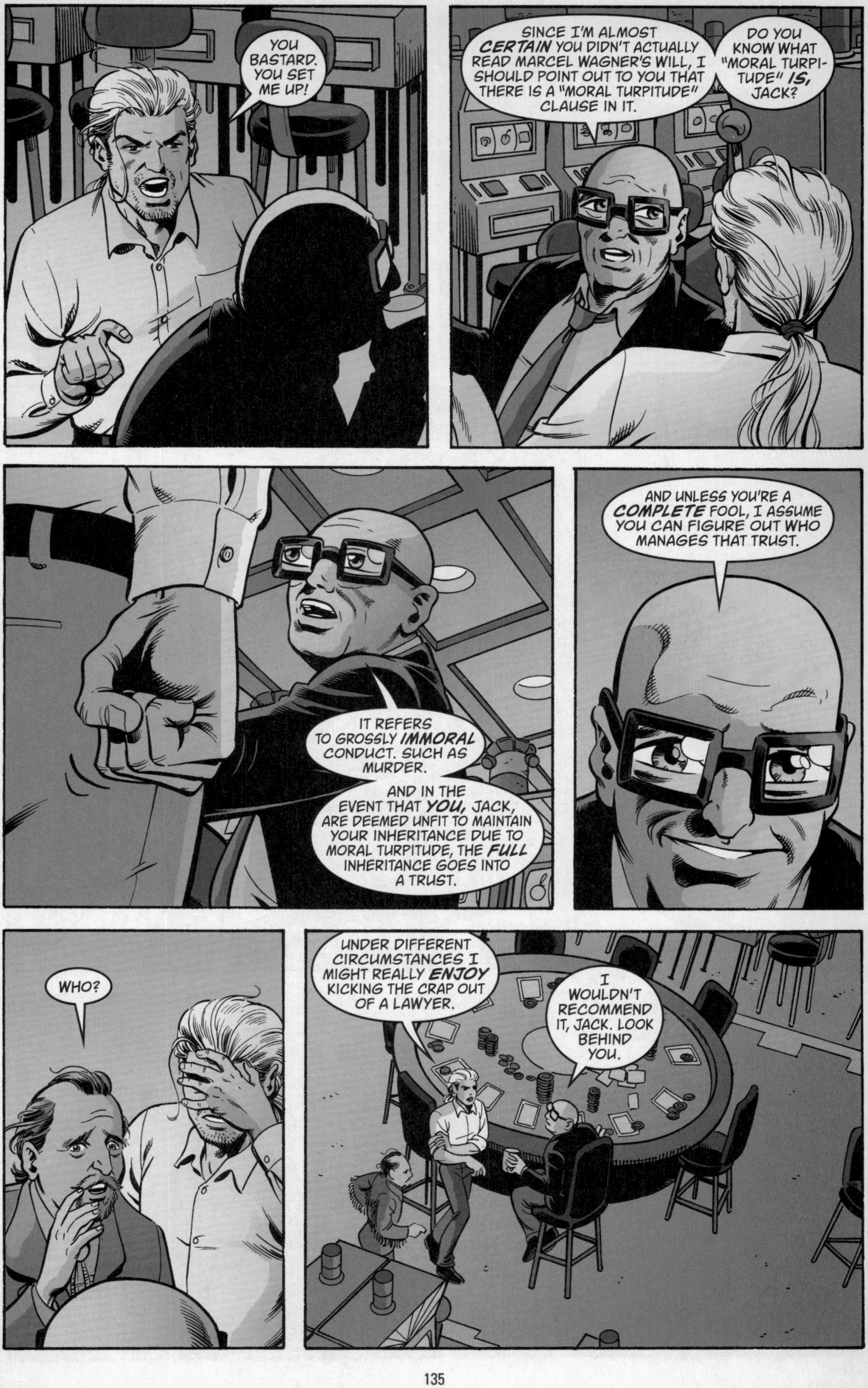
YOU BASTARD. YOU SET ME UP!
SINCE I'M ALMOST CERTAIN YOU DIDN'T ACTUALLY READ MARCEL WAGNER'S WILL, I SHOULD POINT OUT TO YOU THAT THERE IS A "MORAL TURPITUDE" CLAUSE IN IT.
DO YOU KNOW WHAT "MORAL TURPITUDE" IS, JACK?
IT REFERS TO GROSSLY IMMORAL CONDUCT. SUCH AS MURDER.
AND IN THE EVENT THAT YOU, JACK, ARE DEEMED UNFIT TO MAINTAIN YOUR INHERITANCE DUE TO MORAL TURPITUDE, THE FULL INHERITANCE GOES INTO A TRUST.
AND UNLESS YOU'RE A COMPLETE FOOL, I ASSUME YOU CAN FIGURE OUT WHO MANAGES THAT TRUST.
WHO?
UNDER DIFFERENT CIRCUMSTANCES I MIGHT REALLY ENJOY KICKING THE CRAP OUT OF A LAWYER.
I WOULDN'T RECOMMEND IT, JACK. LOOK BEHIND YOU.

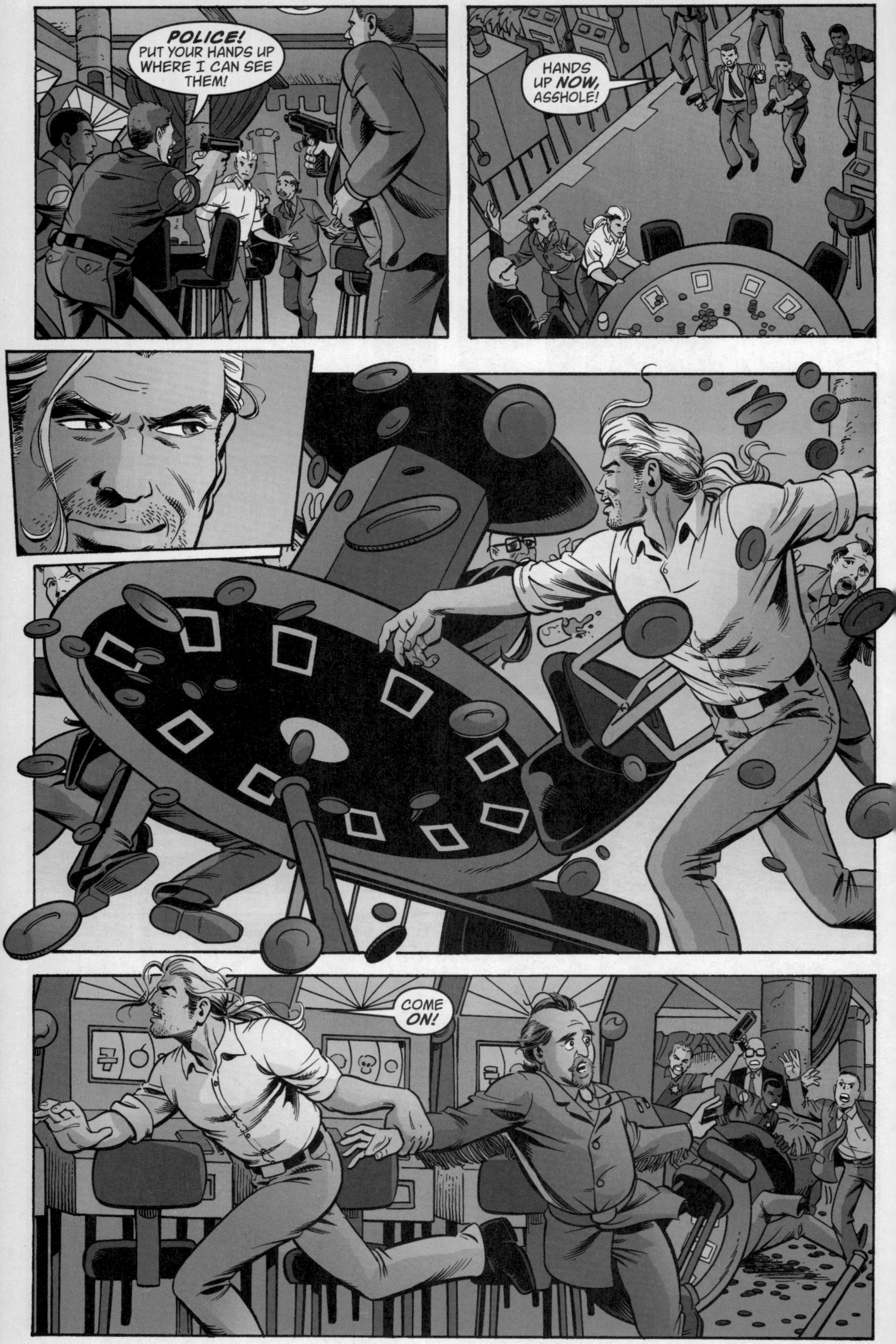
POLICE! PUT YOUR HANDS UP WHERE I CAN SEE THEM!
HANDS UP NOW, ASSHOLE!
COME ON!

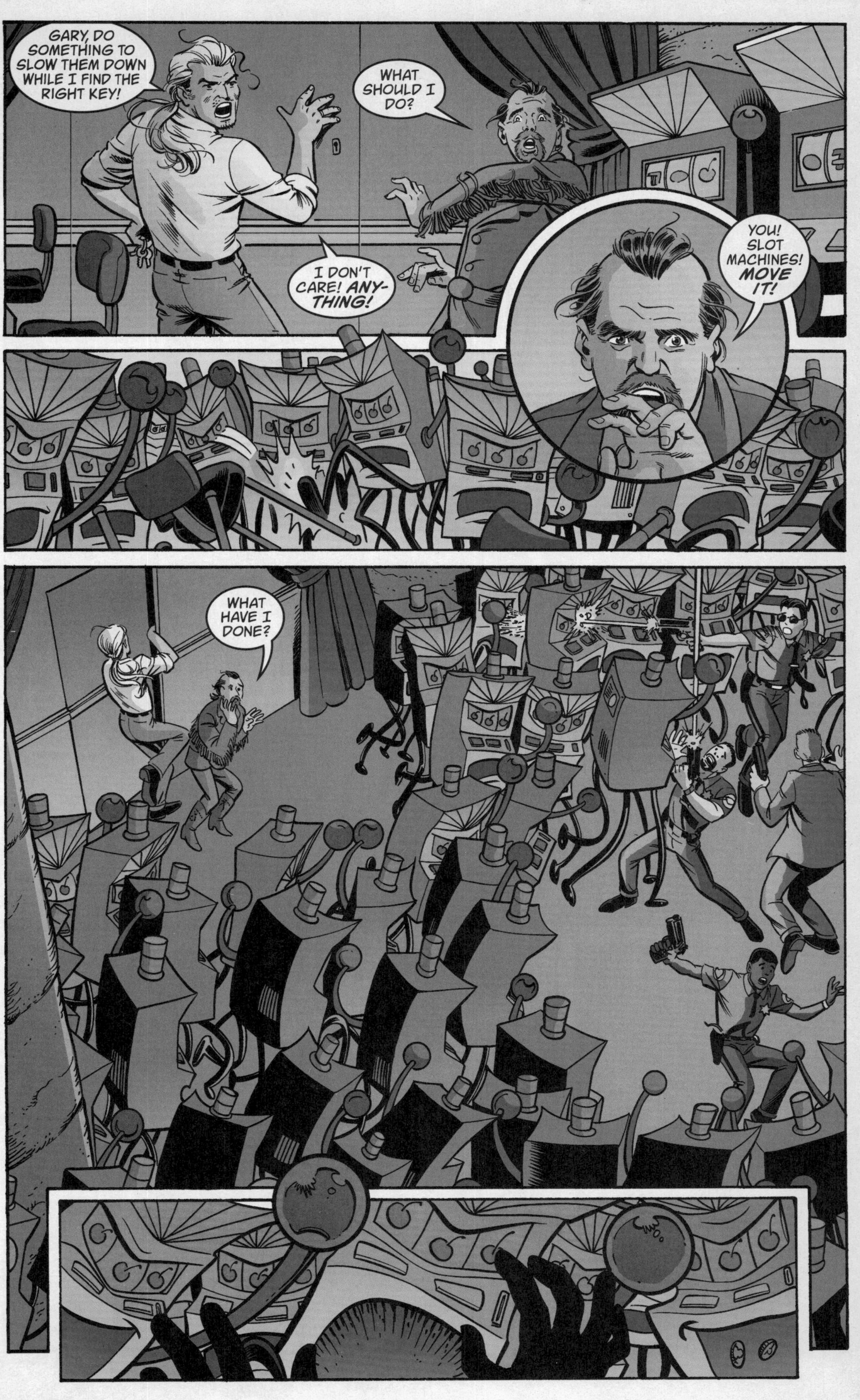
GARY, DO SOMETHING TO SLOW THEM DOWN WHILE I FIND THE RIGHT KEY!
WHAT SHOULD I DO?
I DON'T CARE! ANY-THING!
YOU! SLOT MACHINES! MOVE IT!
WHAT HAVE I DONE?

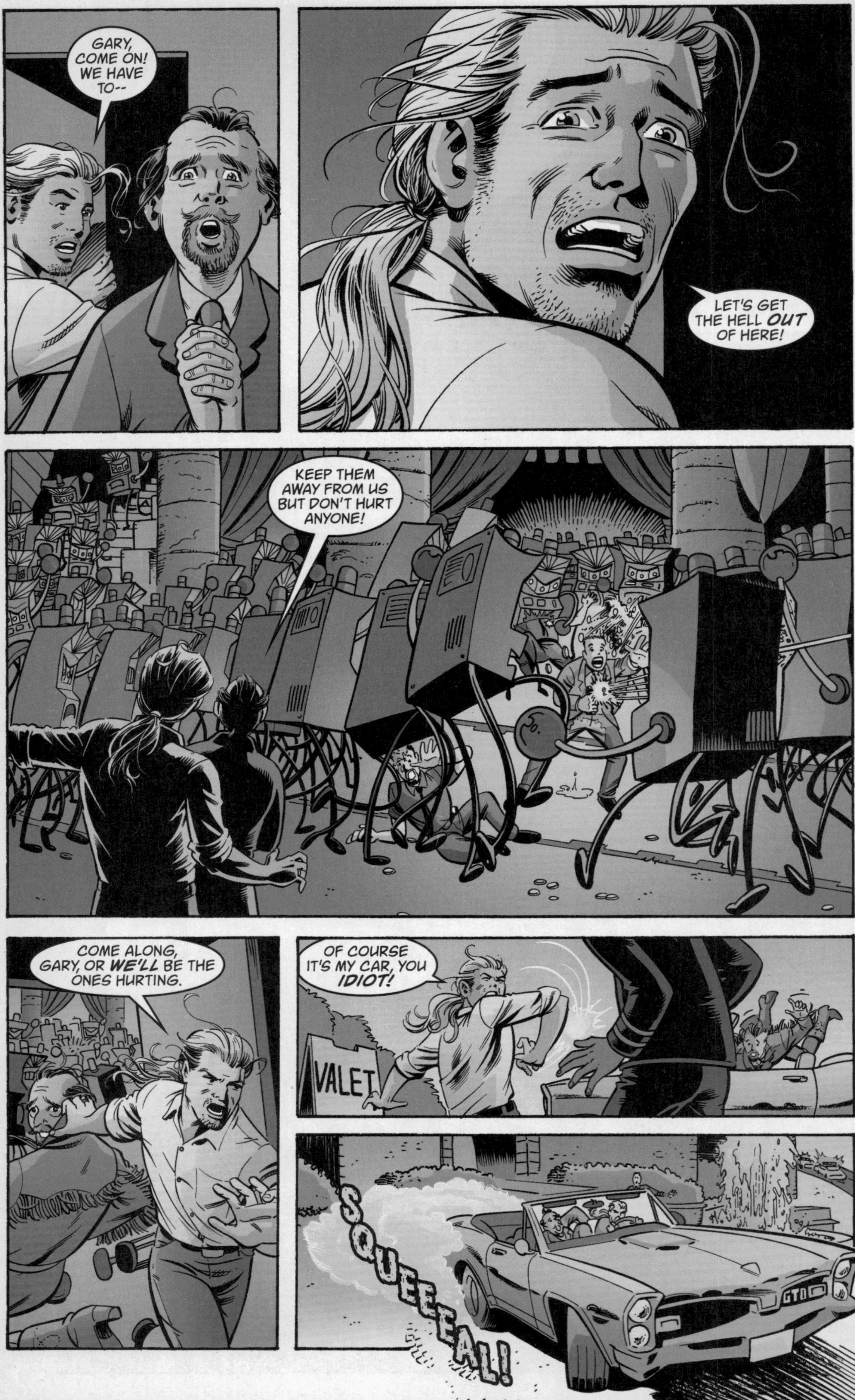
GARY, COME ON! WE HAVE TO--
LET'S GET THE HELL OUT OF HERE!
KEEP THEM AWAY FROM US BUT DON'T HURT ANYONE!
COME ALONG, GARY, OR WE'LL BE THE ONES HURTING.
OF COURSE IT'S MY CAR, YOU IDIOT!
VALET
SQUEEEEAL!
GTO

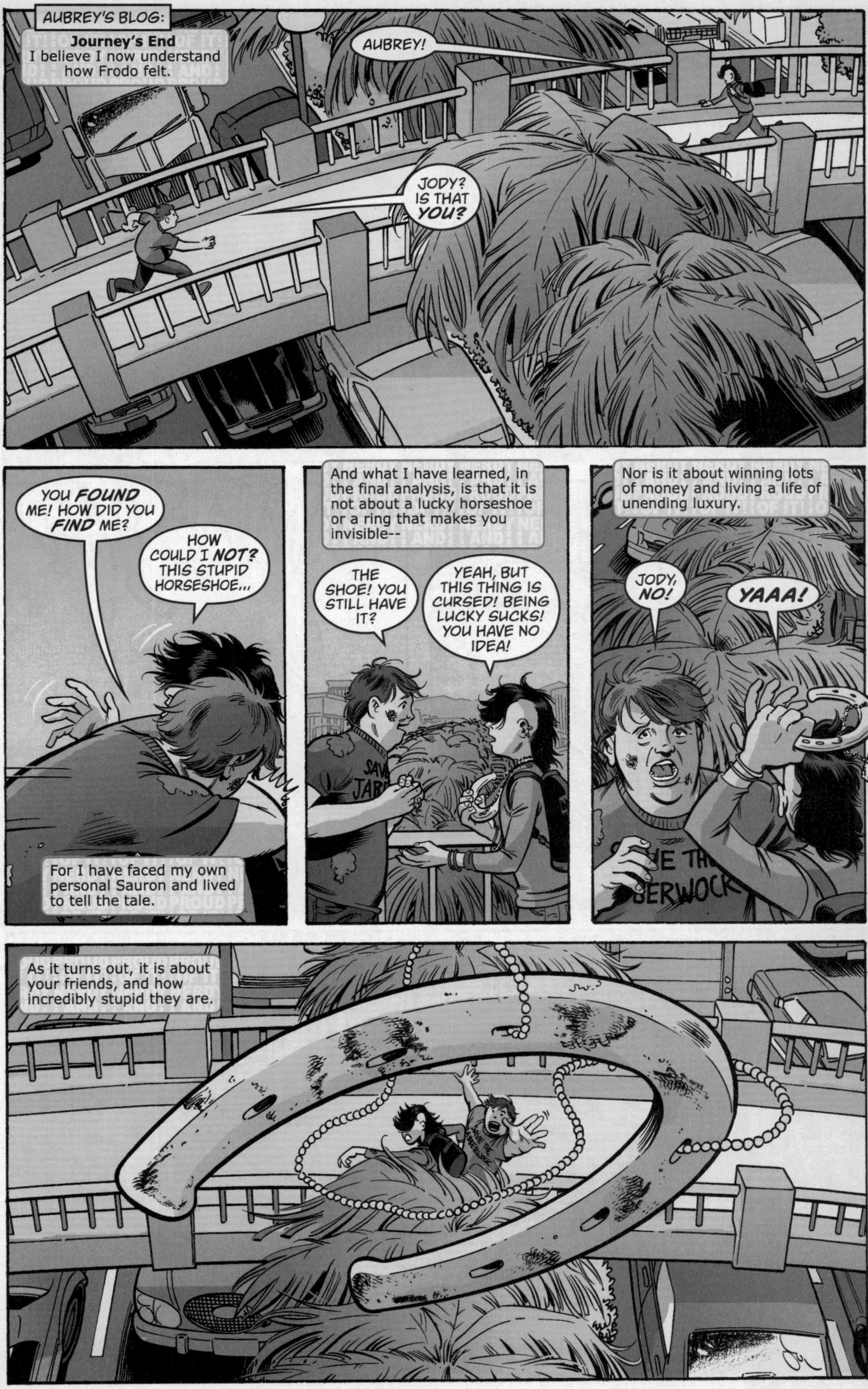

AUBREY'S BLOG:
Journey's End
I believe I now understand how Frodo felt.
AUBREY!
JODY? IS THAT YOU?
YOU FOUND ME! HOW DID YOU FIND ME?
HOW COULD I NOT? THIS STUPID HORSESHOE...
For I have faced my own personal Sauron and lived to tell the tale.
And what I have learned, in the final analysis, is that it is not about a lucky horseshoe or a ring that makes you invisible--
THE SHOE! YOU STILL HAVE IT?
YEAH, BUT THIS THING IS CURSED! BEING LUCKY SUCKS! YOU HAVE NO IDEA!
Nor is it about winning lots of money and living a life of unending luxury.
JODY, NO!
YAAA!
As it turns out, it is about your friends, and how incredibly stupid they are.

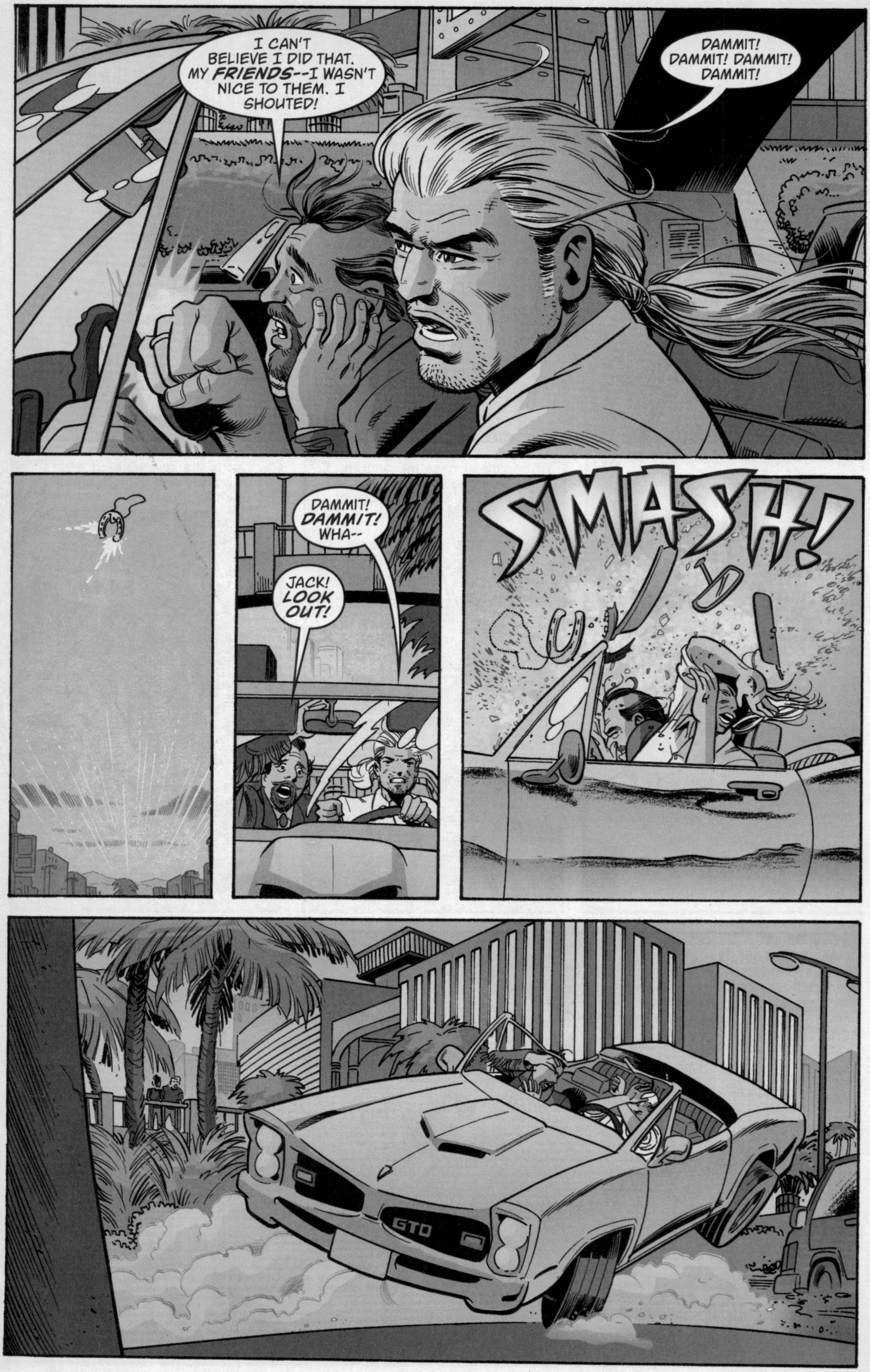
I CAN'T BELIEVE I DID THAT. MY FRIENDS--I WASN'T NICE TO THEM. I SHOUTED!
DAMMIT! DAMMIT! DAMMIT! DAMMIT!
DAMMIT! DAMMIT! WHA--
JACK! LOOK OUT!
SMASH!
GTO

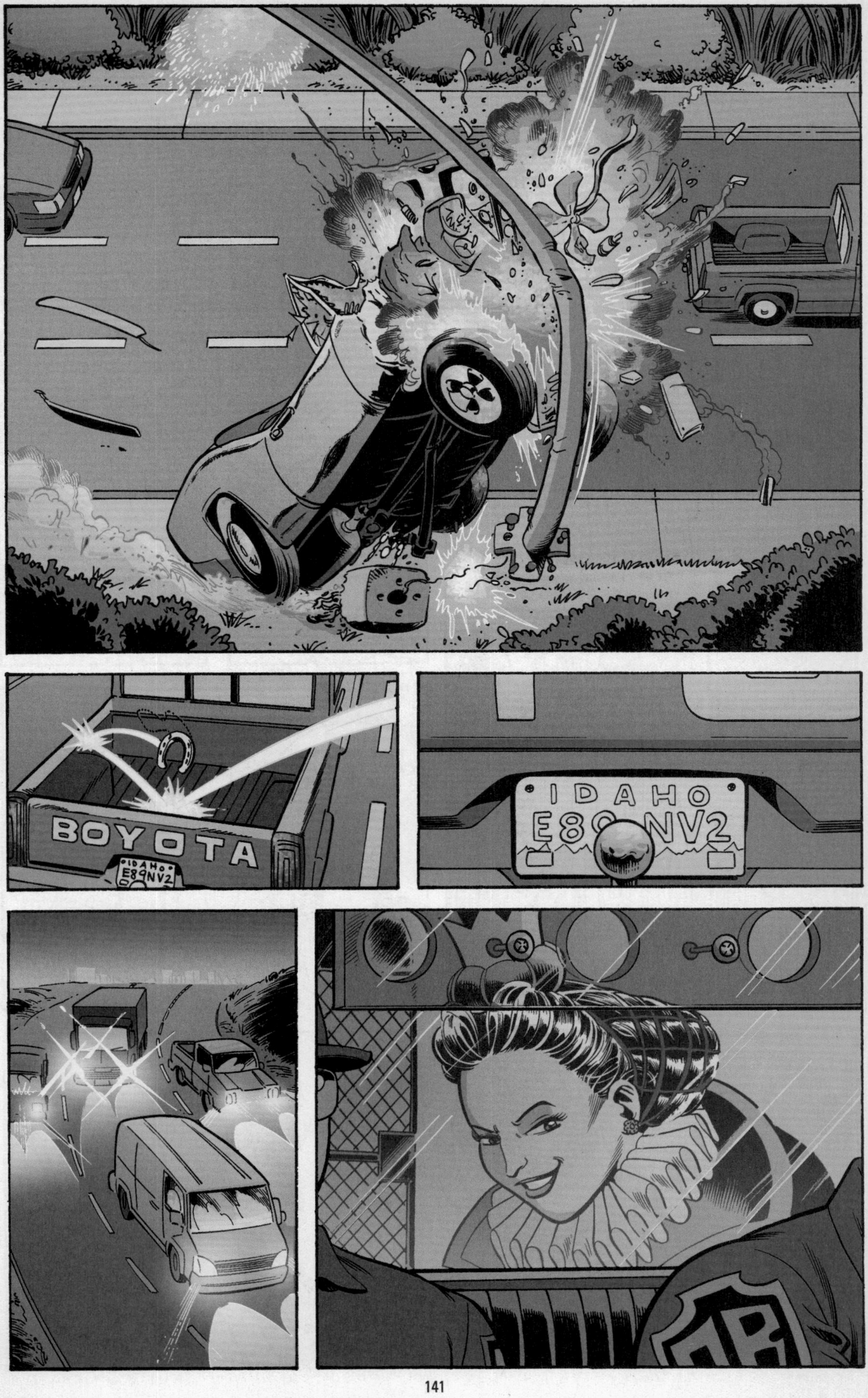
BOYOTA
IDAHO
E89NV2
IDAHO

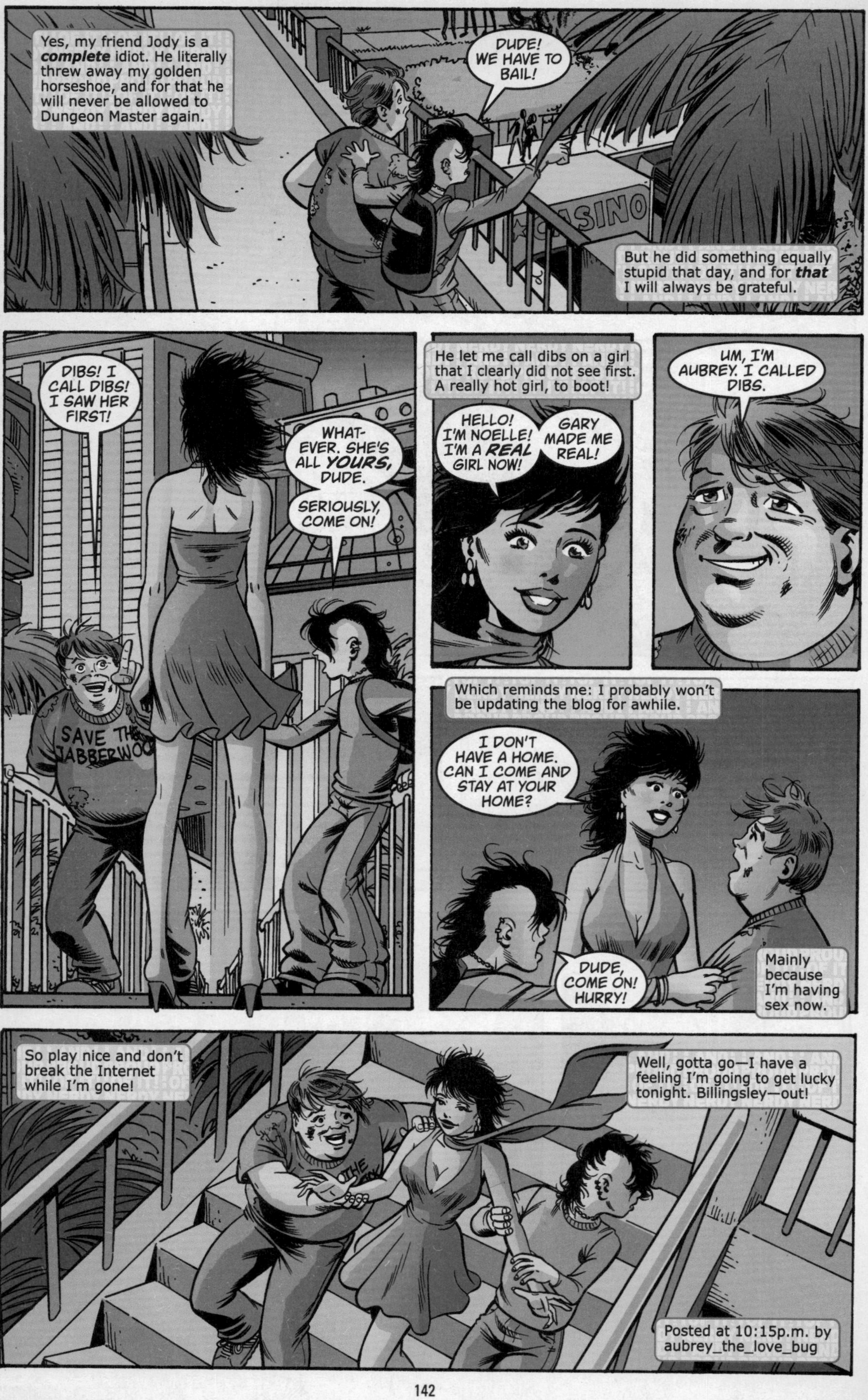
Yes, my friend Jody is a **complete** idiot. He literally threw away my golden horseshoe, and for that he will never be allowed to Dungeon Master again.
DUDE! WE HAVE TO BAIL!
CASINO
But he did something equally stupid that day, and for **that** I will always be grateful.
DIBS! I CALL DIBS! I SAW HER FIRST!
WHAT-EVER. SHE'S ALL **YOURS,** DUDE.
SERIOUSLY, COME ON!
SAVE THE JABBERWOC
He let me call dibs on a girl that I clearly did not see first. A really hot girl, to boot!
HELLO! I'M NOELLE! I'M A **REAL** GIRL NOW!
GARY MADE ME REAL!
UM, I'M AUBREY. I CALLED DIBS.
Which reminds me: I probably won't be updating the blog for awhile.
I DON'T HAVE A HOME. CAN I COME AND STAY AT YOUR HOME?
DUDE, COME ON! HURRY!
Mainly because I'm having sex now.
So play nice and don't break the Internet while I'm gone!
Well, gotta go—I have a feeling I'm going to get lucky tonight. Billingsley—out!
Posted at 10:15p.m. by aubrey_the_love_bug

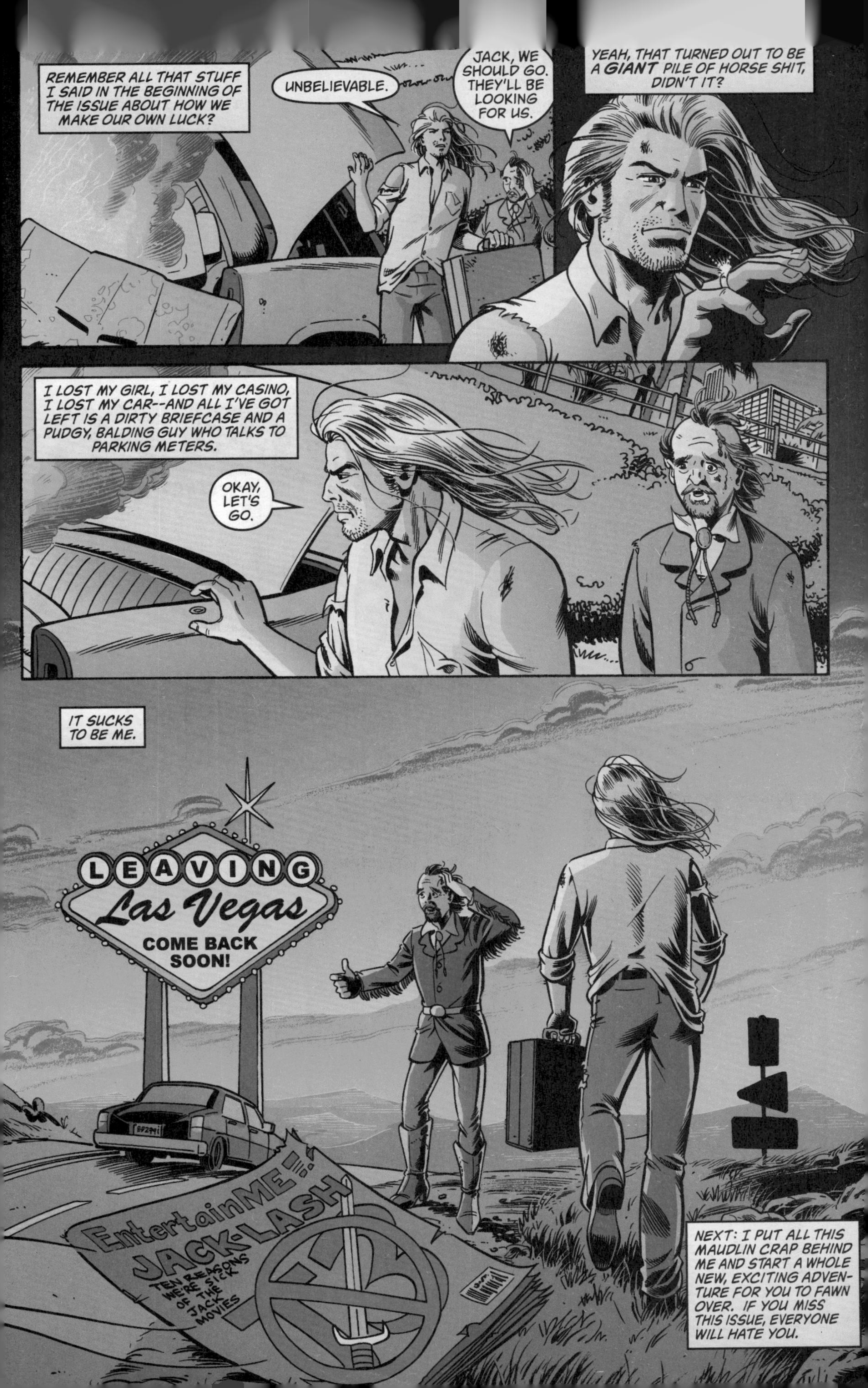
REMEMBER ALL THAT STUFF I SAID IN THE BEGINNING OF THE ISSUE ABOUT HOW WE MAKE OUR OWN LUCK?
UNBELIEVABLE.
JACK, WE SHOULD GO. THEY'LL BE LOOKING FOR US.
YEAH, THAT TURNED OUT TO BE A GIANT PILE OF HORSE SHIT, DIDN'T IT?
I LOST MY GIRL, I LOST MY CASINO, I LOST MY CAR--AND ALL I'VE GOT LEFT IS A DIRTY BRIEFCASE AND A PUDGY, BALDING GUY WHO TALKS TO PARKING METERS.
OKAY, LET'S GO.
IT SUCKS TO BE ME.
LEAVING Las Vegas COME BACK SOON!
EntertainME!!
JACK-LASH
TEN REASONS WE'RE SICK OF THE JACK MOVIES
NEXT: I PUT ALL THIS MAUDLIN CRAP BEHIND ME AND START A WHOLE NEW, EXCITING ADVENTURE FOR YOU TO FAWN OVER. IF YOU MISS THIS ISSUE, EVERYONE WILL HATE YOU.

THE IMMORTAL CHARACTERS OF POPULAR
FAIRY TALES HAVE BEEN DRIVEN FROM THEIR
HOMELANDS AND NOW LIVE HIDDEN AMONG US,
TRYING TO COPE WITH LIFE IN 21ST-CENTURY
MANHATTAN IN THESE COLLECTIONS FROM
WRITER BILL WILLINGHAM AND VERTIGO:

FABLES

VOLUME 1:
LEGENDS IN EXILE

ALSO AVAILABLE:
VOL. 2: ANIMAL FARM
VOL. 3: STORYBOOK LOVE
VOL. 4: MARCH OF THE
WOODEN SOLDIERS
VOL. 5: THE MEAN SEASONS
VOL. 6: HOMELANDS

"[A] WONDERFULLY TWISTED CONCEPT."
— *THE WASHINGTON POST*

"GREAT FUN."
— *BOOKLIST*

ALL TITLES ARE SUGGESTED FOR MATURE READERS.

SEARCH THE GRAPHIC NOVELS SECTION OF
www.VERTIGOCOMICS.com
FOR ART AND INFORMATION ON ALL OF OUR BOOKS!